Youth and
Social Change

Youth and Social Change

edited by

Morton Levitt
University of California at Davis

Ben Rubenstein
Marlboro College

Published for the American Orthopsychiatric Association
Wayne State University Press / Detroit 1972

Published simultaneously in Canada
by The Copp Clark Publishing Company
517 Wellington Street, West
Toronto 2B, Canada.

Library of Congress Cataloging in Publication Data
Levitt, Morton, 1920-   comp.
   Youth and social change.
   "Published for the American Orthopsychiatric Association."
   Includes bibliographical references.
     1. Radicalism—U. S.—Addresses, essays, lectures.
     2. College students—U. S.—Political activity.
     3. Youth—U. S.—Political activity.
     4. Conflict of generations—Addresses, essays, lectures.
     I. Rubenstein, Ben O., 1914-   joint comp.
    II. American Orthopsychiatric Association.
    III. Title.
HN90.R3L48   301.43'15'0973   73-157414
ISBN 0-8143-1450-3

To the memory of
Gordon H. Scott

Contents

The Adolescent Search

Introduction

America has been undergoing violent change in the last decade. All sections of the population are affected, the adult group perhaps less than the young. Today's adults grew up in a relatively stable society and their characters, as a consequence, tend to be fixed and settled. The young people with whom this anthology deals were born in a period of global flux and have been both more vulnerable to and more responsive to forces which make for social alteration. In addition, the very process of adolescence is one which encourages change and experimentation.

As old forms and traditions have fallen away, the adults continue to move along familiar paths and often seem to refuse to look at the surrounding rubble. In an attempt to find individual definition and social purpose, today's youth reject the old road, but are thereby caught up in the chaos of the times. Some become disaffected and angry, and a relatively small number even dedicate themselves to destroying society. A much larger group are living in a nonproductive but personalistic life characterized by heavy drug use and open sexual experimentation.

Because we can make no final judgments of an ongoing process, an "objective" view is impossible. Perhaps the most benign view of the matter can be found in a statement made by Martin Luther King when he was leading the open housing march in Illinois, "Better that the hatred comes out into the open." It seems to make little difference whether the exotic young are militant radicals, literate and reflective activists, drug-ridden academic copouts, or long-haired, exotically dressed penitents in search of an ephemeral Shangri-La, the simple fact of their nonconformity has brought a vicious storm of hatred—and sometimes bullets—down upon their heads.

It is not surprising that this group has provoked so much hostility from the workers and lower middle class. Their contemptuous disavowal offends the materialistic ambitions of the lower classes. A surprising *folie à trois* has developed. Liberals, rediscovering their old fantasies in the acts of the young, beat their breasts, exclaim *mea culpa*, and wave them on. The students rush along only to find themselves confronted by the politically reactionary right, or by the hardhats who view the students as bums and suggest that "all they need is to be taught a lesson." But it is not the conservatives who earn youthful enmity; it is instead their supporters in the liberal ranks.

After each episode of provocative nonnegotiable demands, liberal support, confrontation, and counterattack from the right, the young retreat into communes, pads, tents, or tree houses—congregating, congressing, and rapping like groups of puppies. It has been suggested that one severe economic drought could end the movement. Vast sums of money are spent on drugs, which create a traffic in ancillary services; i.e., purchases, repossessions, arrests, bail, lawyers, doctors, psychiatrists, judges, jails, deans of students, and probation. From this perspective we can see a horrible waste of human beings, resources, and time and energy involved in dealing with just one small aspect of the problem.

Some contend that society's difficulty with its children reflects the disintegration of American family life and values. Those who support this idea refer directly to the college student population who have responded most quickly to the stresses of our civilization and who are the first to articulate their sense of the issues. These students have backgrounds which have given them a sense of options, of resources, of rights and a vision of the future. Moreover, concerned adults are not far away and are ready to respond to pleas for help or counsel.

Much less is known about another group who have been subjected to much the same sort of pressure, but who do not have the sophisticated knowledge of those events and little sense of options, rights, resources, or vision. These are working youth from the lower middle class whose homes were the first to be destroyed by the technological revolution. They have been exposed to social pollutants which have dulled and weakened them. The breakup of both ethnic and regional cultures dissipated their hopeful orientation, and their parents quickly turned these children over to a society which had already lost its own way and which was angry at those who pointed out its failure.

Schools which are not geared to such academic material provide the setting for their inevitable failure. Students who are not college bound soon become faceless in institutions with usual middle class aspirations. A few may get to college, but most are shunted toward vocational classes. The latter are a humiliated minority group, and they accept their status. It is this broken quality, coupled with the boring atmosphere of the high school, that creates a frightening similarity to the factory life that looms ahead for them. They submit to the system and learn to "soldier" like factory workers to get through stultifying days.

These students are likely to spend the hours after school in bowling alleys or driving about city streets consuming whiskey or beer. Because the car often becomes the center of this limited universe, it creates its own demands. Oppressive jobs provide the money for its purchase and upkeep. The initial excitement soon disappears, and the familiar sense of boredom is apt to surface once again. The irony is that this group, the registered losers, those who have been put down by everybody, are the first to react to any movement which provides some hope of freedom or independence. Inarticulate and pained, they seize upon any simplistic slogan which offers an opportunity for activity, beating up blacks in racially shifting

11

neighborhoods, and marching against all who protest the sorry nature of their own existence.

Still the lower class group is not entirely separate from college students, for drug users belong to all classes. Moreover, the radicals have given young people of all classes and ages slogans to express their hatred of their own educational experience: "The school is a police state," "they don't even know us," or "the teachers are jailers." If the manifestoes are to be believed, the middle class has stimulated a new way of thinking for this depressed group and has given them at least transient membership into an elitist organization. Nonetheless, activist and liberal youngsters carry the brunt of the battle for social change, and those from impoverished classes are likely to join the opposition when they enter the working class.

The two groups also come apart on the issue of the draft. Middle class radicals can, with few exceptions, find a multitude of ways to avoid military service. The Vietnam war has been fought by working class youth and by blacks, and perhaps this is why no permanent liaison seems possible. Little mention can be found in this collection, or elsewhere for that matter, of the problems facing lower middle class white youngsters, yet their difficulties certainly demand the same kind of attention offered so willingly to their more economically and educationally favored colleagues.

Standing apart from either of the two segments described above are blacks of all economic and social persuasions. The growing polarity in the culture reinforces the isolation of black youth, leaving those at the upper end alienated and uncertain of their loyalties. Forced to choose between H. Rap Brown and Thurgood Marshall, the black adolescent is apt to discard traditional American values, finding no satisfaction in becoming an academic or economic success.

This youthful segment, or really the nature of the internal conflict to be found in this group, has attracted the widest attention among college radicals. Here an uneasy and often tenuous connection apparently has developed. Still, some who profess to have looked beyond the slogans and the pictures see a more complex relationship. In the Autumn 1969 issue of *The American Scholar,* Michael Lerner wrote:

> When white . . . students denounce the racist university or racist American society, one has little doubt about what they refer to. One also has little doubt about the political leanings of the speaker. He is a good left-liberal or radical, upper-class or schooled in the assumptions of upper-class liberalism.
>
> Liberal-to-radical students use these phrases and feel purged of the bigotry and racism of people such as Chicago's Mayor Daley. No one could be further from bigotry, they seem to believe, than they.
>
> But it isn't so. An extraordinary amount of bigotry on the part of elite liberal students goes unexamined. . . . Directed at the lower-middle-class, it feeds on the unexamined biases of class perspective, the personality predilections of elite radicals, and academic disciplines that support their views. . . .
>
> In general, the bigotry of a lower-middle-class mayor toward a rioter is not viewed in the same perspective as the bigotry of an upper-middle-class peace matron toward a lower-middle-class mayor; or of an upper-class university student toward an Italian, a Pole or a National Guardsman from Cicero, Illinois—that is, if the latter two cases are called bigotry at all. The violence of the ghetto is patronized as it is "understood" and forgiven; the violence of a Cicero racist, convinced that Martin Luther King threatens his lawn and house and powerboat, is detested without being understood. Yet the two bigotries are very similar (p. 439).

Lerner's statements cast a certain doubt upon the purity of radical motives with reference to those they seek to rescue from the ghetto. Finally, it has been said all too often that no one really understands what is going on in the black community today. This sad fact is confirmed by the fact that papers from the symposium on which this volume is based include no essays bearing directly on the problems of blacks, and the editors were forced to look elsewhere for material on this subject.

If one takes the short view of what is going on in the country, he may conclude that the nation is heading rapidly for disaster. The younger generation is out of control, and leadership in the executive branch of the federal government has passed from the hands of one madman to another. The opposing view is much more reassuring, but has a certain wishful quality associated with it. Things are not worse; they are much better. It is best to have the issues out in the open, and what is happening on the campus, in places like Chicago in the summer of 1968, in New Haven in 1970, and in politics everywhere, is a healthy and inevitable sign of the need to change, to reorganize our country.

The revolt of youth against their elders is not a new phenomenon. It is doubtless one of the conditions needed for cultural change. The right of one generation to challenge or examine the conclusions of another is too well accepted to require documentation. Without it there would have been no Renaissance, no Reformation, and mankind would truly have been the loser. The long view, however, is difficult to attain in this country where most know little of history and care nothing for philosophy. The youth movements with which we are familiar are the more traditional ones, those which operate within the expanded framework of our society. We are comfortable with Young Republicans and Young Democrats, and with the Boy Scouts. We even understand, although reluctantly, movements which want to change society, but once again within the established political framework, as in the case of the Communist Youth Groups and even the Hitler Jugend. They belong to the revolutionary movement, but operate in a clearly defined way in support of a political philosophy.

Our own youth conflict in this country apparently had the same roots. Students protested the treatment of blacks, the war in Vietnam, the use of the campus for recruiting, and their small voice in academic policies. Society's first reaction was one of repression and delay. We did not really hear, and we had little disposition to act. The ensuing conflagration brought the message home, and society's institutions began slowly, as they must, to change. It was at this point that a peculiar "newness" manifested itself. The changes did not bring an end to the revolt; they only brought a

14

new series of demands. A few were once again serious, but some verged on the absurd. The feeling slowly grew that we were dealing with a strange and new idea, revolt for its own sake. This, then, was not a movement which sought to change society, but rather one which seemed bent on society's destruction. The above statement applies only to a small segment of all who profess activist aims. In fact, the student movement has become fragmented, and in retrospect we can now distinguish between the radicals and moderate activists.

The case for the young is well stated by Hugh Trevor-Roper, the sympathetic provost of King's College in Cambridge. He argues in an article "The Revolt of Youth: Society's Cancer or Cure?" in *Réalitiés* in April 1968 (*no. 209*) that "society ought to surrender to the young, and abolish the family against whose strictures the young have risen in justified rebellion" (p. 52). But here again, the historian brings some reassurance. There were other periods of history when the gap between generations loomed so large that social restraints were violently cast off, when a generation's experience was so different in some powerful way from its predecessors that the attendant tension was too great to tolerate. The sixteenth, seventeenth, and eighteenth centuries all provide examples; the religious struggles in which whole generations were used up is only a single illustration.

Trevor-Roper takes a pleasantly sanguine view of today's difficulties: "Just as in a family, the revolt normally lasts for only a brief period—the young man who rebels at eighteen becomes a conformist, with only a slight difference, at twenty-two—so in society tradition is broken only to be reasserted, again with slight difference. This toughness of tradition, its capacity to reassert itself, even in radically changed circumstances, is something of a historical mystery; but it is also a historical fact."

This is in effect what we stated in the *Yale Review* in October 1967 when we first wrote on the growing youth upset. When youthful dissent is viewed this way, it is possible to construct a reassuring picture in which one need only insert the proper elements in the

15

various squares, see the puzzle whole, and wait for it all to subside. Thus, we have the parent generation, raised in the Depression, products of the terrible uncertainties of that era, the stultifying emotional climate, the frantic fight for survival, the merit badges we all now proudly wear. We sit in our affluent houses and vie with each other in horrendous recollections of that era while our children sit about us with bored looks on their faces.

Our children are indifferent to us, and they wear different labels. They are the Pepsi generation, raised in convertibles and often off to Europe before their parents have been there. We have sent them to the colleges we had no thought of ever attending and have dressed them the way we wished to be dressed in our own fantasied youth. They are young, attractive, speak far better than we ever did, and we are caught up in their charisma. Structural-defect specialists, as the young always are, they can easily tell us what is wrong in society, and most of us agree with their analysis.

This, of course, was never quite true before, neither here nor in Europe. Age is the culturally venerated period throughout mankind's history, and as a corollary, the stability of society has always been regarded as an absolute necessity for progress. Today we find ourselves agreeing with the young that change, in and of itself and of almost any variety, is a good thing. This state of impermanence is neither good nor bad. It is different, and it creates different sets of expectations in the disparate groups. But even more striking is the notion that youth has certain rights and privileges which automatically accrue to it. This last is surely a novel development, and we doubt that the historian really can find precedents. History does demonstrate that children were never more affluent, never more concentrated in single places like large universities, and never more encouraged to think well of themselves and their ideas.

In a cultural sense we can say that today we have an exaggeration of normal occurrence—youth separating itself from its elders. This may be the consequence of the special circumstances discussed above. In any event, we are now in the midst of the struggle, and we must live with it. Its excesses (and the special circumstances which

16

encourage them) should be reviewed carefully by both those who support society's institutions and those who mean to overturn the institutions. From this dialog we may find the means to encourage the healthy need for individuation, while avoiding the psychopathy. As Trevor-Roper trenchantly stated it: "In our complex society one generation has too much to teach another for the dialogue between them to be abandoned. In a healthy society, what I have called 'the dialectic of generations' is not vetoed, as in Russia, nor uncontrolled, as in America, but contained."

The forty-sixth annual meeting of the American Orthopsychiatric Association was devoted to a measured consideration of these problems. In his welcoming speech Dane G. Prugh, the president, stated the charge:

> Together we will explore the contributions of mental health workers to changes in our social and educational institutions which can permit our deeply concerned young people to play a vital role in determining the destiny of our society. As professionals alone we cannot solve the crisis of racism, purge our country of violence and bitterness, remove the scourge of poverty, nor erase the blight of our cities. We can open our ears to youth, however, in company with our distinguished guests from professional and public life. From the ensuing interchange of ideas, we can enrich and enlarge our mental health contributions, with the promise of some help resulting for our faltering society in responding to youth's challenge—our most precious asset and perhaps our only hope.

Ears were open to youth, both formally and informally, and the unscheduled, intramural performances were very exciting. Some meetings were picketed by a student caucus, led by a radical psychiatrist who was a member of the association, and several meetings were reduced to shambles and then canceled by the chairmen after hooting interruptions from the floor. Some members professed to see these things as a healthy sign of organization growth, and others were troubled to find a frightening similarity to pre-World War II Germany. Here as elsewhere in this land of the free, the reader is invited to "pay his money and make his choice."

17

The papers which follow represent the publishable yield from that meeting, along with a classic or two from elsewhere. John Bunzel's article, which first appeared in *The Public Interest* in 1968, deals with at least one aspect of this matter. Certain other papers of major importance were similarly added to broaden the scope of this volume. In this category fall Brzezinski's analysis of revolution, which originally was published in *The New Republic* (June 1968); Nathan Glazer's commentary on Berkeley (*The Public Interest*, Fall 1968), and Friedenberg's observations on social class (*New American Review*, no. 6, 1968-1969). The papers appear here in slightly different form from the original versions and are used with permission of the original publishers. A careful reading will convince anyone that sadness and pessimism are the characteristic ambience of the professionals, while those under age thirty remain, for the most part, cynical and disillusioned with society and with our efforts to change it. The collection has a mildly misleading tone, for it has not, unfortunately, caught the angry sarcasm which was often heard from the other side of the speaker's podium. The tone of the organized presentations was sober and reflective, while student behavior often seemed to some to resemble a floor fight at a Students for a Democratic Society convention. In an effort to catch this flavor, the editors interviewed some of the informal participants both at the meeting and back at their campuses as well. These vignettes will be found in the prolog, midpiece, and epilog.

Lastly, it should be noted that no solutions to the problems raised by youthful dissent can be found in this collection, which simply intends to appraise in a current sense a process which has been afoot in the land since Berkeley in 1964.

Morton Levitt
Ben Rubenstein
September 1970

Prolog

The Week That Was

Monday, August 18, 1968 was an extremely warm day, the kind that is becoming commonplace in this country with the approach of Labor Day. I am sure that the weather bureau, with its impressive instrumentation, can disprove this subjective idea of days becoming warmer at the end of summer, but my own notions about climate date from the *Farmer's Almanac,* which I read while passing time in drowsy fashion in my father's barber shop in the middle 1920s. That doughty journal routinely warned its readers about Labor Day weather and, like many things associated with my past, I remain attached to its predictions in simplistic fashion.

Someone had approached me that morning with the news that Russia and four Communist nations had invaded Czechoslovakia. Since the same campus humorist had tried me once with a story that the Israeli Army had shot down our Early Bird satellite, and that we were going to war to rescue the country's television empire, I was not much concerned. I sighed wearily, waved my hand in amused fashion (thus covering all exigencies), and went about my business.

Later there was an informal faculty meeting. Two students had been accepted as members of the curriculum study committee, and one was readily identified as a malcontent. The evidence was incontrovertible: he wore a thick beard (still something of a rarity in medical school) and was known to be dissatisfied with his education (or of our efforts). The faculty's first proposal was simple: ask for two more choices from the Student Council. How to explain it? Just say we don't like the nominations! Get clean kids, get bright kids; there were countless attributes and student names to fit them. They all added up to a description of what we know as the campus squares, students who behave like the students of five or ten years ago.

My efforts at persuasion were only mildly successful. The group agreed to accept the nominees, but one faculty member insisted that the students be informed that they had only advisory functions, that they were to think before they spoke, etc., etc., etc. Another compromise was necessary. The students were to be voting members (after all, there were only two of them to eight faculty), but previous decisions reached by the committee were to stand and were not subject to reconsideration.

The faculty meeting was over, and members stood in small clumps. One angry voice asked: "What do they want from us? Don't they think we know how to do our jobs?" By natural progression, the discussion shifted to the war, to the countless anti-Vietnam war posters (described by one physician as un-American) on the corridor walls, to the McCarthy petitions on all sides of the building. Again the plaint: "What do they want from us? We didn't make the war. What's it all got to do with medicine?"

Evening came. The late afternoon dogfight on the expressway was replaced by a martini, and mild anticipation of hearing how mature and sober Walter Cronkite saw the world "the way it is" that evening. But there was no Cronkite. Instead, the Security Council of the United Nations was debating a procedural matter, whether to make the Russian invasion of Czechoslovakia an agenda item. Startled, I heard myself say: "the Israelis have shot down the Early Bird satellite."

How to explain this strange juxtaposition? I would not believe the first story, I could not believe the second. But it was true. Undersecretary of State George Ball was speaking. I did not like him; I had no reason save why would anyone willingly join a lame duck president knowing he had to support an unpopular war in the corridors of the U.N.? I also confused him with someone else with a similar name, a younger man, an economist, who left President Johnson to return to Columbia. Was he Ball or Bell? No matter, this was George Ball and, while he was not an Adlai Stevenson, there was something solid and attractive about him. Without false virtue, he was lining out in clean, muscular prose a strong condemnation of the Soviet Union. Of course, I thought, we can afford virtue here; we have so little left in Vietnam. What would the Russians reply? I found myself thinking that there had to be some plausible explanation—summer maneuvers that overshot their mark, overzealous commanders disobeying orders, a series of semi-tragic errors that would now be rectified, the troops were even at that moment being ordered home, even perhaps a confession of an honest mistake.

Nothing of the sort. Soviet Ambassador Yakov A. Malik spoke with broad sarcasm and a cutting bitterness. A small matter, he said, hardly worthy of any kind of fuss. We were sent for, he contended, but furnished no names, addresses, nor phone numbers of the hosts. We will do our business quickly, he promised, and once we have taught those turncoat Czechs their lesson, we will leave quietly. An internal matter, a family fight, he offered, really not a matter of international borders at all.

My sons sat around me as I listened, two wearing beards and the other hoping to. No one said anything. None of them seemed concerned by the apparent fact that someone had to be lying, that an amazing *trompe l'oeil* was taking place. It was, I was told when I inquired, the way politicians were. And concern for the truth? I asked. What of the expectation that nations at the bar of justice must be expected to speak honestly? No chance, they said. Politics, they answered again.

A year ago I was walking through the Yale campus with a faculty adviser on our way to one of the dining halls. I commented about a bulletin board notice I had read that day which removed the requirement that jackets and ties be worn in the dining halls. The adviser nodded sadly and added that he regretted it; to him, "the university would never again be the same." Later, around the table, faculty men noted empty places and spoke of the declining prestige of dining hall membership for the faculty. In the past it had been a coveted badge of status. Now they mentioned the name of a professor who received membership and had never taken advantage of it. I looked around the lovely hall and agreed that it would never again be the same.

Later that evening, I spoke with a group of students who had recently returned from the Peace Mobilization March in Washington. Several of the young men were in the divinity school; others were in general studies but all were influenced by the Yale chaplain, the Reverend William Sloan Coffin. They were bearded, wore turtlenecks, and, out of deference to my age, wore ties over the turtlenecks. There was an air of quiet fraternity about them. Two of them had been beaten by the police in Washington but had not been intimidated. Determined to continue their nonviolent resistance, they showed impressive dedication and militancy. One young man said that Jesus gave him both example and courage. They did not speak with hatred, and yet I felt 'hat there was an underlying danger. One student said that he was not afraid to die because he believed that he was a part of a noble cause based upon the principles of brotherhood, compassion, and love as enunciated by Jesus. I sensed in the group a feeling of both moral superiority and quiet arrogance.

The next night the picture cleared in some ways while becoming more muddied in others. Cronkite was back, pointing out that time was of the essence, that the Soviets were about to locate and identify their hosts. Three of the ten members of the Czech Presidiur̄ were reported to have sought outside intervention. Meanwhile, Alexander Dubcek, the prime minister, and other members were rapidly disappearing in armed vans enroute to Moscow where they were in time-honored Russian fashion being labeled as traitors. Television pictures smuggled out showed thousands in Prague's streets pelting Russian tanks with fruit and paint while shouting "Go home." A national strike was being threatened for the next day.

And here in America? Several miles of chainlink had been erected around the International Amphitheatre in Chicago to keep demonstrators out of the Democratic party convention, and that wise young-old sage Eric Sevareid was now telling it the way it was. President Johnson, proclaiming his readiness to go to Moscow any hour of the day or night to settle this "monstrous international crisis," had intended to go to Moscow all the time, Sevareid said. The President's hope for greatness was based in final spasm upon the hope of a Russian *entente cordiale,* now shattered by the events of the last two days. Moreover, Johnson was alleged to be annoyed by the dovishness of his ambivalent Vice President and was leaning toward the Republican candidate, Richard Nixon, whom he had formerly denounced but who now greeted each of the President's belligerent statements with whoops of support.

What were the youth of the nation to think of this spectacle? Where were the solid links in the chain? What was the right and what was the wrong? When would the Russian tanks begin to shoot and ruin the whiskey courage of the tiny Czech nation? When would Chicago Mayor Richard Daley's police force give in to those internal impulses and start this summer's issue of what was fast becoming an annual civil war?

It was truly a world out of control, with our folly in Vietnam now matched by Russia's madness on her own borders. Worst of all, the whole thing was inexplicable. Russia, the Hungarian holocaust of 1956 almost forgotten, was fast becoming a respectable world power. Our warlike posture in Asia and China's intransigence was giving Moscow a peace-loving reputation. Some immense miscalculation must have taken place for anything so untimely to have happened.

A few years ago, we wrote an unpopular article (unpopular enough for the journal which published it to invite someone else to refute it) entitled "The Children's Crusade" (*American Journal of Orthopsychiatry,* 38 (July 1968). The paper posed a number of questions:

> Should the university with its traditional goals—the search for truth and the transmission of knowledge—accept the program, behavior, and methods of the rebels as an integral part of the educational process? Are the consequent confrontations the kind of educational experience which the university wishes to encourage? What are the philosophical and historical implications of a victory of violence over rational discourse?

It should now be interesting to see how student activists would react to this most recent imbroglio. Surely there would be strong condemnation of the Soviets, placards, street parades, and protest meetings. Granted that there was a political convention in Chicago, that Tweedledee and Tweedledum were hopefully to be upset by Senator Eugene McCarthy, a doomed man with a charisma among youth. The Americans were therefore to be allowed a week for finishing tasks already begun, and then the real international work would begin. Shoulder by shoulder with English youth, the French, the Japanese, and the Italians, the bloody legions of last spring would reform, up would go the barricades, out would come the paving blocks. Soon the helmeted police would arrive, and the now familiar scene of youth in revolt would pass in review once again.

Strange to say, nothing of the sort happened. Where were the world builders? Working on Cape Cod, waiting on tables in national parks, sunning at Santa Monica, and traveling in Europe. A few were still reported to be in New York to hear what happened to the newest anti-Christ, Grayson Kirk, president of Columbia University, who resigned a week later.

Occasionally, a contretemps of similar magnitude to the Soviet error in Czechoslovakia occurs. A South Vietnamese general is pictured in the nation's press in the act of shooting a desperate Viet Cong guerrilla who appears to be fourteen years old, or U.S. Marines set fire to a village in Vietnam because the enemy were reported to be in the vicinity; or American U.N. Ambassador Arthur Goldberg offers ringing assurance to the Security Council that the *Pueblo* had "always and constantly" been in international waters while Secretary of Defense McNamara is to be heard 200 miles away saying that no one knew where the *Pueblo* had been for at least ten days before its seizure; or President Eisenhower denies any knowledge of U-2 flights over Russia only to find that the State Department has confessed. Although the incidents mentioned here relate to the United States, each of the world's large nations suffers its share of painful exposures.

At issue is the matter of morality. Shall the truth be told, no matter what the consequences? Shall errors be frankly confessed? Can a man's or a nation's motives be discussed and analyzed openly? These are the compelling questions of this era which must be honestly answered.

Let us digress for a moment to the week begun above. Dubcek and Czernick are back from Moscow alive and well. A compromise has been struck; the Czech government will be allowed to remain in office, but the Communist armies will stay and liberalism will be curtailed. A "victory" proclaim the country's political leaders, but the people cry sellout. Still, not much happens as thousands mill about the streets muttering vaguely about a general strike that will paralyze only the country itself. This typically bourgeois gesture will undoubtedly demonstrate Czechoslovakian unity to the world, but it will scarcely impress the invading armies who are in no case dependent upon the Czech economy. Will there be any real war, will street fighting begin, will we have an uprising like Hungary in 1956 or Warsaw in 1942? Not likely, because the enemy military power is to be found on all sides, and Eastern Europeans of all ages and persuasions have learned to be wary of life and death issues. "Lie back," is the official word, "let's see what happens now."

And the same week in our own country? After a promising start, the Eugene McCarthy and George McGovern forces fall in disarray while Ted Kennedy says once and for all that he is not the one for this hour. Vice President Hubert Humphrey, a man for all seasons, turning and twisting to cover all positions and all exits, clearly carries the day. The drama is stark, and the struggle between good and evil is fought over each issue in the lengthy convention. The only winner, as might be expected, is expediency, and political compromise, badly disguised as virtue, triumphs over all. Humphrey proclaims that he wears no man's collar but also proudly announces that he is running on Johnson's program. He is for ending the war promptly, but the peace must be honorable, one which assures enemy capitulation. We are for self-determination, but we cannot abandon the Vietnamese to the forces within their own country.

The bitter fights over delegations are, with a single exception, resolved in favor of the status quo, but we are informed that this has been an "open" convention. And finally, after the hatred is spent and the furor subsides, we are told by Humphrey that the bloodletting was good for the spirit of the country, that such family fights are healthy and really a part of the tradition of the Democratic party, that everyone will kiss and make up as ranks close and the party goes on to its eighth victory in its last ten tries.

And youth? Outside in the streets surge our country's hope. None manage to penetrate the convention hall, although their efforts keep police and National Guardsmen occupied throughout the four days. On the first two days they enthusiastically demonstrate, and their very presence makes the delegates uncomfortable. They stand outside hotels on Michigan Boulevard and plead humorously through bullhorns to be invited into delegates' bathrooms "to wash up for the day." Later that day, and less humorously, they provoke the police into mild displays of brutality, but the gains and losses are small, and more than 2,000 delegates serenade Mayor Daley, whose orders the police are following, with a hearty "happy birthday" greeting. It must be admitted that the youth groups' activities on Monday likely kept Lyndon Johnson from a similar hootenanny, and that Humphrey would soon indicate that he is on their side, too, in another amazing feat of legerdemain, but student comments in Chicago as of that moment were instructive. Some felt that no matter what happened, it was a worthwhile experience. Others reported that they had made their presence felt; that is, the fact that they were opposed to the Vietnam War gave support to the minority position in the platform fight. A number expressed bitterness at their treatment by the Chicago police and threatened vengeance at the very next opportunity.

Several days before the Democratic convention I visited the Students for a Democratic Society headquarters located near the Columbia University campus. It was easily identifiable by the huge red flag hanging from a pole in front. There were some young men outside waiting, I discovered, for Mark Rudd. When he appeared, I found him abstracted, intense, and very much involved in stimulating young people to move on to Chicago. Rudd said he was working on an ideological article, and I said that we would like to print it. The matter of an author's fee was important, for money was desperately needed. It was also clear that he needed a platform from which to express his ideas. I was sent to the third floor to meet other SDS members. The foyer was plastered with anti-war posters, announcements of meetings, and four-letter words.

A boy named Dave and two girls in the messy room were talking on the telephone. There was an urgent need for cars and money for the trip to the Democratic convention. Dave and I spoke as he followed the telephone conversations with a worried air. Shirtless, he scratched his chest in an abstracted fashion while he explained the goals of SDS. At one time a girl interrupted us, saying (with annoyance) "That damned phone company. They always break in to ask the calling number." The others commiserated with her, but after a moment, the other girl said reflectively, "Maybe it has to do with that $200 call someone made to Paris. We don't know who made the call."

I asked Dave about student strategy last spring. If Columbia had granted their original demand for amnesty, would they have negotiated the other issues? After some reflection, he said no. Initially they had no idea of strategy or direction. They felt that they must be treated as equals by the faculty and administration, because their grievances were just. Events made it clear that there would be more to gain from confrontations than from negotiations. What took place later, as he saw it, proved the point. The police brutality served to radicalize the uncommitted students.

Dave did not feel that the conflict about Columbia's plan to build a gymnasium was a contrived issue. He named a Harlem group led by a minister as one which had fought to bring Columbia

27

to reconsider its building plan. In addition, the Morningside Heights community project had initially fought the gymnasium but later widened their scope of action to include other institutions in the area. As a consequence the role of SDS in the community action program has been weakened. The community project now concentrates on fighting tenant eviction and the Columbia University's "arrogant" drive to change the present character of the area. Dave said that the sole interest of the Board of Trustees of Columbia University is in the development of the real estate holdings. He asked if I had read Who Rules Columbia?

"We are revolutionists," Dave continued, "even if Columbia granted amnesty this spring we would have continued to fight." The university should be seen as a training ground to prepare radicalized students for work in community action programs. Campus liberals are of little value in effecting social change, and the faculty is impractical. Dave quoted Stalin: "Liberals are people who are guilty because they are not radicals," and felt that those he identified as "the reformers" have been unable to push "the administration" into making any changes. Columbia Vice President David B. Truman was said to have rubbed his hands recently this summer as he said, "Things are back to normal," which Dave took to mean there was no longer any interest in students.

SDS wants to move out of the campus into the community. They recognize that social issues are larger than the campus struggle and they have no purchase in the neighborhoods. They hope to work with organized labor. The plan of action is unclear. Dave enthusiastically described SDS's plans to sponsor an international meeting of student radicals at Columbia in October. They want to bring in Wolf from Berlin, Cohn-Bendit from Paris, and many others. But again they need money, which they wish to borrow and repay by sending the foreign leaders on a tour of college campuses. Dave asked whether I had any money to lend for this worthy purpose.

In Grant Park on Wednesday morning the Guerrilla Theater rehearses its productions. Dirt and grime on their faces are covered by chalky makeup, and several dozen demonstrators march in a mock birthday celebration for LBJ. Looking strangely like children dressed in their parents' clothing, they walk in top hats, morning coats, and long dresses, chanting in moving fashion:

"Happy Birthday, Hell B. J.!
Happy Birthday, Death!
Happy Birthday, Atrocity!"

A not-too-gifted mime is shown addressing the Democratic convention. In Senator Claghorn fashion, he poses several questions to the delegates. One has to do with youthful dissent and a second with minority groups. In answer to both queries, the players shout "Kill, kill, kill!" The president then congratulates the convention for the selection of "Humphrey-Dumpty, whom I raised from a pup." Onlookers laugh gently, and the whole setting has a bittersweet, end-of-summer quality. Afterward a television commentator interviews a red-haired, freckled-faced twenty-three-year-old girl who is one of the players. She is from Wisconsin and has come to Chicago to act in the company. In response to the routine question about wanting to be in the theater, she answers negatively. The announcer is incredulous. "Why are you doing this then?" he asks. She quietly answers, "It's the way I can show how I feel about this country." The unadorned answer seems incomprehensible to the commentator, and the interview founders.

As the third day wears on the political machine gathers momentum and the permanent chairman, Congressman Carl Albert, known as "The little Lion from little Dixie," gavels motions and votes to quick decision. Depression is seen in the faces of the McCarthy-McGovern supporters, and several ugly incidents develop between security guards and delegates.

Outside, the mood has changed ominously. Hundreds, perhaps thousands of young people stand in the street outside the Conrad Hilton Hotel. The police suddenly charge, and a bloody melee develops. The police chase, catch, hold, and hit demonstrators. Many are thrown to the ground and beaten. On television film we see newspaper men and photographers struck by the police, ministers wearing clerical collars manhandled as they are loaded in the police wagons, and one girl demonstrator knocked down by police and kicked continuously as she tries to roll away. Well dressed bystanders are similarly attacked, and the whole terrifying performance is accompanied by the demonstrators' derisive chant: "Seig Heil!"

Mayor Daley sits calmly at the helm of the Illinois delegation and denies any knowledge of what is happening in the Loop. When a reporter points to the telephone at Daley's elbow and requests that the mayor make a call, Daley insists that the reporter mind his own business. This stratagem succeeds for only a few minutes, for new reports of serious trouble keep coming into the hall. The mayor finally speaks: "The police are all family men, the finest men who wouldn't react with violence." This satisfies only the mayor, and soon the New York, Wisconsin, and Colorado delegations are trying to move that the convention be adjourned because of the disorder outside. They are defeated on parliamentary grounds (no roll call vote may be interrupted for any reason), and the convention goes on to nominate Humphrey. More film is shown on television, McCarthy and McGovern are reported to be incensed by the police brutality, and we see pictures of the hundreds of wounded as the fight goes on.

Finally this night is over. There are talks of a walkout, of a sit-in for peace, of a caucus for a fourth party, of a delegate march all the way to the Hilton Hotel in protest against the police brutality. The usually mild Cronkite places the blame squarely in the lap of Mayor Daley. It is now 3 a.m. Thursday. A week ago Czechoslovakia was invaded. Dubcek and Svoboda are back in Prague, but their popularity is in peril. The militant youth of the last week who threw fruit and paint at the Russians march down the Prague streets carrying a coffin simply marked "Czechoslovakian Nationalism." An English-speaking Czech in Wenscelas Square is asked whether there will be "a war, a fight" now that the Russian terms have become known. He answers apologetically, "No fight, sorry, no rebellion, sorry, only resignation, sorry." They are sorry there, and we are sorry here. It is in the nature of life.

A grain and a half of seconal—the middle-aged "fix"—brings four hours of restless turning and twisting. Back to the television. This time NBC. There in Chicago sits Hugh Downs, Barbara Walters, and Joe Garagiola. All look clean and fresh-faced. Friends in the entertainment business have told me that Downs makes more than $400,000 a year hosting the "Today" show, because he is the least controversial man in television. If this is true, Miss Walters is a perfect counterpart. Once after commenting that her elderly mother watches the show and criticizes her when her slip inadvertently shows, Barbara apologized to her own mother, for saying something about her which might sound uncomplimentary to this fine woman, and to all mothers everywhere who "really love their children."

Garagiola is a former major league catcher. The jock incarnate; his tortured syntax is improving, but his jokes bear the stale smell of the winter baseball banquet circuit, where they undoubtedly originated. I once heard him interview a black athlete who had decided not to compete in the Olympic Games. Outraged, Garagiola asked him why he did not move to another country, as if Olympic competition was obligatory for American citizens. Despite the well-manicured appearance, all three are concerned with the trouble in the streets the night before. Downs reports that tear gas had wafted into the windows of Humphrey's suite, obliging the Vice President to take a shower to get rid of the sticky feeling, thereby interrupting his television viewing. Downs is all for law and order, while Miss Walters is full of womanly sympathy for the demonstrators, Garagiola, however, is quite interesting. He had been disgusted by what he had seen outside his window last night. "Wait a minute," Downs says, "they were asked to get out of the street, weren't they?" Annoyed, Garagiola asks, "Are police supposed to take a 'shot' [to hit] at kids? How about that?"

Sensing a controversy, Hugh backpedals skillfully, "Now, wait a minute, Joe, sit right where you are. Let's stop for a word from 'Ball Blue Book.' " Struck dumb by the transpositional possibilities of that name, I fail to find out what the product is and soon the discussion continues. Downs develops an involved argument about streets versus sidewalks and concludes, "We all do agree, don't we, that those kids shouldn't be on the street, they should be on the sidewalk, that's the issue, isn't it?"

Before anyone can respond Hugh turns us over to Barbara, "with a message about athlete's foot." Suddenly the excitement mounts. The big winner of the night before makes his appearance with his pleasant wife. The Vice President also looks clean and rested and he makes the expected victory disclaimers. No bad feelings, a congratulatory call from Nixon, shore up the dykes, etc., etc., etc. It's all top-drawer Humphrey until we get the issue of the street fighting on the night before. The Vice President's easy manner fades: he thinks it is terrible. Hugh suddenly asks an embarrassing question. It has to do with Mayor Daley's responsibility for the mess and its effects upon Humphrey's chances for election. Without missing a beat Humphrey neatly sidesteps: he and his wife "have suffered some real insults from these people as we have traveled around the country. Some are idealists, some came with helmets looking for a fight, they're all mixed together."

Downs nods sympathetically, and the Vice President continues, "We shouldn't confuse dissent with disarray, with bad manners, with all the things that happened downstairs last night. I happen to feel students are justified by the way they are not brought into campus life." This is a most difficult sentence to parse, but perhaps Humphrey's confusion about these matters reflects what most of us feel. The candidate is offered the best wishes of the cast of "Today," and with Humphrey's fixed visage still on the screen, Downs begins to talk up the next commercial "the case of the lazy eye, ambiopia."

I had been given Joan's name by an SDS member at Columbia who said that she had been involved in the sit-in at Hamilton Hall. This was the place where the blacks had rejected the white students on the first night of the Columbia riot. Joan was described to me as a sensitive Negro girl who wrote poetry. I telephoned her at her job in one of the Columbia offices, and she agreed to meet me at the university gate. She described herself as "skinny, look like a sixteen-year-old, but I am older and I am slightly brown." We met and walked to a nearby student restaurant. Joan was thin, almost emaci-

ated in appearance, depressed and sardonic. She was a curious mixture of pessimism and strength. She had grown up in Cambridge and came to Barnard College, where she received a degree in French literature. She went to graduate school at Columbia after working for a year. Later she dropped out, saying: "I felt I was not going anywhere. My work did not mean anything." She struck me as a withdrawn person caught up in the drug game. Joan had been politically active throughout college in civil rights and antiwar projects. She reacted sharply when I tried to make any categorization ("The Establishment encourages categorization in order to fragment actions groups; If red baiting won't break you up, you will win.") and she deeply distrusted organizations. Although committed to SDS goals, she did not trust the group.

She holds two jobs. One is at Columbia, which "doesn't disturb my mind," and another is as a union organizer for office workers. Although Joan works with SDS, she regards the group as undisciplined middle class youngsters. "Did you see that mess in those rooms? They don't understand that if they are not tightly organized, they are through. They don't understand about violence. I do not mind murder but one has to know why he is murdering. "The SDS'ers," she continued sardonically, "look for a new Bolivia every day. There is no Bolivia here. They want the highs, not the nitty-gritty lows of scrounging for signatures on petitions and recruitment cards."

Those young people, she felt, were captured by the charisma of Castro, Cuba, Ché Guevara, and Bolivia. She described the tragic comedy of many young radicals who believe that their own situation is identical with that of their heroes. Joan is equally critical of her black colleagues. "Those cats were constructing a new history. They saw themselves at the barricades. Each one of them described their childhood spent on the streets of Harlem making the drug and crime scene. Not a word of it was true. They didn't come from Harlem. Those kids are middle class people who never had to worry in their lives. They would sit around all night making great plans for revolution."

33

"What are they doing now?" I asked. "They sold out. Ford Foundation gave their group a summer grant. They are reading history books and are being paid for noting the distortions of Negro history. They are all through."

"Why did they ask the white activists to leave?" I asked. Joan said it was a simple decision. They decided that if they kept their racial separatism, the authorities would never use force with the shadow of Harlem at their backs.

Joan has great respect for the Black Panthers but said that they did not come on the scene until after the confrontation. She had difficulty being arrested because the confrontations occurred while she was at work. Joan is committed to revolution and although she feels it will not come in her lifetime, she has no choice but to prepare for it. "The liberals will accomplish nothing."

On the way to work that morning, I heard David Dellinger being interviewed on the radio. He led the march on the Pentagon last fall. Although the FBI has called him a Communist, he is a graduate of Yale's Divinity School, and I am confused by the apparent contradiction. He has been in Chicago as chairman of the National Mobilization Committee, and said, as I recall his comments, that the protestors achieved ". . . a tragic kind of success. . . . I think that the American people have seen the repressive nature of the city of Chicago, what happens to people who try to legitimately protest this country's involvement in Vietnam. I can't ask these people to stay here and be beaten again tonight [Thursday]. The dirty deed has been done by the Democratic party. They have nominated another loyal militarist and I am asking my people to go home and work against him and all the policy he stands for."

The local morning newspaper had a reporter in the successful candidate's suite the night before. Humphrey sits in front of the television screen (like the rest of us) as the votes are counted. He frequently bends forward and pulls the front of his coat down so his shirt will not stick out. Mrs. Humphrey is at the International Amphitheater. I saw her on and off during the previous evening on my television and felt she looked tired. Hubert watches her, too, from where he sits and when the state of Pennsylvania puts him over the top with its 103 votes, he, according to the paper, races to the television set and says "Mom, I wish you were here." Reporting that he kisses the screen, the morning paper commented (perhaps unnecessarily), "They have a thing going, those two!"

Thoroughly shaken by this tale of connubial bliss, I limped through the day and came home to watch the rest of the mess. A drink in hand, no passes to show, no challenges, no angry Andy Frake guards, no fights for food. My still-silent sons sat around me. No summer soldiers, they apparently would see the whole thing through. Cronkite sat at his usual station, and there with him was the man with all the "clout," the mayor of the city of Chicago. It appeared that he had been hurt by Cronkite's condemnation of last evening and had asked for equal time. Daley's stance was, I think the word is, conciliatory. Perspiration beaded on his florid face, but his manner was easy. He was either the friendly policeman on the beat having to rough up a few neighborhood drunks, or perhaps a teacher of delinquent children explaining in an earnest fashion why they had to be punished for their transgressions. The whole incident was television's fault, he maintained. People see a camera in the slums and come out to make trouble. Not only was the television industry responsible, but television continued to foment the trouble by reporting it. Cronkite, insouciant as ever, asked the mayor whether he really felt the news media was responsible for last night's mess. Daley responded, "Well, the press were part of the riots, were rioting, were acting like hippies." Cronkite offered, "You mean the underground press?" "The press," Daley said firmly. The police were maligned, the mayor contended. Rioters had called them "pigs" and other four-letter words and had used language "which you wouldn't hear in a brothel house, Walter." Daley wanted to know why there were no pictures of injured policemen. Some fifty-one were reported to be lying on the ground somewhere, one had a broken leg, and the other "a back," the mayor said. "The administration and the people from which I come would never stand for that," the mayor contended. In a fascinating slip Daley thundered in his honest-John fashion: "The people of Chicago and the police department have never and will condone violence." He continued: "Certain people planned to assassinate the three candidates. Also certain leaders, including myself." The mayor is now very sober and quiet. "Too bad you T.V. people didn't know that, Walter, you'd have treated us different, Walter." Then he volunteered the statement: "I wouldn't do nothing different, not even if I had the chance." The rioters were Communists, Daley said, as Cronkite slowly appeared to wake up. "Communists," he inquired, "are you sure?" Came Daley's prompt reply, "They're against the war, aren't they?" But did that make them Communists? Cronkite wanted to know. Daley was majestic: "You're too smart a man to believe that, Walter."

The interview was over. What did that last statement mean? Was it a gigantic put-on in which Cronkite and the rest of us were being taken in, or was Daley's sentence construction at fault? No matter; a simple judgment had been rendered by my sons: no man who talked that poorly could expect to be Vice President. Of course, that must have been Daley's ambition. He would bring law and order to Humphrey's liberalism. What a team! I'm flabbergasted.

I later talked with a young woman who had graduated from a small, conservative Eastern college and entered graduate school at Columbia. Before Columbia, Claire had never been "involved." She had indeed not been confronted with issues demanding a choice before—"We did not have one single Negro!" The graduate faculty in English at Columbia had little interest in literature but were heavily invested in criticism. Some reform of the department had been discussed by students, but the faculty was essentially uninterested. She had joined SDS because the group was involved with meaningful issues, although she did not care for their rhetoric or their uncomprising tactics. She found compatible boyfriends in the group, because she would not have been interested in fellows who thought differently.

Claire was frightened when the sit-in began, although the group did not believe that the administration would bring in the police. Nevertheless, although she would not want to relive "those nights at *Avery Hall," she would do it again. Strangely, she did not feel that the protest made any difference. "It has been a disorganized mess."* Yet action had to be taken, and the experience at Avery was described as the most meaningful of the year for her. *Learning had not been relevant, "not even the literature I was reading."* She was attractive, blonde, smartly dressed, and well mannered; yet she conveyed a feeling of hurt, anger, and confusion at the state of affairs on campus. *Like the others in the group, she claimed that the police brutality had radicalized here.*

The evening wears on. I soon discover that Senator Edmund Muskie has been tapped for the second place on the ticket. He is opposed only by the attractive black from Georgia, Julian Bond. When Bond shyly confesses that he is too young for national office, the audience can sense that here is a real winner, surely someone to be reckoned with in the future. The voting is perfunctory, and Muskie is soon on the dais. Only his wife is with him. His family is still in Maine, for he found out too late that he was Humphrey's choice. My home team of television viewers snicker. It has been known all day, they allow. Muskie compounds my doubts by telling what his old Polish mother said when asked earlier whether she intended to vote for her son. "It depends upon whom he's running against," she answers. If a man's own mother is not sure, I say : . . nonetheless, he is an engaging man who perhaps can be of some help to the listing Democratic party fortunes.

The night in Chicago appears to be quieter. There are some pictures of minor skirmishes, but the unpopular police are nowhere in sight. Instead we see gas-masked members of the National Guard. There is less fighting but more tension and more tear gas; in fact, the television screen creates the impression of a heavy fog shifting into a light snow. During the day a weary Eugene McCarthy has walked out to Grant Park to make a farewell address to his troops. He will not support the ticket, but will continue to work within the traditional political process. Newsmen are puzzled by his mixed reception, apparently not realizing that many of those spending the week in the park are not *for* anyone, only *against* the Establishment, wherever it is to be found.

37

Two marches develop during the day. Several thousand people of all persuasions participate, but both groups are turned back by the police at 16th Street. They are told that they have no permit for a parade, and they peacefully disperse. The old fight is seemingly gone, but Tom Hayden, a leader of the mobilization committee, says the struggle has already been won. Its purpose has been to "radicalize" the people and strengthen the anti-war movement. Sober reflection makes it hard to quarrel with his assessment.

An interesting development in the afternoon march is the participation of the deputy police commissioner of Chicago. As he walks along, he carries on a running dialog with the protestors. Patiently he repeats over and over a comforting litany: "The streets are for vee-hicular traffic and the sidewalks are for free movement of foot traffic." This is his explanation for the carnage of the preceding evening. Oh, yes, it is also "a matter of communication, we had people here acting as individuals, but moving in concert." The last word is pronounced like "cancer," and only after I see the footage again on another station do I finally make out its meaning. Strangely, the marchers respond positively to him. "This cat is O.K.," they say. "He's here with us, not at city hall or at the convention." The policeman smiles broadly, but I am flabbergasted. He utters the most arrant nonsense, but the young demonstrators are beguiled by him.

At the convention the band strikes up the "Minnesota Rouser," a song I associate with Big Ten football, with Bernie Bierman and the Golden Gophers of the 1930s, Hal Van Every, Bill Daly, Julie Alphonse, Bruce Smith, and that fabled horde of all-American linemen who stood seven feet tall and answered to names like Svenson, Nomellini, or Widseth. In comes Humphrey, looking strangely out of character with the football song. His face has an ashen quality, and the bright television lights create the appearance of much scar tissue around his face and eyes, like an old boxer who has suffered honorably over long years in the ring.

The speech was predictable. Humphrey was the same as Johnson, but he was also different. He said in what was probably the only quotable statement: "The policies of tomorrow need not be the policies of yesterday." Someone had sold the Democrats on an orchestra that punctuated Humphrey's statements with a loud chord and the effect was grotesquely disconcerting. A wind machine kept the American flag at attention through the proceedings. When it was all over, McGovern joined his old friend on the platform, but McCarthy opted out.

The next morning was "show and tell" time on the "Today" show. Hugh asked the regulars to describe their impressions of Chicago. Barbara spoke first from prepared notes. She got more than she reckoned on, she confessed. She learned what blood on the street looked like and what tear gas smelled like. She was still distressed by police brutality but gave the National Guard high marks. They and the rioters respected each other, she felt, and, in fact, when she and Joe Garagiola had been taking a stroll last night, a National Guardsman had called, "Hi Joe, how's Yogi?" Program regulars know that Yogi is Yogi Berra, the former New York Yankee catcher and manager, whose antics Garagiola has chronicled for years. How this question evidenced respect for the protestors was not made clear. A woman had phoned Miss Walters the night before from Atlanta. The woman was unknown to Miss Walters but had a son who had enlisted in the Army and was now awaiting shipment to Vietnam. What was he to think of the rioting? Barbara did not have the answer, but both women wept a little and each felt better for the experience. Barbara wondered about her own baby, now ten weeks old, whom she had not seen for a week. Hugh and Joe agreed that a week was a long time out of the life of a ten-week-old infant, and Miss Walters passed the "what did you think of Chicago" ball to Garagiola.

Much to my surprise, Joe was almost speechless. He did not know what to say . . . he had lived in Chicago himself . . . he had friends in Chicago whom he had seen last night . . . what was happening was terrible . . . . I was genuinely moved. Garagiola, so ready to dispatch black athletes to the boondocks, was truly troubled.

For Downs, "The hours were dwindling down to a precious few. Don't blame the basket for a few rotten apples," and then a commercial. Hugh brought news of some early morning trouble. The police had come up to the McCarthy headquarters on the fifteenth floor at the Hilton and had arrested some of the senator's young supporters for throwing things out of the windows. A fracas had developed in the lobby enroute to jail, and McCarthy was shown inspecting the damage in his campaign headquarters, as well as in the lobby. There were some pictures of youngsters with bloody heads being rushed out by the police. McCarthy looked particularly grim, I thought.

Hugh Downs was fair about the incident. He did not know what or even if anything was coming out of windows on the fifteenth floor. He was higher up in the hotel, and there were plenty of things coming past his window from floors above him. I wondered aloud how the police could tell where things came from in the hotel. One of my sons offered: "Angle of incidence equal angle of reflection. It's all very scientific, Dad." It was apparent I was being had, and I turned back to the program. Senator Muskie came on saying some relatively innocuous things, and then the program ended with a recording of Frank Sinatra singing "Chicago, My Kind of Town," while background pictures of the fighting in the streets were superimposed on the screen.

It was the end of summer and there were few people, issues, or even things to become entangled with. At lunch someone reported a great fight on television the night before between Gore Vidal and William F. Buckley. One network had been pairing these two antagonists as a commentator team, and I had meant to tune them in and see what was going on. There evidently had been a real rhubarb (as Garagiola would say) the night before. There had been some allusion on Buckley's part to Vidal's lack of masculinity. Vidal responded by calling Buckley a neofascist, and Buckley, after identifying himself as an infantryman in World War II, threatened to punch Vidal in his "goddamn face" according to the local respondent. Vidal countered with the fact that Buckley had seen no combat in the war, and apparently the whole thing ended there.

Time was running out for the convention. Charles Kuralt was sitting in for Cronkite, as he had all week. Neither Huntley nor

Brinkley was to be seen. The whole thing reminded me of a *New Yorker* cartoon showing a woman saying to her husband, "You know it's summer when Charles Kuralt is sitting in for Roger Mudd who was sitting in for Harry Reasoner who was sitting in for Walter Cronkite who is on vacation."

There was still revulsion about police brutality, but with youth and delegates leaving Chicago in large numbers, the whole matter began to be regarded with the fatalism associated with the second day after an airline disaster. A bad thing had happened, but what was now important was to pick up the pieces and go about the business of living. The Democratic ticket was viewed as roughly equivalent to the Republican with Humphrey-Nixon at six to five and take your pick and Agnew-Muskie seeming to be Siamese twins.

Czechoslovakia was in deep trouble. CBS reporter Morley Safer, who earlier in the day had been expelled from the country, said that there existed a list of 2,000 Czech intellectuals who were about to be arrested. The underground newspapers and radio stations were no longer in evidence, and the Presidium was meeting to choose a cabinet which would be acceptable to the Russians. The newspaper, *Literarni Listy*, which had spearheaded the liberalization movement, had put out its last edition. It contained a cartoon showing a Soviet soldier standing atop a tank and holding a machine gun. The caption read: "Workers of the world unite—or I shoot you!"

A short, slight, smartly dressed white girl with cropped hair came into the room at SDS headquarters. She was welcomed by the others, and I was introduced to her as a man who "is writing a book about us!" The phone rang and one girl, who is from a college in Ohio and working for SDS the summer, answered it. She listened, then whooped while clamping her hand over the receiver, "It's the newspapers! They want to know what we think about the Russian invasion of Czechoslovakia." There was a momentary silence in the dirty room. Clearly it was a historic moment, and I suddenly realized the meaning of the aura of arrogance which I had felt before. These youngsters were living out history. In their own minds they were at

41

the barricades personally struggling against the enemy—the Establishment, LBJ, Dean Rusk, et al. Perhaps this intense feeling of involvement was the "relevance" they sought.

An excited discussion began, but Dave quickly imposed order stating, "Tell them we have no statement." I asked, "What do you really believe?" He said, "We don't like what the Russians did but that is not relevant. We believe that the issue is why they do not send their tanks to North Vietnam." Then he turned me over to Trudy, a new arrival, who was to give me copies of SDS literature.

We walked to a back room where Trudy kept her files. She was proud of her file case. The rest of the room was in utter disorder. The walls were covered with latrine poetry, a vestige of the previous fraternity occupancy, and the newer slogans were in the new argot: "Up against the wall, Mother Fuckers." But Trudy's files were in immaculate order, much like her own appearance.

She is an eighteen-year-old Barnard sophomore from the deep South, and her parents are divorced. She had previously attended exclusive private schools. Bluntly she said, "My mother is a fascist-racist." Her father is a liberal, "an honest one." Throughout her adolescence she believed that there was a world out there which had more meaning than her empty one.

The moment that she entered Barnard she knew that she was free and running. She became acquainted with the activists. At the time of the sit-ins at Columbia her French history class was discussing the ideal character of French education. She had functioned last year at a "B" level but believed that she had learned little of value in college.

When sit-ins began in May, Trudy was frightened because she feared police retaliation. After the police assault she recovered quickly and, in her own words, "has no fear of the police" and has become "radicalized." Her mother, seeing her picture on television, sent a telegram to Columbia asking that they expel her. Moreover, she cut off all of Trudy's support.

She has withdrawn from Barnard and has secured a full-time office job. She works all of her spare time for SDS and finds her life mean-

*ingful and exciting. She glowingly described individual incidents of
rehabilitation observed while attending Liberation School. A well
known Cuban economist who was in a state of depression began his
lectures and research again this summer after his involvement with
SDS. Trudy's own plans are uncertain. She may never return to
school since the degree means nothing. While she does not agree with
the revolutionary role of SDS as defined by Dave, she does agree
that it is more important to change the total society than to concentrate upon campus affairs.*

Friday morning reporter Robert Trout said that he liked
Humphrey's speech, saying it had a religious ferver that used to be
characteristic of the old Humphrey. Still he felt the Democrats were
in real trouble. Someone else felt that the Vice President had once
again let his enthusiasm lead him astray on Wednesday night when
he publicly confessed his love for his leader: "Tonight, Mr. President, I say thank you, thank you, Mr. President."

McCarthy was staying over another day to investigate what
happened to his headquarters. Kuralt showed film of the injured
parties in McCarthy's group. They had, they said, asked the police
on what grounds they were being arrested. "Coffee grounds," was
the answer. It was clear that Mayor Daley was not abashed by anything that happened in his city, that he truly meant that he would
do nothing different the next time around.

That night *The New York Times* carried the small notice: "The
radical leaders of the Columbia University student strike have
called an open rally to protest against the Warsaw Pact occupation
of Czechoslovakia. The rally is to begin at 2 P.M. tomorrow in front
of the Plaza Hotel at Fifth Avenue and 58th Street."

The next afternoon we had a Pugwash Conference in our back-
yard. It is an idea we have easily stolen from Cyrus Eaton, and in
my family, it has omnibus implications. It covers everything from
quarrels over allowances to trouble with girls. As titular head of our
party, I had called this one myself. The agenda was simple and concise: 1) what about the Democratic party convention? and 2) what
about Czechoslovakia?

The answers were equally simple and concise. The convention was a farce, a show representing only the elitist elements in our country. It proved nothing, save that the people had no voice, no unity. And Czechoslovakia? Nothing to say really; crises come and go in the world and this was no different from Vietnam, from Santo Domingo. And lastly, (a nonagenda item) what about right and wrong? No difference, it just depends upon whom you talk to in the world. The evening paper on Saturday carried the headline: "Tough Warning to Soviets is Issued by Johnson."

Defining a
New Generation

Social Class Factors in Generational Conflict

Edgar Z. Friedenberg

The widely publicized marijuana raid effected January 17, 1968, on the dormitories of the State University of New York (SUNY) at Stony Brook has dramatized certain basic conflicts between American universities and the rich but toxic substrate that reluctantly supports them more clearly perhaps than any event since Senator Joseph McCarthy's campus incursions. Much more important than the use of marijuana on the campus is the power struggle between local authorities—especially the police—and the cosmopolitan interests of a university. Particularly at issue is whether the university is a "privileged sanctuary for lawbreakers," an allegation SUNY officials indignantly deny.

What seems oddly muted in the conflict is any suggestion that a university is indeed a sanctuary for certain kinds of activities and relationships which are socially valuable; and that unless these are privileged against gross violation by zealous and punitive officials, they will be lost from the society. Society, moreover, is diverse and pluralistic; and it is conceivable, though uncongenial to the American ethos, that there may be real conflicts of interest in it. It is possible—indeed, it is not unlikely—that to the police who busted Stony Brook to haul twenty-nine bewildered students out of bed before dawn and take them away, handcuffed, for booking, while the press and television cameramen they had notified recorded the scene, no function of a university has value. But a social institution

47

need not be valuable in the eyes of every member of a society to merit protection from violation by its enemies. If any institution were, it would not require protection.

Such an event could have occurred on any one of many university campuses in this country; somewhat similar events continually do, which is why the matter is worth considering. There are, to be sure, certain aspects of the situation at SUNY that contributed to the development of hostile relationships between the community and the university which finally exploded in the raid; these are worth considering as examples of factors which serve this destructive function. But a still more fundamental question is why, as a people, we permit our universities to be continually harassed on one pretext or another but always in a manner that expresses the same pattern of punitive shabby-gentility. Anti-intellectualism and an intrusive hatred of free and distinctive culture are old and persistent characteristics of American society, and one would have thought that so pragmatic a people would by now have evolved some practical means of dealing with them.

If there is any way for an American university to defend itself against pot busts, investigating committees, irate legislators, and indignant citizen's groups, we ought to have learned it long ago. The ambitions and anxieties that rock a mass society which has grown accustomed to regard the academic community primarily as a source economic opportunity for its more docile children and low cost technical advice for its economic enterprises are as predictably noxious to college and university life as heat, noise, and air pollution are to life in an industrial city. Yet, curiously, few comparable measures seem to have been taken to reduce their influence and minimize their effects. Those adopted have been almost entirely public relations measures, intended to increase the understanding and elicit the support of antagonistic groups, usually by compromises that sacrifice certain aspects of the integrity of university life. Administrators consent to the presence of undercover narcotics agents on campus, sometimes allowing them to register as students without even requiring that they meet the usual entrance qualifications. Records of conversations between students and faculty members or administrative officials which at the time were believed to be confidential are later turned over to staff investigators. At a more general level, less offensive morally but perhaps even more inimical to the university in the long run, efforts are made to convince the public that the university is "their university," that its services benefit them directly, that the ethical and esthetic standards that prevail in the university community are fundamentally the same as theirs, although occasional breaches of taste and decorum are to be expected in view of the immaturity of the students.

This attempt to win over the university's adversaries by insisting that they share its interests, and vice versa, is basically disrespectful of both the university and of its critics. There is no more reason why a university should be a public amenity than a steel mill or an Army camp. These facilities are not commonly defended as having to conform to the tastes and demands of the neighboring community. They are defended—if, indeed, they are attacked, as they rarely are —as generally serving a useful social function, though admittedly at somewhat greater profit to their own personnel than to the community at large. It is acknowledged that to the community at large they may be substantial sources of pollution. And although they may and usually do maintain public relations offices to develop the best relations they can with the community and still get what they regard as their job done, they do not expect active community support. The management—or command—assumes the political responsibility for neutralizing and containing such hostility as, it is assumed, will arise from time to time.

The argument that the university is uniquely dependent on public support and therefore more vulnerable is not logically tenable. The university *is* more vulnerable, because the public is far less critical of the military-industrial complex and less inclined to intervene in its affairs; and the university derives much of its support from state sources rather than federal sources, and state revenues are more subject to local influence. But both are dependent on public support, and the major universities may derive more than half their budget from federal sources, although these funds received under grants and contracts are largely unavailable for the university's traditional purposes and serve, indeed, to divert it from them. Nevertheless, popular disfavor is potentially as threatening to the military or to industry as to the university; but one cannot imagine disfavor actually being directed against the military or industry in as effective a manner.

In any society the essential systems of communication function to preserve the central organs of power from effective attack or even scrutiny. The public schools and the other mass media not only preserve a favorable image of the military-industrial complex, but they rather effectively prevent most people from conceiving that it could be fundamentally different, so it is not remarkable that steel mills and Army plants have little trouble with their constituencies. The last serious possibility is that they might have vanished with the incorporation of big labor into the Establishment. But universities, too, are a part of the Establishment. President Eisenhower, the former president of one of our greatest universities, might as well have referred to the military-academic as the military-industrial complex. Why, then, do universities not share in the Establishment's relative immunity to local harassment?

There are several reasons, but the most relevant to the kinds of hostility under discussion here derives, I believe, from the university's specific function of developing certain kinds of excellence in its students. This is what the society demands of it; and as long as the excellence is conceived in terms of the mastery of a body of knowledge and skills to be used competitively in an open society, there is no problem. The development of this kind of excellence is conducive to equality of opportunity and the elimination of privilege, although the selection of candidates for development is perpetually complicated by the fact that even purely cognitive, technical skills are expressed in the language and by the mental operations characteristic of the social class that has usually displayed them. It is perfectly true that the ability to take tests is an expression of a character and personality type more commonly developed among middle class children than among the culturally deprived; so that even training for competition in the open market may tend to reduce equality of opportunity rather than increase it, on the principle that the middle classes are more test-and-training prone. This is usually thought of in America as a technical rather than an ideological problem, however. The tests must be changed and new methods of instruction devised that give lower status applicants a better break; or the compulsory school attendance age lowered so that their minds will have less time to develop independently of middle class norms.

Certain of the kinds of excellence the experience of college or university attendance is expected to develop have very little to do with competitive achievement and are doubtless inimical to it. I refer here to the traditional fruits of a liberal education: independence of judgment, emotional sensitivity, taste, the imagination needed to perceive what is happening to other people and the breadth of knowledge to understand it. These sound so old fashioned that it may be unrealistic to say that university attendance is still expected to develop them. It is probably more accurate simply to note that though the traditional fruits of liberal education are no longer much cultivated in American colleges and universities, their growth is still favored a little more by certain conditions that occur within the university community than by those found outside it. Despite the pressure of grades and the Selective Service, careerism among both faculty and students, and admissions policies that are as competitive and universalistic as the state and the state of the art can contrive, there is more community on campus than off. The student body is still made up of people, many of whom have a great deal in common in terms of age, experience, level of culture, and the artificially low standard of living imposed by student status, which excludes otherwise middle class people from the economic opportunity to sustain even a working class standard of living. The result is that in college young people find it relatively easy to communicate among themselves. The larger and more heterogeneous and mechanized the university, the less true this will be, but even in enormous public universities the conditions for community may usually be met by fragmentation into congenial, conflicting groups —activists, hippies, fraternity men, jocks—each of which develops norms and patterns of intimacy that sustain its own members.

This opportunity to feel oneself a part of a community is rare and joyful in America and constitutes an absolute advantage in the quality of life, not merely a competitive advantage. But I believe it is precisely this advantage that arouses the bitter antagonism of the citizenry and activates their legislative and police sanctions. Most Americans accept as legitimate the university's function in promoting social mobility for students who accept the goals and opportunities provided in the larger society. Many students enrolled in the university ask no more of it than this, and even become very uneasy if it offers or demands more: the adapted ambitious in science and engineering, where the opportunities are now to be found; the adapted unambitious in education and social work, where the risks are low if you do not make trouble; the commuters, many part-time, who want limited and specialized, often technical training. These constitute no community and are too little committed to one another to build a community. And it is they, by and large, who appear to the public to be making legitimate use of the opportunity the university provides them, instead of wasting their time and their parents' and the taxpayers' money in dubious and often anti-social behavior. Between students who use the university primarily as a sheltered territory in which to relate to one another, formulate values, and explore their feelings and the meaning of life, with whatever aid the curriculum can provide in the process, and those who use it primarily as an anthrodrome in which to prepare themselves and compete for external rewards, likewise with such aid as the curriculum provides, there is a real conflict of interest. This involves not only goals, values, and personal animosities but the immediate deployment of the university's resources and, ultimately, the kind of place it is. The current conflicts over permitting the armed forces and war industries to recruit on campus provide an almost ideal example of this. The proponents of the anthrodrome do not attribute any educational value to the recruitment process; they merely insist that an efficient placement service is a proper function of the university, which their experience in American society led them to expect and which they are unwilling to relinquish. It is also chiefly the proponents of the anthrodrome who insist that the university as such must not take specific moral positions, such as condemnation of the Vietnam war. Those who argue against this on the grounds that the university is corporate and is comprised of individuals whose views would be misrepresented by any single moral stand, see nothing inappropriate in the state itself establishing an official policy that is abhorrent to many, perhaps most, of its citizens. But this is not the real issue. The problem is that they see the university as an arena in which competitions are held and want the university to eschew any partisanship of its own that might discourage either contenders or those in a position to offer prizes. If possible, they would prefer that the kinds of students and faculty who make prize-givers nervous be banished from the campus altogether as injurious to its image and to its effectiveness as a source of opportunity; and they see this as no invasion of civil liberty—it is just a matter of keeping the anthrodrome clear for the runners and making the spectators comfortable.

But the populace not only prefers, but feels more comfortable with, the university as anthrodrome. The public has a specific hostility to the university as community, for it is well aware that to feel oneself a member of a community is a rare privilege, as well as a necessary condition for just those aspects of liberal education that have always aroused ambivalence in American society; the more so as it becomes more and more "mass." To have friends one can to some degree trust, genuine intellectual interests, a basis in shared experience for moral judgments, personal tastes, and political goals is to be, by prevailing standards in this society, very much a privileged character. Public policy seemingly does not intend to provide the young with such privileges, which certainly surpass anything they might be entitled to as an aspect of equality of opportunity and which interfere with the quest for opportunity by making the rewards granted for successful achievement seem shoddy and worthless and the life of the successful achiever empty. This view of the conventional life in America has become cliché. But part of the damage done by clichés is that, as they become familiar, we are led to assume that something must have been done about the conditions to which they refer. American life remains expensively wretched and without dignity. All kinds of minor experiences which in a halfway decent society would be either pleasurable or at least no trouble become a real drag or genuine threat here. I am not thinking about big deals, but little things, such as plane trips or a walk through the part of town where blacks live. The plane trip is really worse; because the people of Masten do at least have enough sense of community to make it clear to the occasional white visitor that he is not one of them. Flights to California have now become sheer anomie, a melange of drunken salesmen trying to exhibit a rather unconvincing sexual interest in a stewardess who is serving bad but pretentious food she cannot pronounce to anxious retired couples on their way to Hawaii who are wondering how they can afford it and whether the Polynesians are not some kind of niggers when you see them up close.

Such people, who become terrified and furious at the mere thought that they might have some moral responsibility (aside from that of punishing various kinds of delinquents) for the conduct of the society in which they live, are the mainstay of our social institutions, which everywhere defer to them. And at this stage in their lives they certainly are not going to allow a university campus to provide students with the security and genuine nurture that a real campus community affords.

A pot bust, like that at Stony Brook, must be understood primarily as an assault on the sense of community the campus might have developed. To call it instead an attempt at law enforcement begs this question, because law enforcement is always, among other things, an effort to use the power of the state to crush kinds of communities deemed anti-social either by the more powerful elements

54

of the community or the enforcement officials themselves. The point that I am trying to make explicitly is that for a large part of the American populace a university is an anti-social community, and the prevalence of drug use simply goes to show how anti-social it is. But what makes it anti-social is the fact and the degree to which it is a community, with its own norms, sanctions, sources of self-esteem, and capacity to resist the judgments and demands made upon it by those who reject these. Liberal education must be rooted in the idea of community, which is probably one reason that such education is but feebly rooted in American life. The antithesis between community and society, or gemeinschaft and gesellschaft is one of the classical insights of sociology, and America has one of the most determinedly gesellschaft societies that has ever existed. An emphasis on equality and impersonality has served since Andrew Jackson's time to distract attention from fundamental questions about the quality of American life to pragmatic questions about the distribution of opportunity, and of sanctions, within it. If this emphasis on equality of treatment exacerbates envy, it also provides the means for controlling it by continuous assertion of a relentless egalitarianism which promises that the state will police away any undue advantage, and, particularly, any undue advantage in the quality of human experience. A privileged pattern of life may provide attendant risks of leading those who enjoy it to think they are privileged characters.

What results from police action is clearly stated by Francis X. Clines in *The New York Times:* "A loss of contact between students and faculty members because of fears that confidences might be betrayed to legislators or police investigators;" "A fear that authorities may try to 'punish' the campus by means of budget cuts or forced dismissals;" and "Concern that the administration may overreact with tight controls that erode the students' self-responsibility."[1]

The article continues:

> Nine faculty members declined to answer questions about the narcotics problem last month before the Joint Legislative Committee on Higher Education. They did this "to avoid testifying to confidential

matters disclosed to them by students," according to Dr. Bentley Glass, the noted geneticist, who is the academic vice president here.

Dr. Glass, who is national president of Phi Beta Kappa, says the professors will not have the same protection before the grand jury [as accused students].

"The judgment with which they are faced," Dr. Glass declared in a recent letter to *Science* magazine, "is like that of the Athenians upon Socrates, whom they accused of debauching their youth. One must drink the hemlock."

Peter Nack, the leader of the student government, continues Dr. Glass's allusion in describing the undergraduates' concern.

"We should also keep in mind that under similar pressure Aristotle fled Athens," the philosophy senior from Long Beach, L.I. asserted. The main danger, he said, is that in "placating" its critics the university may be "retreating" and taking on the police mentality. . . .

Last month, the administration issued what was described as a tightened set of rules of student conduct. Faculty and student members of the University Committee on Rules and Regulations immediately resigned.

"We were not consulted," declared Robert Weinberg, assistant professor of physics. "Rather than trusting us, the administration treated us like a facade," he said.

This week, Dr. Toll [university president] had to assure the students that the new regulations which provide for unannounced room inspections and a closer watch on campus visitors, would not interfere with their right to protest demonstrations.

This may have been difficult, for last fall in the emotional wake of the massive protest demonstrations at the Pentagon and in New York City, construction workers on the Stony Brook campus attacked student demonstrators without arousing, so far as I can determine, any indignation among members of the surrounding community. There are many reasons why SUNY at Stony Brook should currently be exposed to an unusual degree of community hostility. Not only is the Stony Brook campus new, but there has never before been a university center on Long Island, and Suffolk county resembles Southern California in its fulminating rate of growth and diverse, discordant demographic pattern. In area, most of it is still highly agricultural; this is where Long Island ducks come from; there are specialized truck gardens and some of the strawberry farmers who sell their berries at roadside stands will let nostalgic city visitors pick their own and bring them over to be measured into pint baskets —at no reduction in price for doing their own labor. Further out on the island there are acres of potato farms that depend on migrant labor, so that at harvest time rural Suffolk county looks like Virginia. But Stony Brook and the adjacent villages of old fields like the Hamptons, on the South coast, are still solidly and conservatively rich. Into this political unit which combines the two traditional sources of conservatism there has been a dual intrusion. From the east, as Nassau county becomes more and more indistinguishable from Queens or Brooklyn, the rootless, predominantly lower middle class tracts push out into Suffolk. The original Levittown was in Nassau about four miles from the Suffolk line, but it has been duplicated many times in Suffolk. Stretching across the middle of the island from the ocean to the sound at what, for the moment, is the eastern end of exurbia with farmland beyond, is the large, predominantly rural township of Brookhaven, in which both the State University at Stony Brook and the Brookhaven National Laboratory—linked centers of cosmopolitanism—are located.

The New York Times article I have quoted previously also reports:

> "This place is fake New England," commented Jim Harrison, a professor who, in the course of teaching creative writing, disputes the value of narcotics to the artist. "There are aggressive American types here who prefer to be shielded from Jews and Negroes," Mr. Harrison said, seated in a pantry-sized faculty office. . . .
>
> In an editorial after the raid, The Three Village Herald declared: "We never particularly liked the sight of some students from SUSB slinking through our community looking like hideous hippies—dirty, unkempt, smelling like a backed-up sewer."
>
> This started a stream of anti-university letters that continues. . . .
>
> And an issue that stirred more anger than the narcotics raid, Mrs. [Ann Smith] Coates, [president of the local chapter of the American

Assocation of University Women] continued, was the university's attempt two years ago to get permission to build student apartments off campus. "All the civic groups fought that," she said.

In view of this intense and protracted hostility of the populace to the university, which in slightly different form has probably been experienced by most universities, it seems to me that a very serious question of public policy arises: must this sort of harassment and humiliation continue? To many this question will seem irrelevant on the simple grounds that marijuana was found in the raid and the law must be enforced. But law enforcement, too, is public policy; it must be authorized and paid for, and it presumably serves some social end. That Americans would find unusual difficulty in distinguishing circumstances when law enforcement would be socially useful from those in which it would be a dangerous nuisance is one of the many remarkable aspects of our life that Tocqueville predicted 140 years ago:

> The Americans hold that in every state, the supreme power ought to emanate from the people; but when once that power is constituted, they can conceive, as it were, no limits to it, and they are ready to admit that it has the right to do whatever it pleases. They have not the slightest notion of peculiar privileges granted to cities, families or persons; their minds appear never to have foreseen that it might be possible not to apply with strict uniformity the same law to every part of the state and to all its inhabitants.[2]

This is still true—truer than ever—as far as the conception of a privileged sanctuary is concerned. Yet, in practice, our legislative codes do establish major areas of operation to which the ordinary processes of law cannot be applied. These are not, however, justified as specially privileged areas, but as exemptions made necessary by the peculiar social function of the exempt agency. Military reservations, for example, are not subject to the civil authorities, even for pot busts, although the use of marijuana is known to be common in the services and Vietnam is a prime source of prime grass. If local officials executed pot busts on Army camps with the zeal they bring to university campuses, and if such raids were followed by relentless demands for the demotion and transfer of their officers and punishment of their men, American military policy would become even more demoralized than it is now. The Central Intelligence Agency consistently directs its agents to refuse to testify in litigation involving the agency's activities, making it virtually impossible to protect oneself or obtain redress from it in the courts. For the shadowy marksmen of Dealey Plaza, the National Archives have become a sanctuary. Legislators themselves enjoy immunity from lawsuits that might otherwise arise from their comments on the assembly floor. All these exemptions are justified, or at least rationalized, as in the public interest rather than as privileges for those protected. But the functions of colleges and universities are held to be in the public interest too, obviously, for they are granted tax exemption. Male college students, moreover, have been granted one very important form of exemption from a form of discrimination to which others of their age and sex are subject: the student deferment. This too is viewed not as a concession to the students' interests or needs but to the supposed manpower needs of the nation and the undoubted political convenience of coming to terms with middle class ambition. The student deferment, notably, protects the anthrodrome; it concedes nothing to the social value of liberal education. Its function is to permit the Selective Service System to control vocational choice at the college level and channel students into occupations useful to the military-industrial complex. "Freedom of choice under pressure," as former draft director General Lewis Hershey observed in just this connection, "is the American way." Nevertheless, tax exemption and the student deferment are enough to establish that even the university campus is officially recognized as socially useful, and where that usefulness requires privileged treatment—for the good, in the official view, of society—even students are given it.

But is exemption from pot busts and close surveillance in the public interest? The difficulty is that the public interest is far from monolithic; it is pluralistic. I stated previously that I saw no reason

59

to suppose that the university's adversaries were deluded; but that there are real conflicts of interest in our society; what is good for the police, the ambitious district attorney, and the aging entrepreneur is not necessarily good for the whole country. I wish merely to emphasize that this conflict exists and appeal to scholars to ask themselves whether their social interests are not better served by an open and confident university community than by a cautious and intimidated one. There is no single answer to this question. But there is, I think, no possible question that raids like those at Stony Brook destroy any chance of maintaining an environment conducive of education, at least liberal education, and I believe this is what the regents are required to maintain.

No reasonable person, certainly, would argue that a university campus should or could be permitted to enjoy an absolute immunity to police incursion without regard to the nature of the alleged student or faculty conduct or the threat it might pose to other members of the community. But I believe a very strong case can be made for the proposition that a university should protect its members against harassment, whether from the police or from an outraged and presumptuous public opinion. Precisely because that opinion has so consistently been punitive and constrictive, colleges and universities have been very reluctant to abandon the substitute parent principle and continue to claim the authority and responsibility to regulate the private lives of students with respect to sex, drugs, and other personal habits. The authority to control implies, however, the responsiblity to protect; families and communities that do not protect their young against hostile attack lose their love and loyalty and fall apart.

This falling apart has been happening to families, universities, and other communities with conspicuous frequency during the past few years. Experienced observers of the college scene have attributed student unrest and the decline of community in colleges and universities in part to the students' widespread perception that the bureaucracy in which they have lodged themselves will never deserve the title alma mater, because it has abandoned its responsibility to nurture while retaining its authority to punish and constrain. As Nevitt Sanford observes in *Where Colleges Fail:*

> Another source of student unrest is the new meaning of the old conception that colleges stand *in loco parentis.* Originally, the conception implied not only discipline but generous personal help. As colleges have grown and 'raised their standards,' however, the nurturing functions of the college have been eroded or neglected while the control and punishment functions have been maintained. This in itself creates a revolutionary climate. . . . Students for many years surrendered their rights as citizens in exchange for the special care and attention that parents or colleges were expected to offer. Now, with the care and nurturance gone, students not inappropriately demand their rights.[3]

In recognition of the justice of such observations, there is a current trend among universities to relinquish, or pretend to relinquish, the parental claim, mutual distrust being not so far advanced as to make the converse way of dealing with the problem by restoring genuine nurturance unthinkable. This requires the university to assert that students will no longer be subject to special university discipline for actions off campus or unrelated to education. Conversely, the university administration also then asserts that the campus will not be a sanctuary from the law or from other forms of community pressure. This position, if carried through in good faith, relieves the student of double jeopardy. But, in practice, the university usually breaches its undertaking if the conduct at issue is judged to be sufficiently offensive to the community. Cornell and the University of California, and many others, have adopted the position that the use of marijuana, off campus or on, subjects the student to suspension as well as to prosecution. Similarly, most universities continue to monitor their students' dormitory bed life in response to community even after a show of abandoning the parental principle, though a shadow of legitimacy is usually achieved by transferring this function to the student government and making the dormitories a kind of pseudo-autonomous Bantuland.

What seems impossible in America is a simple act of generosity, trust, and good faith expressed in a policy that would assure students that their mentors will not, in fact, betray them. The nine Stony Brook faculty members apparently have not done so, and for this I commend them. I know, too, that, if Glass is right, it must be a comfort to them to know that hemlock, although a dangerous drug, is not addictive. This is something we must all bear in mind in these troubled times, when the fatherland seems so determined to destroy its children—among others—that the war in Vietnam has come to seem less a tragic error in political judgment than an expression of a need deeply rooted in the American social and economic structure, and perhaps the American character as well. With so graphic an example of American police action before us, commanding our participation and support, who needs pot busts, anyway?

Notes

1. "Stony Brook Fears Distrust Left by Raid May Do More Harm than Narcotics Problem," *The New York Times,* May 11, 1968, p. 44.

2. Alexis de Tocqueville, in *A Documentary History of the U.S.,* ed. Richard Heffernan (Bloomington: Indiana University Press, 1968), part 2, book 4, section 53, p. 291.

3. Nevitt Sanford, *Where Colleges Fail* (San Francisco: Josey-Bass, 1967).

Revolution and Counterrevolution (But Not Necessarily about Columbia!)

Zbigniew Brzezinski

A revolutionary situation typically arises when values of a society are undergoing a profound change. The crisis in values in its turn is linked to profound socioeconomic changes, both accelerating them and reacting to them. For example, the transition from an agrarian to an industrial society produced very basic changes in outlook, both on the part of the elites ruling the changing societies and also of the social forces transformed by the changes and produced by them. Similarly, it can be argued that today in America the industrial era is coming to an end and America is becoming a technetronic society, that is, a society in which technology, especially electronic communications and computers, is prompting basic social changes (see "The American Transition," *The New Republic,* Dec. 23, 1967). This automatically produces a profound shift in the prevailing values.

The crisis of values has several political consequences relevant to revolutionary processes. First of all, it prompts ambivalent concessions by the authorities in power. The authorities do not fully comprehend the nature of the changes they are facing, but they are no longer sufficiently certain of their values to react in an assertive fashion. Concessionism thus becomes the prevailing pattern of their behavior. Secondly, increasingly self-assertive revolutionary forces begin an intensive search for appealing issues. The purpose is to further radicalize and revolutionize the masses and to mobilize them against the status quo. Thirdly, limited claims begin to be translated into more fundamental claims. Expedient escalationism of demands is a typical revolutionary tactic, designed deliberately to aggravate the situation and to compensate for initial revolutionary weakness.

A revolutionary situation is a combination of objective and subjective forces. Revolutions do not come by themselves; they have to be made. Unless a ripe revolutionary situation exists, revolutionary efforts can be abortive. Abortive efforts can contribute to the creation of a revolutionary situation, but a truly revolutionary situation arises only when a society is ill at ease and when established values, legitimacy, and authority are seriously questioned.

In that setting, confrontations, the test of will and power, become more frequent. Revolutionary forces engage in repeated probes to test the reactions of established authorities, while searching for appealing issues around which to rally. The initial phase of the revolutionary process thus involves a protracted game of hide-and-seek. The authorities try as skillfully as they can to avoid a head-on confrontation: they concede in a limited fashion while trying to avoid confronting fundamental issues. The revolutionary leaders, by their probes, seek to identify weak spots and to provoke a head-on clash.

The critical phase occurs when a weak spot has been identified, appealing issues have been articulated, and the probe has become a confrontation. At this stage the purpose of revolutionary activity is to legitimize violence. If the initial act of violence is suppressed quickly by established authorities, the chances are that the revolutionary act itself will gain social disapproval; society tends to be conservative, even in a situation of crisis of values. A revolutionary act is likely to be condemned by most, provided it is rapidly suppressed. If the revolutionary act endures, then it automatically gains legitimacy with time. Enduring violence thus becomes a symbol of the authorities' disintegration and collapse, and it prompts further escalation of support for the revolutionary act.

Simply by enduring defiantly, the initial act of revolutionary self-assertion becomes legitimized, and it contributes to further escalation of support as latent social grievances surface and are maximized. In every society latent grievances exist, and a social crisis brings them to the forefront. Equally important is the manufacturing of grievances and demands to express unconscious resentment of authority. Most individuals and groups resent authority to some extent; a defiantly enduring revolutionary situation brings out this unconscious resentment and prompts the manufacturing of grievances and demands which are designed to define an anti-authority posture.

Legitimist reformers and intellectuals play an important role in this revolutionary process. Intellectuals by their very nature are unwilling to pick sides, because they are better at identifying gray than siding with black and white. In a revolutionary situation they are particularly concerned with not being stamped as counterrevolutionary conservatives. They want to prove their reformist convictions, even at the cost of compromising their posture as reformers and becoming more closely identified with revolutionaries. Moreover, many intellectuals tend to be frustrated power seekers, and a revolutionary situation creates a readymade opportunity for the exercise of vicarious statesmanship.

In a revolutionary situation their desire for power, plus their inability to take sides, leads intellectuals to adopt a third posture, that of interposing themselves between the revolutionary and anti-revolutionary forces. In doing so, they often place their intellect in service of emotions rather than using emotions in the service of intellect. Many intellectuals are highly excitable; their political weakness and lack of organization inclines them to rely on demagogy in a revolutionary situation. At the same time, because they are accustomed to dealing with established authorities, they are more experienced in coping with the authorities than with the revolutionary forces. In the process of interposing themselves, they are inclined to apply most of their pressure against the established authority, with which they have many links, than equally against established authorities and the revolutionary forces on behalf of reformist appeals. Irrespective of their subjective interests, the legitimist reformers and intellectuals objectively become the tools of the revolutionary forces, thus contributing to further aggravation of the revolutionary situation and the radicalizing of the overall condition.

When faced with a revolutionary situation, the established authorities typically commit several errors. First, because they are oriented toward the status quo, they display an incapacity for immediate effective response. Their traditional legalism works against them. Faced with a revolutionary situation, they tend to procrastinate and seek refuge in legalistic responses instead of striking immediately and effectively. Second, in so doing, they tend to opt for negotiating with the new interposing element, thus obscuring the clearcut confrontation. An early confrontation would work to the advantage of the authorities because mass support begins to shift to the revolutionaries only after the situation has been radicalized. Third, while negotiating with the interposing element, the established authorities tend to dribble out concessions rather than making them dramatically and thereby gaining broad support. Fourth, when force is finally employed, the authorities rarely think ahead to the consequences after force has been used, concentrating instead on the application of force to the specific challenge at hand. They thus neglect the important consideration that the use of force must be designed not only to eliminate the surface revolutionary challenge, but to make certain that the revolutionary forces cannot rally again under the same leadership. If that leadership cannot be physically liquidated, it can at least be expelled from the country or area in which the revolution is taking place. Emigrants can rarely maintain themselves as effective revolutionaries. The denial of the opportunity for the revolutionary leadership to rally again should be an important ingredient of the strategy of force, even if it is used belatedly. Fifth, in the application of force a sharp distinction should be made between the direct challenge and the masses which the challenge has tended to bring out. In the event of violence in a specific setting, the first objective of force ought to be the clearing of the area of those not directly committed and not involved in the revolutionary process. Only after the direct revolutionary partici-

66

pants have been fully isolated should force be used directly against their strongholds. Moreover, if isolated for a period of time, the revolutionaries themselves may be more inclined to bargain. Finally, established authorities often fail to follow effective violence with immediate reforms. Such reforms ought to be designed to absorb the energies of the more moderate revolutionaries, who can then claim that although their revolution has failed, their objectives have been achieved.

For every revolution that succeeds, at least ten fail. It is not always a matter of abortive revolutionary situations. Frequently, the revolutionary leaders themselves are guilty of errors, typically tactical ones. Under the pressure of dramatic events, they tend to make excessive demands, designed to radicalize and politicize specific grievances. In so doing, they often outrun their supporters and end up losing mass support. Also, they often engage in incorrect symbolization, focusing on personalities rather than on basic issues. Such personal symbolization does not have staying power, and it gives the other side the option to change or to keep the personalities involved. Revolutionary leaders also frequently overdo their reliance on emotional appeals. For example, the condemnation of violence by revolutionaries is too transparent to be long effective. If sincerely meant, it stamps the revolutionaries as naive, for violence necessarily accompanies a revolutionary process; if used as a tactic to mobilize support, it tends to backfire because it eventually becomes evident that the revolutionaries themselves court violence in the hope of further radicalizing the situation. Finally, there is a tendency, and this is very important, of the revolutionaries to overestimate the revolutionary dynamic that they have set in motion. Revolutionaries tend to operate in a fishbowl atmosphere and to assume that their context and their appeals have universal validity. They thus underestimate the nonrevolutionary context of their own specific revolution. The French revolutionaries expected their revolution to sweep all over Europe; so did the Bolshevik revolutionaries. In most cases this does not happen, and the revolutionaries, because they lose touch with reality, increasingly become separated from the reformers on whose support they desperately depend for their long-range success.

In that setting, the task of the reformers is to isolate both the revolutionaries and the reactionaries as extremists. This is difficult because in a revolutionary situation there is little room for reformers. Accordingly, they must formulate tangible and attainable reforms, together with highly concrete action programs. It is only through positive involvement that the reformers can begin to gain broader support. They also must not participate in activities designed to keep the pot boiling, for this, if successful, will benefit the extremist revolutionaries; if it fails, it benefits the reactionaries. If the revolutionary process is itself in motion, the reformers must decide whom to trust more. If they trust the promises of the authorities, they have little choice but to side with them until the revolution is crushed; if they do not trust the authorities, they must side with the revolutionaries and eventually let the revolution consume them. Either way they should not mislead themselves into thinking that by staying in the middle they will impose a middle solution.

A crucial consideration in judging the validity and significance of the revolutionary process is to determine whether it is historically relevant. Some revolutions, which related themselves to the future, clearly were. This was the case with the French Revolution, with the 1848 Spring of Nations, and the Bolshevik Revolution. They all were part of and ushered in new historical eras. But very frequently revolutions are the last spasm of the past, and thus are not really revolutions but counterrevolutions, operating in the name of revolutions. A revolution which either is nonprogrammatic and has no content, or involves content which is based on the past but provides no guidance for the future, is essentially counterrevolutionary.

Most revolutionary outbreaks are of this character; they respond to the past, not to the future, and ultimately they fail. Examples are the Luddites and the Chartists in England, who reflected the traumas of an agrarian society entering the industrial era; their response was spasmodic and irrelevant to the future. Peasant uprisings, whatever the merit of specific grievances, essentially fail, for they do not provide a meaningful program for the future. Anarchist revolutions fall into this category. More recently the Nationalist Socialists, the Fascists, and now the Red Guards in China are essentially counterrevolutionary. They do not provide meaningful programs and leadership for the coming age on the basis of an integrative analysis which makes meaningful the new era. Rather they reflect concern that the past may be fading and constitute a belated attempt to impose the values of the past on the present and on the future.

If America today is ceasing to be an industrial society and is becoming a technetronic society, then it is important to decide whether some, though not all, of the crises and violence of today add up to a meaningful revolution or whether some manifestations are counterrevolutionary. A revolution which has historically valid content for the future and which provides an integrated program for the future is historically relevant. In that sense, the civil rights revolution is a true and a positive revolution. Similarly, the important function of Marxism was that it made meaningful the revolutionary activities of Communists by providing them with a sense of historical relevance and a pertinent program.

No such broad integrative idealogy exists today in the United States, a country which confronts a future which no other society has yet experienced. Some of the recent upheavals have been led by people who will have a diminishing role to play in the new technetronic society. Their reaction reflects both a conscious and, even more important, an unconscious realization that they are becoming obsolete. The movements they lead are more reminiscent of the Red Guards or the Nazis than of the Bolsheviks or the French revolutionaries. Thus, rather than representing a true revolution, some recent outbursts are in fact a counterrevolution. Their violence and revolutionary slogans are merely the death rattles of the historical irrelevants.

The Student Revolt: Totem and Taboo Revisited

Morton Levitt and Ben Rubenstein

> If the real facts were more familiar to you, you would very likely not
> have thought that there was a case where a father did not let his sons
> develop but you would have seen that the sons wished to eliminate
> their father, as in ancient times.*

Imagine a recent meeting of a psychoanalytic society on the
campus of an Eastern university. Student unrest was the subject.
An investigator of patterns of violence reported that the student
variety was part of a continuum of violence in America. The president of one well known university took strong exception to the
thesis that administrators were repressive. He told of endless efforts
to mediate issues with students and his concern over the rigid
tactics of the militants. Next a psychiatrist described activists as
frantically trying to bring to a halt the machinery that was inexora-
bly moving them from the campus to Vietnam. His study convinced
him that students' use of radicalism was determined in part by the
manner in which the significant tasks of childhood were mastered.

A second analyst who felt that no one listened to students commented that he spent a great deal of time sitting on a bench on his
campus talking with anyone who stopped. A leading authority on
student activism said the the period of adolescence was now endlessly extended and that old theoretical constructs were no longer

---

*Freud replying to G. Stanley Hall's suggestion that Jung's split with Freud was
a classic case of adolescent rebellion (*Time,* Sept. 5, 1969, p. 32).

valid. He also believed that intrapsychic investigations were of little value, and that student militancy was simply a mild reaction to extreme adult provocation. This speaker warned against the dangers of countertransference, defined here as the anger of fathers toward sons. The chairman of the meeting commented that he was envious of the assurance of the previous speakers, for he was less certain of his own judgment of these issues. The dean of a professional school was the last speaker. He was concerned about the violent nature of the radical movement and expressed the wish that adults dealing with militants would be more principled and not retreat under pressure. He felt sorry that Freud was not at the meeting to offer a larger vision.

A few months earlier another such meeting took place at a midwest campus. The *piece de resistance* that day was the last speaker, a young man from a nearby university who represented the student viewpoint. He arrived wearing a beret, which he kept on, and a ski jacket, which he wore zipped throughout the warm afternoon. He sat silently until introduced, then stood up, looked out at the audience for almost a minute, and then suddenly sat down, saying softly, "I can't say anything. When I look out, I get lightheaded." He was given a glass of water, and adults hovered about him with concerned looks on their faces. An effort was made to allow the young man a second opportunity. The chairman, using a time-honored psychological ploy, asked: "What would you have said, Nelson, if you could have talked to us?" The student looked derisively out at the audience and said loudly, "You all make me sick." This utterance apparently struck some responsive (or masochistic?) chord, for it evoked a burst of applause.

Student revolt is both too complex and too recent a subject to permit ready explanation. Since the effort to understand radicalism must cut across areas of culture, politics, socioeconomic class, morality and ethics, the observers' value judgments in these areas are apt to be very significant factors. Those who are clearly identified with both the radicals and their goals are inclined to sociologize their own psychological insights. Thus, the issues drawing

71

radical support are seen as just and the activist as honorable and good. Other scientists focus on the psychological features of the radical, and it can be similarly contended that they are inclined to psychologize history. These men feel that the first group is naively virtuous and solipsistic in accepting the essence of violent activism. Those so condemned reply that their opponents use psychological assessments to avoid the necessary political commitment and that the ivory tower is where yesterday was.

We have tried before to explore these contradictory psychosocial positions. In a paper in the *Yale Review* we argued:

> The conflict appears at this distance at least to be part of the age old struggle of the young and the old. . . . Student rebellions the country over draw upon energy generated from typical adolescent collisions with society's mores. . . . The institution can and must serve as a representative of what is psychologically and culturally important. . . . If [they] fail in this obligation, the results of this "folie a trois"—the college replicating parental abdication of authority—may be unclear until the next generation makes its appearance, but the potential for social destruction is immense.[1]

In a later paper our concern at that time was stated in the simplest terms:

> Can we support a minority group which unlawfully occupies buildings, holds hostages, and disrupts the society? Are the consequent confrontations the kind of educational experience which the university wishes to encourage? Can the accelerated capitulation of the academic community to ultimatums which are based on threats of violence and on immunity from consequences ever be defended as good mental hygiene for either the academy or its angry subjects?[2]

These articles were written quite early in the storm, and we were uncertain about reaction from our colleagues. We did not, on the other hand, expect to be compared (as we were) to "the final solution to the Jewish question, the Stalin era, Churchill's decision to bomb civilians, colonial wars for plunder, the OAS, the lying politicians."[3]

Clearly we had gored someone's ox, but the intensity of the reaction surprised us. What we ought to do, it seemed, would be to try to find in our own theoretical harbor, psychoanalysis, an explanation which offered an order in behavioral terms for our growing body of observations on student dissent.

We believe strongly that psychoanalytic speculation offers only one of several explanations for campus disorder. Moreover, we must limit the boundaries of our expertise. We are discussing only white radical students. This group must not be confused with the support troops—the moderate students, or the activist student group who comprise the most reasonable and largest segment of the student rebellion. Our focus is directly upon the 2 or 3 per cent who comprise the top leadership cadre and who often move from campus to campus as new issues develop throughout the country. Moreover, we have had no experience with black student radicals. The introduction of the black power movement into the campus revolt was not only a most explosive issue, but also one which confronts all of us with a problem about which we know very little. Even one of the very simple observations—that white students often try to "out-radical" blacks in order to win black approval—is so complex a phenomenon that it staggers our clinical imagination.

Stated simply, then, the current campus situation can be reduced to several common denominators:

1. There has been on the part of some young people a profound and growing disenchantment with society's institutions.
2. Probably because it is the place where youth congregate in largest numbers and because it is characteristically benign in its reactions, the university has become the major arena for the expression of this feeling.
3. As the bounds of propriety are threatened by increased demands and destruction of property, there is a societal backlash which takes the form of increasingly severe sanctions against the youthful rebels, and this generally serves to intensify the conflict and to polarize the sides.
4. There is real reason to fear that the consequent loss of control for all who are involved will destroy many of our civilization's institutions in a violent, revolutionary fashion before evolutionary change can take place.

In converting these developments into psychoanalytic terms, we can identify discontent with civilization expressed by small groups in ways which bring them into conflict with societal taboos over issues clustering around authority. It is a very small ellipse to Freud's *Civilization and Its Discontents, Group Psychology and the Analysis of the Ego,* and *Totem and Taboo.*

One of Freud's first references to primitive behavior was his identifying of savages as "hapless children of the moment, less influenced by personal memories than we are" (1905, p. 342).[4] *Totem and Taboo* was written in 1912 to explain the origins of civilization, and its central thesis was that all societies share a dread of incest. Here Freud and James Frazer stood together in stating that strict universal laws exist only for crimes toward which a strong temptation exists, but Freud pushed further when he contended that such precautions were inseparably bound up with the male head of the family. Ernest Jones summarized this condition:

> Hostility to the father, with the corresponding wish to kill or castrate him, is the active counterpart of the forbidden incest longings; they constitute the two halves of the Oedipus complex. Freud suggested that the totemic worship so often accompanying the practice of exogamy was an example of the same taboo, the totem representing the father, or ancestor, who must be preserved and not injured. The totemic feasts where this rule was periodically broken in an orgy, he explained, as a temporary "return of the repressed," a bursting through under certain specific social conditions of the original hostile impulses against the totem, i.e., father.[5]

Freud traced the beginning of a community life to this set of circumstances. The consequences of the overthrow of authority was remorse, repression, and inhibition, all reorganized as a kind of conscience designed to prevent the repetition of the totem act. Freud referred to *Totem and Taboo* as a "just-so story," but he continued throughout his life to find in the infantile, as well as in the neurotic, mind impulses of murder, cannibalism, and incest, and he stated finally that "the beginnings of religion, morality, social life, and art meet in the Oedipus complex."[6]

Earlier Freud had commented that the more civilized one is, the more energy one devotes to avoiding pain rather than to the pursuit of pleasure. He later came to regard this as a characteristic of civilization. He also wrote: "Civilization consists of progressive renunciation."[7] Implicit in this statement is the conviction that the compensation for such renunciation is the intellectual development of mankind, or that restrictions in the sexual sphere provide the energy for more civilized purposes.

In *Civilization and Its Discontents* Freud discussed for the first time in any extended fashion the social relations which he viewed as the beginning of civilization:

> The substitution of the power of a united number for the power of a single man is the decisive step towards civilization. The essence of it lies in the circumstance that the members of the community have restricted their possibilities of gratification, whereas the individual recognized no such restrictions. The first requisite of a culture, therefore, is justice—that is, the assurance that a law once made will not be broken in favor of any individual (p. 340).

Freud saw the conflict between the claims of the individual for freedom to obtain personal gratification, and the demands of society in opposition to them as never-ending and irreconcilable, and he continued pessimistically:

> Civilized society is perpetually menaced with disintegration through this primary hostility of men towards each other. . . . Culture has to call up every possible reinforcement in order to erect barriers against the aggressive instincts of men. This aggression is the most powerful obstacle of culture, and is an innate, independent, instinctual disposition of man (p. 341).

Freud wrote that the only way aggression is managed in civilized society is through guilt, which has as its origin the fear of loss of parental love, and then came his strongly worded conclusion: "It is my intention to represent the sense of guilt as the most important problem in the evolution of culture, and to convey that the price of progress in civilization is paid by forfeiting happiness through the heightening of the sense of guilt."[8]

75

In *Group Psychology and the Analysis of the Ego* Freud described group behavior as often irrational, intolerant, illogical, and deteriorated in moral standards and suggested that this strange functioning was a regression to a more primitive level.[9] Freud was struck by the thought that something "mysterious" in the group composition limits freedom of thought and judgment of an individual member and felt that this could be explained by analogies to the earliest group—the individual's family. More importantly, he linked the group to the primeval horde described in *Totem and Taboo* and tried to explicate group behavior in terms of the old psychoanalytic constants—conscience, fear, guilt, and libidinal bonds.

The task we have set for ourselves in this paper is to try to make psychoanalytic sense out of student behavior by speculating on what in the developmental mix of these young people allows for the release of violence of such proportion that it parallels revolution. And so we must return to the familiar ground, to Oedipus and Laius, to the shaky relations between the child and his parents, to the nature of the binding of aggression by affection, to identity, and to kinds of resolution of the sexual and familial struggle that are produced in our society today. Psychoanalytic theory states in an unequivocal fashion that the major task of adolescence is the dissolving of infantile emotional ties to the parents and the assuming of responsibility for one's own behavior. The adolescent resolution cannot occur without ego and drive regression. The process of disengaging from parents brings on other upsetting changes, such as ambivalence and primitive aggression, which contribute to the lability and contradiction in thought, feeling, and behavior. The marked exhilaration that accompanies the growing independence from parents is usually mixed with some depressive trends, because the process is associated with both infantile and contemporary aspects of the parental relation.

The adolescent is most irrational, erratic, and stormy at the very point when the individuation process is most intense. Such actions frequently represent the opposite of parental expectations, and this same pattern obtains in relation to law, tradition, and convention. The manner in which the adult world manages these transient states in many instances determines whether adolescence process is brought to a natural conclusion, a premature end, or is allowed to continue for too prolonged a period.

The adolescent growth process is a struggle between infantilism and differentiation, between regression and progression, and the final form of the adaptation is constructed out of the nature of the resolution of this conflict. Because the normal adolescent must give up those adult objects who have served as early supports and replace them with more contemporaneous models, and because this process is rarely simultaneous, he often experiences a strange feeling of personal impoverishment. During this time he can find relief in peer groups, which provide affective experiences of intense excitement. In the substitute organization for the family, the youth finds those qualities of empathy, devotion, and belongingness which are so necessary to him. Since the group permits transient role playing, experimentation, and severance behavior without the intense individual guilt children experience in childhood, peer relations pave the way for the establishment of a new identity.

What is the relevance of the preceding material, none of it new, to the particular life style of the contemporary student radical? Although adolescents have always taken part in collective peer experience, replete with idiosyncratic symbolism and style, the attack upon tribal authority totems and sexual taboos is an integral part of the process today.

Sociological studies after the campus revolt in Berkeley in 1964 began to flesh out pictures of the student radical and his family. The following summary comes from combining the work of M. Brewster Smith and associates and Richard Flacks. 1) The radical movement involved the most advantaged sector of students; 2) activists were good students who were in a position to achieve significant careers and status; 3) they came from predominantly upper middle class professional homes which emphasized strongly democratic, egalitarian relationships with a high degree of permissiveness; and 4) intellectual, esthetic, and political values, rather than achievement, were stressed in the home.[10]

It is fair to ask whether these youngsters would find it difficult to fit in with institutional expectations requiring submissiveness to adult authority, respect for established status distinction, a high degree of competitiveness, and firm regulation of sexual and expressive impulses. It seemed incomprehensible to modern parents that warmth, protection, and experience with reason in problem-solving could fail to ensure a shining future for their offspring. Freud commented in *The Future of an Illusion:*

> It will be said that the characteristic of human masses depicted here, which is supposed to prove that coercion cannot be dispensed with in the work of civilization, is itself only the result of defects in the cultural regulations, owing to which men have become embittered, revengeful and inaccessible. New generations, who have been brought up in kindness and taught to have a high opinion of reason, and who have experienced the benefits of civilization at an early age, will have a different attitude to it. They will feel it as a possession of their very own and will be ready for its sake to make the sacrifices as regards work and instinctual satisfaction that are necessary for its preservation. They will be able to do without coercion and will differ little from their leaders.[11]

Later in the same work he said with equal certainty:

> It is in keeping with the courses of human development that external coercion gradually becomes internalized; for a special mental agency, man's super-ego, takes it over and includes it among its commandments. Every child presents this process of transformation to us; only by that means does it become a moral and social being. Such a strengthening of the super-ego is our most precious cultural asset in the psychological field. Those in whom it has taken place are turned from being its vehicles. The greater their number is in a cultural unit, the more secure is its culture and the more it can dispense with external measures of coercion (p. 18).

Only at first glance is there a contradiction in these quotations. Children are to be brought up "in kindness and taught to have a high opinion of reason," but there must be "external coercion" and "commandments" which lead to a strong superego which is "our most precious cultural asset." So here it is laid bare; love, yes, but restriction as well; reason, yes, but repression and internalization also. What do we really know about the intimate familial life of hardcore radicals? Was there love, but restriction as well? Reason, but repression and internalization also?

We are now precisely at the eye of the hurricane. Freud spoke persuasively for the healthy effects of guilt and renunciation, but this is the very psychic real estate over which the most bitter battles are currently taking place. Any of the familiar street signs of today's youthful struggle—the revolt of the blacks, the sexual freedom movement, the widespread use of drugs—bear a characteristic striation; a denial of both the utility of the past and of the efficacious uses of guilt and renunciation in healthy growth and development.

Few psychoanalysts have had clinical experience with student radicals, because this group generally regards treatment as an integral part of the Establishment and rejects its compromising efforts between the individual and society. However, we have talked at considerable length since 1964, while serving as consultants to college mental hygiene clinics, as well as to the Peace Corps, with many in the radical movement about their own lives and have compiled an uneasy outline of family life—uneasy in the sense that it is a reconstruction of largely anecdotal recollections of early life with only a few opportunities to test the thesis with genuine clinical material.

Our profile of the composite student radical family includes these features:

1. The homes from which they come were strongly child-centered with the mother usually maintaining this orientation and with the children's behavior often being the main topic of family conversation.

79

2. The youth saw both parents as sources of gratification. The children felt that the parents' omnipotence was always at their service and that their problems could usually be solved.

3. Conflicts were most often managed by discussion and only rarely was there punishment or deprivation.

4. Psychoanalytic influence of a peculiar kind was common in most homes. Parents were apt to be over responsive to contemporary issues in child development, and unconscious behavior was often interpreted directly to the child.

5. Neighborhood or school problems were usually managed by either moving or changing schools, and since each setting was strongly child-centered, children had little need to discriminate between institutions in terms of their own behavior.

6. Fathers tended to be permissive by default rather than through reason. The majority were liberal, but uneasy and ambivalent because of their economic stake and guilt over the inherent contradiction between their principles and life style.

7. While the conscious management of the child was permissive and reasonably free of taboos, with sexual issues being treated in a non-moralistic fashion, the majority of parents were actually engaged in the process of extricating themselves from their own guilt-ridden Judeo-Christian backgrounds.*

This outline describes a generic grouping of young people, but the profile probably falls apart, as do all such efforts, when applied in totality to any individual. What do these things add up to when converted to the classic psychoanalytic denominators? A number of speculative pathways are open. Let us try, with some real question about the correctness of the directional thrust, the one closest at hand, the oedipal construction, recognizing at the same time that other possibilities may attract different investigators. To convert the familial trappings of radical students into a clinical format for an oedipal crisis, we begin with the assumption that the less direct and firm the father, the more fearful the child. During the early

*We recall that sociologist Phillip Rieff has described the developmental climate outlined above as "amounting to permission for each man to live an experimental life."

development of the young people we studied, symbols of authority were frequently ridiculed. Realistic confrontations were rare, and aggression was usually avoided in father-son relations. The father did not often exhibit strength, and the result was that the characteristically ambivalent love-hate quality was often replaced by a peculiar flatness in their relations. Writing in 1957, we described the consequences of this factor in the father-son equation. "A dual image of the father is likely to emerge, i.e., both a weak loving man and a huge menacing figure."[12] The resolution of the oedipal conflict is deferred until some later date, and the normal struggle to disengage from parents likewise goes underground. The latency period in this group of young people is prolonged, and in early adolescence they are likely to be regarded as very well adjusted. When they get to college, they are free for the first time. Responding to a developmental set regarding the naturalness of sex and the egalitarian nature of familial life, they initiate open sexual relationships and organize their campus life into the permissive style that they had previously experienced at home.

The sexual activities and the communal life may well revive the dormant oedipal conflict, for, as we understand development, some price apparently has to be exacted for postponements. The renewed conflict produces fantasy, guilt, and anxiety. The radical now holds two options: renunciation of these feelings or destruction of the authority figures. Their previous life style comes to the fore, and the environment has to change.

From the psychoanalytical point of view, the radical may well be struggling with aggressive expression within the disengagement process from the primary objects. The most common psychic discharge mechanism available to him is acting out, which is a fairly organized activity, a pantomime, a nonverbal communication of some part of past life experience, energized by a crucial unconscious memory which serves as a drive representative. Rational dialog provides no discharge of feeling, because it recalls intense memories of helplessness, while acting out represents the greatest amount of discharge with the least amount of binding.

81

The new heroes (Castro, Che Guevara, Ho Chi Minh) symbolize the specific character of the youthful struggle because they are men of action who help diminish the sense of helplessness in face of the paternal castrator and because they are more satisfying heroes than the youths' politically impotent fathers. Martin Duberman has written: "The enemy [of the radical] is not as the uninitiated may suppose, George Wallace, or Max Rafferty, or General Westmoreland—but rather that latest figure of left demonology, the Corporate Liberal."[13] The civil rights struggle and the anti-war movement, both campus-based, offered a rational, symbolic option and a mode of active management of helplessness against repressive forces. The implacable hostility, the use of forbidden words, the symbolic desecration, and the absence of any spirit of compromise are aimed at the total destruction of the temple and the tablets of law.

The foregoing material may appeal to psychoanalytic purists but must offend other scientists with strong ties to community and historical interests. Each group should ask a particular question. The former have the right to inquire whether the oedipal construction has a high enough explanatory value to cover the vast radical landscape, while the latter require an answer to the question of why college radicals choose to identify with their parents' political liberalism while opposing many other features of their upbringing.

The first group can be answered fairly directly. We are not entirely happy with the oedipal explanation for such a multifaceted subject as student radicalism, because we cannot offer that which is crucial to the argument, the particularities, i.e., why some in a generation accommodate easily to society, why others rail verbally at its limitations, and why a few actively revolt. Until this link can be clearly elucidated through copious clinical material, perhaps the diacritical style of our title should be changed to read *Totem and Taboo Revisited?*

The second group (those interested in psychohistory) refuse to be satisfied by intrapsychic explanations for social phenomena such as the student revolt, contending that radical behavior is not acting but living out and that it is now necessary to abandon the timeless fixity of definitions relating to character structure and to substitute instead a concept of identity as process connected to historical events. Viewed this way, psychoanalytic constructs do not explain historical sequences and hence must of necessity obscure the giant step from the intrapsychic to external social actions.

Writing in reference to the supposed resistance by psychoanalysts to leaving their offices for more active roles in society, Robert Liebert offers the following judgment:

> The psychoanalytic movement, instead of being a major force for understanding and helping conflicted people of all generations in a complex world, will in succeeding years find its "analyzable" patients getting older and older, and sadly, the Analytic Movement will move towards obsolescence and irrelevance, while remaining pure.[14]

Where can one find a safe position in this scientific controversy? We will attempt to sort out these matters and provide a complementary approach.

If student rebellion is to be seen solely as a political act, there is no need for psychological investigation. If, however, it is at least in part an adolescent rebellion, then we should try to understand the behavioral manifestations of that phase. The psychoanalytic effort will involve extensive clinical work and review, and we hope it will lead to the answers for the following questions: 1) is the struggle of the student radical with society an expression of the continuing influence of the infantile or neurotic character of the Oedipus complex? and 2) is the struggle at the service of growth or regression, i.e., is it adaptive or maladaptive?

Erik Erikson's psychohistorical approach, which examines a psychological process at a given moment, has been brilliantly exercised in his studies of Luther and Gandhi. Erikson refers to it as "an area in which nobody as yet is methodologically quite at home. There will be those who will rush to apply psychoanalytic insights to history and vice versa."[15] Because of the newness and the vagueness of this tool, its proponents must sustain its operational hypotheses. Otherwise the "psycho" part may get lost in history, and history may become stylized and tailored to fit the psychological formulations which accompany it.[16]

In the consideration of student dissent, psychohistorians have selected an area that is by nature charged with extreme emotion. Similarly, the heavy-handed application of classic psychoanalytic techniques to a profound behavioral expression is at best a speculative and shaky enterprise. Much as is true for a symptom, we are all dealing with overdetermined psychic constellations. Traditionally, case studies are presented in depth and then a possible link emerges to some common external manifestation. In the instance of the student radical, it is clear that additional years of analytic observation are needed.

The oedipal explanation can be supported when viewed from one vantage point. Preliminary clinical material from work with student radicals conveys the ambience of a revived oedipal struggle enlivened by a happy consonance of passion, idealism, defiance, and communicability which provides the first strong sense of identity in adolescence, the one defined by Erikson as the "this is me!" feeling.

Anna Freud recently stated that analysts should continue to concern themselves with the study of man against himself, rather than against society. Statements reflecting classic positions, as we have seen, have drawn criticism from investigators who quarrel with its narrow perspective. When such modest positions are contrasted with Kenneth Keniston's forthright comment: "It is clear that I (like Levitt and Rubenstein) perceive and interpret today's student radicalism through a lens that includes not only my scientific training and assumptions, but my political convictions and personal values,"[17] we begin to recognize the source of some of the controversy. Although we resist the gratuitous inclusion above, there are an increasing number in the behavioral sciences who support this position. Keniston's point of view enlarges the scientific operational field in a startling fashion and there is even some question about whether what he describes is a scientific position at all in the commonly accepted use of that concept.

We feel that all researchers in this field need to make clear both their observational platforms and their basic premises, because each of the points of view should be scientifically congenial. We believe, however, that the matter of countertransference (a change leveled at almost everyone who expresses anything but strong support for student radicals) obtains in both groups of investigators. The psychohistorians appear firmly identified with the goals, tactics, and passions of the radicals and, we would suggest, with the infantile components of these attributes. The more classic psychoanalytic critic might well be associated with the defenses against these infantile components. We are not critical of the existence of countertransference (or even transference, or repression, or any of the other psychoanalytic constants) in either case, but we do feel that it is a given in each situation which should be recognized.

Perhaps all of us in the scientific commonwealth should stand together and hold the campus soap box steady so that we might hear in concert what is being said, and then make a unified response. Since we shall not likely be able to stand alone in these matters, we had best put our two visions together, in Janus-like fashion, to understand the student phenomenon. Until that day comes, papers like this will require two endings, each reflecting its own vision of the internal-external equation.

The psychohistoric view is presented first.

Student radicals come from warmly supportive families which have stressed freedom of expression. For a variety of social and political reasons these young people have reacted strongly against the tenuous quality of modern life. When their singular efforts to achieve change bring them into inevitable collision with the world around them, they have demonstrated a willingness to abandon both their education and careers in order to dramatize their conviction that life is hollow. Their life styles give psychoanalytic clues to their basic character structure, but to concentrate on this to the exclusion of the social goals involved is a futile intellectual exercise. While they suffer from the same agonies as we, they are apparently determined to effect meaningful change in the human condition. Those bold enough to look hard at the goals sought by these courageous youngsters will not be misled by either the threatening rhetoric or violent tactics. In the final analysis, nothing much can be expected of an older generation which, at best, is committed by outmoded tradition to the course of gradualism and due process, and which at worst, dismisses the efforts of the young to change the world as a kind of naive idealism that will ultimately be tempered by membership in the PTA, the country club, and the Unitarian Church. Under these circumstances all who are truth seekers will join the effort, either actively or idealogically, because it is, in Erik Satie's phrase, "thirteen o'clock in the night" for the human race.

A second summary is offered on behalf of those who stand on the sidelines peering through the flames in an effort to understand the phenomenon of fire-setting.

We have been a party to a frightening happening in the living theater. A very special section of youth has engaged in acting out in an attempt to communicate symbolically the particular flavor of their adolescent struggle. The conflict is, at least in part, an unresolved oedipal one. However, the choice of the stage, i.e., the campus, as well as the particular time in history, has confused actors, audience, and management. As an audience, we failed to insist that the activity be kept within the confines of the theater for the players' own protection. If indeed what we are seeing is really life itself rather than drama, we must advise the participants to leave the unreal theater-campus arena and develop action programs in the world outside where life is really lived. Moreover, we become easily confused because the plays deal with issues which are signficant and disturbing to us. The transposing of the play with reality similarly confounds both actors and management. As the actors sense the loosening of old bonds, they begin to destroy the theater, and the management becomes hesitant when the audience approves. Now the theaters all over the country are in turmoil. The audience has failed both the actors and the managers by not helping to maintain control.

Writing with rare foresight a full generation ago at a time when youth was commonly regarded as both self-satisfied and disengaged from social issues, Herbert Muller said in 1952:

> I am assuming that the modern world is in fact as revolutionary as everybody says it is. Its profound contradictions are not due to mere perversity or simple folly. They are due to the extraordinary developments in science and technology, which have led to far more rapid and radical change than any previous society has known, and than our society had been prepared to deal with. And because the paradoxes of our age are so violent, men have been violently oversimplifying its issues. On the one hand, many political and business leaders are celebrating the triumphs of technology, science and free enterprise as if there were nothing fundamentally wrong with our civilization, and the world depressions and world wars were unfortunate accidents. On the other hand, many intellectuals are ignoring the obvious triumphs, seeing only a monstrous folly and evil.[18]

We have assumed that it might be helpful to view our world with both pride and alarm, each tempered by historical sense.

Notes

1. "Rebellion and Responsibility," *Yale Review,* Fall, 1967, p. 30.

2. "The Children's Crusade," *American Journal of Orthopsychiatry, 38:* 597-98 (1968).

3. Alfred Freedman and Marcia Freedman, "Responding to Student Protest," *American Journal of Orthopsychiatry, 38:* 780 (1968).

4. *Totem and Taboo* (New York: Random House, 1938).

5. *Life and Work of Sigmund Freud* (New York: Basic Books, 1957), *3:* 322.

6. Ibid., *3:* 329.

7. Ibid., *3:* 335.

8. *Civilization and Its Discontents* (London: The Hogarth Press, 1929).

9. *Group Psychology and the Analysis of the Ego* (London: The Hogarth Press, 1948).

10. M. Brewster Smith, Norma Haan, and Jeanne Block, "Social-Psychological Aspects of Student Activism," *Youth and Society, 1:* 261-88 (1969); and Richard Flacks, "The Liberated Generation: An Exploration of the Roots of Student Protest," *Journal of Social Issues, 23:* 52-75 (1967).

11. Sigmund Freud, *The Future of Illusion* (London: The Hogarth Press, 1927). 1927).

12. "Some Observations Regarding the Role of Fathers in Child Psychotherapy," *Bulletin of the Menninger Clinic,* no. 1 (Jan. 1957), pp. 16-27.

13. Martin Duberman, *The New York Times Book Review,* June 22, 1969, pp. 1,7.

14. "Towards a Conceptual Model of Radical and Militant Youth: A Study of Columbia Undergraduates," *The Psychoanalytic Forum* (in press).

15. "On the Nature of Psycho-Historical Evidence: In Search of Gandhi," *International Journal of Psychiatry, 7:* 451 (1969).

16. See note 10, above.

17. Kenneth Keniston, personal communication, May 7, 1969.

18. *The Uses of the Past* (New York: Oxford University Press, 1952), p. 11.

Youth Culture:
The New Sensibility

Edgar A. Levenson, Arthur H. Feiner,
and Nathan Stockhamer

The original title of this collection, "Youth in Transition," reflects its inherent biases as well as its best intentions. Youth is not in transition; it is not going anywhere. Youth is, quite simply, somewhere else. Were the title "Psychotherapy in Transition," it would more accurately reflect the real state of affairs, for we are living in a period of unprecedented social and technological change which has created a world in which young adults are indigenous and psychotherapists the strangers. We must suspend our traditional ethnocentricity and ask not what is happening to the young adult in our world, but where and how we fit in *his* new world.

This is what Susan Sontag has called an applied Hegelianism: seeking one's self in the other.[1] And if this foggy pursuit were not in itself sufficiently offensive to the social scientist, we must violate still another cherished tenet, namely, the *hard fact*. Scientists, even social and behavioral scientists, are as devoted to the hard fact as the Internal Revenue Service. But hard facts can be delusive, especially in diachronic studies, studies examining change over a period of time. For example, there is considerable evidence that unmarried college girls are engaging in sexual intercourse more frequently than a decade or two ago. The fact is they are having more sex; but according to a recent extensive survey, they are enjoying it less.[2] They are actually less promiscuous and less hedonistic than their antecedents, who were conspicuously less selective in their extensive backseat petting, often to the point of orgasm. What then do the facts reveal about the changes in sexual mores? Are girls sexually freer than they used to be, or are their sexual acts experienced differently? A fact is, after all, only an event or an action viewed from a particular epistemological position.

What we need is not more facts, but a new perspective. Marshall McLuhan, who has made some cogent observations about changing cultures, has pointed out that in periods of radical change there is a tendency to view the new as nothing but an extension of the old and familiar.[3] This might be called the "horseless carriage" fallacy. It was not at first recognized, for example, that automobiles were a radical technological innovation, creating what McLuhan has called a new "environment," entirely changing its world. America, especially California, is a society radically changed by the presence of the automobile. Even great innovators, prophets in a way, are contaminated in their world view. Thus, Da Vinci conceived of man's flight, but he flapped feathered wings. Jules Verne predicted the submarine and the space capsule, but both of his creations had paneled Edwardian living rooms and carvings on the hulls.

Similarly, psychiatrists invoke their own "nothing buts" in dealing with youth culture; from the Victorian dynamics of the oedipus complex to the benign paternalism of Erikson's concept of "identity crisis." The young adult seems fair to become the new white man's burden. This point was well taken by Edgar Friedenberg in *Coming of Age in America*[4]; and, it is worth mentioning that Fanon noted that in the African families which he had observed over many years, he could find no trace of the white man's oedipus complex.[5] Our concepts, then, may well be tied to our own paradigms. To really *see* the new requires a shift in basic perspective. We will give an overview of this alleged cultural revolution and then say something about its consequences for the nature and relevance of psychotherapy.

We are living at the juncture of two great technological revolutions. Up until now man has been involved in technological developments which culminated in the first industrial revolution: the re-

90

placement of natural engines (human beings and animals) as sources of mechanical energy with artificially constructed engines. These have ranged in sophistication and technical complexity from simple planes and levers to the wheel, to hydraulics and gasoline engines, and jet propulsion. In each case the work done was mechanical, involving a transformation of energy. What Rapoport has called the second industrial revolution was rooted in the technological problems of World War II, with the development of machines to process not energy but information; for example, Norbert Wiener's cybernetics, which grew out of efforts in World War II to make machines that anticipated the future position of a moving target.[6]

These new machines reap not, neither do they sow. They do not process energy; indeed, the energy exchanges are infinitesimal. Instead they examine patterns of signals by which information is transmitted. Information steers action, and a circular relationship exists between the two. This is the new world of electronics, computers, and servo-mechanisms. It is the science of communication and control. Weston LaBarre, an anthropologist, has stated that man is the only animal that has transferred his evolutionary development from his own body to his technological extensions.[7] If that is so, then one might say that the first industrial revolution was an evolutionary extension of the musculo-skeletal system and the second industrial revolution an extension of the central nervous system. This is essentially what McLuhan has claimed in *Understanding Media*.[8] One further step in understanding is necessary; one must recognize that this technological revolution is reflected in every aspect of the culture—in its science, its esthetics, even in its forms of aberration. There emerges what could be called a pervasive paradigm of the epoch. Until recently the paradigm has been mechanical, but it now becomes informational.

Our psychiatric concepts are traditionally of the mechanical paradigm. Even the lexicon is mechanical. We talk of force, work drive, damming up. Certainly our terms are energetic, regardless of orientation, whether libido or self-realization. The concepts of psychopathology are equally mechanical; people are supposed to have commonly held basic machinery which works the same way, universally. Pathology, therefore, is a breakdown in the machinery, and cure is a restoration of smooth operation. Freud's patients had disturbances reflecting the prevalent paradigm; to wit, they broke down or developed sexual difficulties, obsessions, or anxiety. They "couldn't function, spun their wheels, were stuck on the same track." Psychoanalysis was the viewing of behavior as conflict, as Kris commented.[9] Newton, Marx, and Freud were the prophets of this mechanical paradigm, and their ideas dominated through the first industrial revolution.

What of the new paradigm? In the world of information processing, energy transfers are minimal and irrelevant. This is the world of negentropy and the contingent patterning of events. Patterning, or organization of data, is more important than content in an age of electronics. A telephoto picture is nothing more than a transmitted pattern of uniform dots. We have become less interested in basic machinery than in private experience. Instead of dynamics we now pursue phenomenology. In this paradigm pathology is *not* a breakdown in machinery but an idiosyncratic attempt at problemsolving. Cure is *not* a restoration of original function, it is *not* a going back. It is a change in the patterning of the patient's responses. This is achieved not by understanding basic mechanisms, but rather by extending the patient's awareness of his interpersonal experience as it is manifested in his history, his present life, his dreams and fantasies, and the imprinting of his patterns of experience on the therapy situation. There is an axiom of information theory that states that informational overload results in pattern recognition. The function of the therapist, it could be said, is to increase the information tolerance of the patient so that he can deal with more data without overload, without premature resorting to closure (a reductive mechanistic explanation). Neurosis might be called a state of informational banality. It has been said that the neurotic knows only one way of doing things and that does not work. Therapy can and often does perpetuate that banality by reductionistic interpretations. The experienced therapist extends information, and the beginner extends metaphor, regardless of his theoretical orientation.

Von Bertalanffy, Miller, and Rapoport in general systems theory; Levi-Strauss in anthropology (parenthetically, the famous debate between Sartre and Levi-Strauss is precisely the struggle of these two world views); Bateson, Ruesch, Parsons, Cantril, Grinker, Shands, and Buckley in the social and behavior sciences; Cage in music; Cunningham in dance; Sontag in literary criticism; Goddard in cinema; in a word, the new sensibility or new culture reflects this informational paradigm.

The young adult is the man of his times. Much of his behavior, which we older adults find irritating and incomprehensible, is totally consistent with the new world. He is like the penguin, on land a waddling pomposity and in his true medium, water, a technical masterpiece. His language, for example, is electronic: "turn on, tune in, blow your mind, freak out," are the lexicon of the vacuum tube. At first contact his speech seems stereotyped, limited in affective and descriptive range, flat. It is replete with grunts, "you knows," and "beautifuls." One notes that while it is not a content-oriented language as is ours, it is a formal language with its own patterned rhythm and structure. This highly stylized language serves the function of excluding content-oriented adults. Blacks have developed an almost identical speech style, which confuses and excludes content-oriented whites. Because computers and young adults talk the same language, it is not surprising, as Justine Jerome has pointed out, that most professors are as illiterate in the language of computers and other skills of the new technology as was medieval man in reading and writing. Much of the new science, general systems theory, or even the new mathematics is more readily accessible to the young than to us (as any parent of a ten-year-old can attest).

The electronic revolution also has extensively changed the esthetic and moral considerations of our society. But small wars in far-off places, that Orwellian prediction come true, are becoming intolerable precisely because of television's immediacy and involvement; the shrinking of the world through instantaneous communication systems; and the highly idiosyncratic behavior of the young, who are unresponsive to sloganizing and at the same time aware of their collective power. Free of the Protestant Ethic of work, unwilling to be part of the machine or the team, the young are, in the epithet of their elders, "amoral"; yet, oddly, much less apathetic and more committed than their elders.

What psychotherapists are seeing increasingly in their offices, as a consequence, is less pathology of the machinery and more pathology of role. Increasingly, patients of all ages are presenting mildly sociopathic disturbances. (We use this term in its most literal sense—pathology in the area of social functioning). Patients come because of commitment problems, drug abuse, dropping out. Others, who have no neurotic symptoms in the traditional sense, who are able to function and enjoy themselves, come for consultations because they want out. Many refuse or are unable to couple competence with the appropriate social role.[10] The hysterical cannot get an erection, the obsessional can but does not enjoy it, and the new patient can *do* both but does not see his place in the work or marital scheme. Philip Roth's hero Alexander Portnoy is the exemplar of the new malaise. He suffers what Erikson has called the problem of fidelity.[11]

The psychotherapist, by virtue of both his age and training, is essentially a traditionalist. His paradigms are largely of the mechanical era, regardless of his metaphor (Freudian, Rogerian, Frommian, Sullivanian). He is most comfortable confronting malfunction. How then does he deal with his obsolescence when he must treat people who talk a different language, have different symptoms, and are not satisfied with traditional solutions? How does he deal with his own irrelevance?

At the Young Adult Treatment Service of the William Alanson White Institute in our three year study of college dropouts we found it difficult to establish clearcut diagnostic categories or clinical entities.[12] Nor could we establish a convincing profile of the dropout in terms of his work habits, school abilities, intelligence, or use of drugs. Dropouts could be distinguished from those who did not drop out not by objective characteristics or dynamics but by their patterns of experience. The problem in malfunction is to restore function. What is the problem in malfeasance? Should a dropout go back to college? Is college necessarily good? Should we ignore the dropping out behavior and treat him for something else, a clearcut neurotic symptom? That clinical evasion usually does not work. When the machine fails, the function and moral obligation of the mechanic is clear; he repairs it. When the mechanic walks out of the napalm factory, what then is the moral responsibility of the therapist? Is the patient an object to be ordered into the therapist's mental scheme of categories? The therapist can stay in his safe but anachronistic world. He can sustain his tautologies by treating patients who have anachronistic symptoms. If he goes into the brave new world, then he must be prepared to have not only his concepts, but the very idea of his own relevance and purpose challenged.

If psychotherapy is not prepared to limit its applicability to middle class, middle aged whites, it must work with the emergent society. Therapy, as any essentially artistic endeavor, must remain revolutionary. Butterfield has said that "it is not irrelevant to note that, of all forms of mental activity, the most difficult to induce . . . is the art of handling the same bundle of data as before, but placing them in a different system of relations with one another by giving them a different framework."[13] Psychotherapy is no body of eternal truths, but reflects changing aspects of a changing society. Our patients, their symptoms, and our concepts are in continuous flux. The young patient is to the therapist as the canary is to the coalminer. His sensitivity may be excessive or exorbitant, but he augurs the winds of change. In this rapidly changing world the patient is often more contemporary than the therapist. We had best learn from him.

In this brief effort at perspective, it is not possible to suggest in any detail the consequences of this change in paradigm for clinical technique. It is, at best, a caveat, an attempt to avoid the old fogeyism implicit in our efforts to understand a new and contemporary phenomenon in the language of the old paradigm.

95

Notes

1. *Against Interpretation* (New York: Noonday Press, 1961), p. 69.

2. William Simon and John Gagnon, "Sexual Behavior in the College Student," paper presented at the Academy of Psychoanalysis meeting, New Orleans, 1968.

3. *Understanding Media* (New York: McGraw-Hill, 1964).

4. *Coming of Age in America* (New York: Random House, 1963).

5. Frantz Fanon, *Peau Noire, Masque Blancs* (New York: Grove Press, 1967). Quoted by J. E. Siegel, "On Frantz Fanon," *The American Scholar, 38:* 89 (1968-1969).

6. Anatol Rapoport, "Foreword," *Modern Systems Research for the Behavioral Scientist,* ed. Walter Buckley (Chicago: Aldine Publishing Company, 1968).

7. *The Human Animal* (Chicago: University of Chicago Press, 1963).

8. Herbert Marshall McLuhan, *Understanding Media: The Extensions of Man* (New York: McGraw-Hill, 1964).

9. Ernst Kris, "The Nature of Psychoanalytic Propositions and their Validity," *Freedom and Experience,* ed. Sidney Hook and M. R. Konvitz (Ithaca: Cornell University Press, 1947), p. 241.

10. Edgar Levenson, Nathan Stockhamer, and Arthur Feiner, "Family Transactions in the Etiology of Dropping Out of College," *Contemporary Psychoanalysis, 3:*134-52 (1967).

11. Erik Erikson, *Insight and Responsibility* (New York: W.W. Norton and Co., 1964).

12. Levenson, Stockhamer, and Feiner, "Family Transactions."

13. Herbert Butterfield, *The Origins of Modern Science* (London: Bell Press, 1949).

Hippies as the Focus of Violence; or, Disaffected Society and Its Stand Against Youth

Robert A. Klein

During the 1950s the larger cities of the United States were plagued by gangs and gang wars. Periodic "stomping" murders and/or flamboyantly psychotic killings such as the "Capeman" incident in New York City in 1959 were common. Rivalries at that time were marked by their essentially hit-and-run nature, with clearcut provocations and boundary (turf) lines making it relatively easy to pick out one's leather-jacketed adversary in the street. When a member of one gang violated the turf or girl of a rival gang, retribution was generally predictable, including a scheduled confrontation between the opposing factions; switchblades and zipguns settled the feud, if the police had not beforehand. Usually this practice was sufficient: swift, clearly defined, relatively brief, and to the point. It was a stimulus-response interaction (provocation-retribution) and not callously brutal (except for the occasional psychotic episodes).

The sociological and political context in which these interactions occurred is extremely important. Law and order were not yet being challenged as Establishment bulwarks in those Eisenhower years; indeed, we all "understood" how to deal with transgressors so unselfconsciously that the gangs themselves accurately reflected the larger society's crime-punishment, right-wrong, the-law-is-the-law philosophy. And because we were able to satisfy ourselves that we did more or less comprehend what was going on, because the observed behavior was in miniature much like what we as a nation were involved in, we were not threatened by this style. Not only was there hardly a vile epithet directed by a policeman toward an Amboy Duke or Fordham Dagger; on the contrary, the police organized ball teams for them in the afternoons and dances in the evenings. Nevertheless, it took many months of coaxing before New York's ninth precinct police agreed to play a game of softball in Central Park with some of the local long hairs (the police, of course, won the game).

Currently, however, unlike ten or fifteen years ago, an easy recognition of the "adversary" is neither explicit-purposeful (that is, it is no longer for reason of delineating and identifying the feuding gangs), nor universal (that is, dress is now idiosyncratic and whimsical). While the clothing worn by groups such as the hippies is certainly self-expressive, it can in reality also become self-destructive, for fear of the strange and an aura of violence are psychological handmaidens. Nor are long-haired, long-bearded, and beaded people the only whites on the receiving end of multi-attacker aggression. (Witness the Bonnie and Clyde-type multiple murder in Michigan, or the boastful brutality of New York longshoremen who attacked a draft resistance picket line, or the grand classic of them all, Chicago in August 1968.) The incursions have usually taken the form of concerted mass aggressions against an *identifiably* helpless group of individuals whose stated philosophy—in the case of the hippies—is a kind of laissez-faire pacifism. The attacks and attackers are often almost pathologically hateful and vicious, strikingly unlike the frequently evenly-matched, arranged, and clearly delineated combats of the 1950s when increasingly successful Youth Board workers even managed to impede the violence by having each of the two warring gangs choose its best fighter to compete in a supervised boxing match. "Normal" anti-social behavior is always the flipside of contemporary social behavior, and its perpetrators can therefore call on accepted ways of expressing and satisfying their own demands—socially accepted, that is, but not legally sanctioned. In this way, after all, they are only reflecting the covert mores of the society from which they sprang. Hippies, in contrast, have no such lineage and thus no corresponding sanctioned exit from their anti-social dilemma. Coincident with the times, both past and present, personal facesaving was the implicit motivation for the former (hence the permissibility of the boxing matches), while impersonal patriotism is inevitably invoked by the detractors of the latter.

But none of the above is uniquely identified with the hippies, who as a group exemplify the inherent strains and frustrations of the late 1960s, not only as a group per se but also as a goad to and indeed a mirror for the larger whole as well. (Hippies laugh at the attempt of the media to fit them into a discernible and recognizable category and have even held elaborate death-of-the-hippie rites in mock-serious efforts to exorcise this peculiarly midcentury American devil.) Less than eighteen months ago any accurate reading of the life style of either individual hippies or hippie tribes would have had to describe them as relatively nonpolitical (certainly ideological), passively alienated human beings whose overtly nonaggressive rituals generally consisted of pelting passersby with flowers as one manifestation of their chaotic but peaceful response to a chaotic and often violent world. Subsequently, and at first subtly, the tenor of hippie behavior became increasingly militant, drawing toward itself as inevitably as the flame does the moth the violence their carefully planned encapsulation had hoped to escape. At first inadvertently provocative in their gaudy, jangling dress, they progressed to a somewhat self-conscious level of put-on until now, finally, a new brand of militantly aggressive hippie has been forced to emerge from the flames of busts, and busted heads, at Tompkins Square Park, Columbia, Chicago, and elsewhere. What is astonishing is that they, with the appropriate aid of the Establishment's ignorance and insensitivity, have brought many others along with them. It is this transition—some would call it revolution—from an attempt at a withdrawn peacefulness, which was both antithetical and frightening to the older macrosociety, to the ultimate "decision" to match stridency with stridency, violence with violence that has

99

most visibly marked recent years. I hope in this paper to place this transition into a meaningful perspective.

Perhaps the first incident dramatically to call attention to the subterranean tensions between the hippies and the immediate community in which they resided was the aftermath of a large arrest-in which occurred in New York's East Village on Memorial Day 1967.[1] About 200 barefooted, Hare Krishna-chanting, bongo-drumming youngsters (not by any means all of them full-time Bohemians) were sitting on what there is of grass in the small, city-block-sized Tompkins Square Park, surrounded both by "Keep Off the Grass" signs and, eventually, more than 100 law officers, including large numbers of the city's so-called elite, riot-trained Tactical Police Force (TPF). After much haranguing of the police (summoned by a park employe who had been offended by the misuse of the grass), as well as deliberately provocative behavior by both sides (the hippies laughed at the policemen, shouted "Heil" at them, and refused to move; the police told the hippies to get a bath and/or a haircut), the police moved in suddenly and viciously, swinging nightsticks and bloodying the resisters, some of whom cursed and bit back (passivity was already beginning to become passé). Almost two score were arrested for trespassing and resisting arrest; virtually all were later released, after promising not to sue the city for false arrest, and the city unofficially apologized for the harshness surrounding the incident.

Within a week the hippies were back in the park, and the city had removed the "Keep Off the Grass" signs. To celebrate their victory the erstwhile trespassers brought along, openly and aggressively, their own "grass." Without concern for who was present or observing (the area was crowded with appropriately dressed citizens, distinguished by the little green lapel pin which identified them as police, as well as the more obvious kind), the hippies psychedelically went about their business of smoking the currently prohibited grass on the previously prohibited grass. It was a sight not often found elsewhere, and no one was arrested! (A similar smoke-in with no arrests was held at about the same time in San Francisco's

Haight-Ashbury district.) The significance of this immunity may be missed by middle class whites, who, with or without the proper connections, have never been harassed, humiliated, or jailed by local law officers for whatever reason, including having a dark skin or a strange accent. The local Puerto Rican and black communities stopped their sporadic but increasingly volatile feuding and aggressively joined forces to complain, in effect, "Who the hell are these white bastards intruding on our restricted and ghettoized play area (that's bad enough) and are allowed to sit on the grass (we've done that before and no one removed the signs; all we got was a good kick in the ass) and who smoke illegal marijuana with immunity (we can't even jaywalk without getting busted)?"

Furthermore, as West and Allen point out, these despised whites were blatantly rejecting exactly what the blacks were attempting to attain.[2] "This poses a deeper threat to the black rebels than does white racial prejudice, because it allies these strange whites with many of the attitudes of the black rebels' parental generation—a gentle, patient, loving, accepting, and basically religious adjustment to uncomfortable and deprived circumstances"—but while simultaneously maintaining their middle class relationship with the law.

The nonwhite community was incensed. Interestingly, the white Jews, Poles, and Ukraninians still in the area were less vocal, probably because they were less vulnerable and had long ago withdrawn into their social clubs and still-cohesive social ways. The nonwhites were at the time intent on mobility and becoming part of the American dream and in their pursuit became increasingly aggressive and hostile to the white long hairs; knifings and other physical assaults became even more commonplace in this area with an already very high incidence of crime including the allegedly provoked chasing and stripping of a terrorized white hippie girl on the perimeter of the park; she finally found refuge wrapped in a blanket in a police patrol car. Additionally, eight- and nine-year-old Puerto Rican boys became discriminating themselves, when, in broad daylight, they neglected pocketbooks for the more exciting thrill (it was hardly a challenge) of feeling up the loosely clad and identifi-

101

ably hippie girls in the neighborhood. At least this particular tactic worked: the exodus of whites from the East Village began in earnest, although some postponed the move by acquiring large, vicious dogs. East 12th Street, in particular, was known for its varieties of canines, and many of the female owners were acquainted with certain Puerto Rican and black leaders, to whom they went for surcease when the young molesters became frighteningly obscene.

The anger of the nonwhite community was now out in the open; one black man expressed his disgust, and frustration, in the now famous remark that "when whitey gets tired of living with the rats down here, he can always go back to Queens; man, we got no choice; this is where we live." And where some die at the hands of the very angry: the brutal deaths of nonaggressive Groovy and Linda hastened the exodus and made national headlines at the same time.

The second and third points overlap somewhat and are implicit in the foregoing. Hippies, by their own definition, were physically defenseless. They preached and practiced pacificism and love and expected that these psychological defenses would be sufficient protection. They offered flower psychology, not power psychology, but nevertheless displayed flashes of ambivalence and fright about their position with such combination phrases as "flower power" and "make love, not war." (The SDS Weathermen have recognized this predicament; they have changed the slogan to "make love *and* war.") But they were proven wrong and resented their own misperception. In the U.S., power without violence has proven to be a myth, they slowly discovered. In an inversion of Whorf's linguistic hypothesis, Americans can dismiss and misunderstand the self-immolation of Quaker Norman Morrison as the response of a crazy man while sympathizing with the same act by a Czech youth. So the hippies became confused, then withdrawn, confused again, and, lately, militant. Furthermore, they proved different in an important way from the Beats or the gangs. The hippies, once they understood, readily acknowledged the changing scene, the context in process; they knew that their time was rapidly ending, and so they adapted and rolled with the punches, both given and received.

102

They were the educated and insightful reflectors of society's death wishes toward them, not to be coopted and incorporated the way Kerouac and the others were, and the way most self-interest groups are. They were the underground now generation, moving, as the guerilla works with the terrain, into direct confrontation if that was what the moment dictated. They were determined not to be enshrined as dusty poets-in-residence at leading colleges; they instead became radicals-in-residence at free universities (except for Carl Oglesby, who became a radical-scholar-in-residence at Antioch, but Oglesby is an SDS radical and Antioch reportedly is a quasi-free university). Roving bands of guerrilla theater groups emerged, creating a living theater of the streets by confronting the straights with the fruits of their deeds. One such group enacted a murder so real that the observers reacted in testimony to its apparent veracity: they ignored the screams for help. (One forerunner of certain types of guerilla theater can be traced back to San Francisco hippies who ran alongside sightseeing buses holding mirrors up for the passengers to gaze into. Subsequently, tours were organized for hippies to sightsee in middle class sections of New York.) And as a kind of salute to Ken Kesey and his Hell's Angels-hippies parties, as well as the ultimate acknowledgement of where it's really at, a group of motorcycle-hippie types called Up Against the Wall, Motherfucker is now pleasantly terrorizing New York's East Village (nee Lower East Side).

In March of last year a gang of vigilantes set fire to a commune of three houses in a small central Vermont town. The bitterness of this episode is evident from a letter writer who asks plaintively: "I ask, what can one do? Call in the man? Forgive and forget? Find the people responsible and burn them? Still, should I feel Hate? Love? Uncertainty? What do the diggers (hippies) do when the local Puerto Ricans bust up their store? What does the spade do when he sees the man shoot his brother, or while he watches the Establishment screw him? What should we all feel? Love?"

Furthermore, and this is the third point, at peace rallies, be-ins, and the like, the police frequently arrest anyone, when they do arrest, with long hair, beads, or painted face. (The exception, after

103

the fact, the Memorial Day detente notwithstanding, the similarity of police treatment in regard to hippies and nonwhites begins and ends right there; in more ways than one does a society insist on its inhabitants being clothed in a conforming, bland manner.)[3] In fact, during the draft resistance activity at the Whitehall Induction Center in lower Manhattan in the winter of 1968 bearded reporters from *Time* and the New York *Post* had difficulty persuading officers of their identity as they were led to the paddywagon. One of New York Mayor John Lindsay's top aides, in the role of official observer, also narrowly escaped arrest only after satisfactorily explaining his "student-looking" appearance. At still another demonstration, this one held in New York's Grand Central Station to celebrate the arrival of spring, the police manifested "the worst display of police brutality . . . ever seen outside of Mississippi," according to a New York Civil Liberties Union lawyer. Hippies were shoved through plateglass windows, forced to "run a police gauntlet," and were attacked without warning. Many of those clubbed were not even among the fifty-six who were arrested at what is described by many of the participants as a police riot. Among those who required a half dozen stitches to close a bloody head wound was a bearded newspaper reporter who had his press credentials pinned to his jacket.

The term "police riot" gained official credence with the issuance of the Walker Commission report on violence at the Chicago convention. It was there that the radicalization of. many of the young took place, and where, perhaps, "reactionalization" of many of the old, watching on television, also occurred. One phase of the transition from a protected middle class majority to an attacked fringe minority was taking place before the disbelieving eyes of the country. The police, of course, are only staunch guardians of the status quo and were doing what was asked of them when they too lumped the enemy into a conglomerate of Negroes and yippies. Jules Feiffer warns us that it is wise to remember that "if we judge policemen harshly now, someday policemen may be judging us." The now-politicized hippies (yippies),[4] the new niggers, have learned, as the blacks have had it emblazoned on their skin, what it means to be busted just for walking down the street. The point is, we are all niggers now and it really isn't a big step from violence in Chicago to overt refusal of Long Island railroad riders to pay for the man's insulting service. After all, there is hardly a man today who is not wearing sideburns.

It is interesting to note that those segments of the population, such as the police who sanction and allegedly participate in brutality and the longshoremen who are permitted by the police to engage in illegal physical assaults—these highly masculine segments of society are just the ones to react with the most violence. Uncertain of their own feelings, these men revel in vilifying the flowing dress of the hippies, with class strains threatening their self-concept of what is or is not pleasurable. Long hair in particular seems most likely to bring out rage, confusing for them the psychosexual identities they have struggled so long to separate out. If the secondary sex characteristics can no longer be relied upon to make the appropriate distinctions, then what remains as the defining difference becomes too fearful and stimulating to accept. It reminds one of the story about the small child who was taken to a nudist colony for a visit. When he was asked which were the boys and which were the girls, he said he could not tell since they did not have their clothes on. West and Allen suggest that those most fearful of and threatened by the hippies may be "struggling with whatever is stirred up inside themselves through stimulation of fantasies of freedom from responsibility, escape from the frustrations of rigid life situations . . . and uninhibited sexuality without the necessity for interpersonal commitments."[5] Similarly, a colleague relates the fantasies of a female patient of his who in her middle class neurotic condition intensely envies the hippies and begrudges them their freedom. This investigator recently had an occasion to lecture to a group of middle aged nurses, all of whom had or would soon have teenaged children. Their horror at the possibility that their sons or daughters would run off to Greenwich Village was pathetic and revealing, especially in the light of a class visit they had taken to a Village free store. "We are the people," says hippie nonleader Abbie Hoffman, "our parents warned us against."

And finally, in a clear display of what Edgar Z. Friedenberg in a different context calls "ressentiment," the mass media explain for their middle class audience (composed, to a significant extent, of the very parents of the hippies), that somehow, when hippies get beat up and bloodied, it is their fault for being attacked, while the attackers are excused if not forthrightly praised.[6] The medium indeed is the message and the hippies are quickly learning that in our headlong dash toward 1984, verities (external or otherwise) have become dangerously inverted, not the least of them being the confusion and contamination of the roles of victim and executioner. When Beatle Ringo Starr was asked if he were a mod or a rocker (two opposing British styles of behavior and dress), he replied, "A mocker."

The passivity of the hippie—or passivity in general—is the most appropriate place to begin to understand urban, post-midcentury American violence. The hippies proclaimed themselves defenseless; they are the perfect target for bullying, cowardly violence (a similar model can be explored the case of Vietnam), and as such are even lower on the allowable retaliation scale than are nonwhites. (The case is somewhat different, but nonetheless relevant, in regard to the Hell's Angels. This marginal group would also ordinarily be low on the retaliation scale, but in fact this retaliatory mechanism is used ingeniously by certain police departments. For example, it was alleged that the Oakland police encouraged a group of Angels to break up an anti-war rally. If this is true, it further supports the argument that the least resistant are the focal point for studying violence, sanctioned or otherwise, particularly in the case of the attacking group's having "an ethnocentric inability to understand the behavior of different groups.")[7] In short, society has been provided with a defenseless group of human beings which has voluntarily rejected exactly what the disadvantaged are striving for (see, for example, Davis).[8] But the larger society may have outsmarted itself. In making the hippies so visible (and seemingly willing) a victim, the result has been overkill, both literally and figuratively. For the very hippies who extolled their own virtuous physical defenselessness and who came to rely on a kind of naive psychological defense have themselves become caught up in the fever they inadvertently spawned. More and more hippies, reflecting the growth and acceptance of mass violence throughout America, are now taking to violence as a way of life, many of them carrying psychedelic switchblades when once they carried flowers. The Establishment treats them as the faceless enemy, draining them of the last residue of self-respect; following the classic history of the minority, they have begun to identify with the aggressor. The media have so perverted their life style that in self-defense a half-mocking, half-serious new term had to be invented: yippies. (One imaginative writer of letters-to-the-editor suggested that the new term be "human beings," relishing the thought of such headlines as: "Human beings protest war" or "Police club fifty human beings in anti-war demonstration.")

One can point to the Chicago slaughter as the event at which ritualistic passivity became clearly violent confrontation. But that would not be giving enough credit where credit is due. The hippies never envisioned the violence that they inadvertently but inevitably spawned. They withdrew only to be pursued by men with microphones, little green lapel pins for identification, and ultimately big police clubs. The American tradition, exemplified by the big showdown in the movies, was and is being played out. The much provoked ex-gunslinger takes all kinds of guff until in the last scene he finally whips out his six-shooter while the audience cheers wildly. And in like fashion the viewers at the hippie zoo have finally pierced that flower myth of insane passivity. You are what you eat, and the hippie-yippies, who were fed the same food as their audience, have only recently walked away from the trough.

And one can point, too, to the parallel exercises on campuses and streets all over the world. The church is being confronted; the state is being attacked, and youth in Davenport, Iowa are wearing long hair, smoking pot, and demanding to be treated like human beings. But, although certain parallels can be noted, in the United States identification with the aggressor is not yet 100 per cent complete; in very few places of the world would such a violent confrontation as those at Chicago or Columbia University leave the police virtually without injury. Not in Tokyo, not in Prague, not in Paris, not in South America would the police escape unscathed, but only in America. But not for long; the demonstrations at Nixon's inauguration, where some policemen were pummeled to the ground, may have changed all that. The strain of authoritarianism runs deeper than we non-Freudians have guessed; the hippie-yippies may still be as helpless as when they first emerged, but they are now struggling openly with authority and power, where previously they were utterly (strange as it seems) cowed by it. If violence sustains power, then it can be dealt with, and the crescendo of Fanonization (a term used by Etzioni[9] to indicate the insurgent's realization that extreme behavior—for example vulgar epithets—only provokes human, not superhuman, responses from one's adversary) will garner intensity. Marcuse notes that our society permits dissent, as long as it is not threatening, but it is also true that our society incorporates and dilutes differences in a sort of self-preserving identification with the aggressed-upon. Fanon, of course, died before the convulsions of the present decade.

Unnerving, too, was Madison Avenue's pirating of the best of the many creative ideas developed by the different hippie tribes and the movement in general. Mixed-media television programs and psychedelic magazine covers, not to mention clothing styles for both men and women, all had their origin somewhere within the psychedelic-hippie morass. It is amusing to listen to those who condemn hippies as "parasites" who live off a community of hardworking citizens, especially when these citizens are reaping the financial, social, or leisure time rewards without so much as a thank you to the innovators. It is America's unique knack to absorb and distort what it can materially identify with and accept in its excommunicants, leaving only the dregs undisturbed by rejection.

Perhaps saddest of all was the slow but inevitable demise of a brightly decorated Digger Free Store on East 10th Street in New York, where everything (food, clothing, and talk) was free, with absolutely no questions asked. (The Diggers were a group of service-oriented hippies originating on the West Coast.) At the end its doorway became a drab, greasy motorcycle runway, while its plateglass windows were smashed with large rocks and pipes thrown by the angry ethnic minority from *their* restricted slum roofs across the street. There are no more joyous happenings or be-ins (labeled "pro-life" by their participants); mass gatherings now are more focused and goal-directed: anti-war, anti-draft, anti-Nixon.

Open season has been declared on hippies and yippies, and the hunters have responded. Many of the more pacifistic youth have opted for the hills and a semblance of communal living, leaving the police to cope with the remaining hardliners along with this year's aggrieved minority, the restless blacks who have learned the lesson of the hippies and do not expect to be pushed off the grass for smoking pot. New York's *Village Voice* raises the specter of marginal groups and collective violence. "They are talking about the possibility of youth riots . . . on a scale unheard of in my lifetime," columnist Richard Goldstein notes.[10] "From [the flower child's] ashes, a militant psychedelic left has arisen. . . . They are commonly lumped together with the Negroes, the Mexicans, and the communists, into a composite image of The Threat. Already, a dominant police attitude toward the hip community has emerged: they must be hit hard before they toughen up like the spades, and they must be destroyed as a movement once they are down."

The interdependency is not only real between the goads to violence and the unique and specific role of the victim, but it also describes the ultimate and perhaps inevitable congruency of the two in late mid-twentieth century America. The merger is as American as apple pie, and it is frightening, though not surprising, that "the flower children have developed thorns."[11]

Notes

1. Not to be ignored are the designs of the commercial and real estate interests which, forecasting the business and economic value of this influx, promptly affixed a high income, high rent priority on the area by calling it the East Village, since rents in the West Village (Greenwich Village) were three to four times higher than those across town. Residents in the community who had been

living, they thought, in the slum-ridden Lower East Side were surprised and aggrieved to learn that the hippie influx not only had changed the sounds and smells of their neighborhood (from lox, cabbage, and cuchifritos to pot and incense) but its very name as well. Of basic psychological significance was the establishing of ownership by giving something a name or identity of one's own choosing—obeisance to animism found many means of expression among the hippies.

2. It was apparent during this time that friction was growing between the non-whites and the middle class hippies (less than 1 per cent of whom were black). Town hall meetings were held in the local coffee houses and daily (sometimes twice daily) mimeographed fliers were printed and distributed informing the populace of any police-community incidents; explaining that the authorities were trying to encourage black-white tension to detract from such real issues as poverty; and, in general, exhorting all concerned to play it cool. This daily flier was a well organized, informative propaganda publication worthy of study in its own right. Participatory democracy was a serious and meaningful factor in those heady days.

3. Hunter Thompson, *Hell's Angels: The Strange and Terrible Saga of Outlaw Motorcycle Gangs* (New York: Ballantine Books, 1967).

4. Paul Krassner, "Activists, Radicals and Yippies," *Careers Today,* Jan. 1969, 22-28.

5. Louis J. West and James R. Allen, "Three Rebellions: Red, Black, and Green," in *Science and Psychoanalysis,* ed. Jules Masserman (New York: Grune & Stratton, 1968), *13,* 99-119. Quote from p. 118.

6. *The Dignity of Youth and Other Atavisms* (Boston: Beacon Press, 1966).

7. Thompson, *Hell's Angels.*

8. Fred Davis, "Why All of Us May be Hippies Someday," *Trans-Action, 59,* no. 2 (1967), 10-18.

9. Amitai Etzioni, "Confessions of a Professor Caught in a Revolution," *The New York Times Sunday Magazine,* Sept. 15, 1968, pp. 25, 109.

10. Richard Goldstein, "New Babylon," *The Village Voice,* March 11, 1968, pp. 1, 10.

11. Krassner, "Activists."

The Conceptual Importance of Being "Far Out": or, The First Humanists, Too, Were Alienated Beyond Redemption

Mark Messer

Alienation is a diagnostic concept. Unlike such medical diagnoses as appendicitis and leukemia, however, which point to quite distinct maladies and call for quite distinct treatment and prognosis, alienation has become such a pervasive diagnosis that it is difficult to distinguish the disease from the patient. When alienation is no longer alien, it ceases to be a meaningful concept. To diagnose a female patient as a woman is tautological. I want to suggest here that it is almost as tautological and meaningless to diagnose the youth of our society (or, for that matter, our society itself) as alienated.

Nevertheless, we continue to characterize ourselves as victims of alienation. The persistence of meaningless diagnosis itself attests to the pervasiveness—the one dimensionality—of our disease, because meaninglessness and alienation are synonymous. At the risk of sounding unnecessarily enigmatic, I think that our tendency to engage in meaningless diagnosis is itself a meaningful diagnosis, and it is here that we should focus our attention.

Alienation, like all pathological concepts, carries with it the strong connotation of redemption. To say that we are alienated is to imply that we can reclaim ourselves, we can pull ourselves back in, we can get to feeling better. We need concepts like alienation to make us feel less alienated. But some of us need more than the false comfort which comes from saying the word. Some of us want to know the prognosis as well as the diagnosis. The prognosis for a disease which is as extensive as the patient, however, is a hard thing to get sorted out. What are we going to reclaim? What body are we going to pull ourselves back into? In short, we ask the question which is now a cliche, from what are we alienated?

Let's hold the question for a while and say something about youth in this context since this is an essay on alienated youth. It is my contention that most contemporary youth are less alienated than the rest of us. At least many of them have worked out what Keniston calls a style which helps to manage alienation.[1] Because of when they entered history—after Hiroshima perhaps—young people sense more keenly than the rest of us that the present historical condition has made the condition of future history unpredictable.

This uncertainty has contributed to a style of unneurotic future-lessness, a style which most of the rest of us find hard to get behind. Since the young people are going to occupy the future, this style (if, as I hope, they do not outlive it) may in a rather paradoxical way be a self-fulfilling prophecy. The future will still be there, but it will cease to preoccupy attention to itself. If this turns out to be the case —notice that I am preoccupied with the future here—then our Promethean-Faustian, goal-oriented, time-centered culture will have undergone a transformation too radical to be called a revolution. The struggle for existence, goal-orientation, will have been replaced by pacification of existence,[2] or something like what Kurt Wolff calls "surrender."[3]

If alienation is the condition of our time so that none of us is left unaffected by that condition, some people in our culture share the orthodox alienation which we all understand. These people want some things which are already valued in the overall culture but they do not have time—things like jobs, money, and power. It is a more unorthodox kind of alienation that I want to discuss here, however, the kind of alienation shared by people who already have that something but no longer want it; it has become valueless for them. "What else can you show me?" is the kind of question which boggles the conceptual minds of social scientists.

It seems to me that this more evasive concept of alienation is to be found in three kinds of victims: the culturally blind, the culturally schizophrenic, and a category of people I shall refer to as freaks. These categories correlate roughly with age, not I think because of age as such but because of historical location which is as much a spatial as a temporal notion. All three—the blind, the schizophrenic, and the freaks—can be diagnosed as alienated, but, depending on "where they are at," from what place they see the world, the alienation has a varying degree of meaningfulness.

The culturally blind are alienated because they do not feel alienated. Rather, they feel integrated with a normative system which is no longer founded very firmly in social reality. Marx called this kind of alienation false consciousness; Marcuse's indictment is more insidious, and he calls it "happy consciousness." We might argue that a person cannot be alienated unless he feels alienated, but only, I think, if we are also willing to say that a person cannot be psychotic unless he feels that he is split from reality.

The culturally schizophrenic are alienated because they relate to two coexisting but diametrically opposed myths, two very different socially constructed realities.[4] Reality is a myth, but myths are very real. One mythic reality gives cultural schizophrenics their consciousness, their language. This is the socially constructed world view into which they were born. But they have an intuitive awareness of the emergence of another real myth which has outgrown the language with which they are equipped to describe it. Cultural schizophrenics, then, engage in tautologies like calling our culture alienated. Francis Bacon was concerned with idols of the mind, a kind of sixteenth-century alienation. He was a cultural schizophrenic because he lived at a time when the medieval and the modern world pictures overlapped. In retrospect, we call this period of history the Renaissance. The Renaissance was too radical to be called a revolution. Most of us here are concerned with alienation and we are culturally schizophrenic as well because the modern and the post-modern world pictures overlap. What this age will be called in retrospect is a moot question because it is not clear that history will be a meaningful concept in the next world picture.

A freak, as I use the term, is a cultural mutant. Mutation is a diagnosis which contains its own prognosis. A cultural freak, like a biological mutant, does not so much get better or get worse as he remains just different, radically and qualitatively different. I have a clear feeling that there are more freaks in this culture right now than most of us want to admit or care to count.

By cultural mutation I mean that the present culture can be replaced by another which, in the words of John Seeley, "will not be, cannot be, in content, organization, aim or spirit, anything like a continuation or culmination of what we have hitherto nurtured or know."[5] This would be a culture invented and occupied by people as freaky to us now as humanists must have been to fifteenth- and sixteenth-century clerics.

Freaks are alienated, but they are alienated beyond redemption. To suggest that this is "just a stage you are going through" or to say that "you are alienated" to a freak is about as meaningful for him as to say "you are a heretic" to Erasmus of Rotterdam. Labeling Erasmus a heretic was an attempt to coopt humanism into the prevailing one dimensional culture (medievalism) by including it within, that is, subordinating it to, the meaningful discourse of that culture. It was a symbolic game, and symbols are our most important cultural tools. To call behavior heretical is to answer a medieval question and thereby assert the dominance of a medieval or theological perspective or world view. But humanistic behavior, as we are able to see in retrospect, was not an answer to a medieval question at all but the asking of a qualitatively different question. Likewise, to call freaks alienated is to answer a modern question and the implication is that they can be brought back in—that they can be redeemed. But these people are asking a postmodern set of questions, and in so doing, they are, I think, redefining reality. They are inventing a new myth. It is the questions asked and not the answers given that characterize the spirit of the times and the world view of cultures. It may well be that the answer we seek in our alienated culture is best found by asking some new questions.

If a young person says to me that "the times they are a-changing" or "you are old-fashioned," I might not like what I hear but at least I understand it. But what if I am told that I'm not "where it's at" or "we are in a different place"? Now I neither like what I hear nor do I understand it unless I translate (which I readily do) this accusation into the former one, namely that I am outdated, outtimed. But is being outtimed the same thing as being outspaced? When does a generational gap (temporal) become a cultural gap—a different place from where one sees the world? The ease with which I make the translation may conceal the importance of my having to translate.

The style of my culture is to evaluate things in terms of time and volume; "So much to do, so little time." I am interested in "timely" questions and "productive" work. If I listen carefully to the freaks, however, I sense a different style, a different language. Not so much volume in time, I hear an evaluative mode more like weight in space. How "heavy" is the trip and how "far out" the place?

Again, the ease with which I make the translation may conceal the importance of my having to translate. I think this may be "where we are at" in terms of our preoccupation with alienation. We simply find it more comfortable to translate than to mutate. The freaks are alienated, but in the same sense that the early humanists were heretical. They are beyond redemption because they have lost interest in the question.

Notes

1. Kenneth Keniston, *Young Radicals: Notes on Committed Youth* (New York: Harcourt, Brace, and World, 1968).

2. Herbert Marcuse, *One Dimensional Man* (Boston: Beacon Press, 1967).

3. Barrington Moore and Kurt Wolff, eds., "Beginning: In Hegel and Today," *The Critical Spirit* (Boston: Beacon, 1968).

4. Peter Berger and Thomas Luckmann, *The Social Construction of Reality* (Garden City: Doubleday, 1966).

5. J. R. Seeley, "Remaking the Urban Scene: New Youth in an Old Environment," *Daedalus, 97:* 1124-39 (1968).

115

Midpiece

A la recherche du temps perdu

The fall began officially today. It is the only pleasant time of the year in the Midwest where falling leaves, sunny skies, and low humidity bring Indian Summer. The leaf colors are striking, and whole families work together on lawns completing the last chores. The pleasant haze of burning leaves is on all sides, and the radio on Saturdays brings the familiar voices which for years have described the football destinies of the University of Michigan. This week Michigan is playing the University of California, and some 70,000 persons are in Ann Arbor watching the game. The spectacle of these two monolithic universities, where there has been so much student trouble in recent years, playing football on a sunny afternoon is intriguing.

How many of the 70,000 are students? There are almost 35,000 students on the University of Michigan campus alone. How many go to the football games? How many of those who go are political activists? Probably very few. How do the militant activists spend warm Saturday afternoons in the fall?

When I went to college, Saturday afternoons in Ann Arbor were full of excitement. The streets were lined with traffic, and the city police force (now seen almost daily in confrontations at the local draft board and with demonstrating ADC mothers) made its single weekly appearance on street corners directing traffic. Busses and trains disgorged girls in large numbers, and fraternity houses had hand-rigged loudspeakers blaring music from upstairs windows. Sometime around 12:30 the tempo quickened as Michigan's Marching Band formed in the street. As it began to step smartly in its strangely stilted cadence down State Street to the stadium, hundreds of students and alumni fell in behind singing "The Victors," and when the familiar refrain which ended the song, "Hail, Hail to Michigan (often sung as "Mitch-cha-gin" by the cognoscenti who knew this was the way the great Michigan coach, Fielding H. Yost, had pronounced it) "the Champions (always pronounced "Champeens" by all) of the West," it was hard not to be moved.

I had begun at Michigan with a football scholarship, had done poorly, and had lost it. Forced to leave, I continued my education elsewhere, doing some athletic odds and ends with no great distinction, but finally managed to return to Ann Arbor just before the war began in 1941. As a jock, then, I was fairly "blooded" and moderately cynical about intercollegiate athletics. Yet on Saturday afternoons that whole town tilted toward Stadium Boulevard as 80,000 people approached the game, and the excitement was a palpable thing.

Often as the years have passed I have taken my children back and spent a sunny afternoon in the stadium. We usually park on the university golf course, eat lunch off the tailgate with the middle aged, and walk across the street to the huge bowl. Every once in a while, I've parked in town, eaten at the Union, and there down the street comes the Michigan Band. The crowd following is much smaller (or is that only the familiar phenomenon of diminution associated with the past?), and surely many of them are town children. The students who follow along seem to affect a deliberate shuffle as if marching is passé. A few of the alumni walk in time to the music, but they wear the tipsy look of the American Legionnaires or Masons at the annual parade, and there is something both defiant and furtive about their demeanor. The music is still exciting, and the colors are vivid, and occasionally one of my sons will comment with detachment, something like, "It's not a bad place, pretty good school, really, isn't it? But it's too big. I wouldn't want to go here." End of story.

I try to remain noncommittal. I'm caught up in my own past, so

117

let the young create their own dilemma. I had returned to Michigan in 1941 to rewrite my own history. Perhaps all parts of the puzzle could be reassembled to make a more pleasing whole. At least that was what I thought. The athletic stew remained indigestible. They remembered me, knew I had been found wanting before, discovered that I had been elsewhere without making much of a splash; there was even a story of the brief use of another name at a Southern school. I was young and easily confused. Caught up in a truly adult problem, I held doggedly to the position that I had never *said* that I had used another name. "But had I *done* it?" they asked. "Ah," I foolishly answered, "that's another story."

Tired of the argument, recognizing the possibility of eligibility trouble, and with little initial enthusiasm anyway, they soon cut me from the squad. Was I cut or did I quit? I can't really recall; I'd like to think the latter, but I suspect the former. Nonetheless, I was around long enough to recognize the immutability of that particular piece of my fate. Long enough, also, I later discovered, to sit for a team photograph—was it the first day, perhaps?—for twenty years later, a medical student saw the picture in a store window in Ann Arbor and asked if it were I. Caught by surprise, for I have tried to forget the whole thing, I could only nod solemnly. When he wanted to hear more, I mustered a melancholy sigh, a wry smile, and the evasive statement, "Those were the old days, yes indeed!" Yet, I was very buoyed by the whole encounter, as if the picture offered palpable proof of success. How the memory does fade.

Mark came from a small family in New Jersey. During the summers before and during college, he had worked as a bartender, bouncer, and lifeguard. His father was a supervisory employe in a chain of food stores in metropolitan New York. Mark had always regarded him as "a benevolent despot" and communication between them had been limited. He later grew to respect his father because of his patient care of his wife, who suffered from a terminal illness. Mark wore his hair in a crewcut, was short and stocky and on the strength of his athletic prowess in high school, had received an athletic scholarship to the University of Michigan.

118

He was an all-state selection in high school, but was surprised by his lack of status at Michigan. Although he played during the fallow years at Ann Arbor, Mark was midway in his senior year before he started a varsity game. Throughout it all he doggedly persisted, coming out to practice day after day, always hoping to catch "some coach's eye." Although solidly unimaginative, he was insightful enough to recognize that his first movement after a good play was to look around and see if it had been observed by a coach. Mark was plagued by the idea of being watched, or really of being under observation at all times. He walked tall, wore a clean shirt daily, and wore a tie to dinner each evening. During the winters between fall and spring practice he worked out in the fieldhouse, lifting weights and plodding around the track. This ascetic regimen finally caught the attention of the line coach, and small glory soon followed. The big times were at the kickoff in the stadium on Saturday afternoons. Everybody standing and shouting, the roar from the crowd filling the field, both benches standing, the tremendous excitement. Mark liked the trips all over the country with the squad, even liked Friday nights before home games which were spent in uncomfortable cots at the University Country Club. The coaches drifted in and out, talking quietly to the individual players. It was, he said, like one big family. In school Mark did fairly well. Some of the courses he took were handpicked by the athletic staff, but it was nothing like it had been before the war. Then, the coaches had said, it was possible to find professors who would pass a football player without ever seeing him. Things were different now. Football players were called "beasts" by many students, and some of the younger faculty seemed to dislike athletes. There were even some classes where it was a mistake to wear a letter sweater.

Mark had applied for admission to a service academy, but had failed the entrance examination. The war in Vietnam was, as might be expected, no big thing to him. He became interested in the diplomatic service and majored in government. When the sit-ins began in the Administration Building in his senior year, Mark tried to organize the athletic faction. His idea was to go in and ask the students to leave. If this failed, they were to be warned, and, finally, the athletes, dressed in shirts, ties and sports coats, were "to get to work."

Mark discovered that there was fair enthusiasm for this stratagem, but before anything could happen, "the word came down from the coaches to 'cool it.'" Which coaches? How did the "word come down?" Mark didn't know, "Maybe it was just an impression, but we knew we weren't to do anything." Did he personally know any of the demonstrators? No. Was he angry at them? Yes. Why? Mark paused for a long moment and twisted his large monogram ring with the gold block "M" on the bright blue background. Finally, he answered, "Because they were trying to destroy the University and Michigan has been good to me."

And the other effort to rewrite past failures that year? There was the matter of a girl. It had been a liaison of long standing. She was ambitious and I was clearly going nowhere. When I tried to leave, she would become uncertain and cling to me; when she struggled to be free, I held on. The entire issue was complicated by "religious differences" (what a naively simple term that sounds like today). Neither her family nor mine cared much for the idea of the relationship, and both were manifestly relieved when I manfully packed my clothes and returned to the scene of an earlier crime.

I had read Somerset Maugham's *Of Human Bondage* that year in a class. I saw myself as Philip, limping to and from medical school, while Mildred coolly destroyed my life. I also saw the movie and wept when Leslie Howard finally found lovely Frances Dee and was freed from the toils of Bette Davis. I even practiced limping, but became disconsolate when an older and more sophisticated friend informed me that the story was autobiographical, that Maugham suffered from a speech defect which he displaced onto his major character as a foot deformity and that either or both symptoms were to be understood as symbols for impotence. The book had a peculiar hold on me all through college, but today it is scarcely to be found on reading lists. My children bring home *The Autobiography of Malcolm X*, Claude Brown's *Manchild in a Promised Land*, Norman

Mailer's *What are We Doing in Vietnam?*, Selby's *Last Exit from Brooklyn,* and Stokely Carmichael's *Black Power.* Are these better books, or worse? I don't know but surely they are different.

I lived alone in a small apartment in a rooming house, and mourned the girl I had lost. It was not an easy thing, and my athletic failure seemed to bode ill for all the rest. As the weeks went by, I found some solace with a graduate student who lived in the apartment above mine. She was older than I, attractive, and far less complicated than the former girl. We struck up an easy friendship, talked a great deal, walked the streets of the quiet town on cold nights, holding hands. I liked her, she liked me, it all seemed so simple and direct. There was, however, the other girl stuck away uneasily an hour's drive away. There was also a war looming somewhere in the future, but no one really expected the Japanese to upset the National Football League's championship game in New York early in December.

And so the fall moved pleasantly along until the girl from back home decided that she was too lonely to live comfortably without me and came to Ann Arbor to reconcile without, of course, any warning. I was not at home but she waited for me to arrive, and to fill the time, she cheerfully tidied up my rooms.

In the flat above, now seen clearly as in the stage setting of Arthur Miller's *Death of a Salesman,* awakens the graduate student. She has passed an important examination earlier that morning, and on the way home has purchased some steaks and Chianti. This girl also has a surprise for me; she is going to cook the steaks, bring the wine, and we're to celebrate her success. Although it is now over thirty years ago, I can also reconstruct that picture very well. She is blonde, has the kind of coloring one associates with English girls, and has napped in pleasant anticipation of a nice evening. The sounds of housekeeping below bring her eagerly to my door, steaks safely in refrigerator but wine in straw basket held firmly in hand.

The confrontation is brief. "Who are *you?*" "Who are *you?*" Both quietly leave; one drives back home, the other returns upstairs. Her door remains locked to me, and she averts her face when we meet

121

at the mailbox. Later, each writes me a note, I am a bad person, it seems; a "trifler" says one, "unfaithful" says the other. Each suggests that I interest myself in her rival, for neither has any personal interest in me any longer. It is apparent that no one thinks I can exist alone; the whole world must regard me as badly in need of help.

To this day I find it difficult to reconstruct the heinous crime of which I was convicted. I had given up one girl incompletely and taken up another, also incompletely, but these were internal things, things that have to do with the delicate nuances of the mind, with shades of meaning, and I meant neither any ill. Nevertheless, the trial was over and my punishment was clear. How terribly moral it all seems now, almost like a scene from a Harold Lloyd movie, "The Freshman" perhaps. The girls wear dresses which hang almost to their ankles, I am wearing gray buck shoes, a double-breasted coat with pleated back, and the only thing missing is a white straw boater. Why was the matter in the rooming house so serious? Why were all of us finished with each other forever? No matter, it was serious and we were finished with each other forever.

Last year the U.S. Olympic track team held its final trials high up near Lake Tahoe and one gold-medal winner of 1964 who had decided to give world-class competition one more whirl failed to make the team. He had worked for two years, training endlessly and putting aside his career while his wife worked to support him. Now it was all over, and as he walked slowly around the track, he was asked by reporters how he felt. He said softly, "This is the first day of the rest of my life." What a tremendous reply! Truly in the Hemingway tradition, and if spontaneous, it was worth twice its weight in Olympic gold medals.

My travail ended less sensationally. I had neither girl, I was not an athlete, I had not been to class in weeks, and I was indeed going nowhere. I waited around Ann Arbor for a week or two drinking German beer at Metzger's at night, walking the cold streets during the day. After several false starts and spurts of indecision, I took a Greyhound bus to Detroit, took another bus to Windsor, Ontario, walked across the street to the Prince Edward Hotel, rode the elevator to the eighth floor, walked into an office and enlisted in the Royal Canadian Air Force. It was the day after Thanksgiving in the year 1941.

Frank was one of the leaders of an activist group at the University of Michigan. He was the only son of a middle class professional family, and his father was active in liberal causes. He lived in monastic style in an attic room in a dilapidated rooming house on campus. The other tenants were members of the movement, and the house was a field headquarters. Bikes, motorcycles, boxes, and debris littered the entrance. His current girlfriend occupied an adjoining room and was expected to pay rent for it, clean the house, and do his laundry. His clothes were threadbare, but were enlivened by an expensive jacket sent to him by his mother. "Everything above my belt is my mother," he said, "everything below is me." He was enraged by authority figures. "It has to do with father images. They must be destroyed. Children should be raised collectively in kibbutzim." According to his plan, four or five sets of parents would be in charge, and the children would not necessarily know their natural fathers.

He was arrogant, dogmatic, and romantic. It was easy to visualize him in the role of a knight seeking the Holy Grail, or a hero on horseback bringing justice to the oppressed and truth to the ignorant. When I told him I was a psychologist, Frank was deeply suspicious of me and said bluntly that "psychology is a lot of horseshit." Its purpose was to force people to adjust to "the rotten Establishment." He viewed his group as constantly harassing the administration to bring awareness. Frank said it was all the same. He had an unshaken belief in his simplistic analysis of American society and in his assertion that it was to be destroyed. His sense of mission was both curious and frightening. Somewhat later he asked me to describe vocational possibilities in psychology, his current major, as if he had completely forgotten his earlier rejection.

As Frank spoke, young women wandered in and out. They were students who were active in draft resistance and civil rights groups, and they talked with candor. The organizational life also provided

123

their social life because their boyfriends were involved in the same activities. There was a lot of sleeping about—"it's not a big thing," they said. Questions about promiscuity brought little overt response. The whole matter of sex was "rather open," they said. There were some long relations, some short ones. Sometimes there were hurt feelings when changes were made, sometimes not. It all depended. People who couldn't "hack" that kind of openness got out. As we talked about this, I slowly recognized that I was the one who became uncomfortable; the whole thing seemed quite unremarkable to them.

These girls did not participate in usual campus activities but found ready friends among the young teaching assistants at the university. The latter accepted them as peers, and it was difficult to distinguish between the two groups either by clothing or manner of speech. It was a closed world, and it carried with it again a sense of mission, a "we-they" feeling, as well as an air of penultimate superiority. Although the girls did passing academic work, they rejected the idea of a college degree for either economic or vocational reasons. Their patois was made up of terms such as "relevant" or "genuine," and they worked only in courses that they liked. There was little interest in good grades, in disciplined programs of study, or in getting summer jobs which paid a good salary. Instead, they were romantically involved in a happy marriage of ideology and love.

It has been almost a month since the Democrats nominated Humphrey and Muskie. The campaign has begun in earnest. The candidates zigzag all over the country by jet and helicopter. They are able to speak in Philadelphia in the morning, Springfield, Illinois at noon, Independence, Missouri at 3 P.M. and be back in New York for a fund-raising dinner by 8 P.M. Although this is an election which all admit will be won or lost on television, Nixon has attracted larger crowds as he moves about the countryside.

Humphrey has been distracted by young dissidents who try to break up his meetings. Pictures of his tight grin and creased forehead as he begins his "my friends" monolog in an effort to talk over the racket have become commonplace. The interference has led

Humphrey to new highs in rhetoric. Yesterday he said "we will win the victory, reach the goal, capture the gold medal"—all of this having to do with either Vietnam or any other issue he is speaking on. The *New Yorker* faults him on the grounds of something called "pleonasm," which they define as the rhetorical term for the use of more than one word when one will do. They allege his speeches are sprinkled with such pleonasms as: sorrow and distress; quietly and silently; capacity and ability; force and brutal power; prudence and caution; ways and means; tolerance and forbearance; hedging and equivocating; and finally, law and order, which he is reported to have used three times in a single speech. Moreover, Humphrey seems to be addicted to the use of an extraordinarily high proportion of sentences beginning with "And." The Vice President is also being trailed by a Republican Truth Squad, which corrects what they allege are his misstatements (otherwise called "untruths").

More important, *The New York Times* finds him ahead in only six states, far behind even Wallace (sixteen states), with Nixon leading in all the rest. The Vice President is not dismayed; he has kept to his promise not to call Nixon "Tricky Dick" and, moreover, he has gone to Independence to take a cram course from Harry Truman who has advised him "to tell the truth, even if it hurts." Nevertheless, it is apparent that Humphrey will not tell the Vietnam truth. There is even a report that high ranking Democrats suggest that he resign as Vice President to free himself from Johnson's control, but no one regards this as a serious possibility. Humphrey made a single effort to say something concrete about the war, and it got him into immense trouble with his chief. Last week he said that he "could confidently predict that some American troops could start coming home within months." Questioning from reporters brought something close to a retraction from his press aides, but several hours later on a plane bound for Texas, Humphrey triumphantly flashed a newspaper bearing the headline "Some Marine Units to Return Home Soon." When it was disclosed that these were war-weary troops routinely scheduled for return, press aides again stressed the hopeful and general nature of their chief's comments. "But the newspaper, why did he hold up the newspaper in the plane as if it confirmed his statements?" they were asked. "No comment" was the terse reply.

The next day President Johnson chastised all those who allow sentiment to interfere with hard and sound military judgment in Vietnam. We will, he repeated, be there until the victory is won, and there was little question whose ox was being gored at that moment. So the Vice President continues to run far behind because he cannot dissociate himself from the unpopular President, but each day he thunders after Nixon because the Republican candidate, wise and cautious man that he is, refuses to answer Humphrey's demands that they debate the issues.

Issues, indeed! There is only one palpable issue, the Vietnam war, but Humphrey is Johnson's captive while Nixon states that he is reluctant to disturb the sensitive negotiations still going on in Paris. Nixon is smooth and seasoned, and has been turned away at the door too many times to risk everything by making another mistake. So he runs on platitudes, promising committees to solve all kinds of problems, even bipartisan committees at that. Russell Baker, *The New York Times* humorist, portrays Mrs. Nixon asking her husband what he wants for breakfast. The candidate thunders, "Don't expect me to take a position on that!" Occasionally, he is beset by hecklers bearing signs which identify him as "Super-Hawk," or suggest other ambitions, such as "Nixon for Sheriff." But the best one of the entire campaign appeared in Philadelphia on September 21 and bore the hostile inscription: "Vote for One: Hubert Nixon, Richard Humphrey, or Lyndon B. Wallace, or join Voters Anonymous!"

There's too much to be heard from one of the running mates, too little from the other. Agnew has evidently been sentenced to do the heavy work for the Republicans. He has been unable to throw off his "law and order" statements at Miami, and Negro leaders regard him with deep suspicion. Moreover, he offended even Nixon when he referred to Humphrey as being "soft" on Communism and has had to recant publicly. Nonetheless, Agnew still takes the hard line, and reveals an immoderately large gift for saying the wrong thing.

But wrong or right, the governor of Maryland creates some excitement in an otherwise lackluster campaign. His opponent from Maine has said very little, or really very little that makes sense. In Wichita, Kansas, the Maine senator offered the following facts: 1) Alabama has the highest murder rate in the nation; 2) states with Democratic governors since 1960 have had much lower crime rates than states with Republican governors; 3) Maine, with a Democratic governor, has the fifth lowest rate of violent crime in the country; 4) Maryland, the home state of Gov. Spiro T. Agnew, the Republican vice presidential candidate, has the highest violent crime rate. When asked if this meant that the Democrats are more responsible in combatting crime, Muskie answered, "No. . . . it just means that there are no simple answers to the problem [of crime]." About Vietnam, he has taken to blaming Eisenhower for beginning the mess in 1954 and lauds Humphrey by saying that "the Vice President's record on the war has been continuously toward peace *except for the ambiguity of the last four years*" [italics added], whatever in the world that means.

Meanwhile, there is tremendous excitement in Manhattan where 10,000 men crowd both Broad and Wall streets in front of the New York Stock Exchange to see a nice Jewish girl from Brooklyn, Francie Gottfried, walk to work. Miss Gottfried is substantially endowed (43-25-37) and wears tight sweaters, but 10,000 men? The police are out in full regalia with bullhorns and tear gas, but the crowd is cheerful and this time there are no confrontations. The lady in question works for the Chemical Bank New York Trust Company, and one advertising man has proposed "full-page ads." "Float her around to Chemical's 141 branches," he adds. The method of propulsion is not stated, but no one questions Miss Gottfried's buoyancy. The bank wisely decides to send her home for a few days, but all agree this has to be seen as a counterdemonstration to the recent tension in the country.

Walter Cronkite is back at the usual place. He has had a brief vacation following the Democratic convention, and now the lines on his face are less deeply etched. There is more detachment in his

127

stance, and Mayor Daley's caterwauling about mistreatment at Cronkite's hands seems far in the background. Tonight's program revolves around four issues.

The first is Czechoslovakia. Morley Safer has been declared *persona non grata* by the Russians (or Czechs?), and now Daniel Shore stands in Prague in his place. The passage of time has brought many surprises, and it has become increasingly difficult to sort out the issues. The UN General Assembly opens this week, and the Soviet invasion is the top item on the agenda, but rumor has it that the Soviets wish to use Czechoslovakia as a standoff in the matter of the United States and Vietnam. I am confused about how this will operate, but the newscasters apparently understand. There has been, in other Czechoslovakian matters, a curious ebb and flow. Repressive measures are followed by loopholes, the Russian troops leave Prague but do not go very far out in the countryside. There is to be another summit meeting with Moscow, but it is postponed because the invaders are not yet satisfied that all their conditions have been met. Dubcek and Svoboda tour the countryside explaining what is going on, and while it sounds like they are men seeking support for a sellout, more experienced observers see the matter quite differently. Safer views the two men as forging ahead in plans to resist Soviet pressure for more control of the country. This team evidently plays a double game, giving into the opposition on some issues, but continuing skillfully to rally the country on others. No one knows how long these tactics will be allowed to continue, and this, the reporter tells us, is the central question.

My home television viewing team, having given up talking about the issue last month, cannot be induced to talk about it now. This is apparently true for the rest of our country's youth, for no one else in that generation seems to be talking about Czechoslovakia now or before. Two weeks ago, while walking near the campus of McGill University in Montreal, I came upon the consulate of the U.S.S.R. on Ontario Street. Several windows were broken by rocks, and for a brief moment I had the feeling that here was a change in the wind, here were students who were openly expressing their opposition to the Eastern European takeover. A call to the *Montreal Gazette* brought disenchantment. The rioters who had assaulted the consulate, who indeed stood in the streets and cursed Soviet personnel, were Canadian citizens of Czech ancestry. But it was practically on the campus of the university, I said, no students at all? "Oh, there were a few standing around, even a few who joined in the fun, but they weren't really a part of the fight," the newspaper's librarian answered.

Back to Cronkite. Agnew is apparently in trouble again. He has called a sleeping reporter on his campaign plane a "fat Jap." Agnew is confused by the growing reaction and says testily, "The reporter and I happen to be good friends and kid each other a lot about that," but other reporters who have covered Agnew's campaigns in and out of Maryland are unable to remember ever having heard that term there. Agnew thereby becomes a two-time loser in this particular area, for he used the word "Polacks" in a Chicago press conference. He had passed off the first incident with a rather stuffy "my Polish friends have never apprised me of that [the unpleasant connotation of the term] when they called each other by this appellation." Now he is in deep trouble because he's enroute to Hawaii where remarks about Orientals are likely to bring small currency.

Taking the spirit of the fall season, Agnew offers a football explanation. His statements, he says, are "similar to the slang that people on an athletic team use affectionately among themselves." Then he calls for a "national sense of humor," saying: "How important it is that we in the United States of America, one of the few countries in the world where it's safe to laugh, don't lose our sense of humor."

And finally, he turns tough. Agnew tells his Hawaiian audience that he is fed up with this business of being misquoted, of reporters taking things out of context. He lists his own impeccable credentials in the minority group: 1) only Greek family on block; and 2) saw his father come home tired in the afternoon and climb down off the vegetable truck to be ridiculed by certain people. The cameras pan out over the faces of the audience. The speech is at a luau, and the people stare uncomprehendingly. Cronkite explains the blank looks:

129

the group knows nothing of the recent charges, and Agnew's oratorical flights seem like routine campaign talk to them.

Dinner is over, and we sit at the table drinking coffee. "What do you chaps think of them apples?" I say in a sprightly fashion. "Beatlebum" they reply. "What's that mean?" "Elliott Sugarman says it." "Who's he, no, forget that, what's it mean?" "Oh, my God," one groans, "everyone knows what that means. It means baloney, it means balls, it means that Agnew is uncool, that nobody in his right mind would support him, he's dead." "But," I ask, "Why 'Beatlebum'? Why don't you say it out? What's the connection between that remark and the explanation?" There's no answer, and the program goes on.

We next see Humphrey; he is speaking in what looks like a rural setting, perhaps in the Midwest. The Vice President has his jacket off for the day is apparently quite warm. He is being heckled for a change, and has become very angry. Finally, he shouts, "There are some hardcore hecklers and demonstrators back there. They're highly disciplined members of a minority which seeks to destroy our country." Humphrey pauses dramatically, and the chanting voices can be faintly heard, and then the Vice President concludes triumphantly: "I am privileged to be the target of this minority, call them what you will, and I warn them, the more they pursue me, the more pleased I am. I have no intention of being driven away from a public meeting or platform. I will stand my ground. In fact, I consider their animosity and their hostility to be a tribute to my character, to my purpose and to my program." There is some cheering, and Humphrey now steps back and shakes hands with admiring friends on the platform.

This time, at least, Nixon wins the prize for brevity. Recognizing like the rest of us that politics and fun and games are really the same thing, Nixon's peroration is blessedly brief in Anaheim, California: "Step up, hit the ball! We're going to win for America! Let's go!"

Cronkite is almost finished, and time for only one more note of good cheer remains. When it comes, it is startling. We switch to

130

Mexico City where we are told that sixteen people have been killed and more than a hundred wounded in student-police rioting. It is the sixth day of a struggle involving the occupation of the University of Mexico campus by both military and student forces. The facts in the dispute are unclear. In quick review to a background accompaniment of pictures of police machine guns being fired at buildings and student rifle fire in response, we are told that 5,000 students have marched upon the federal penitentiary vowing to release two jailed labor leaders, but have been turned back by machine-gun fire; that at the Santo Tomás Vocational School people on rooftops are "shooting at everything below," while the police fire back with rifles, pistols, and tear gas; and that the new rector of the University of Mexico, who only a short time ago replaced a rector who had resigned because of a two-month student strike, has himself resigned. Rector Javier Barros Sierra's resignation is self-termed "irrevocable" but his reasons have to do with his anger at the government's decision to send troops onto the campus to dislodge the barricaded students.

The program ends, and if this is "the way it is today," there is little to cheer about. The student revolt in Mexico City, even allowing for Latin impulsivity, may end up as the granddaddy of them all—sixteen dead, more than one hundred wounded. The mind is stunned by these figures, and these are not students being dragged away by New York police; these "children," as they were called repeatedly on the convention floor in Chicago, are being shot to death. The stakes in Mexico are obviously higher than in this country, although the Mexican government is regarded as the most stable in Latin America. Maybe there is even an inverse relation between government stability and student revolt. However, it is absolutely impossible to imagine relations so deteriorated that people can kill each other over educational problems.

In late spring of 1968 I had visited Edinburgh University in Scotland. It was a college similar to my own in appearance, situated in the heart of the lovely old city. Its buildings represent so many different centuries of architecture that side by side can be seen strik-

131

ing examples of sixteenth- and twentieth-century planning, yet the whole rambling establishment had a visible coherence. To an American the air of permanence and tradition was overwhelming. England and Scotland are not as far removed from the youth revolt as we in this country think, and beards, long hair, sandals, and blue jeans were common. Malcom Muggeridge, the English critic, had recently served as rector (an elective position at Edinburgh, as at many European institutions, with the students nominating and electing the recipient). The rector is expected to represent the students directly on the university councils, but Muggeridge resigned after a very brief period, sharply criticizing today's youth for their attitude toward birth control pills and drugs, if I recall it correctly. He confessed to personal disillusionment and hurt, but my daughter, then a graduate student at Edinburgh, described him as "a complete ass!"

The ashes of the struggle had hardly settled by the time I arrived on the campus. After a short, and to me disappointing, presentation to my own discipline, I went to the faculty club to be the luncheon guest of the university administration. Present were the vice principal of the institution, the executive dean of the medical faculty, and an interesting assortment of the senior faculty of the medical school. The faculty club had beautifully varnished walls, hung with pennants representing 600 years. Scottish lunches are pleasantly unhurried, and apple-cheeked girls came in and out of the dining room filling martini glasses with artless enthusiasm. By the time we sat down to eat, most of the feeling of pain had dissipated.

The talk soon turned to my impression of their student body. I made the usual noncommital comments. There had been "a real incident" the night before at a meeting of the executive faculty, and because I reputedly was knowledgeable in the matter of student unrest, I was asked to evaluate the issues. The dean of the medical faculty was the narrator: "Well, we're not used to it here, maybe you are, but its quite new here. We've this meeting of the executive faculty a few times a year. The executive faculty here consists of the department chairmen of the colleges of the university and the prin-

cipal is in the chair. We're all in our academic robes, you see. Well, last night the meeting is going along, I'm sitting up near the principal, kind of dozing away if you know what I mean, when I hear some kind of commotion.

"On his feet is a man who is asking for the floor. He is bearded, kind of a tall fellow, but I have never seen him before. Well, the principal says 'state your name and business,' and the fellow says, 'I'm Mick Brown and I'm a medical student.' I could have fallen out of my chair. The principal asked did I know him, and I had to say I did not. I have only been back at the college now a year, you know. Well, the principal says, what in the devil do you want, how'd you get in? Cool as anything, the fellow says, 'I walked in and I've a statement to read!' Well, I can tell you, that threw the chair all right, caught him right in his starkers, as it were. Soon he said to the chaps, 'Shall we let him speak?' and some said yes and some no. Finally, someone wanted to know what Brown wanted to talk about, that is, what did his statement say, and then another fellow who was also a student got up next to him and said courteously as you please, 'If you let Mick read his statement, you'll know all about it!' I have to hand it to the chair. He said crisply, 'Mr. Brown, you've got five minutes,' and then sat down. Brown came up with the paper and began to read this stuff. What was in it? Oh, the usual blether, give the students a voice in governance of the college, put them on committees, that sort of blether. After a couple of minutes the chair stood back up and said, severely, 'How many pages do you have there, young man?' Well, Brown was shaken, I can tell you. He said he had eleven pages and was now on page five. The principal said, 'You've three minutes more, either throw some out or read much faster.' It was soon over, and the two thanked the faculty for allowing them to speak and went out. What happened then? It was quiet for a bit, and then Walter here (the vice principal) got up to speak. He felt the students had some right on their side, and that things were changing a bit over the world, and maybe we'd better change, too. Most of the others were annoyed, feeling we have our business to do and they have theirs and what's it all about? What

133

was worse was that they were medical students, and that's a bit em-barrassing, you know. How do you chaps put up with the fuss in the states, and do you think we should?"

I try the "Today" show the next morning. Things are much calmer there, and much of the uncomfortable chatter is gone. Hugh Downs is on vacation and has been replaced by Frank McGee, the calm NBC anchorman of the space-shot programs. Barbara Walters sticks to show-business interviews with Hollywood celebrities, Joe Garagiola is back telling Yogi Berra jokes, and sane and sober Frank Blair is even more so. McGee sits at the large desk, talking about odds and ends, but everyone has recovered from the Chicago crisis.

The news is quite brief and uneventful this morning. Humphrey is once again in his shirtsleeves, now in Toledo, Ohio. He is not LBJ's prisoner, he says: "Whatever you may want to accuse the President of, he has not captured me. I am a man of the future, I'm not locked in by the past." If his own views should happen to differ from Johnson's, "so be it" says the Vice President philosophically. Then the now free and philosophical candidate cracks out again at Richard Nixon over his ambivalence on the Supreme Court decision on school segregation in 1954. Nixon, it will be recalled, is for the decision but against its implementation, a cool position even for that cool man. The newly released Humphrey flails away at such reasoning: "That's like a husband saying he loves you, but won't give you money to buy a dress or get your hair fixed. Some lover." And so for the first time in memory the issue of sex has been directly inserted into a presidential campaign.

The other story on the program moves me in a strange and melancholy fashion. A group has broken into a Milwaukee draft board and stolen 27,000 draft files, then burned them in a city park. The draft board indicates its work will be slowed. We see the small group standing around the draft card pyre. Several are middle aged priests; a number are young men. They read poetry, selections from the Bible, and sing as they await arrest. Their voices are soft and uncertain, like Cub Scouts who must sing solo at a pack meeting.

Frank Blair tells us that the FBI has entered the case, and all those accused are in jail with bond set at $25,000 to $35,000 each. Barbara is eager to bring on a singer, and the bad news ends.

Although saddened by both the war and the impossibility of ending it, by the incessant attack and counterattack, I limp through the day and return again at night for another refreshing view of the absurd character of modern existence. The major part of the Cronkite program is given over to the films released by North Korea on the *Pueblo* incident. Pictures show the boat, and I am surprised at how small it is. Obviously, there is little relation between size of the offending object and international crises. We see pictures of life in the prisoner-of-war camp, and then begins a horrifying sequence. Rank by rank, members of the crew are brought to the microphone to speak their piece. There is no mistaking the authenticity; while the North Korean announcer sounds like a bad 1930s film version of Warner Toland playing Fu Manchu, these voices have the flatness of the American Midwest, the Southern softness, the New England nasality. These are the men of the *Pueblo,* all right, but their messages strike terror on all sides. They are all international criminals, all have sinned, but are now being well treated, all miss their mothers, fathers, wives, brothers, sons, or daughters, and all want to come home. Each pleads with the United States government to admit its guilt, so they can get on with the business of living. The story of what the *Pueblo* was ostensibly doing in North Korean waters is told with disarming simplicity, and then again they plead with Johnson to confess, to secure their release.

I find myself standing right at the television set, looking each man in the eye as he speaks. Is there evidence of brainwashing? As far as I can see, the men stand up straight, talk clearly, and look directly at the camera. Some smile sadly, others look sober, but surely their affect seems normal, at least to this untutored eye.

What a calamity! American sailors caught in some kind of international hocus-pocus pleading for their lives. What about those World War II intelligence lessons? Name, rank, serial number: "Sir, I am Captain Dumbjohn, John, N.M.I., United States Army Air

135

Force, Serial Number 0583357. By international convention, I am obligated to give only name, rank, and serial number." How many times I practiced the little catechism. At night in bars, in quonset huts, in canvas tents, marching down dusty roads, never when it really counted, of course. "Sir, I am Dumbjohn, John, N.M.I., and no matter what you do to me, sir, I will never reveal the names of my comrades, my commanding officer, or how many homeruns Babe Ruth hit in 1927."

Now these solemn men stand and tell it how it is. The newscaster helps but little with his reassurance that "what we have seen was propaganda film produced in North Korea." Deep in my "heart of hearts" (as our Vice President has taken to saying in the hustings), the whole performance rings with authenticity. These are frightened human beings caught up in an impossible situation, trying to save their own lives by what?—telling the truth?

My own panel is scattered tonight. Only my oldest son is here. Misery loves company, it is said, and we sit silently for a bit. Since I cannot explain the world to my children in any meaningful way (the existential dilemma today), perhaps he can help me. He has changed somewhat over the weeks of our vigil. His long red hair and bushy orange beard have diminished; they are not gone by any means, but the hair has been cut and the beard trimmed. He looks not unlike the young Freud, but with autumn coloring. His clothes, however, are another matter. Dressed now for a date, he is wearing mountain-climbing boots, tight white jeans, a bright yellow Brooks Brothers shirt and no tie, and a double-breasted, padded shouldered, pinstriped suit jacket, which his younger brother recently bought at the Salvation Army store in Traverse City, Michigan. Admittedly, the jacket resembles at some distance the one his father wore twenty years ago, but times have changed, have they not? The costume is completed by a large Australian bush hat with one brim pinned to the crown. The whole effect is overwhelming, but not unstylish. Moreover, sensing (I think) my own growing confusion about life's meaning, he has become more thoughtful, perhaps even contemplative.

Now I turn to him, "What's it all about?" He answers, "What, the North Korean business?" He thinks for a bit, and then begins to gently lecture me. "The North Korean leaders state that they will release the crew of the *Pueblo* if the U.S. admits the ship was sailing in Korean waters for purposes of spying. Our government does not reply. We must therefore infer that the government expects the ninety survivors to pay the highest price, that is, their freedom, for our so-called freedom. As your mighty President sees it, our country's honor comes first, our men second."

"Do you agree?" I break in. "No, of course not. Life for honor, never! Life's too important, you have it only once. Why give it away for a silly war that no one supports?" "Would you fight in any war?" I ask. He quickly answers, "Depends on the war. Do you remember the story of Achilles in the *Iliad?*"

I confess to him that I do not, and, with a suggestion that I read it soon, he starts to leave. By now his two younger brothers have entered. Then ensues an unfunny parody of their father's television-viewing habits. Turning to his right, my eldest son says to his brother David, "Eric?" while this second boy looks back and says "Walter?" Having thus done the Cronkite-Sevareid thing, they next move on to a "Good evening, David; Good evening, Chet" routine while their younger brother sings "Huntley is grumpy but Brinkley is twinkly" and I leave the room in quiet despair.

My television-viewing experiences have not only been unnerving, but certainly debilitating in an intellectual sense. There is something hypnotic about that square box, the large screen, the authoritative voices of the performers. My last show of this season is the new style "Today" show. Frank McGee is still in the conning tower, and as I gulp breakfast down, I discover that today's guest is none other than my old friend Jack Vaughn, director of the Peace Corps. I have worked for that organization for more than five years as a selection consultant, and although I have never met my chief eyeball to eyeball, he often writes letters to me which address me by my first name. On one occasion I wrote a "Dear Jack" answer. Now Vaughn is in New York to make a speech in defense of youth and has agreed to appear before the early morning viewer. Before Vaughn begins, Frank Blair gives us the news. There are two new pieces of intelligence. Humphrey "has shifted somewhat away from President Johnson's positions" [Blair's statement] by saying that the United States cannot play the role of world policeman. Moreover, Humphrey would stop the Vietnam bombing today if he thought it would end the war, no matter what Johnson thought.

On come Frank McGee and Vaughn. My first impression is that the Peace Corps director looks very bad, probably from getting up at 5 a.m. There is little question that Vaughn has seen this show before because he starts out in the usual easy fashion by blaming the Establishment for youth's troubles. When McGee expresses mild curiosity, Vaughn speaks winsomely of the "sham of education, of big business, of mass production, all factors which alienate youth," and then complains that "the universities are not related to the community, and that's also bad for the young." Frank starts slowly, "But that's another problem isn't it, Mr. Vaughn?" What does it have to do with big business or mass production? Undaunted, Vaughn rides on. He tells about interviewing a Peace Corps trainee who had been smoking marijuana because he was forced to "regurgitate information in college, was bored, was lonely, and so started smoking marijuana."

> McGee: Wasn't it always that way? Didn't all of us have to regurgitate information, weren't we lonely and bored in college, and we didn't smoke marijuana?

> Vaughn: The whole mix was changed. There's isolation from the community, from war, from civil rights. It's galling for the young people. If they're old enough to die in the war, they're old enough to have a say in society. They want a piece of the action and we're not giving it to them.

> McGee: How do you know? And what's this got to do with the university?

VAUGHN: Well, I'm impressed with the sign that appeared on the door of the French university, the Sorbonne, last May during the student riots. It read, "Imagination has seized power."

McGEE: So, what's that got . . .

VAUGHN: That's why so many apply for the Peace Corps. There were 94,000 last year alone and one of the few mistakes I have made in the past is to doubt the ability of the young to survive, to surmount.

McGEE: Yes, I see, but what about the universities?

VAUGHN: Well, the prime function of the university is to get youngsters ready to assume full citizenship.

McGEE: I thought the role of the university was to teach students how to live.

VAUGHN: Well, yes, that too, but that's why they've been disappointed.

McGEE: Where are they disappointed, Mr. Vaughn, and why haven't they told us before? Why has this thing begun just now?

VAUGHN: Well, it began really in Berkeley, was it three of four years ago?

McGEE: Well, I was disappointed in college and so were you. We talked about it but we didn't destroy the university. Where have these youngsters talked about it and to whom?

VAUGHN: They've been talking to themselves mainly, to their student councils, mainly in the high schools and colleges, about how they've been disappointed by the country.

McGEE: But where have they been disappointed by the country?

VAUGHN: All over, they want a piece of the action, as I've said.

McGEE: But for heaven's sake, Mr. Vaughn, where, where, where have they been failed?

VAUGHN: Well, why would one-half million apply for the Peace Corps, for VISTA, for other programs?

McGEE: Mr. Vaughn, isn't there a great danger in their arrogance, their feeling that we have a right to do this or that because its right?

VAUGHN: Oh, yes, our surveys show only 4 per cent, we've surveyed the campuses and only 4 per cent are extremists. We don't want them in the Peace Corps. We want reverence.

McGEE: Thank you very much.

The whole thing is too preposterous to contemplate. Sargent Shriver, first director of the Peace Corps, brought an attractive charisma to the position. I have no personal knowledge of what he really was like, and I must admit that the Shriver reflected through the eyes of his subordinates was something less than awe-inspiring. Mark Harris's *Twenty-One Twice* gives a somewhat jaundiced view of the man, but there was something about the Jack-Bobbie-Sarge-Steve-Teddie entente that was undeniably different.

When I first came into the Peace Corps orbit in 1964, there was plenty of excitement. Recruiting officers were to go after campus activitists, and many of the full field clearances on trainees indicated arrests for sit-ins and peace marches, and we rarely thought too much about these items in an applicant's record. What we were looking for was dedication, enthusiasm, and ability. It was a very affecting time for the "old China hands" in the program, and we all worked hard and enthusiastically for a cause that we believed in.

I recall with considerable pleasure the time a young artist in a Nigerian training program—he wore his hair in a pageboy, had a beard, drank a bit, wore jeans and sandals on all occasions, and had lived in a common-law marriage with a girl throughout his four years at Philadelphia Academy of Fine Arts—came up with the slogan "Fighting for peace with peace." There was considerable excitement at the training site, and even excitement in Washington where the phrase was transmitted. I do not know whether it became part of the official legend of the Peace Corps, but no one questioned the young man's haircut, his clothing, or even the fact that he had at one time used what in those days were called "narcotics."

Shriver left and Jack Vaughn took his place. I was at a training site at Dartmouth College shortly after the change. The new director had been there the day the first training group arrived. He is reported to have looked out of the office window at a group of young men throwing a football around. They wore beards, *T*-shirts and cutoff shorts. He said, or so it is alleged, that "I surely hope that our trainees won't look like that." The end of the story is, of course, already visible. The young men were Peace Corps trainees, and later at a speech to the staff Vaughn gave his views on dress. Beards, *T*-shirts, and cutoff shorts were to be discouraged, not only overseas but on local training sites as well. These young people were, no matter where, official representatives of our country, and were to be dressed properly.

It is always interesting to stand on the outside and observe external changes as an organization's internal goals change. First, the difference is felt on the executive echelon, then the men on the assembly line slowly discover that a new hand is on the tiller, and finally the product itself is changed. This has certainly been true in the corps. The director is reported to be concerned with economy and safety, and his new staff reflect his philosophic preoccupations. Bit by bit new facets of the plan became evident, and those in the field note changes in the wind direction. The Peace Corps volunteer is a markedly different person today, really quite pallid when compared to his predecessors of three or four years back.

The easy questions asked of selection officers about trainees in the Shriver administration—will it hurt the Peace Corps' objectives if he goes and will it hurt him personally if he goes?—have now gone by the boards. They have been replaced by what at first glance is a more progressive question: What does he have to contribute in a positive sense to the role of the Peace Corps overseas? But like many things which ring like fine glass on first try but emit a blurry sound the second time around, what the whole thing translated into was: don't take kids who make trouble. The word was out—the old "high-gain, high-risk" category, where we used to be able to hide all manner of interesting young people, was viewed with official suspicion. In other words the gain potential had better far outweigh the risk.

Were these things ever flatly stated? No, but they were surely felt in the ambience of the organization, and the old *espirit de corps* slowly dried up. Even young people sensed the change, and recruiters began to comment upon the lack of enthusiasm for the program on campuses. The refusal of some draft boards to regard Peace Corps service as a deferment contributed to the problem, but the corps has really lost some of its appeal for the youth of the country. Was this Vaughn's fault? Probably not, for the Peace Corps (right or wrong) has come to be viewed by activists as an Establishment organization, and there was a real question about whether the Johnson administration could ever arouse the happy dedication of the Kennedy era.

A few months ago I spoke to a young woman who has been around from the beginning of the Peace Corps. She was one of the few people who had stayed through all the changes. "It's all money," she said. "That's all you hear these days. The director goes to Congress and tells how cheaply we can produce volunteers, how he returned so many thousands of dollars from his budget to Congress last year, what fine Americans these young people are, what high morale they have in the field. Then we send them out, half of the time there are no jobs in the host country for them, at least not the kind of jobs we trained them for. Then a lot of field supervisory positions are eliminated for economy reasons, so there is no one to support them. So the kid sits around for a while doing nothing and then writes to the country director and maybe someone is available to go out and maybe not. So the kid rots out there for a few months more, and maybe he decides 'to hell with it' and wants to go home. Well, that's all right, but then Washington makes the volunteer pay his own transportation home, even if there was no job, even if there was no backup support for him to make new plans, even if he hadn't a thing to do for months. Can you imagine? Making him pay his own way home! Why even the Army sends men who don't work out home at the government's expense, for God's sake!

"And the kinds of kids we get to send these days. You get the notices. If he has ever smoked pot, he's got to be seen. If he's smoked it four times, he goes out. Well, you can read it as well as I can, what did it say, where is it, oh, here in italics, 'Without exception no one for whom we have evidence of hallucinogens use "will go overseas or be sworn in as a volunteer without an approval from Peace Corps/Washington." ' If there is any, but any question of trouble, an arrest for a sit-in, a march on the Pentagon, it has got to go to the director's desk for his personal approval. General counsel sees all kinds of things now that they never saw before. If a young person has applied for the diplomatic corps as well as the Peace Corps, general counsel gets into it. And homosexuality, what a fuss! Well, you remember, you were asked to get someone out because there were reports on the full field, which is all right. I don't disagree, but then you were not to tell the individual where the information came from. You could not mention the full field, you were to pretend, what? That the stork brought you the word that he was gay? Well, I don't say that homosexuals should or shouldn't go. But the whole world doesn't have the same attitude we have, there are even some places where it is completely acceptable. But what I really want to know is: where were all these cases of pot and homosexuality before? Did we just handle them quietly? Did we decide whether the guy was a good trainee or a bad one on the basis of what we saw in twelve or sixteen weeks, without national policy being threatened?

"Oh, it's a mess, I tell you! You know there's a big move to do away with background investigations for Peace Corps applicants? Oh, not for the reasons you think. It has nothing to do with the in-

*vasion of privacy but on the basis of money. The government has
found out it costs $400 to $500 per background check, and it's too
expensive. That's the operant word around here these days—expense! I've heard people speak very clearly on budgets—"keep 'em
low"—and on policy—"be careful"—but I've been here since 1963,
well, with Vaughn since what, 1966 maybe, and I can tell you that
things have changed."*

*I finally interrupted to ask "why do you stay on?" "Oh, ho," she
replied, "you think I'm going to say something inspirational, like I
won't let the bastards grind me down, or even better, that I'm still
sold on the idea. Hah, I'm still here because my husband is in analysis, and I've got to pay for it. He was pretty clever getting my father
to fix my teeth before we were married, but I never thought of requiring his mother to pay for the trouble she caused him. So here I
am."*

I have finally seen Vaughn eyeball to eyeball on the "Today"
show, and it has been interesting. According to the inside word,
Peace Corps enrollment has decreased significantly. Vaughn speaks
in one place of "one-half million" and in another, of "94,000," but
maybe he has lumped VISTA people with Peace Corps trainees.
Oddly enough, and I suspect this is where the trouble lies, the director does not define whether he is speaking of young people who
have expressed an interest, or those who have applied, or those who
are in training. Somehow the figure of 8,000 sticks in my mind; I
think that's the size of the entire volunteer group today, and that is
down, if I recall, from something like 10,000 last year or the year
before.

Reviewing the McGee-Vaughn confrontation, one would never
know that the Peace Corps's appeal to youth is on the wane, nor
would one know much else. What was Vaughn trying to say? That
he is for the young, that they have a right to "opt" out, that society
has failed them? If this is so, why does he want to send such disillusioned citizens out to represent us? Well, no matter, it is all too
hard to figure out. One thing is certain; Vaughn ought to join the
political tours dashing around the country this fall. His sober ambiguity makes him a natural in either the Nixon or Humphrey camp.

144

The New York Times on September 28, 1968, under the heading "L. I. Students Seek Wider Campus Role," called attention to the interesting fact that "Student government leaders at the State University center here have circulated a preliminary set of proposals to create joint student-faculty committees and eliminate grades, credits, rigid course structures and requirements."

The University
as a Medium

Politics and Culture
in the University

James Hitchcock

Politics and culture are related in obvious ways and also in profound and subtle ways which historians and political scientists have largely ignored. Yet it is also true that a close harmony of the two is usually unhealthy. Such harmony is really the ultimate aim of the totalitarian state, and it is only insofar as men insist on the autonomy of their culture, their right to divorce it from politics as they see fit, that they are able to remain free.

In the United States the political aims of student activists, with some exceptions, are benign and highly desirable—world peace, justice for American blacks, food for the hungry all over the world, the redistribution of corporate and personal wealth for critical social expenditures. For the most part the practical consequences of the student movement have also been beneficial to American society, again despite scattered extremist actions. The burgeoning of the peace movement, which in time resulted in the negotiations in Paris, was brought about by activist students and faculty more than any other group in society.

As the war may be in the process of settlement, however, and as students feel excluded from domestic political activism by militant black power, their discontents escalate on the American campuses. The confrontations of 1969 at San Francisco State and Cornell were more extreme and dramatic than those at Columbia, and there have been many more such occurrences. Within a few years scarcely a college in the United States has escaped upheavals of some kind.

Since the university is the chief repository of high culture in our society, it is here that the principle of separation from politics becomes applicable. This paper will argue that many of the attitudes, purposes, and programs articulated in national politics by the New Left are not only inappropriate to the university but profoundly harmful to it and to American culture as a whole.

Any discussion of the student movement must carefully distinguish its various levels. In its most immediate form this rebellion is a healthy and probably overdue push by students for a voice in their own educations, particularly through membership on important university committees. Those interested in such measures probably constitute a majority of activist students on the campus, but they naturally receive far less publicity than the more radical. The moderates are also often scorned by the radicals for their meliorism and their apparent indifference to larger issues.

A second group is primarily political in its concerns. Its obsessions are war, racism, and poverty, and its aim is to influence the society beyond the campus, to purify the university itself from immoral political influence, and to mobilize the academic community into a progressive political force. There are great extremes within this group, ranging from Eugene McCarthy liberals to would-be Maoist revolutionaries. Because they are more interesting and because they may represent the wave of the future, I will consider only the more radical students. A great dilemma arises within the radical group. Even relatively moderate forms of student political activism tend to blend politics and culture, which is at least a faint warning of totalitarianism, not a totalitarianism of American society as a whole, which students are obviously unable to effect, but a totalitarianism of the university and of high culture generally.

This danger can be seen clearly in the demand for relevance, a central feature of student discontent. No one can object to this demand in principle; unquestionably there is much within the university which is irrelevant to any kind of humane education. However, student leaders have a distressing tendency to define relevance in rather mechanical and shortsighted fashion, equating it with con-

150

temporary social problems. Whatever is directly related to these problems is deemed relevant; all else is rejected.

On one level this concept of relevance and the militancy which supports it is a kind of professional and intellectual imperialism by the social sciences. A disproportionate number of activist students are social science majors, and social science faculty members seem on the whole more sympathetic to student demands than most other professors. In some cases these professors actually betray ambitions to lead these new movements. Professional imperialism reveals itself in the fact that if the curriculums of the universities were reconstructed to become relevant, as that concept is often formulated, perhaps 90 percent of the courses now in the universities would be abolished and a fantastic proliferation of courses in sociology, economics, and political science would replace them. All else would be relegated to the fringes of the curriculum.

This drive for relevance is intellectual imperialism in the strong tendency of students and faculty members to subsume all knowledge under sociology. Values related to religion, nationality, family, political beliefs are seen only in a quasi-Marxian way, not as ideas to be espoused or rejected in their own terms but merely as the emanations of social class. "Bourgeois hangup" or "middle class ideology" are epithets which make it possible to dismiss ideas contemptuously rather than to come to terms with them. This tendency is profoundly, though unconsciously, anti-human, because it implies that we are all merely creatures of social class and our perceptions have no significance apart from that fact. (An example of this is the assertion of some radicals that classical music, novels, art are expressions of a bourgeois society and as such have no permanent validity.)

This intellectual imperialism approaches totalitarianism in the implicit belief that all of culture must serve political ends, albeit progressive and ostensibly democratic ones. Students drawn to the traditional liberal arts or the creative and performing arts now often feel guilty that these studies do not relate directly to social problems. Folk and rock music have totally eclipsed classical music in

151

the interest of the young, because folk and rock music appear to be politically relevant. Some attempt to radicalize organizations like the Modern Language Association. The whole validity of high culture is being called into question. Certain student programs for educational reform would in fact make the university a totalitarian community, in which all members would be pressured to associate themselves with progressive politics, and all interests and activities not directly relevant to politics would at the very least fall under general disapproval. Art would degenerate into propaganda, and scholarship would consciously serve partisan ends. This crisis goes beyond the university, as in former director Thomas Hoving's stated belief that the Metropolitan Museum in New York cannot rest contentedly as a repository of the classics but has to play a progressive role in the great social struggles of our time. (It is perhaps worth noting that the political awakening of the campus during the past decade does not seem to have enriched the students' total political awareness. Ten years ago there were some extreme leftists on campus, although not many, plus some extreme rightists and many opinions in between. The sudden radicalization of the campus, however, has made irrelevant nearly all classical political philosophy, and political debate is carried on almost entirely as a sectarian conflict on the left.)

The politicization of our students confronts us with a fact which our society prefers to overlook, that except for occasional fortuitous exceptions (who often do not look so exceptional the closer they are studied), political success usually goes to the most ruthless and singleminded. If the student desire to effect change is highly laudable for its idealism and caring, there is also in it a kind of vanity—the student's belief that he is too moral, too talented, too aware to confine himself in a social role which is less than central ("mere scholarship") and relatively without power. In the campus rebellions at Columbia and San Francisco State we also have evidence that moderates, those with too many scruples, will inevitably lose control to those whose only restraints seem to be whatever they can get away with. Often such people appear invincibly self-righteous, utterly

152

contemptuous of those who disagree with them, and totally manipulative in their relationships with other people. They reject an American society which makes people cogs in an economic machine, but they are ready to make their fellow students cogs in a revolutionary machine of their own design and construction.

In a peculiar way this kind of student activism is very American and mirrors some of the worst features of our culture, especially its philistinism. Like his businessman father, the student radical has little use for "culture" and a great deal of contempt for those whose bent is meditative and inactivist. He scorns his liberal professors for the same reasons his father scorns them, because they are intellectual, indecisive, ineffectual, and unproductive. Certain student rebels worship action and respect only success.

However, student activism has long harbored a current which is not primarily political, despite appearances. The initial puzzlement of liberals at the apparent hopeless utopianism and breathless disregard for political realities of some New Leftists has at last yielded to the understanding that certain radicals are in fact not primarily interested in politics at all but in the most fundamental kind of cultural revolution, of which politics is merely a part. This is the third general category of youth rebellion, and in a sense these rebels are at the opposite pole from the second group, because the third category rebels promise a totalitarianism in which culture controls all and politics is subordinate. Unlike certain of their colleagues, they are not pragmatic to a philistine degree and are not particularly interested in measurable success.

We are experiencing a second romantic revival, very similar in many ways to the first, and it is well to remember that romanticism is both a drive toward freedom from convention and a search for absolutes and hence for authority. The gap which so many older intellectuals now sense between themselves and the young derives primarily from the older generation's formation in the tradition of the Enlightenment, especially the belief that ironic, detached, rational probing is the proper task of moral man and the necessary starting place of a valid politics. The young have come to look upon ration-

153

ality as sterile and are now inclined to rely on instincts, feelings, and obscurely sensed intuitions as the best impetus for action. For many students the political reawakening of the 1960s was less than genuinely political; it was a constant search for liberating and transforming experiences, the constant sustenance of particular emotions and perceptions. Certain segments of the New Left seem held together less by stated political goals or articulated ideologies than by shared feelings about the world which cannot be expressed adequately in public language but are intuited in other ways by those who are properly sensitive. Hence such things as clothes, music, and speech have a significance for the New Left which they did not have for the old. It is here that the glimmerings of a possible new totalitarianism can be seen in that the student rebels, at least by their exclusions, have created a rigidly conformist subculture. Descriptions of psychedelic experiences bear a sinister similarity to some descriptions of brainwashing experiences, and we have not begun to discover the potentialities for manipulation inherent in the new culture.

The divergence of the hippie movement from the New Left was the first clear sign of the distinction between the movement for cultural revolution and that for political revolution. There are still New Leftists who are less than interested in politics (for example, Abbie Hoffman and Jerry Rubin). The final expression of this phenomenon has been given clear form by the yippie Abbie Hoffman, active in the 1969 Chicago demonstrations but now proclaiming that politics itself is a hangup and that the bourgeoisie must first be assaulted not in its institutions but in its fundamental consciousness. The aim of the yippies, only tangentially political, is total revolution in the lives of the middle class, in which every assumption concerning taste, beliefs, truth, and morality will be subjected to a "transvaluation of values."

Insofar as this movement exists on the campus it seeks not to restructure the university, even in a revolutionary way, but to destroy it, since the university is literally a prison in which students are force-fed according to old thought patterns. This criticism of the

154

university goes far beyond charges of subservience to the status quo, conservative political biases, and cooperation with the defense establishment. What the new group of revolutionaries oppose is the whole Western intellectual tradition, high culture, respect for history and for science, and certain underlying assumptions such as linear time and three dimensional space. In this view of reality the university, not because it has betrayed its purposes but precisely because it fulfills them, is the chief enemy of education, standing in the path of the new psychedelic consciousness. Robert Brustein of the Yale Drama School, an early admirer of the newer art forms, now admits to his fear of the nihilism he senses in some student radicals.

These attitudes are shared at least tentatively by many student rebels and faculty sympathizers who are not yet as thorough as the yippies. They are of course quite explicit in the thought of Marshall McLuhan, who has exerted a deep influence over some students. They have even been celebrated in the pages of *Look* magazine by its education editor. Implicitly certain student demands reach the extreme of relevance, the requirement that the university become a microcosm of the larger world, a total environment in which virtually no human experience is denied to students. As an ideal of education, this holds great attraction, but it suffers from a fundamental romantic fallacy—the failure to realize that certain experiences cancel out certain others, that to live a highly involved, activist, deeply sensual existence may prevent one's living a meditative intellectual life, that total commitment to certain political goals requires the surrender of one's critical faculties with respect to these goals and the means used to attain them. (There is surely no merit in the refusal of so many student radicals even to listen to speakers whose opinions they do not respect and their attempts to prevent others from listening, also.) Finally it might be questioned to what extent the concept of the university as a total environment, a microcosm of all worldly experiences, is at all possible or viable. The university occupies limited physical space, has relatively few members compared with the larger world, and is equipped to deal with only certain kinds of learning experiences. As students insist on reaching out to include more and more of "life" within their educations, the ultimate logic will dictate the abandonment of the university altogether or its reduction to a convenient place for young people to meet for exchange of information about worldly experiences. The neoromantic temperament regards all formal learning as valueless and will be satisfied by nothing less radical than a totally unstructured and unacademic education.

Many students, however, have a profoundly ambivalent attitude toward the university. They demand to be treated as adults, but they also resent bitterly the largeness and impersonality of the university. An appropriate response to this complaint is to point out that in our mass society, so highly mobile and rapidly changing, it is precisely a mark of adulthood to accept impersonality and largeness and to forge one's own meaningful personal life rather than expecting society to provide it. Many students seem to want a university which offers an intimate familial atmosphere and is, at the same time, free of all paternalism and normative guidance. This is a contradiction which extends to the entire notion of relevance as the students employ it. They seem unable to decide whether the university is simply irrelevant to the real world, as they sometimes charge, or rather all too relevant, a mere factory processing students for the needs of capitalist society. The contradiction in these charges is implicit also in the students' desire, on the one hand, to imbibe all worldly experiences, to be free of hangups, to admit to no stifling boundaries, and, on the other hand, to cleanse the university of all unsavory influences. A totally reformed university, according to the student vision, apparently would be one in which no element of tyranny, stupidity, backwardness, or immorality would be allowed to exist and such unpleasant realities as the ROTC and Dow Chemical Company would never penetrate. Such a university would indeed be an ivory tower, and students who spent four years in such an institution would find themselves unable to live in the real world after graduation.

The root of the student rebellion seems to be an extraordinary thirst for life experiences, again a manifestation of a neoromanticism which makes intellectual and cultural activities seem boring and insignificant by comparison. This attitude has been spawned in part by the knowledge explosion—students despair of ever attaining an intellectual mastery of the world and therefore seek other roads to truth. They also recognize that the accumulation of human knowledge has not led to a deepening of human meaning. It also stems in part from the fact that within the last few decades higher education has ceased to be a privilege and for many students has become a duty, almost like the draft. When one is virtually forced to spend twenty years of his life in formal education, it is inevitable that serious doubts about the process will arise. We should heed the advice of Paul Goodman and others to develop other respectable modes of growing up in addition to formal schooling. We should also restructure our system so that young people will interrupt their formal education at various points to engage in worldly activities, returning to the campus when they themselves feel the need for quiet thought in an attempt to place their experiences in perspective.

It seems doubtful, however, if this expedient, even if adopted, would redeem the university in the eyes of its most radical critics, and we can expect an intensification of student rebellion into the forseeable future. In a very real sense the ideal of liberal education has been grafted onto American culture; it is not a native plant, and the success of the operation is very doubtful. For some decades, when higher education was largely the preserve of a semi-leisured elite, the classic ideal of the liberal arts was paid lip service, even if relatively few students were deeply affected by it. This ideal was upheld by the constant insistence of intellectuals themselves, who took a resolutely anti-philistine line. Now, however, young people appear to be in the vanguard of a cultural revolt which affects mature intellectuals as well, and across the nation many professors have lost confidence in themselves, the validity of their own disciplines, and the very ideal of education to which they have given their lives. A Princeton graduate student, replying to George Kennan in *The New York Times,* perhaps took the pulse of this phenomenon in saying that the students' demands for relevance, and their impatience with meliorism in politics, is related to a consumer society in which people are systematically taught to seek instantaneous gratification of their wants. Thus, the charge that liberal education at present is largely meaningless evades the classic notion that man spends his entire life in the search for meaning, that it is found in flashes and fragments, never whole, and that to achieve even this requires the endurance of many days and years of relative darkness. As many people have pointed out, the interest in drugs among the young reflects the hope that somewhere a short-cut to meaning can be found, that the struggle and discipline which since the days of the Greeks man has believed are essential to his life are no longer required. The classic notion of liberal education has been the planting of seeds which will mature slowly. But American society, always interested in speedy and concrete results, has never accepted this ideal, and the student rebels do not either. Hence their education, the results of which they cannot see, is to them a failure.

Despite its rebelliousness, this generation of students manifests disquieting signs of the crowd mentality, perhaps no more so than previous student generations but more disturbing precisely because this is a generation superior in its seriousness and sophistication. It is still true, as it always has been, that student tastes in books and music, styles of dress, commonly held ideas and values are standardized and predictable. Despite their iconoclasm they are, in George Orwell's phrase, a herd of independent minds. (Whatever criticisms can be made of the older generations of intellectuals, they manifest much greater diversity of taste and opinion than do students.) The constant search for the new and stimulating, the distrust of rationality and the desire for ecstasy, the refusal to see events in perspective and the lack of interest in the past—in a word the utter preoccupation with the moment, the "now"— also make this generation potentially susceptible to the worst kinds of manipulation, and this manipulation seems already to have taken place in some colleges. (Significantly, the concept of the "now generation" does not derive from the student movement or from any intellectual movement but from Madison Avenue, and that the notion behind the concept—of living entirely in the present, for the sake of immediate satisfactions—is the heart of advertising psychology.)

The cult of youth, which has gained so much intellectual respectability (young people are the noble savages of this particular romantic revival), was also in origin a Madison Avenue invention, although it is also an aspect of romanticism, as advertising itself reflects the romantic frame of mind and is most seriously challenged by Enlightenment skepticism. It was in advertising that we were first taught to believe that the loss of youth is the greatest misfortune. Ultimately, this same belief permeates a good part of the student movement, and it implies a horrifyingly negative view of the human situation, despite its superficial optimism. For in their contempt for so much of the past, whether in politics, education, art, or religion, the student rebels imply the impossibility of significant human achievement in the future. If past generations have failed so miserably, there is no reason to suppose that this one can succeed. Man himself is thus as absurd and tragic as the existentialists see him. We may wonder if the almost obsessive need to devour experiences, to seize power, and to transform the world does not come from a deeper need for young people to prove to themselves that such achievement is in fact possible. For at this ultimate point, the most alienated of the young seem literally not to believe in the possibility of human growth beyond a certain early point. "Don't trust anybody over thirty" is the clearest distillation of this attitude, and it persists. Many students seem convinced that once their student days are over, they have no possibility for happiness, meaning, or moral integrity. Only degeneration and regression lie ahead. The extreme cynicism of this view has had a deeply corrosive effect on all aspects of our culture. As Norman Mailer said in receiving the 1969 National Book Award, "We are . . . poised upon the lip . . . of a spiritual revolution that will wash the psychic roots of every national institution out to sea." And again, " . . . no longer do we know where we go, or whom we fight."

The Dissident Cause: Antioch Student Culture

Conrad Hilberry

In the fall of 1968 one semi-rebellious student said: "If we're going to sink the ship, I'd like to have a canoe nearby, in case I can't walk on the water." Almost everyone who has written about disaffected students has noted, in their rhetoric, the absence of a "program." The students are not Marxists or Fidelists or agrarians or any other recognizable thing. They want the war ended and ghetto misery relieved, but the war and racism are both offered as symptoms of a society that is too big, too mechanical, hopelessly beyond the reach of simple feelings or moral choice or common sense. The prescription for the universities—and by implication for the society in general—is to "bring the whole thing to a standstill," or more dramatically "to get a traveling yippie guerilla theater band roaring through college campuses burning books, burning degrees and exams, burning school records, busting up classrooms, and freeing our brothers from the prison of the university."[1] Except for black students, who do frequently advance quite specific programs, the goal of student rebels appears to be disruption. They will sink the ship, giving no thought to the canoe.

But perhaps this reading of the matter results from a too narrow notion of what might constitute a program. Certainly many of the more quotable rebels are indeed anarchists or have, at least, turned their attention to tactics—how to create the greatest disturbance with the fewest men—rather than objectives. Certainly, too, the

160

great majority of students are not rebels at all, although they may not be exactly happy with their university or their world. But in between the more or less contented majority and the very few students genuinely devoted to chaos stands a considerable congregation of disaffected students who, in a sense, do have a program. Neither they nor their elders have described it as a program, because it is not a political nor economic nor academic plan of action, not something that can be plotted or campaigned for. It is a new order, but not one that can be achieved by legislation or coup. It is a web of social customs, attitudes, habits, preferences, convictions—in short a culture—that has spread with revolutionary speed from campus to campus until the most conservative colleges shelter at least a piece of it. The mores and values of this culture are remarkably consistent across the country. Although the anti-establishment subgroup at Western Michigan University is less strident, more open to accommodation than its counterpart at Columbia or San Francisco State, it departs from standard American culture in the same direction. And although the dissident student culture borrows much of its ideology, its idiom, even its tone of voice from black ghetto life, the two subcultures are not by any means identical, as both have been sharply aware since the dismissal of white radical students from leadership in SNCC. Confrontation, a willingness to be violent if pushed, is part of the culture, but only a small part. The Vietnam war has in a sense created the culture, but its tenets extend well beyond the war. Although the rebels may not have a cause in the accustomed sense, they have a way of life, and a coherent one, that presents an exhilarating or threatening challenge to the habits and assumptions on which American society has been built.

Adults are already acquainted with dissident student life, but our acquaintance is likely to be scattered or superficial, adding up to an impression of hair, free love, and violent set-to's with recruiters, or with faculty members doing research on government contract. I will argue that these fragments of behavior are often knit together into a fairly elaborate culture that enforces and sustains a coherent pattern of values and actions. Student life at Antioch College in Yellow

161

Springs, Ohio is a convenient example because on that campus the dissident culture predominates, setting the tone and defining the prevailing expectations. I am aware that student life differs dramatically from campus to campus. And I know the Antioch program gives special emphases to student life. Nonetheless, I believe that Antioch student culture is closely related to dissident subcultures on all sorts of campuses and that these subcultures collectively are a significant force in American society. This description of Antioch comes in two parts: first, a sketch of the assumptions and social patterns that seem most conspicuous to an outside observer, and second, excerpts from notes made by Sue Keese, then a Wittenberg sophomore, during a three-day visit to Antioch in January 1967. These remarkable notes, included elsewhere in this volume, will give a sense of the texture and complexity of the place as the more generalized sketch cannot do.

At graduation in 1967 an Antioch College senior, Peter Adair, issued a two-page mimeographed statement, headed: I REJECT MY DEGREE. The statement opened:

> I have decided to reject my degree. Not only has the honor itself become odious to me, but by accepting it I would also be giving passive support to a system in which I no longer believe.
>
> I consider the granting of degrees little more than a medieval rite signifying that the novitiate is now a part of the elite of society. Peter Adair, B.A. 'He must be literate.' 'He must be genteel.' 'He must make a better employee than Joe Smith who never got his degree.' I am not going to be genteel . . . I am not going to be 'literate.' And I will not be judged by any letters on the end of my name. If my time spent at Antioch has had value for me, and I have become a little bit wiser as a result of it, then why does it need official recognition?
>
> I am also refusing my B.A. as a gesture to protest against the direction in which this college is going. I want to stress, however, that I think this college is perhaps the best in the country, and that I love it. Otherwise I probably wouldn't bother taking the time to try and change it. I am not objecting to those elements of Antioch which are

unique to her, but rather that element which this school shares with all other colleges and universities in the country, the academic establishment.

Adair went on to detail his discontent with the academic Establishment: its refusal to learn except within its own closed-loop system; its neglect of television and other news media, both as subjects of study and as tools to be employed in education; the "creeping monasticism" that prevents the colleges from taking a public stand on the Vietnam war. Adair invited other graduating seniors to join him in turning down their degrees, or to protest in whatever way they chose.

Earlier in the spring term at Antioch Adair showed an hour-long documentary movie he had made of a snake-handling religious sect in West Virginia. Before undertaking the project, Adair had done professional film work, and, to gain access to the sect, he had spent his weekends for nearly a year with the people in the West Virginia hollow. Most of the picture, called *The Holy Ghost People,* was filmed during actual religious services; at the film's climax, the preacher himself, whom we know by that time as an open, appealing, and persuasive person, is bitten by a rattlesnake. The film is an extraordinary piece of work—professional in its technical quality and very remarkable indeed in its content.

There are not many Peter Adairs at Antioch or anywhere else, but he displays many of the attitudes that the Antioch student culture promotes: a distaste for rankings, honors, and ceremonies; a tendency to disparage the old and hunger after the new; utter confidence in one's own judgment and willingness to act on it, despite discomfort to oneself or others; and admiration for creativity, meaning any number of things but particularly the ability to do arresting work in an art form that has not become traditional or tightly disciplined. In refusing his degree and castigating the educational and political establishment, Adair was roughly in accord with the precepts of Antioch society: President James Dixon, in the commencement ceremony, took respectful notice of Adair's defection.

163

Antioch College enrolls about 1,800 students, unusually bright ones, largely from the Middle Atlantic states and the Midwest. It is distinguished by two programs. The first is a work-study (or co-op) program, which sends students off campus every other quarter to jobs in offices, laboratories, hospitals, schools, social service agencies, and so forth. Two separate student bodies, called divisions, take turns occupying the campus and never meet, except when individual students change divisions. The second is a first year program, introduced for all freshmen in 1965, which invites students to follow their own interest without the intervention of conventional academic organization: they take no courses and receive no grades. They may attend presentations and engage in seminars of varying lengths, but no contract binds students to either presentations or seminars. They choose those they feel they need, or none at all. Besides presentations and seminars, they have available to them programmed materials, tapes, films, reading lists, books, autonomous laboratories, and studios. Each student is assigned to a faculty preceptor to help him plan his work, find resources, and evaluate the results. These programs give curricular embodiment to many of the values emphasized in the student culture: the desirability of experience, rather than just academic work, as a way to education; the importance of individual need, rather than external pressure, as a motive force; the distrust of anything that appears artificial or rigid or removed from life.

Although I believe Antioch student life is built on a number of positive values, a visitor to the campus likely will be struck first by a sense of formlessness, as though there were no groups, no routines, no customs. And indeed Antioch does slight a great many of the forms that organize life at more conventional places. For example, the college seldom obliges a student to be in a given place at a given time. No chapel calls students together every morning or every week. They need not show for meals at a specified time. If the cafeteria is open when they are moved to eat, fine; if not, they can take their meal tickets to the coffee shop at any hour. The dormitories never close, and students may come and go at their pleasure.

Classes probably organize time as strictly as any campus structure, but they allow leeway, too. Students are expected to do impressive quantities of work, but they are seldom required to attend classes. Lectures in the first year program are recorded and the tapes filed in the library so that late sleepers can hear the 8:30 a.m. presentation at a more civilized hour.

Time is similarly unmarked over the stretch of a year. The ends of quarters, of course, are sharply marked: examinations, papers, the end of courses (except in the first year program), the switch to a job. But aside from this, there are few of the expected events that organize the school year elsewhere: no homecoming, no Greek week, no football games on Saturday afternoons, no regular intramural competition among houses or sections of a dormitory, no annual Christmas pageant, no May festival. I do not wish to overstate the point. The newspaper, the Antioch *Record,* does appear once a week, the theater puts on a certain number of major performances in the course of a year, and commencement comes up each spring, though without academic garb or processions. But the events that, in retrospect, give shape to the year are not annual and predictable but rather single events sizable enough to draw the notice of the whole campus: a national conference on draft procedures, the showing of Peter Adair's movie, or an all-day anti-war demonstration climaxed by the burning of a lifelike gasoline-soaked figure in the center of a Yellow Springs street.

This informal sense of time and place pervades Antioch courtship, too. Students seldom telephone ahead for dates for a particular night. Men and women are much more likely to meet in the cafeteria, where one can find knots of students drinking coffee and talking at all hours of the day and night, and simply go from there to a movie at the Little Art Theater in town or to the Old Trail tavern or to a workshop play or the midnight movie at the college. Though most Antioch students must have been accustomed, in high school, to a system of prearranged dates, once at Antioch they seem ready enough to dismiss the calendar and the telephone as artificial impediments, destroyers of spontaneity.

Conspicuously absent, too, are the devices by which students ordinarily measure themselves against one another, the honors and offices that publicly recognize student achievement, perseverance, or popularity. Grades have disappeared. The college pins few medals on its members. It has not applied for a chapter of Phi Beta Kappa, believing that such honors are likely to be arbitrary and superficial. Because the college has no intercollegiate athletics, no one is publicly celebrated as a letterman or a breaker of the pool record or a most valuable player. Recently some Dayton disc jockeys challenged Antioch to a basketball game and the students created a coed team for the purpose—the athletic event of the season. There are elected officers of community government—a fulltime community manager, assistant community manager, and so forth—editors of the *Record,* and student members of the influential administrative council and community council. But there are no class officers, no sororities, fraternities, eating clubs, or literary societies that establish one as *in* or *out,* and no honorary fraternities recognizing leadership or accomplishment in a particular discipline. The honors ordinarily recorded in a college yearbook do not exist: Antioch has no yearbook.

At most institutions, regulations lay some order on students' lives. They must not drink or smoke pot in the dormitories; men are permitted in women's rooms or women in men's rooms only during certain visiting hours; certain occasions demand shoes or a skirt or a tie; students must live on campus; they must not own cars during their freshman year. Antioch provides little of this ordering. Rules call for shoes in the cafeteria, and for something besides jeans in the Antioch Inn, which serves the public at large, but beyond that, dress can be thoroughly informal, even bizarre. (Dress is subject to the same skeptical analysis as everything else in this introspective island. Marilyn McNabb, a student observer from Earlham College elicited this story from one Antioch student. When Whistler went to visit Degas, Whistler wore an outlandish costume. Degas greeted him by exclaiming, "My dear man, you dress as if you had no talent!" The storyteller felt the observation was applicable to Antioch:

some students, in their bizarre outfits, dress as if they had no individuality.)

Sometimes pressure is strong to violate law or regulation. Without question, marijuana is part of Antioch life, and it would take determination for a student to resist it altogether. One senior, bound for Harvard and not at all a hippie, expressed surprise at finding a fellow senior who had never tried pot. All the freshmen he had worked with in a preceptoral group had tried it by the end of the first quarter. Many students sample it and let it go at that; others smoke marijuana the way many students drink—in small groups two or three times a month or once or twice a week. In fact, Antioch students probably drink less than students at many campuses. But it is a "wise" campus. There is little sign of heroin or opium, and LSD is taken with far more caution and by far fewer people than marijuana.

Sexual relations, too, are relatively free of regulations or constraint. Little public observation or excitement attends Antioch courtship. Women are not likely to run jubilantly to their housemates after a man has called them for a date, and they do not sit conspicuously neglected while others go out on weekends. An upperclass preceptoral fellow reports that freshmen men and women "play games" with each other for only a few weeks before they drop into more informal interaction. "It takes the romance out of it," he concedes, but he thinks this is desirable because it makes way for more genuine relationships.

Partly because courtship is surrounded by so little public ceremony, both men and women at Antioch feel real pressure to have sexual relations. Other conditions contribute to this end: dormitory rooms are open to men and women all day or a large part of the day (by vote of the hall itself), terms on campus are short and intense, any externally imposed code is suspect, education tends to be equated with experience, and intimacy, "really knowing" another person, is universally acclaimed as good. Virtually all students claim to respect individuality and personal choice, but a woman may feel pressure not only from men but from other women as well, though this differs from one dormitory group to another. A third year student described herself when she came to Antioch as "pretty narrow minded, opinionated, ironclad—'straight' is the word we use now. I was determined not to lose any of my high moral standards or to do anything that might detract from my integrity or dignity. But I didn't have a very clear understanding of what those terms mean." A "straight" girl can get along all right, she says, especially if her moral standards have a basis in strong religious commitment. But "a straight girl gets hammered at." In her case the hammering was done "by the guys I was dating, but also by other members of the group, particularly my roommate . . . as one by one they threw over bits and pieces of the ethic. That was really the most powerful influence. A guy is pretty easy to dismiss as someone who's just out for what he can get and is willing to say anything to con you into doing it. But when somebody I respected and trusted as much as my roommate would say the very same things, in more general terms, but essentially the same, mainly that I was just insulating myself against something that I was afraid of because I didn't know anything about it, then it was pretty hard to shrug it off. In fact, it was impossible." Asked about the effects of this process, she says, "I think so much depends on who does it. I don't know what would have happened if I had let the breaking down be done by the guys I was dating. I'm almost sure I would have felt guilty and abused or misused and conned. But somehow accepting the advice and the fruits of experience from peers is a lot more palatable and easier to integrate."

It may be that Antioch students are less preoccupied with sex than students elsewhere. Sexual activity is more a part of their lives, less a glorious or fearful promise. But it can be a source of anxiety and practical difficulty here as elsewhere. The *McDowell Weakly*, a mimeographed newspaper not remarkable for literal accuracy, reports on the logistical problems following upon the adoption of hall autonomy in 1966. Previously "displaced" roommates had little trouble finding an empty bed on a Friday or Saturday night when weekend guests disrupted normal sleeping arrangements. The routine has changed, however, to one something like this:

> X has girlfriend in overnight
> X's roommate goes to Y's room
> Y has girlfriend in, too
> X's roommate goes to a girl's room
> Girl's roommate goes to Z's room
> Z's roommate goes to . . .

The dean of students' office at Antioch does little policing. When standards or regulations must be enforced—which means when someone is making it impossible for other people to go about their business—the enforcing is usually done informally and on the spot. A student gives this account:

> Most halls informally agree on hours when the volume on record players and radios is to be turned down, conversation confined to common rooms, and athletic events are to cease. If a person forgets these rules, he is usually asked to decrease the volume. If he is a constant offender, the sanctions against him become stronger. One example shows the full spectrum of methods used to obtain relief. After repeated requests to turn the record player down, a pair of roommates were requested to attend a hall meeting on noise. When this failed, a spontaneous display of affection was staged for their benefit: the trash buckets and assorted cushions from two halls were emptied through their transom. The situation was finally resolved by individual action. Our normally mild-mannered and easy going hall adviser (an upperclass student) kicked in their door (not such a spectacular feat in South Hall) after being awakened at one in the morning and roared, "You turn that damn thing off and the next time I hear it after twelve, I'll throw it out the window." The boys transferred to another hall at the end of the quarter, but remained quiet while they stayed in our hall.

The customary social structures are gone. But underneath these absences lie what may be more distinctive values. The first of these is creativity, ranked as high as any virtue in the Antioch code. Creativity is not by any means the same thing as artistry, a word not often heard at Antioch. Although the students recognize that creative production may require highly polished skills, they believe the essential ingredient to be a kind of looseness, a freedom from conventional forms and disciplines, an ability to imagine and construct something new, ideally something that cannot be accommodated in any recognized genre. One piece of statistical evidence supports the observation that Antioch increasingly respects "creativity": in January 1964, on a College and University Environment Scales questionnaire, 36 per cent of the respondents agreed that "students (at Antioch) often start projects without trying to decide in advance how they will develop or where they may end." By summer 1966 the agreement had risen to 65 per cent. This conviction pulls together much of what one sees at Antioch: the first year program attempts, among other things, to clear away the conventional expectations, leaving some open space for creativity; psychedelic drugs are thought to break the tight boxes in which logic and habit have held our minds; and if creativity is good, surely the sexual act must be good, the archetypal act of creation.

Creativity appears in many forms, many of them small scale. Posters, announcements, and advertisements are likely to show an extraordinary flair. One bicycle on campus has been altered so that the back hub is eccentric; the bike rises and falls like a merry-go-round horse with each turn of the wheel. Graffiti have become a minor art form.

Other pieces of creativity require elaborate preparation and become the most memorable events of a quarter. A production called "Distances" brought together slides of people, places, objects on the campus, fragments of conversation, personal confessions or appeals, brief quotations, and a bit of drama spoken by a man and woman from balconies on opposite sides of an auditorium. The whole thing spoke about loneliness, about protecting and covering oneself from other people and the world, about Antioch. It was a skillful piece of work—the photography of professional quality, the play successfully skirting sentimentality, and the fragments of talk held together by recurring themes and phrases. The production drew capacity crowds for at least three performances, and talk of the show reverberated for weeks afterward. Other quarters turned up similarly

170

ambitious and unorthodox pieces of theater. Using documents that the Antioch theater department inherited from a long defunct burlesque company, students during the summer of 1966 staged a burlesque show, complete with chorus lines of various descriptions, dozens of dirty jokes delivered with fitting gestures and leers, and a thoroughly sexy striptease. In the spring of 1967 the producer of the burlesque show turned to movie making, producing *Antioch Adventure,* a pastiche of parodies (of everything from the Keystone Cops to *Blow-Up*), all translated into Antiochian. It did not have the poise and polish of Peter Adair's *Holy Ghost People,* but it had energy and humor. The campus embraced it enthusiastically.

Marijuana, LSD, and other psychedelic drugs are taken seriously, not just a means to pleasure or ecsape but as means to creativity or religious discovery. A student gives this account:

> One friend of mine was smoking hashish. He was in New York at a friend's house and got very, very high until his head fell over in his lap. He was sitting in that position for quite a while and sort of pulsating with a strong kind of feeling. After a while he wandered off into the next room and apparently he had some notion enter his head; anyway he said, "Oh, wow!" And hearing himself say "Oh, wow!" in that typically hippie way of saying it was so nauseating to himself that he just felt disgusted. But then thinking about it he said, well, you know, after all I really did have a great idea there and I really did deserve to say that that way. And suddenly he realized that he was forgiving himself for having said that—that it was really okay, that there was no need to feel nauseated by the whole thing. Then he thought about lots of other things he had always had little guilt feelings about, and he forgave himself for all these things, very systematically, not just arbitrarily forgiving them all but he sort of realized one by one that it wasn't a question of whether you do it that way—if you say "Oh, wow!" or if you say "My God!"—it's a question of whether you really should be concerned about the way you say it or which way you do it. He began to realize that there was a chain of endless forgivingness, and he said out loud. "Endless forgivingness, wow!" He said to his friend in the room, "Hey, look at this endless forgivingness." My friend said it was just then that he realized those phrases that they use in

the Bible that sound like endless forgivingness must have had a great deal of meaning to the people who originally set them down and therefore must be very, very important. So indirectly he developed a kind of religious experience and willingness to accept religious terminology and biblical kinds of writings.

The student conceded "you don't have to get a religious experience, you can get a hellish experience, too." And Antioch has had its share of casualties. Physicians at the Yellow Springs Clinic, which serves the college, are far from casual about the effects of LSD.

It is not far from creativity to simple eccentricity, and Antioch is inclined to honor any behavior that is sufficiently odd to catch its attention. During the spring of 1967, for example, the common room in one of the women's dormitories was known as Harlow Hall, after a student named Harlow who had taken up residence there, sleeping on the floor or on a sofa. More often the college will create a legend out of someone who mixes eccentricity with some kind of entrepreneurial genius. In spring 1965 students in two dormitory halls, set in motion by the bizarre energy of a student, Dennis McDowell, combined to form the McDowell complex, which, among other things, publishes the mimeographed, often outrageous *McDowell Weakly*. A story in the *Weakly* about the origin of the complex states:

> This turned out to be one of the most chaotic, financially mismanaged, spirited, comic, productive, disorganized, creative social groups ever to crop up in the annals of Antioch. Dennis McDowell served as the insane inspiration. Aside from such quirks as taking a martini to his 8:00 class he displayed an unbelievable flair for organizing parties. The initial Viking-Gunsway party featured inordinate amounts of beer, 100 pounds of peanuts, a Pepsi machine with six canisters of soft drink, and enough potato chips to cover the floors of both halls to a depth of eight inches. As the parties grew bigger and bigger he seriously considered 800 lobsters from Maine one weekend.

McDowell dropped out after a year or so, but the complex lives on.

This admiration for creativity has something to do with the structure of Antioch student society. The idea of status or prestige is alien to the campus; students deny any consciousness of rank among their fellow students. This may follow from the emphasis on creativity. On a campus that honors organizational skill, social aplomb, or straight intellectual, artistic, or athletic competence, students may achieve a fairly stable position of prestige. The person who holds important offices or who is the best French horn player, chemistry student, fullback, or actor on the campus can count on certain status in a culture that values those accomplishments. But where the criterion is creativity, whether artistic or social, status can hardly be stable. By definition a creative work must be a new conception, not just another evidence of established competence. Having been creative once, a person may be expected to be creative again—but not with much assurance. It is ground too shifty to sustain a hierarchy.

Along with creativity, the Antioch culture prizes intellectuality. Here again a distinction is called for: intellectuality is not to be mistaken for scholarliness, academic perseverance, or the ability to get good grades. Antioch students undoubtedly read a great deal; on the average they check out of the library seventy-five books apiece each year. But diligence in one's studies is not looked upon as a virtue. Many students, in fact, are inclined to condescend to physical science majors who spend long stretches of time in the laboratory. They must be narrow and uninteresting. Intellectuality means the ability to call up information and plausible conjectures about a wide range of subjects, the ability to analyze a situation, a person, or a problem, or to criticize someone else's analysis. Students from other schools are consistently impressed with the amount of talk at Antioch and its quality: they notice the Antioch students' skill in moving from the abstract to the concrete and back, citing examples, manufacturing theories, sketching graphs or charts on the nearest napkin. Test and questionnaire data confirm these impressions, and Antioch students score well above average on Scholastic Aptitude and Graduate Record area tests given by Educational Testing Service. The College and University Environment Scales show Antioch extremely high in both "awareness" and "scholarship."

173

The college's propensity for talk often finds an institutional structure, at least temporarily. Conferences, for example, on Vietnam, on drugs, on college ranking for the draft, or on the decision-making process at Antioch, occur often and draw in a considerable proportion of the student body. Sometimes they attract students from throughout the country. The college newspaper, the *Record,* is energetic in reporting campus controversy, getting the talk on paper. Occasionally a mimeographed journal appears as a vehicle for dispute. In a different way students make an institution of discussion through student-initiated courses, or even a student-initiated professor: In 1966-67 the community council appropriated funds (from student fees) to bring Carl Oglesby to campus as activist-scholar.

Impressive as this intellectuality is, not everyone at Antioch is enamored of it. A bright, handsome senior from a rural high school reports that he has never felt able to keep up with the "intellectuality" of Antioch students, although he has had excellent grades and job reports. He has been more comfortable on jobs and studying at the University of Aberdeen in Scotland than at Antioch. Though he sometimes goes out with Antioch girls, he assumes that most of them would be bored with him. He has been working with the Peace Corps training program at Antioch and has found a girl there more congenial than any he has met on campus.

Faculty may feel dissatisfaction of a slightly different kind. Two Antioch professors, after interviewing candidates for Woodrow Wilson Fellowships, reported their impressions of Antioch students as compared to those from other schools: "I overheard one of my fellow interviewers comment that the Antioch students were mature, sophisticated, and revealed remarkable gaps in their knowledge. . . . We do not emphasize fundamentals: Our students are not taught blocking and tackling, but the virtue of taking the ball and running; and not bulling through the line, mind you, but those brilliant, wide end runs which cover so much distance and gain such little yardage." Antioch has done well in the Woodrow Wilson competition.

The absence of structure in the Antioch program, coupled with the demands for creativity and intellectuality, makes self-examination inevitable. The first year program asks a student repeatedly, persistently, "What do you really want to do?" That is not an easy question, and many students spend weeks or months pondering it, going over yard by yard the ground on which their habits and ambitions have been built, the question becoming more urgent the longer it goes unanswered. Social liberties have much the same effect: Shall I sleep with this man tonight? Shall I try LSD? Why or why not? How do I decide such things? Who am I anyway? This is not an accidental byproduct of the Antioch system, but a conviction on which much of the program depends. Education is experience, self-definition, not just the mastery of skills and information. If, after six undisciplined months, a sense of purpose takes hold of a student, this may be counted an educational achievement. A freshman wrote: "The only significant learning is achieved by self-discovery; education is involvement. On my first coop quarter, I went through a complex, intense gestation in which every day brought revolutionary insights and radical upheavals of past assumptions and values." He may be exaggerating what happened to him, but he has stated the doctrine flawlessly.

Antioch students sometimes describe themselves as neurotic. Unquestionably, they brood about their problems more than students elsewhere. Whether they actually are more disturbed remains a question. At more conventional schools, where students' lives are more organized for them and where they may be expected to appear cheerful, do students have fewer problems or are they more deeply buried? "Does a problem exist," an Antioch student asks, "if you're not aware of it? If you keep piling roses on top of the problem, is it there at all?" The question becomes more than a rhetorical one when this same student, a girl from a traditional Southern family, defines the content of these problems:

> Basically, it's whether or not we're going to accept the world as it is. Now if we reject it I don't know what that means—go back into our own world or go out and try to change this one. But that's a question a lot of people our age consider. Do I like the social standards of the United States or anywhere else, do I accept sex standards of the

175

world, do I accept the political behavior and ideologies, do I accept war? Plenty of basic questions that you don't think about when you have a test in psychology but you do think about at other times to a greater or lesser degree. And then of course personal problems like setting up your own sexual standards when you haven't decided whether or not you like the ones society has set up, or finding some religious substitute when you haven't decided whether or not you are going to accept religion as it is. Things like this, just living day to day without having agreed upon a foundation. Problems which everybody our age goes through to some degree, but I think there's something about Antioch that makes those problems bigger than they really are or allows them to be as big as they really are. Of the upperclass students and graduates I've known, a lot of them are very stable people who seem to resolve those problems. They seem to be different from the person who repressed them all his life. But I'm really not sure how big a percentage of them ever make it to that mature, stable level.

Freshman preceptoral groups at Antioch sometimes sequester themselves for T-group sessions, and a course in communication is conducted partly by means of T-groups. Sometimes groups record their sessions on video tape so that they can play them back and analyze themselves analyzing themselves—a mirrors within mirrors effect where introspection becomes its own subject. Many Antioch students, especially first and second year students, have been through a T-group. Some remember it as a reassuring experience, showing them that other students were lonely and scared, too, or felt less intellectual than everyone else. For others it was frightening, with people lashing out at each other in the name of honesty. One student observed that T-groups and psychedelic drugs may recommend themselves to students for similar reasons: both produce sharply intensified experience—exaltation or agony—a heightened awareness of oneself.

Accompanying this introspection is a new mysticism, remarked by the Antioch pastor in 1966-1967 and reported since then on a number of campuses. This mysticism takes many forms, but often the point of entry is drugs or sex: at moments of ecstasy the believers feel a union of the self with an all-encompassing self. The experience is almost never interpreted in theistic terms, but it does lead many students to a serious search of theology and metaphysics, and not just existential philosophy or theology, for answers to questions of identity and purpose. The pastor welcomes this return of interest in Jesus and Paul, in Barth and Tillich, partly because an intellectual search, unlike a strictly mystical one, is open to an ethical imperative: Go, therefore. . . . The mysticism itself is asocial, even anti-social or cultic.

A final tenet derives from the previous ones: Antioch students have an unmistakable sense of their own importance and confidence in their ability to make moral decisions and act on them. By observing their gait, gesture, and tone of voice one senses that they feel no need to defer to age, property, tradition, or power; they trust in their own logic and experience, and they expect to be noticed. This sense of individual importance fits logically with the absence of social restraints and the flexibility of the academic program. One senior, enrolled for fifteen units of independent study in group dynamics, commented on the ease with which students can adjust the academic program to accommodate themselves. It fits, too, with the college's pattern of government which places students, as well as faculty and administrators, on virtually all decision-making bodies within the college, including the administrative council which approves the budget, acts on faculty appointments and tenure, reviews building plans, and debates policy issues such as whether or not the college should provide draft boards with the class rank of students.

One episode may illustrate the students' assertion of their place in the institution and their willingness to risk discomfort or rebuke for the sake of their convictions. In May 1967 some fifty students entered a closed meeting of the college board of trustees and distributed themselves around the edge of the room. They were pressing for two reforms: that the college should no longer invest funds in corporations doing business in South Africa (in a referendum the preceding quarter, the college community had voted three to one

177

for "an institutional stand against South African apartheid"); and that the trustees' meetings should be open, ending the board's "self-imposed estrangement from the community." Apparently there had been some earlier negotiation between the students and the board; Theodore Newcomb, board chairman, had offered to allow five students to make five-minute presentations each, but the students rejected this offer. In response to the walk-in, the trustees adjourned their meeting. President Dixon and some other members of the board remained to hear statements read by two students. As remaining board members left the room, students took their places at the table and unanimously approved a motion concerning South Africa. President Dixon stayed to debate with students while the board reconvened in another building. After final adjournment four board members, including Newcomb, talked with students for several hours. Although President Dixon made clear his irritation with the intrusion, he asked the deans to designate three students and three faculty members to sit with three trustees on an "institutional task force" to consider the issues raised by the walk-in. As a convenience to the trustees, the task force held its first meeting in Boston. Since then students have taken other institutional decisions to themselves, temporarily closing the college's Behavioral Research Laboratory because it is financed partly by a Defense Department contract and, presumably as a gesture of protest, conducting a "nude-in" at the swimming pool.

These attitudes, I believe, are the weight-bearing walls of the Antioch edifice—and of similar dwellings throughout the country. Here is a society committed to freedom, creativity, intellectuality, introspection, and individual choice. More social virtues such as restraint, loyalty, order, considerateness, and due process are pushed much further down in the order of priorities. Student observers were consistently impressed with Antiochians' articulateness and their willingness to talk analytically and candidly about themselves and about an extraordinary range of other topics. Yet they felt these encounters usually left little residue of personal attachment or concern. Students go their own ways, look out for their own needs, ally themselves with others cautiously, knowing the alliance will soon disband. Students must find Antioch comfortable, a relief after the thousand petty obligations of a more organized society. Yet they acknowledge loneliness and anxiety. They seek the sometimes violent instrument of drugs and group dynamics to open themselves to others and themselves. Even love affairs are often built on the understanding that three months will bring a new season and who knows what sort of people we will be then? If standard American society, with its formal groups and obligations, proves often to be alienating, this alternate culture, disparaging forms, may turn out to be isolating.

This dissident subculture is not divorced from the American superculture. The students come from high schools where they distinguished themselves as scholars, if not as athletes or social movers. In academic matters they have mastered the system. They have come from the superculture and can return to it, with rewards waiting, whenever they decide to do so. To some extent the main culture's drives remain their drives and its rewards their rewards. When they violate its injunctions, they are liable to suffer its guilt.

But the defection from standard American culture is deep. The Vietnam war, students say, could not have continued and grown if Americans had not emptied themselves of choice, allowing their lives to be organized from without. The virtues of efficiency, self-control, deference to authority, hard work, and respect for social forms and legal process have proved inadequate, pinched, unable to give individual men a generous sense of life or the nation a moral foreign and domestic policy. Although students have been unable to build a nation on the virtues they advance as alternatives, they have built subcultures on these virtues. We may have doubts about the high place given to self-determination, pleasure, creativity, impulse, free-ranging curiosity, introspection, and immediate action, but we must respect this cluster of values as a contestant that may rout the more austere virtues that formerly went unchallenged. This

179

is the cause, the program of dissenting youth. While we have been belittling students for lacking a program, they may have gone far toward establishing it.

Notes

1. Jerry Rubin, in Berkeley *Barb,* February 2, 1968, quoted in Morton Levitt and Ben Rubenstein, "The Children's Crusade," *American Journal of Orthopsychiatry, 38:* 597-98 (1968).

Black Studies at
San Francisco State

John H. Bunzel

On college campuses black nationalism, still only in its earliest stages but emerging with considerable force and purpose, comes in many different sizes, shapes, and even colors. (It is no accident that in many quarters Negro is "out" and black is "in," or that the NAACP is sometimes referred to as the National Association for the Advancement of Certain People.) Yet one thing is clear: just as one finds black artists in the existing theater calling on one another to stop assimilating and imitating white standards, and instead to begin building cultural centers "where we can enjoy being free, open and black, where," as actress and director Barbara Ann Teer put it, "we can literally 'blow our minds' with blackness," so one also finds black students in our existing academic institutions demanding a program of black studies—one that will not only lead to the affirmation of their own identity and self-esteem, but will recognize the new needs of the black community and thereby help to define the concept of black consciousness. Black power, black nationalism, a black society, whatever meaning these terms will have for American society in the years ahead, the curricular idea of black studies will become the principal means by which black students will press their claim for a black educational renaissance in colleges and universities.

It is still too early to tell how the demand for black studies will ultimately be incorporated into different undergraduate instruc-

181

tional programs, but the idea itself represents a formidable problem for American educators. The concept of black studies, at least on many campuses, is as much a political consideration as an educational one. At San Francisco State College the demand for inclusion of black studies in the curriculum has capitalized on an atmosphere of student militancy, black and white, real and potential. One of the reasons the blacks did not participate in a sit-in demonstration organized by the Mexican-American students (and supported in full force by Students for a Democratic Society) was that the president of the college had already appointed a man, chosen by the Black Students' Union, to develop and coordinate a black studies curriculum. The appointment of a black studies coordinator was made by the president alone, without the knowledge of, or consultation with, the vice president for academic affairs, the council of academic deans, or the faculty. The president, characteristically, was candid about what he had done: this college is going to explode, he said, if the blacks do not get what they want soon. (In the fall semester he had suspended four members of the Black Students' Union after they had pushed their way into the office of the campus newspaper and attacked the editor.) The man he had asked to be the coordinator of black studies had recently been fired from Howard University for what the *Negro Digest* called "his militant pro-black activities"; but, the president said, he had a Ph.D. in sociology from the University of Chicago and was anxious to come to San Francisco State. The president had not spoken with anyone in the sociology department about the appointment, because he felt he had to move quickly "if we are going to keep the lid on this place."

The president, John Summerskill, had reacted to what he felt to be a critical situation. His response was a political one, in the most practical and urgent sense of that term. He may very well have been right; no one will ever know. However, in terms of the acutely difficult academic problems involved in developing a curriculum of black studies and its implications for the educational program as a whole, his interest and concern was something less than visible. In point of fact, Summerskill was soon to resign and leave the college.

Many of the major universities in the United States have already taken steps toward developing their own form of black studies. At Yale a faculty-student committee has proposed the creation of an undergraduate major in Afro-American studies that, according to Robert A. Dahl, professor of political science, will involve "an interdisciplinary approach to studying the experience and conditions of people of African ancestry in Africa and the New World." Students would be provided a broad view of the African experience, but would be required to concentrate on one of the relevant disciplines by way of enlightening their understanding and knowledge of the cultural, economic, political, social, artistic, and historical experiences of Africans and Afro-Americans. Beginning in September 1969 Harvard offered a new full-year course in "The Afro-American Experience" and is considering a degree-granting program in Afro-American studies for the future. The course began with the African background and the Negro experience in American history through 1945 and in the second semester considered issues of race relations, psychology, civil rights, housing, employment, and education from 1945 to the present. The course was taught by a faculty group of four, headed by Frank Freidel, professor of American history and biographer of Franklin D. Roosevelt. As a social science offering the course is comparable to the introduction to Western civilization. Parallel to this course, Harvard's Institute of Politics of the John F. Kennedy School of Government offered a series of lectures on the Afro-American experience by visiting scholars, required of students taking the course and open to others. In addition, the Association of African and Afro-American Students offered a series of films and television tapes.

Other colleges and universities around the country are similarly considering the direction of their program of black studies. The problems to be resolved are difficult, but they are significantly different depending on the institution involved. An Ivy League university, for example, will be very much concerned with the academic substance and soundness of any proposed black studies curriculum. Given its educational tradition and philosophy, the heavy

183

emphasis on research among its faculty, and the particular undergraduate constituency it attracts and admits (virtually no underclass minorities of the slums), a Yale or a Harvard can insist on and expect a considerable measure of intellectual discipline in all of its academic programs. Or consider a university such as Stanford. Comfortably located in the white suburban area of Palo Alto, it has little or no sustained involvement with the poverty environment in general (San Francisco-Oakland) or the core city minorities in particular, and therefore has not had to deal with the problem of large numbers of militant blacks renouncing not only the normal curricular offerings, but their whole college experience for being totally irrelevant to their own perceived needs and the needs of the larger black community.

The way a college or university approaches the problems of its minority students will depend in part on the view it holds of its mission as an academic institution. Thus, a black studies program geared primarily to the needs of black students will follow one way if it is designed primarily to develop future academicians, but will move in a very different direction and at a very different pace if its major purpose is to equip and train its students to present the black perspective when they return to the black community to help transform it.

San Francisco State College, a microcosm of the diverse and polyglot urban and suburban society of the Bay area, has seen more and more of its energy in the past few years converge on the needs and demands of its black students. It may be illuminating, therefore, to consider the recent proposal for a department of black studies in what has generously been designated "this tumultuous educational scene."

The academic year 1965-1966 has been called the year of the student revolution at San Francisco State, for it was during this year that changes in the attitudes of a small but influential number of students were consolidated and expressed in new functions of student government and new forms of faculty involvement. The most

184

important of the Associated Students' programs were channeled into three major activities: 1) the experimental college, which offered a diversity of courses never before seen in a college bulletin; 2) the community involvement program, which placed students in neighborhoods throughout the city to help support them in their efforts to work in the communities, principally the ghettos and slums; and 3) the tutorial program, which concentrated on helping children learn to read, to do arithmetic, and to want to stay in school. The programs were regarded as successful, and in the words of a later report, "The experience was earned, the price was paid, and our point was made, the point being that students on this campus wanted forms of education that the institution was not providing." It was the same point that would be made over and over again, reflecting the growing disaffection among black and other minorities on the campus.

In the summer of 1966 the Black Students' Union (BSU) emerged and almost immediately became a major force in the student government. (It should be kept in mind that out of a total college enrollment of 18,000 a good turnout for student government elections each spring is about 3,000-4,000. One other point worth mentioning: the annual budget of the Associated Students, derived from student fees, is more than $300,000.) During the next year it turned its attention to the educational problem of black and other minority students on the campus, which they saw in its broadest terms as the problem of relevance, estrangement, and identity. The high dropout rate, low grades, and general lack of motivation among large numbers of these students was due, they said, not only to a general feeling of separateness, but to the more compelling fact that education from kindergarten through college under the authority of the white community fails to focus on subject matter that is germane to the life experiences of the people in the minority community. The charge was repeatedly made that black and other minority students have little opportunity to place themselves in an identifiable historical and personal context in the traditional curriculum. Disregarding the question of its intellectual worth and value, we can realize that some of the perceptions and feelings of a leader of the BSU on why the present college curriculum is inadequate are revealing:

> One black student told us of sitting in an anthropology class for an entire semester and being interested in the class on only two occasions —once when the instructor offered a lecture on the Negro in America, and again when there was a lecture on Africa.
>
> Few black students are really interested in the western, "classical" music which characterized entire departments of music. Black students have no fundamental cultural understanding of western music. And since a part of many beginning music classes is spent instructing students that the only legitimate music is that of Beethoven, Mozart, Stravinsky, etc., this is seen as a denial of black students themselves. For example, a black student interested in music theory spent his first semester arguing with his instructor for the legitimacy of black musicians Charles Parker and John Coltrane. He lost the argument by receiving a "D" grade and is now out of college.
>
> Black people are not western: they are "westernized," made to be western. So basically their psychology is not Freudian, Adlerian, or Jungian, only so far as they have accepted westernization. Students find themselves enchanted by the schools of psychology, but as they probe deeper they find less and less in an association with their lives. Other black students pretend they can relate to western psychology by "becoming" Freudian. They psyche themselves out as we say, by trying to describe manifestations of every desire by description directly from the textbook.
>
> When black students begin to describe themselves in real situations, they are at times put down. A black woman student wrote a paper on Marxism and alienation in which she said she could not be alienated from a society of which she had never been a part. She had recently joined the Black Students' Union. The instructor attacked the student's basis of thought and gave her a low grade. She soon afterwards had a nervous collapse and has been out of the school for more than a year.

As perceived by the BSU their educational problem at San Francisco State is clear: they read white literature, study white families, analyze white music, survey white civilizations, examine white cultures, probe white psychologies. In a word the college curriculum is white culture-bound.

To remedy the situation, which in concrete terms meant attracting the interest and enthusiasm of the black student, the BSU wanted to develop a black curriculum. The black arts and culture series was instituted in the fall semester of 1966 as a part of the experimental college. The purpose was to introduce a positive focus on the life experiences of black people in America. Classes in the series covered the areas of history, law, psychology, humanities, social science, and dance. One year later the first black studies were enacted, with a total of eleven classes for which thirty-three units of college credit were given. Several hundred students, black and white, enrolled in the courses, which were taught on a voluntary or part-time basis either by members of the faculty or graduate students sympathetic to the program. Among the classes listed in the black studies program for the spring semester of 1968 were the following: Anthropology: Historical Development of Afro-American Studies; Dramatic Arts: Improvisations in Blackness; Education: Miseducation of the Negro; English: Modern African Thought and Literature; History: Ancient Black History; Psychology: Workshop in the Psychology of, by and for Black People; Sociology: Sociology of Black Oppression.

The improvisation of a black curriculum during the past two years at San Francisco State has reflected a growing feeling among members of the faculty and student body that educational innovation starting at the college level be given a chance to remedy the perceived ills of the past and create a model for other levels of education as well. By the end of the 1967-1968 academic year it was taken for granted that there would be a black studies program. The question was no longer whether it would happen, but what direction it would take and how the administration, faculty, and students would choose to react.

Meanwhile, the special coordinator of black studies, Nathan Hare, had circulated a proposal for a degree-granting department

187

of black studies that deserves careful study. The document was his alone, and his particular angle of vision, indeed his basic assumptions and attitudes, are important in interpreting it. He has been described as a man seething with anger about the path of Negro leadership, the duplicity of whites, and the fallibility of many Negroes who "follow" both. A sample of his remarks made in a speech at Stanford University does not belie the description:

> I had expected to speak to a black audience. You can build a wall a mile high, but white people will always climb up and peer over at what you're doing. [He added that he was glad white students were interested in black culture and history, in spite of the environment of the "white brainwashing factory," the university.]
>
> The bourgeois nationalists (among pre-Civil War black power groups) were more interested in personal gain and mobility within their group than freeing the slaves. The main difference between them and the revolutionaries was in their outlook on the world in which they lived. The revolutionaries had lost faith in the routine means of righting wrong. They were crippled, though, by a feeling of power-lessness against the white power structure. It's like today. They say we are too few to fight. We should vote. But I can kill 20 [white] men. I can cut one's throat, shoot another, drop a hand grenade in the middle of a whole bunch. I get only a single vote, and that's between the lesser of two evils.
>
> [On white historians] It is anachronistic for white men to teach black history to black militant students. The white man is unqualified to teach black history because he does not understand it.
>
> [On black historians] Black people must declare void what the white slave masters have written and must begin to write their own history and direct their destiny. Black historians, presenting other than the white viewpoint, are forced into copious footnoting and must accept the conventions of the white academic overlords in order to make our history valid and get it published in white journals.
>
> [On the draft] I was asked if I am an American first or a Negro first; I said I'm a black man first and not an American at all. Since most Americans do not consider me an American, I see no reason to fight for them. I said that before it was fashionable. I did serve six months

in the Army, but that was in peacetime. And I said I couldn't fight for them, and if I did I would shoot as much as possible at the whites around me.

I don't believe in absolutes, so I do not categorically reject all white men, only 99 and 44/100% of them.

The importance of Hare's pronouncements is not that they are angry or bitterly anti-white. This, after all, is the standard militant black rhetoric today that derives its own satisfaction in constantly putting down whitey, including those who have a hunger for humiliation. What is important is that they provide a backdrop against which his conceptual proposal for a department of black studies can be more clearly understood and evaluated in terms of its basic rationale and philosophy.

Hare acknowledges at the outset that the whole idea of black studies is "more far-reaching than appears on the surface." His conversations with academicians across the country on the education of black Americans leave no doubt in his mind that even those who have accepted the idea of black studies do not fully understand its need. "They see the goal as the mere blackening of white courses, in varying number and degree," he writes. "They omit in their program the key component of community involvement and collective stimulation." Their program is individualistic, aimed at "rehabilitating" individual students by means of pride in culture, racial contributions generally, and regenerated dignity and self-esteem. "They fail to see that the springboard for all of this is an animated communalism aimed at a black educational renaissance." Thus many well-intentioned efforts, Hare says, are doomed to inevitable failure. "They comprise piecemeal programs that, being imported, are based on an external perspective," Hare's document continues. Put simply, they are white, not black.

Nor will Hare accept any form of tokenism. He cites the example of an eminent Negro professor who proposed increasing drastically the ratio of black—"by which he meant 'Negro,' " Hare adds—students and professors. "The students for the most part would be admitted with the expectation that, excepting those salvaged by tuto-

189

rial efforts presently in vogue, they would eventually flunk out, the merrier for having acquired 'at least some college.' " This approach, Hare says, is not the answer to the problem. Although he is willing to "endorse the professor's suggestion in fact though not in theory insofar as to do otherwise would appear to condone current tokenism," he dismisses the approach on the grounds that it may be used "to appease the black community while avoiding genuine solutions."

When a representative from a foundation proposed giving full financial assistance to the "talented tenth" and hiring black persons to recruit such students and inform them of the availability of such aid, Hare responded that this is only slightly better than providing no aid at all. "A talented-tenth approach is largely superfluous to the educational needs of the black race as a whole," Hare writes. "Talented-tenth students, for whatever reason, have escaped the programmed educational maladjustment of the black race, just as some trees survive the flames of a forest fire." Such a program, "though noble on the surface, offers super-tokenism at best, but neglects the important ingredient of motivation growing out of collective community involvement. It is individualistic in its orientation and only indirectly, therefore, of collective consequence."

Of concern to many members of the faculty and student body at San Francisco State is the question of separatism, specifically, will a department of black studies result in a college within a college? Hare's comments deserve to be quoted in full:

> Even if it be so that black studies would ring more separatist in tone than Latin American studies, and the like, this is not the issue. The question of separatism is, like integrationism, in this regard essentially irrelevant. The goal is the *elevation* of a people by means of one important escalator—education. Separatism and integrationism are possible approaches to that end; they lose their effectiveness when, swayed by dogmatic absolutism, they become ends in themselves. It will be an irony of recorded history that "integration" was used in the second half of this century to hold the black race down just as segregation was so instituted in the first half. Integration, particularly in the token way in which it has been practiced up to now and the neo-

190

tokenist manner now emerging, elevates individual members of a group, but paradoxically, in plucking many of the most promising members from a group while failing to alter the lot of the group as a whole, weakens the collective thrust which the group might otherwise muster.

A related question is whether or not white students would be admitted into the program. The answer, Hare writes, "must be ambivalent inasmuch as the program has to be aimed primarily at the black student, particularly in its motivational activities involving the black community." Hare is concerned that white students will flood black studies courses.

> One way to draw white students off (and/or care for the surplus) is for existing departments to increase their offerings in blackness as they are doing now under the guise of "dark" (or, as sociologists say, "color-compatible") courses. This would probably result in greater benefit to the white students' needs anyway and most certainly would offset the apparent sense of threat in the minds of conventional departments.

Hare then makes an important admission:

> It may be necessary eventually to distinguish black education for blacks and black education for whites. There is no insurmountable incompatibility or mutual exclusiveness between black studies and ethnic group courses in other departments. Indeed they are easily reinforcing and could make a major contribution to better "race relations" or as politicians are fond of saying now, "the effort to save the nation" in decades ahead.

In a section of the proposal called "Redefinition of Standards" Hare offers some singular observations. He begins by saying that current standards evolved in large part from a need to restrict the overflow of recruits—what he calls "the principle of exclusion"—into existing professional niches.

> This gave rise to occasionally ludicrous requirements. The late social theorist, Thorstein Veblen, author of *Theory of the Leisure Class,* might hold that the liberal arts approach grew out of the leisure

191

class mentality, where it was prestigious to be non-productive and to waste time and effort in useless endeavor. Hence footnoting minutiae and the like. When middle class aspirants began to emulate these codes, the principle of exclusion evolved. However, now we are faced with the educational enticement of a group conditioned by way of the cake of time and custom to being excluded. How do we transform them into an included people? For example, a law school graduate with high honors might fail the "bar" exam (pun intended) because of political views, or fail the oral exam for teacher certification because of an unpopular approach to teaching. . . . Or pass everything required except the "language" exam. It is widely known that languages studied for graduate degrees are quickly almost totally forgotten and are rarely of any use after graduation. Much of the motivation for the retention of this and even more useless requirements apparently stems from the "leisure class" origin of the "liberal arts" approach where, as Thorstein Veblen explains, prestige was attributed to "non-productive" or wasteful useless endeavor.

What Hare is saying is that requirements were devised "to serve the functions of exclusivity rather than recruitment" and that now "we are facing the necessity for collective recruitment from a group victimized as a group in the past by racist policies of exclusion from the educational escalator." The two most "salient qualifications" for professorial rank today are a Ph.D. "and a string of 'scholarly' publications," and Hare wants the freedom "to depart from those criteria without risking the suspicion of 'lowering standards.' " That the Ph.D. is not necessarily synonymous with teaching effectiveness "is accepted by most persons confronted with the question," he says. Less understood is the question of publication.

Consider two candidates for a position in history, one qualified á la conventional standards, the other not. Never mind the fact that articles outside the liberal-moderate perspective have slim chances of seeing the light of day in "objective" scholarly journals. More ludicrous is the fact that the black historian, in adhering to the tradition of "footnoting" is placed in the unenviable position of having to footnote white slave master historians or historians published by a slave-holding society in order to document his work on the slavery era.

192

When it comes to recruiting a faculty, Hare believes that a black studies program would want to redefine the notion of a qualified professor "by honoring teaching effectiveness and enthusiasm more than qualities determined by degrees held and other quantifiable 'credentials.'" Is there to be a role for the white professor? "Their participation at least during the early stages of the program, must be cautious and minimal," Hare writes. He admits, however, that the impracticality of recruiting a sufficient number of black professors may force a relaxation of this principle. But on one point there is no compromising: "Any white professors involved in the program would have to be black in spirit in order to last. The same is true for 'Negro' professors."

Central to Hare's whole proposal is the component of community involvement. To bring about this development, it is necessary "to inspire and sustain a sense of collective destiny as a people and a consciousness of the value of education in a technological society. A cultural base, acting as a leverage for other aspects of black ego development and academic unit, must accordingly be spawned and secured." Students and other interested parties "will be organized into black cultural councils which will sponsor cultural affairs (art, dance, drama, etc.) in the black community and establish black holidays, festivities, and celebrations." For example, a black winter break could begin on February 21, the day they shot Malcolm X, run past George Washington's birthday and end with February 23, the birthday of the late black scholar, W. E. B. DuBois. "This," Hare says, "could approximate the Jewish Yom Kippur." There are many other suggestions: black information centers "to increase communication, interpersonal contact, knowledge and sociopolitical awareness"; a black community press, put together by "members of black current events clubs and students taking courses in black journalism"; a bureau of black education "to provide black scholars mutual aid and stimulation, and to organize black textbook and syllabi writing corps."

Finally, Hare outlines his plan for the black studies curriculum. The initiation of the program is to be accomplished in two stages:

phase 1, involving the pulling together of some of the currently experimental courses into a new department; and phase 2, the inauguration of a major "consisting of an integrated body of black courses revolving around core courses such as black history, black psychology, black arts, and the social sciences" (See Table 1). In addition, as part of the course requirements, there will be student

Table 1.
Tentative Black Studies Major for Fall, 1969

CORE COURSES	UNITS
Black History	4
Black Psychology	4
Survey of Sciences: Method & History	4
Black Arts and Humanities	4
	16 units
BLACK ARTS CONCENTRATION	
The Literature of Blackness	4
Black Writers Workshop	4
Black Intellectuals	4
Black Fiction	4
Black Poetry	4
Black Drama	4
The Painting of Blackness	4
The Music of Blackness	4
The Sculpture of Blackness	4
	36 units
BEHAVIORAL AND SOCIAL SCIENCES CONCENTRATION	
Black Politics	4
Sociology of Blackness	4
Economics of the Black Community	4
The Geography of Blackness	4
Social Organization of Blackness	4
Development of Black Leadership	4
Demography of Blackness	4
Black Counseling	4
Black Consciousness and the International Community	4
	36 units

field work in the black community, involving an effort to transform the community while educating and training the student. (This, Hare observes, is the key ingredient which Yale's program omits.) Although the black studies program "would not preclude electives outside the black curriculum, even for majors, it would seek to care for a wide range of academic training in the humanities, the social and behavioral sciences." Most persons enrolled in black studies courses would not be majors.

Hare says graduates could become probation officers, case workers, poverty workers, or enter graduate or professional schools in preparation for careers as lawyers, social workers, teachers, scholars, professors, research scientists, businessmen, and administrators. "They would, other things being equal—we feel certain—quickly emerge, and predominate in the upper echelons of the black community," Hare concludes.

The specific content of the curriculum as proposed by Hare can be found in his proposal. "Although much of it is expressive" (geared to ego-identity building, etc.), Hare concludes, "the utilitarian function has by no means been omitted. . . . The black race woefully needs concrete skills . . . both for individual mobility and community development."

The proposal will get a full hearing before an academic program of black studies is recommended for adoption at San Francisco State and sent to the State College Board of Trustees for its final approval. The range of opinion and reaction will be wide, from those who see no reason to make special curricular provisions for black students to those who believe that whites are not competent to pass judgment on an educational program for blacks. Some members of the faculty will rush to support whatever the most militant black students want simply to demonstrate that they are not overly anxious about militant black students. Others will oppose black studies with the question: why not a department of Jewish (or Indian or Chinese or Mexican-American) studies? Still others will propose alternate plans, for example, that existing academic departments increase the number of minorities on their teaching staffs and develop course offerings that will meet the different ethnic needs on the campus. Predictably, however, the great majority of the faculty will choose to be uninterested and uninvolved. They will have nothing to say.

Any proposed program of black studies will inevitably produce a flood of questions. The trouble is that dispassionate answers are difficult to come by. Perhaps the most that can be done, in keeping with the commitment of the academic community to the use of reason in the resolution of problems, is to suggest a number of issues that deserve consideration and analysis.

Not long ago the battle was fought to dissuade college admissions offices from requiring candidates to submit a photograph or to state his race or religion. In many colleges and universities the specific target was the so-called "quota system," which had a special application to Jews. Today the new liberal position is that Negroes must not only be identified but admitted to college by special quotas. Race and color are no longer to be ignored. At a number of universities militant students have demanded the admission of specific numbers of Negroes, which increasingly is being translated into quotas roughly equal to the proportion of Negroes in the total population of the locality or of the nation.

Daniel P. Moynihan, speaking for many who subscribe to the old liberal position, has warned that quotas for one group inevitably turn into formulas against another. "Let me be blunt. If ethnic quotas are to be imposed on American universities . . . Jews will be almost driven out. They are not 3 per cent of the population." (This, Moynihan said, would be a misfortune for Jews, but a disaster to the nation.) Undergraduates at Harvard enthusiastically endorsed ethnic representation, if not exactly quotas, on the faculty but had misgivings about applying the same principle to student enrollment. As Moynihan pointed out, if such quotas were to be applied, seven out of eight Jewish undergraduates would have to leave, and much the same exodus would be required of Japanese and Chinese Americans. "America," Moynihan said, "has known enough of anti-Semitism and anti-Oriental feeling to be wary of opening that box again."

196

Virtually everyone is agreed that special efforts should be made to increase the enrollment of Negro students in our colleges and universities. The problem is to find a way to open the doors "without going from the assumption of color-blindness to the extreme of forcing on every institution quotas of racial and religious membership," Moynihan has said.

Many whites have not yet fully understood the psychological meaning and force of an issue that, to many blacks, is even more critical than white racism, namely, pride and personal identification. More than any other component of the racial question, it pervades every discussion of a black curriculum. Its importance and enormous power cannot be minimized. The fact is that black students do respond directly and positively to a black instructor. The relationship is clear, personal, and effective. It is a potent consideration, and it is at the heart of every argument in support of a department of black studies.

On another level of analysis, however, many in the academic community are concerned about its ultimate meaning and implication. At issue, at least for some, is the matter of standards. Is the color of a professor's skin more important than the substance of the course? The black studies coordinator at San Francisco State phoned the chairman of the political science department to inquire about a course in African Government and Politics scheduled for the fall semester. "What color is the instructor?" was his only question. "White," he was told. He was not interested in the fact that she was writing her Ph.D. dissertation in the area of African politics and had received her training under the supervision of a leading authority in African problems at the University of California. His single concern was color. Thus, a fundamental professional question is raised: is color the test of competence? It has only been recently that colleges and universities have succeeded in removing politics as a test for hiring and firing. Now is it to be color?

A department of black studies, it should be said, would make such questions unnecessary. All personnel in black studies would be black, with the sole and avowed purpose of concentrating on blackness.

197

At a time when educators throughout the United States are trying to devise new ways to reach their students on a more personal, individual basis, it is significant that Hare's proposal for a department of black studies is aimed at "collective stimulation"—that is, to get black students to stop thinking individualistically and to begin thinking collectively. Put another way, the black curriculum is not explicitly designed to encourage black students to develop qualities of independence, skepticism, and critical inquiry—to think for themselves—but rather to intensify the motivation and commitment of all who enroll in the program to return to the black community and translate everything to which they have been exposed into black leadership and black power. As a political program for community action it is not to be faulted. As an academic program, or, perhaps more properly, as a program in academic surroundings, it poses some different problems.

For those whose total educational philosophy and concern is contained in the penetrating nugget "Let them do their own thing," there will, of course, be no problems at all. Others, however, will have some questions. Will those who teach in the department of black studies be of the same political and ideological persuasion, or will efforts be made to recruit a black staff that purposely reflects different and opposing points of view? Would black studies hire a black undergraduate to teach one of its courses for credit? Will the department of black studies mirror the views of the Black Students' Union, thereby reinforcing the union's political goals and purposes on campus?

Hare has said: "Black people understand black problems better than anyone else. We are determined to solve our own problems and the important first step is education." Few will dispute the first half of the statement. There may be some question, however, as to what is meant by education. It is certainly not to be confused with indoctrination, any more than tales of heroism, white or black, can pass for genuine history. It is true that for many students in this country the history of man has too often been treated as though it "started in Athens and ended in California," with the Afro-American story simply left out. The question now is whether a department of black studies would substitute propaganda for omission, or, as some have said, new myths for old lies. For example, many highly respected historians view black history in the United States as a problem of deciding where and when the question of race or religion, or any particular characteristic or trait, has historical significance. Would this approach, this form of intellectual discipline, be acceptable to black studies? Would black studies look on a course in African history as an opportunity simply to venerate the great achievements of cultural forebears, or would it also lay stress on, for example, the historical fact that the more advanced African peoples and energetic leaders were often the very ones who sold other Africans to slave traders, thereby helping to bring about Negro slavery in America?

Or we may consider Hare's own book, *The Black Anglo-Saxon*.[1] Writing as a sociologist, he argues that black, would-be Anglo-Saxons are forgetting or denying their "Negroness." However, Professor Troy Duster, a social scientist at the University of California at Berkeley, points out that much of E. Franklin Frazier's scholarly life was spent documenting the fact that the Negro in the United States was stripped of almost every vestige of his African culture, and that his primary substantive culture is an American one. In discussing one type of black Anglo-Saxon Hare states that "their pathetic pursuit of white values is an effort to include their true personal and social identities." But, Duster asks, "Do Negroes really have a separate set of ethical and moral precepts, or separate standards for evaluating themselves and others? If so, what is the wellspring of this distinctly Negro culture if it is not that of the whites who brought Negroes to this country in the chains of slavery?" Would this intellectual position be fully recognized and discussed in a department of black studies? Would open and sharp disagreement over the nature and substance of an American Negro culture be encouraged?

Martin Luther Kilson, Jr., assistant professor of government at Harvard and advisor to Harvard's Afro-Americans, has asked some

199

pointed questions: "What community or segment of black peoples should be used as representatives of whatever the black experience is or has been? Should it be the Republic of Haiti where black power has been oppressive of the black masses? Or black fratricide in Nigeria? Or the black experience with 200 years of white racism in the United States?" Kilson does not hesitate to say that all men, black, white, yellow, and red, are capable of oppressive abuse of power without gaining from such experience any special will or capacity to rid human affairs of oppression. He concludes that "it is a common fallacy to believe that what is momentarily politically serviceable is *ipso facto* intellectually virtuous."

Epilog

Black Studies was a controversial issue at San Francisco State throughout the 1968 fall semester.[2] On September 13 the president announced that he had created a black studies department for which he hoped a curriculum, faculty, and the necessary funds would soon be forthcoming. But in the weeks and months that followed, the Black Students' Union repeatedly charged that "the racists in the administration have been and are destroying the whole concept of black studies" and that "all black student and third world student programs and achievements face extermination on this campus." The accusation was untrue, but that mattered little to those who were heady on the fare of black liberation and revolutionary bombast and for whom the real need was the dramaturgy and psychic release derived from a powerful symbolism. It was not long before black studies was caught up in the mythic language of black pride and identity, of "soul" needs, of black rage and violence. Passionate and explosively charged rhetoric, calculated to mobilize sentiments and generate emotive responses, obscured the elements of reality and made all the more difficult, if not impossible, any serious examination of the proposed black studies program, including consideration of curriculum options and outcomes. In early November, at the invitation of the BSU, Stokely Carmichael came on campus and told an audience of over 800 third world students that "white people have the luxury of being revolutionary, but for us it is a necessity." In helping to give cohesion and direction to the impending strike, he made it clear that "when you are talking about black studies you are not talking about course content, you are talking about methodology and ideology." For someone like myself (and many others on the faculty), who has been committed for three or four years to the development of a program of ethnic studies at San Francisco State, it was not difficult to see that the concern for some measure of academic substance and integrity had long since been swept away in the flood of symbolic arguments seeking symbolic solutions.

There was great pressure to adopt the program of black studies authored by Nathan Hare, although 95 per cent of the faculty had neither seen it nor knew anything of its character and content. So pervasive was the sense of urgency and the fear of an imminent explosion on campus that the paramount thought was to get Hare's curriculum through the necessary committees as rapidly as possible. There was no time (or, as some preferred to say, it was not the time) to be concerned with its quality or direction.

In late October the Undergraduate Curriculum and Instructional Policies committees met jointly to consider for the first and only time Hare's concept of black studies. The members of the two committees sat around a rectangular table. Standing directly behind them two and three deep were members of the Black Students' Union who had packed the room to give visible evidence of their strength in numbers. The final draft of the proposed curriculum was given particular attention (see Table 2).

Members of the two committees spent most of the time asking Hare to explain certain features of the curriculum. "What is black statistics?" "Will only black people be hired to teach in the department of black studies?" "Will white students be admitted into the program?" In little more than an hour and a half they completed their work, quickly voted support of the black studies proposal (the Dean of Academic Planning abstained), and forwarded it to the Academic Senate with the recommendation that it be adopted im-

Table 2.

Proposal for a Department of Black Studies

MAJOR PATTERN

12 units	(core, required)
24 units	(electives in area of concentration)
9 units	(electives from throughout the college, on advisement)

45 units   total

CORE COURSES   UNITS

Black Studies 601	Black History	3
Black Studies 602	Black Psychology	3
Black Studies 603	Survey of Sciences: Method & History	3
Black Studies 604	Black Arts and Humanities	3

                                                                                 12 units

Clarification of number and types of electives, if any, under the proposed degree program including special options:

BLACK ARTS CONCENTRATION

Black Studies 605	The Literature of Blackness	3
Black Studies 606	Black Writers Workshop	6*
Black Studies 607	Black Intellectuals	3
Black Studies 608	Black Fiction	3
Black Studies 609	Black Poetry	3
Black Studies 610	The Painting of Blackness	3
Black Studies 611	The Music of Blackness	3
Black Studies 612	Sculpture of Blackness	3
Black Studies 613	Black Radio, Television, Film	3
Black Studies 614	Black Journalism	6*
Black Studies 615	Black Oratory	6*
Black Studies 616	Black Philosophy	3
Black Studies 617	Black Classics	3

                                                                                 48 units

BEHAVIORAL AND SOCIAL SCIENCES CONCENTRATION

Black Studies 618	Black Politics	6*
Black Studies 619	Sociology of Blackness	6*
Black Studies 620	Economics of the Black Community	6*
Black Studies 621	The Geography of Blackness	3
Black Studies 622	Social Organization of Blackness	6*
Black Studies 623	Development of Black Leadership	6*
Black Studies 624	Demography of Blackness	3
Black Studies 625	Black Counseling	6*
Black Studies 626	Black Nationalism and the International Community	3

Table 2.—Continued

Black Studies 627	The Anthropology of Blackness	6*
Black Studies 628	Black Consciousness	3
Black Studies 629	Black Statistics: Survey & Method	6*
Black Studies 630	Black Economic Workshop	6*
Black Studies 631	Black Political Workshop	6*
		72 units

Recommended patterns of electives in both emphases will be available for guidance.

* Field work and/or off-campus work required.

mediately. There were no surprises. The two faculty committees charged with the responsibility of examining and thereby giving collegewide approval to new academic programs had officially met and deliberated. The scenario had played out.

But at what cost? A number of profoundly important questions having to do with the planning of any black studies program were not considered. For example, a fundamental assumption was made from the outset and virtually accepted without challenge or debate —namely, that if the college is creating a department of black studies, it should place the task in the hands of blacks or, perhaps more exactly, in the hands of black studies specialists who are black. There is a deceptive simplicity in this argument which obscures a basic fallacy. A college or university never places the task of creating a new department (or any significant administrative or academic entity) solely in the hands of those who advocate its creation. The reasons are eminently sound: every self-respecting institution of higher learning recognizes that although there are segments of the academic community that pursue their specialized interests, there is the even more compelling concept of community which must mean that certain values and concerns are held in common. There is, in other words, the larger collegiate reality and distinctness-of-being of which everyone is part and to whose standards of excellence and to whose long-established expectations about white racism. What we want is very simple: we want to be left alone to do our own thing."

intellectual and administrative rigor and clarity they are presumed to be committed.

But there is still another and perhaps even more significant consideration implicit in the original proposition which deserves some attention. Black studies, it is argued, makes a unique claim for acceptance, with perhaps only negligible review, because only blacks can judge the proposals of blacks or because black students can relate only to black teachers. Thus, the argument runs, only black teachers or black specialists can legitimately propose black studies courses. It should be made clear that to state these arguments is neither to validate nor invalidate them out of hand. The point is that at San Francisco State, unlike many other colleges and universities presently considering black studies, these arguments were never seriously examined in any collegewide faculty review committee. For example, no discussion was ever focused on the critical premise that being black is not in itself an absolute qualification for being an expert, any more than being white is in itself a qualification for being an expert. Nor was there any attempt to separate the different educational contexts in which being black might have meaning. A black statistician cannot by definition be a more expert statistician qua statistician than a yellow or white statistician. Either the college or university is a single community with standards of scholarship that make black statistics as repugnant as Lysenkoist biology or it begins a piecemeal transformation into a cockpit of ideologs and fanatics who have abandoned the search for knowledge. The same is true of a black biologist, physicist, or chemist. However, in every one of these and other instances, a black teacher who is a biologist or physicist will presumably be able to relate significantly better to black students than a white biologist or physicist. But even this last point might need to be qualified: presumably black teachers relate significantly better to black students when blackness is the prime subject matter. Acceptance of any broader principle might mean that the college would have to provide a black and a white teacher for every course in every department on the grounds that to do otherwise would be to

204

disadvantage black students. Not only is such a policy pragmatically impossible, but many if not all observers would regard it as pedagogically, philosophically, and politically indefensible.

Among the ten demands of the BSU for which the members went on strike in November (they were all declared to be "not negotiable"), five related specifically to black studies:

1. That all black studies courses being taught through various other departments immediately become part of the black studies department and that all the instructors in this department receive full-time pay.
2. That Nathan Hare, acting chairman of the black studies department, receive a full professorship and a comparable salary according to his qualifications.[3]
3. That there be a department of black studies granting a bachelor's degree in black studies; that the black studies department, chairman, faculty, and staff have the sole power to hire faculty and control and determine the destiny of its department.
4. That twenty fulltime teaching positions be allocated to the department of black studies.
5. That all black students wishing so be admitted to the program in the fall of 1969.

All the demands cannot be discussed in this paper. However, the third one above is one of the most important in that it raises some serious and difficult questions. The nub of the issue is the insistence that those in black studies department have the "sole power" to run it in any way they choose—in short, the kind of autonomy and control not given to any other department in the college. At San Francisco State, departments enjoy a high degree of independence, but their decisions are subject to review by appropriate faculty bodies and administrative personnel. Furthermore, the college and all of its departments are legally responsible to the Office of the Chancellor, the Board of Trustees, and the California legislature. And there's the rub, at least so far as the militant blacks are concerned. As one of their spokesmen on campus put it, "That's the white power structure, and all it means is more white double talk and white racism. What we want is very simple: we want to be left alone to do our own thing."

There is no way of knowing how this demand and all the other will be settled. Perhaps the department of black studies will be grafted onto the rest of the educational program with no difficulty at all. Perhaps it will take its place with the other departments at San Francisco State, which is to say separate but equal but not "more separate" or "more equal" than others. Perhaps the new curriculum, which many regard as essentially one course in blackness flattened out into seventy-two units, will develop into a highly respected degree program. Many people are hoping. But no one is placing any bets.

Black studies is a new venture. One would have thought it plausible, therefore, to suppose that a number of different ideas would have been given at least cursory attention since the forms of organization, methods of analysis, curricular possibilities, and the like are still very much in the process of discovery. But on this subject the political environment at San Francisco State had already been polarized: one either supported in its entirety the specific proposal as outlined in these pages, which reflected essentially the views of one man working alone or one was summarily defined and dismissed as an "enemy" of black studies. It was as if the academic universe had been divided into the "moral" and the "perverse." It should have been possible in principle to accept the notion that alternatives are feasible and that criticism and skepticism are both legitimate and essential in the search for the most viable option. The same principle should apply to specialists in black studies. It may be unfortunate though it is still true that the credentials of such specialists are not as readily identifiable as those of scholars in other well-established fields. All of us must learn to live with this uncertainty without seeing it as the malevolent workings of a power-crazed and intransigent racist majority.

Notes

1. Nathan Hare, *The Black Anglo-Saxon* (New York: Marzani and Munsell, 1965).

2. In the first week of the semester the vice-president for academic affairs at San Francisco State called me into his office to tell me that, as a consequence of my having writen "Black Studies at San Francisco State," I was now a target of the militant blacks on campus. (It had circulated dittoed coppies to a number of my colleagues on the faculty, including Nathan Hare, for their comments and criticisms.) On September 25 the campus newspaper printed a long essay entitled "BSU States Its Philosophy, Goals, and Achievements" in which it was stated that "Dr. Bunzel's article was the cause of the Black Studies Department losing grants totalling up to a half-million dollars. This money would have been used to provide jobs and grants for Black students, and at the same time as salaries for Black faculty." The statement, of course, was false and preposterous, not only because the article had not even been published yet (it was not to appear in print until November) but because there were no such funds to be lost, as members of the college administration, including the president, quietly assured me. It was not long thereafter that I heard myself being denounced as a "racist," a "faculty mandarin," and "a lackey of the CIA and the Democratic party." (I had been a member of the Kennedy delegation from California and had attended the Democratic National Convention in Chicago.)

3. Nathan Hare had been an assistant professor at Howard University and was appointed a lecturer at the salary of associate professor when he came to San Francisco State in the spring of 1968. Thus the demand that he be promoted to full professor was made only nine months after he joined the staff. Regarding this particular matter, three other points should be made: 1) promotion of a faculty member to another rank is the responsibility of the promotions committee; 2) at San Francisco State there is no necessary relationship beween the rank a faculty member holds and the administrative post to which he may be assigned; 3) at the present time there are at least eight departmental chairmen and one associate dean who have not attained the rank of full professor.

The Silent Vigil: A Student Nonviolent Demonstration

Eleanor C. Crocker and Maurine LaBarre

The recent proliferation of literature on adolescence contains numerous fragmented studies and theoretical discussions scantily substantiated by research. Rather than claiming prematurely some theoretical construct or relying too heavily on impressions necessarily colored by our own idiosyncracies, we have documented the events and ideas of a student demonstration from an ethnographic perspective, that is, the participants' own terms as far as possible.

This paper describes and analyzes the responses to the assassination of Dr. Martin Luther King, Jr., by students at Duke University, a small, predominantly white, private Southern university. Their reactions led to a silent vigil, during which 1,500 students gathered on the main quadrangle of the campus and for five days sat, studied, ate, and slept in dignified silence to dramatize their concerns for social and racial justice. The students directed and monitored the vigil with remarkable organization and self-discipline. The university crisis in conscience which this demonstration evoked stimulated many students to self-examination and resolution; awakened the faculty from its self-described "timid apathy"; and pressed the administration and trustees to escalate changes in communicating with students, faculty, and nonacademic employes. This demonstration was, to our knowledge, unique for its nonviolent nature and effectiveness.

North Carolina is in some respects a liberal state. In Durham, a small city of some 80,000 people about one-third of whom are Negro, race relations have been better than average for the South. Slightly more than half of the 5,000 undergraduate and 2,000 graduate students at Duke University come from within the geographic South. The first Negro undergraduate students were admitted in 1963; in 1968 there were about seventy-five American Negro students and one Negro faculty member. Numerous student organizations, notably religious groups, have long engaged in the usual altruistic programs, including volunteer work in poverty areas. There had been some student and faculty participation in the civil rights movement and anti-war demonstrations in the community, some reaching out and dialog between students at Duke and the Negro college in the city, but students had not been moved to demonstrate in large groups over any issue. The number of activists on campus was small.

The assassination of King and the outbreak of rioting, looting, and burning in American cities shocked, grieved, and frightened many of the students. A small group of campus leaders met to talk over what the students might do. "The energy and the motivation and the determination which lay behind the students' actions stemmed from their desire to demonstrate the good faith of the white community toward the black community," and from their belief that "we had the last opportunity we were likely to have to give the black community evidence that peaceful means could achieve results, and that violence was neither tenable nor necessary." "They did not believe that words alone were enough to convey their message in a meaningful, credible way, and throughout the day they sought for specifics, for deeds, and for immediate action that would dramatize the depth of their convictions."[1]

Various memorial actions were considered. It was finally decided to publish in the local paper a tribute to King, calling for racial justice, and to ask faculty members for signatures. The Friday after King's death it rained. The leaders expected that thirty, at the most one hundred students might come out for the canvass, but about three hundred turned up. They marched the mile from campus to the faculty residential section and made house-to-house visits to secure signatures for the newpaper memorial. The students also prepared a petition, requesting: 1) that the president of the university sign the newspaper memorial; 2) that he resign his university membership in a private, segregated country club; 3) that he press for the adoption of the federal minimum wage of $1.60 an hour for all nonacademic employees as soon as possible; and 4) that a study committee of faculty, students, and representatives of the workers be formed to work with the administration and board of trustees to help insure just settlement of problems. (These and other quotations not noted in references are from flyers, tape records of student discussions, interviews, and other documents.)

When the students brought this petition to the president's home on campus, he invited them in and suggested that three spokesman confer with him. Several hours of discussion led to a stalemate, the president being unwilling to make decisions under pressure and the students being unwilling to defer their requests. The students had not planned a sit-in, but when they were told they were welcome to stay, a group remained overnight, sleeping on the floor. As the administration said, students considered University House a university meeting place; the president's private living quarters were never invaded. During the night there was much discussion about what to do next. The student leaders displayed keen awareness of psychological factors in the situation and how they might influence the group's desire to reach a wise, objective, considered decision.

The next day the president conferred with administration officers and made an address at a memorial service for King. In the evening the students were informed that the president had become ill from exhaustion due to overwork and had been ordered into seclusion. The students were at first skeptical but subsequently wrote him a letter, which expressed concern and regret if their visit had injured his precarious health. Student leaders refused "to allow amoral institutions to trap good men. We must do something important now. We are nonviolent, but we will not be moved." Whereupon the group sang the old labor song "We will not be moved."

A rally was held Sunday on the main quadrangle. The group decided, in memory of King, to conduct an ongoing, round-the-clock demonstration which was to be nonviolent, sustained, and focused on pressing for improvement within the university community. The overall plan was "to maintain the educational process, by self-disciplined study and lectures on political, social-economic, and racial issues, and to attempt throughout to form a reasonable, working community on the quadrangle." The students prepared to sleep on the lawn, gathered blankets from the dorms, and borrowed sleeping bags and other necessities from faculty families. Faculty and student wives served a hot supper to 450 students. On Monday night more than 1,000 students slept out. Tuesday the number increased, despite the rain. By Wednesday 1,550 students, more than one-fourth the entire student body, were sitting in straight, and silent rows in front of the university chapel.

Over the weekend tension had mounted in the city. Eleven fires were reported, set at businesses owned by persons maintaining rental property in the poverty areas which black individuals and organizations had long and fruitlessly sought to have repaired in conformity with city housing ordinances. Rumors about the Ku Klux Klan persisted. A city curfew was announced. On the campus, however, all was quiet and orderly. By Monday night the city police withdrew, and the university police strolled the campus, "practically ignoring the student group."

Once the intent and tone of the vigil had been outlined, a spontaneous seemingly instantaneous organization developed. Ground rules were outlined:

1. Remember the national day of mourning.
2. Remember the sense of purpose—we are very serious.
3. No talking.
4. No eating except at group snack and at meal breaks.
5. No sunbathing.
6. No singing except at specified periods under the direction of the song leader.
7. No conversation with the spectators.
8. There should be no response to harassment.

> The monitors are in charge, so please listen to them. We will all remain seated on the ground except during the periods specified for short breaks.

As the student paper observed, the students "ran the demonstration like their daddy's business." Volunteer committees sprang up to handle food, bedding, announcements, a public address system, fund raising, etc. The students were seated in neat rows of fifty; monitors were assigned to the ends of each row to handle requests, calls for doctors for treatment of colds, fainting spells, and, when the weather improved, for sunburns and heat exhaustion; and to maintain patrol shifts during the night. The students occupied their time by silent meditation, study, and writing letters to families, friends, alumni, congressmen, senators, and political candidates. A strategy committee, composed of campus leaders and new leaders who emerged in this crisis, met often. All students were invited and urged to participate, so that everyone's opinion would be heard and decisions would be reached by consensus. During the breaks at each hour brief talks by students, faculty, and community supporters were broadcast. Students sang songs, "to keep up our spirits and let the campus hear us." "We Shall Overcome" was the theme song. Repeated pep talks reiterated the goals of the vigil and reaffirmed their commitment. "Here we are, cold, dirty, grubby, but we will stick it out. We know how important it is for us to be here and demonstrate our commitment and hope in this kind of action. None of us knew how difficult immediate, direct action would be, how many pressures there would be on those who ask for change."

The participants included those both to the right and to the left of the political center. The editor of the student paper, who labeled himself a Goldwaterite, said: "Some of the people whom even I consider reactionary were taking part." And one of the deans, who talked with many students, reported that "the overwhelming majority of the students—and these represented all segments of the student body—were sympathetic to the view that something dramatic needed to be done to show the good faith and determination of the white race to achieve quickly greater social justice and

212

equality. . . . While many students disagreed with the methods being used, and with some of the specific requests placed before the president, even those who disagreed were inclined to be tolerant toward the other students because they held the students' basic motivations in high regard."

The group sense of commitment to a moral cause acted as a tremendous pressure on other students. Some felt they were already demonstrating a commitment by their volunteer work in poverty areas. Some felt they could not risk academic penalties as their parents had made an investment in their education. Others were upset by the pressures of some of the converts, who accused them of being bigots and lacking in moral courage. A number sought counseling from the service set up by the YMCA and the divinity school or the student mental health service. A number joined for extraneous reasons, to keep company with a boyfriend or girlfriend or make new ones, or for "the kick" of sleeping out all night. Some were called for being "glory hogs." The leaders were concerned whether new recruits would "hold" when the going got really tough. One student leader familiar with confrontation tactics said, "I believed in the vigil and its principles and was engrossed in it; but I thought I could 'play it cool'; what got me was the songs, the feeling of the group." Whatever the nature of the stand, it was clear that almost no one was untouched by the demonstration.

On Tuesday the campus maids, janitors, and dining hall workers (with the exception of medical center workers) went on strike, encouraged by the students' stand. The students supported them with a boycott of the dining halls. This development, along with the increasing size of the vigil group, greatly increased the job of the food committee. The committee maintained a list of invitations for dinner in faculty homes and arranged catering services. A local black-owned restaurant provided several hundred hot chicken dinners each day at cost. Out of loyalty some nonparticipating students volunteered services in the campus cafeterias, so that students on a paid board basis or athletic scholarships could get their meals. Cleanup rules and squads for the dormitories were organized, so that complaints could not be made of violations of health regulations. Various campus groups contributed up to $300 each to the vigil and the strikers' fund.

The students did not know what the general faculty and administration reactions to the vigil would be, or whether they might be penalized or expelled. Although the participants missed classes, they never in any way interfered with administrative or teaching functions of the university, occupied buildings, or obstructed traffic. From the beginning a number of faculty were consulted, and increasingly individual faculty manifested interest and support. A faculty group issued a signed statement, assuring the students of their sympathy, concern, and support. Many faculty members cancelled classes; some taught classes on the quadrangle, and nearly all agreed to postpone quizzes and papers for that week. The divinity school was especially active in support; its faculty voted unanimously to forego their annual raises and contribute that money toward increasing the wages of the nonacademic workers. Rumors that fire-hoses might be used to disperse the vigil brought a pledge from this faculty group to form a human barrier if necessary to protect the students. Two new campus groups, the concerned faculty and the graduate students, formed organizations to support the vigil and work for more participation in university planning. On Wednesday the faculty of the law school joined the vigil as a body, marching from the law school to the quadrangle in the rain. The academic council, consisting of the chairman of each department plus elected faculty members, unanimously passed a resolution in support of the principles of the vigil.

Leaders of the Negro community visited the group on campus, made speeches, and sang songs to show their appreciation and support. They stated that the black community in Durham was watching the events on campus very closely, and that they felt the vigil had contributed toward keeping down vandalism and possible riots. "We were given heart," the students reported, "by those who came and said, 'If Dr. King were here, he would be proud of you.'" All but a few members of the student Afro-American Society abstained

214

from taking part in the vigil, doubting that it was militant enough to produce results. But of special significance to the students was a visit from a black activist, well known for skepticism of white liberals, who commended them for their stand, which he felt would have much meaning for Negroes and poor whites.

During these four days of the vigil in the absence of the president, who was in the hospital, no statement from the administration had been made to the students. The board of trustees had convened, and on Wednesday its chairman issued a statement:

1. The points in the student petition about the president were personal and would have to be taken up with him when he was able to return to his office.
2. A committee would be formed, as the president had discussed with students earlier, but its scope and composition would be left entirely to the president and would not be established until his return.
3. Private educational institutions had been given an extension of time for meeting federal minimum wage standards until July 1971. The university had already instituted plans for gradual increases in wages. Now the trustees announced that non-academic wages would be raised to the federal minimum by July 1969, an acceleration of about eighteen months from the previous schedule. (The issue of collective bargaining was largely avoided in this statement.)

After this announcement the chairman of the board of trustees found himself clasping hands with the students and swaying to the words of "We Shall Overcome."

The vigil was moved out of the rain into the campus auditorium, and the students were joined by the entire academic council. Discussion and dissent about what to do next went on far into the night. Some students wanted to remain on the quadrangle, some to move into the administration building, some to keep a token vigil and continue pressure in other ways, and some to abandon the vigil. Some were concerned lest their efforts be nullified by delaying tactics and were worried about their academic status, as the examination

215

period was approaching. The major focus of concern for students and faculty had become support of the right of the nonacademic employes to collective bargaining. One of the students' questions was "whether they could trust the moral intent of the trustees." For a while the movement looked so divided that some thought it would not last the night. After nearly six hours the group decided to get some rest and resume in the morning. They resumed discussion at 8:30 a.m. and reached a decision by 10:30. As one student put it, "No one knows quite how but we came out all in one piece and were made even stronger from having weathered a major crisis successfully." The two points concerning the president were postponed until he would be able to deal with them, and the primary objective now became the support of the nonacademic workers' right to collective bargaining. The students agreed to remove the vigil from the quadrangle, but to reassemble "if at any time the administration appeared to be acting against the workers or if reprisals were made." The group formed a committee of students and faculty, to which representatives of the workers and the union were to be added, to study the situation and submit specific proposals for the implementation of collective bargaining procedures. The boycott of classes was ended. The students planned to help the workers man their picket lines; they provided rides to take men off campus for meals so that the boycott of campus cafeterias, whose workers were on strike, would be effective. They raised money for the strike fund. All vigil participants adopted blue armbands (the Duke color), in place of the black mourning bands for King, "to remind everyone that we are still actively working to help the Negro workers."

The silent vigil on the quadrangle ended the morning of the fifth day with a march to the dormitories, leaving a cleanup squad to erase all traces of vigil occupancy. The students held two other rallies on Thursday night and on Easter morning. These meetings reaffirmed students' support of the right of employes to organize and bargain collectively. By actual count 2,700 people were in attendance on Thursday night.

In analyzing the vigil we have focused on three aspects: 1) the focused goals and nonviolent conduct of this demonstration; 2) the meaning of participation and nonparticipation to various students within the context of adolescent dynamics; and 3) the application of this analysis to the understanding of other student demonstrations. Our data include participant observations; publications released by the vigil committee; coverage in student, local, and national news media; questionnaires and interviews with student leaders, participants, and nonparticipants; private letters; papers written for courses; and a series of audio-visual documents recorded at the demonstration by students.

Students were asked to rank order and indicate degree of importance of eight possible causes for participation in the demonstration. Respondents were sixty-four male and female demonstrators and ninety-seven male and female nondemonstrators. There was a high correlation $(r = .88)$ between the rank ordering of all eight motives by the demonstrators and nondemonstrators (Table 1).

Table 1.
Rank Order and Mean of Factors Causing Participation

FACTORS CAUSING PARTICIPATION	DEMON-STRATORS		NONDEMON-STRATORS	
	Rank	*Mean*	*Rank*	*Mean*
The general crisis in civil rights	1	1.79	3	3.3
Desire to give an active response	2	3.08	2	3.04
The assassination of Dr. King	3	3.17	1	2.57
The four demands (petition)	4	3.75	4	4.82
A feeling of guilt	5	6.21	5	4.84
Response of the administration to the demonstration	6	6.66	7	6.59
The strength of the demonstration	7	6.92	6	4.85
A desire for personal power	8	7.48	8	6.65

A possible interpretation of this data is that regardless of the decision to participate, a large portion of the undergraduate students shared an understanding of the value system operating in the situation.[2] Adolescents need a hero, an ideal image of courage and unselfishness with which to identify. This need is often overlooked in a generation that publicly stresses "playing it cool." King's death dramatized the martyrdom of a modern hero who had the courage to risk his life for the sake of his brothers and to challenge the traditional codes guiding race relations. Set in the context of Dr. King's death, the choice of goals and the strict conduct of the demonstration along orderly and nonviolent lines illustrate an aspect of mourning described by Lindemann, that of imitating some characteristic of the dead person.[3]

A tactical factor which contributed to the relative success of the demonstration was the choice of action aimed at two already defined problems within the university community, those of the federal minimum wage and collective bargaining. Since the textile mills, a major contributor to North Carolina's economy, were still successful in keeping labor unions out of the area, it seemed unlikely that the small group of nonacademic employes would achieve unionization. As the students sought a meaningful and reasonable focus for their deep concern and grief about King's death, the workers saw a potential ally in their struggle.

Another important influence on the demonstration were its student leaders. They were, by and large, elected officials of campus organizations and were expected to function in a leadership capacity defined by the democratic process. These leaders were continually focused on the goals and realities of the current situation rather than being committed to a particular strategy. Throughout the vigil both the leaders and the rank-and-file insisted that, insofar as was possible, all strategy be a product of group consensus. While this process consumed time and energy, it reduced (although it did not completely eliminate) factional and impulsive action and helped the students accept reasonable time-limited progress in achieving their objectives. The students showed maturity in thinking and behavior.

Of great importance was the tactical counsel and support given by the faculty, individually, by departments, and through the academic council, as described in the documentation. The speedy organization of a previously nonvocal, nonactive segment of the faculty bears out the observation by Lipset[4] that student attitudes reflect the mood of many faculty members.

Continuing evidence of student commitment to a quiet and orderly demonstration and the administration's consequent willingness to abstain from restrictive and punitive action were crucial to the maintenance of the nonviolent nature of the vigil. Also important was the administration's willingness to engage in study and mediation. The trustees avoided direct confrontation with the group or its leaders while remaining open to negotiations with authorized students and faculty.

An important consequence of the demonstration's nonviolence was the news media's lack of interest in what was going on. The administration was concerned about the university's image, but the students had hoped that the news media would report the purpose and nature of the demonstration, thereby bringing more pressure to bear on the university to change. The students were angry and disillusioned by their experience:

> Coverage by the national news media has been almost non-existent, while more violent university demonstrations make front page headlines all over the nation. NBC flatly refused to cover the vigil, *because* there was no violence; an NBC official asked students to contact him if violence erupted, and then he might be interested enough to send down cameras. Newspaper coverage, with the exception of some North Carolina papers and a small squib once in the *New York Times* has also been negligible. Letters describing the activities here were sent to over fifty newspapers across the nation, with no result. Just as newspapers select "significant news" about political candidates, so do they select other types of "significant" news for the edification of the masses. Evidently, only violence is significant enough to be brought to the attention of the public.[5]

In a carefully reasoned review of the current literature on youth, Jahoda and Warren point out:

> In almost innumerable journalistic contributions to the understanding of youth, this growing segment of the population is often loosely equated with the trouble makers among the young, be they involved in delinquency or in riotous reception meetings for the Beatles, in any case, with the most visible group among them.[6]

219

It is appropriate to wonder just who determines "visibility." We might speculate on the possibility that, given the instantaneous and often intimate audio and visual nature of the modern communications system, the mass media afford a fantasy vehicle for acting out, synesthetically some of our own unresolved conflicts and less socially acceptable impulses. As Jahoda and Warren have noted, perhaps the adult world's concentration on the most visible section of youth takes on the aspect of self-fulfilling prophecy so that today's myth may play its part in producing tomorrow's reality.

In attempting to understand adolescent dynamics, we believe it to be important that the student's experiences be described in terms of the continuities as well as the discontinuities, the strengths as well as the conflicts. Especially important is the need of the young to establish an individual identity which incorporates behavior consonant with personal and social values and norms and to consolidate peer group identification which reflects these.[7] The concept of role is useful for looking at the convergence of personal and social identity. Responses to questionnaires by sophomores and juniors of Duke's women's college, both demonstrators and nondemonstrators, clearly documented the profusion and diversity of concerns inherent in the role of student as highlighted by this situation. What was crisis for some was catharsis for others; one student's accomplishment was another's problem. The most frequent response to the question of what had been the most important thing which happened since the demonstration began was "the realization of my personal responsibility to act on social problems." Also listed as important were learning to defend opinions, keeping an open mind to all issues, seeing evidence of concern for the university as a community, finding oneself able to stand up for and act on beliefs, becoming more sympathetic to problems of the poor, and concern for grades. One girl thought that the end of the demonstration and the return to ordinary academic routine were most significant. One girl "met Bill," while another said she would never forget cooking a million eggs. Their major personal problems included, in addition to those just mentioned, deciding whether to get married or go to graduate school, interpreting the demonstration to parents, handling peers' misunderstanding of the decision not to participate actively in the demonstration, and keeping a cool head. Several reported that they had had no personal problems. When asked what they thought to be the most significant consequences of the demonstration, besides the wage increase and possibility of collective bargaining, the range of response was slightly more narrow. The most frequent was "pride that a heretofore uninvolved campus could rally such a show of student support and organization." Second highest was "waking up to problems of the real world," recognition of the moral responsibility of institutions, increased faculty involvement in determining university policy, and more awareness of one another as people.

We were also interested in whether the students felt that the experience had affected their general mental health. Again the responses varied. A large number felt that there had been no change. Others listed such things as increased self-understanding and less satisfaction with their ability to make decisions, especially moral ones. Several felt they had more increased self-understanding, particularly a greater awareness of their personal decision-making process and greater awareness of their mental health in general. A few felt improved because of reconciliation between thought and action, and some indicated they simply felt improved. For many the vigil met the adolescent need for dramatic experience and meaningful action in the group context. For these students there were many, sometimes mutually supportive, sometimes conflicting, expectations operating. These became evident during a time of crisis when a decision about behavior must be made and measured against the decision of one's peers.

With the notable exceptions of Freedman's *The College Experience*[8] and the material of Katz in *No Time for Youth*[9] most research is concerned with what the investigators think youth should be or with concepts based in pathology. Jahoda and Warren have noted:

> For research purposes, an essential part of studying the young should be the uncovering of youth's own images and sterotypes,

221

'myths,' and projections of youth and life, for these stand the best chance of shaping the reality of youth and, in due course, adulthood. . . . [The] research literature reviewed is strangely silent on what being young means to the young and on youth's fantasies of being adult. Perhaps this is because the study of personal experiences is unfashionable in much modern psychology.[10]

Why is it that young people are so seldom asked what they think about themselves? Could it be that we are dealing not only with the dynamics of adolescence but also with the dynamics of adulthood? Perhaps the aspects that we choose to examine are influenced, if not determined, by conscious and unconscious memories of our own youth, its pleasures and pain. Such influences, combined with the historical emphasis of the mental health field on pathology, may be a potent force in developing myths about the young and what we see as their many problems and struggles.

One of the obvious consequences of focusing on their discontinuities and problems has been the consistent failure to represent, both in the professional and popular literature, the strengths of youth. We promulgate the idea that adolescence is a turmoil; that young people are still struggling to master qualities of maturity in judgment and groping for a personal philosophy which will herald adulthood. So it is even more difficult for adults to acknowledge that reasoned judgment and creative efforts can also belong to the young. Yamamoto has commented that:

It may indeed be that in our blind acceptance of our favorite myth we have been largely overlooking the positive aspects of present-day adolescents. We may have interpreted their constructive urges and their experimentations in a rigid, institutionalized frame of reference, thus ignoring much of their integrity and potential contribution.[11]

Much has been made of adolescent rebellion, and many are concerned that what was previously an individual process contained mainly within the family is becoming a socially endorsed peer group process. Do not the young have ample reason to revolt? Adolescents have not yet become desensitized, as have many adults

222

whose defenses against the perception of human suffering and injustice have been strengthened through rationalization and intellectualization. Perhaps with the growing code of participation, stimulated through the "you are there" ethos of mass media, student groups may become agents of social change, not because they are the underprivileged revolting, but because they have available psychic resources for strong feeling and conviction and an increasingly articulated model for action.

We believe that a college demonstration may provide an appropriate, significant developmental experience for adolescents in their struggle with the tandem tasks of individualization and socialization. It may provide a context for rebelling against while seeking ways for identifying with authority figures and institutional policies. A demonstration such as the silent vigil also meets the needs of the young for a hero with whom they can identify, a noble cause to which they can commit themselves and participate in meaningful, self-directed activity. Each demonstration should be studied in terms of its own circumstances, and the situational and group process components as they influence and provide a framework for the dynamics of the participants should be understood. The importance of developing such understanding increases with the emergence of student demonstrations as recognized political and social forces in America.

Notes

1. Frank L. Ashmore, "A Crisis in Conscience," paper presented to the Greensboro Alumni Association of Duke University, April 24, 1968.

2. Robin Zaverl, "The Duke Vigil," unpublished master's thesis, Department of Sociology, Duke University, 1968.

3. Eric Lindemann, "Symptomatology and Management of Acute Grief," *American Journal of Psychiatry, 101:* 141-48 (1944).

4. Seymour M. Lipset, ed., *Student Politics* (New York: Basic Books, 1967).

5. Mary A. Mantuani, letter to the editor, *The New Republic,* May 11, 1968, pp. 39-40.

6. Marie Jahoda and Neil Warren, "The Myths of Youth," *The College Student and His Culture: An Analysis,* ed. Kaoru Yamamoto (Boston: Houghton Mifflin, 1968) .

7. Mervin B. Freedman, *The College Experience* (San Francisco: Jossey-Bass, 1967).

8. Ibid.

9. Joseph Katz et al., *No Tme For Youth* (San Francisco: Jossey-Bass, 1968).

10. Jahoda and Warren, "The Myths of Youth."

11. Kaoru Yamamoto, ed., *The College Student and His Culture* (Boston: Houghton-Mifflin, 1968).

A Student's Account of
The Columbia Crisis

Jane Johnson

As the child of parents who voted for Eisenhower in 1956 and Nixon in 1960, my background is far from radical. My father is a reactionary; his prejudices, although basically thoughtless and superficial, are most vocal. On the other hand, my mother at her most conservative moment was a moderate Republican. She maintained that her early preference for the GOP was based on origins in small town North Dakota, where big government was feared and the highest premium was placed on economics. Since then she has developed into a fairly progressive liberal and recently supported McCarthy with vehemence. I might add that during the Columbia strike she approved of my participation, whereas my father called to tell me to come home immediately.

Before going to Columbia I spent four peaceful undergraduate years at Middlebury College in Vermont. I rarely read a newspaper, and any political opinions that I had were based on the most general information. I have always considered myself extremely liberal, have always been intensely opposed to the war, and have been involved to some extent with a civil rights group at Middlebury. Occasionally, we even had peace marches in college. But it is hard to take a radical position on civil rights in a white academic community which considers itself enlightened, which does not admit of any particular prejudices, and which is never confronted. The few black people at Middlebury were middle class Negroes and were totally accepted. Looking back now, I believe that we might have questioned Middlebury's admission policy. While living in the green loveliness of Vermont, I did not feel pressured to confront myself, not to mention the community, on the issue of Vietnam. It was easy to say that I was against the war while marching around the unpatrolled green of a small New England town, where our protest was largely ignored or was greeted with amused looks and irrelevant remarks.

It was not so easy at Columbia. There I was forced to confront myself and defend what I had been thinking benignly for years. A peace march in New York or Washington was somehow more meaningful than in Vermont. I signed petitions against the Dow Chemical Company and the Institute for Defense Analysis. What was more important, people were doing things at Columbia. Students doing volunteer work for Citizenship Council were holding tutoring programs in Harlem; they were working with community groups in dealing with problems of urban housing and organizing rent strikes. Problems which were abstractions at Middlebury were dramatized at Columbia. I now went to "Columbia University in the City of New York," and New York City is as integral to Columbia as is its curriculum. Columbia's geographical location in relation to Harlem cannot be ignored. Theoretically, the university is a model of the society and is therefore to be involved in all aspects of its environment. The law school has its counterpart in the world outside, as does the school of architecture, business, economics, political science, and divisions of the humanities. Ideally, the relation between the university and the world that surrounds it is a dynamic one. For example, the students in the school of architecture have the opportunity to study their environment in terms of social design as well as to study books on the principles of construction. At Columbia especially, the architecture student is confronted with problems of restoration and slum housing. At the same time, the concerned student, as he develops a certain knowledge, feels obligated to utilize his expertise to the benefit of the surrounding community.

The great inconsistency between the academic structure and the larger social structure is a matter of class. For the most part the

226

members of the academic community belong to the same social class. In their call for a free university the students at Columbia were demanding that the university complete itself in terms of the society that it should represent.

Concentrating on English literature rather than a specific social science, I found it difficult to relate what I was studying to my immediate surroundings. There is an ivory tower stance that is dangerously easy to adopt in the study of literature. Although my commitment to literature is also a commitment to education and my interest in writing is based on the assumption of an audience who will think I will have something to say, it was very easy in the graduate study of English to indulge oneself in scholarly talk for its own sake. Frankly, I was bothered during my first months at Columbia by the possible irrelevance of what I was doing there: I was certain that my appetite for poetry would continue regardless of whether or not I was in graduate school. At times I was plagued by the premonition that I was merely involved in literary professionalism.

Whether or not the above narrative explains my state of mind and academic attitude on April 23, 1968 remains for me an open question. It is partly a reconstruction after the fact, but I cannot help feeling that whatever persuasion compelled me to enter Avery Hall on April 24 had something to do with this background.

What happened at Columbia last April was neither a social revolution, an academic temper tantrum, nor calculated nihilism. The students involved had various objectives, but ultimately their commitment was to each other and to the necessary solidarity of the gesture that they were making. Hands held up in the traditional victory sign became a common symbol for radicals, liberals, and even moderates for their common effort to end the oppression imposed by Columbia University.

On Tuesday, April 23, I was not at Columbia, but read the account of the day's events in *The New York Times*. I must admit that my initial reaction was one of amusement. I am now convinced that this amusement resulted from the style of the report rather than the matter. It seems to me that the *Times* followed its own precedent by treating all subsequent events as purely dramatic irresponsibility. This was due no doubt to the editorial disapproval of Arthur Sulzburger, a trustee of Columbia University.

I was not one of those who took Hamilton Hall on the first day of the strike. Up until this time my political commitment had been more sympathetic than active.

On Wednesday, April 24, in the early afternoon a friend of mine called from Hamilton Hall where he had spent the night. A black student from the law school, he had remained there after the white SDS students had left to liberate Low Library. He had been entrusted with the barricade at the door and had been instructed to keep all press and all white people out. At this time Dean Coleman was being held as a hostage, which struck me as humorous and a little outrageous. However, at this point I began to regard what was happening more seriously. I did not immediately go to the campus. Although I was aware of the issues at stake and entirely approved of the current protest, I did not feel that I could identify with either the student Afro-American Society or SDS, both of which were more militant than I was prepared to be. However, at about 7 p.m. on Wednesday another friend called from Avery Hall, the architecture building. He said that students, the majority of whom were in the architecture school, had decided to occupy Avery, which they considered their building anyway, as a gesture of support of the students in Hamilton and Low and of commitment to their six demands. My roommate, a master's candidate in city planning (a division of the architecture school), felt a professional as well as political obligation to join the people in Avery. When my black friend arrived from Hamilton and a discussion ensued, both my roommate and I decided to go over to Columbia, if not to occupy a building, then at least to discover at firsthand what was going on. I took my sleeping bag, which seems to suggest that I had very little doubt that I would stay.

When we arrived at Avery, a meeting concerning the procedure to be adopted in occupying the building was in progress. The students decided not to barricade the building, not to restrict the occupation solely to architecture students, and to accept in full the six demands of the original strikers. The decision not to use barricades in Avery, unlike Hamilton, Low, and eventually other buildings, was typical of these students' more moderate, absolutely nonviolent position.

My reasons for being in the building were fairly simple. Although I had always been opposed to the war and community oppression by institutions, I felt that my protest would be more effective by demonstrating against specific issues in which I felt a personal responsibility. I felt personally involved in the protest against the Institute for Defense Analysis and the gymnasium. As a representative of Columbia University, I had the right and the obligation to protest Columbia's involvement in research on counterinsurgency for the Department of Defense and in building a gymnasium which appeared racist in design and intent. Students, the most essential part of the university, were never consulted on these involvements. In the confrontation the demand for amnesty was at the core of other demands. By setting up a tripartite or preferably bipartite committee composed of faculty and students (administration only if unavoidable), the university would alter the power structure significantly so that its decisions and consequent actions would be representative of those who make up the university.

The interests of students and administrators seemed to me distinctly different. My impression of the administration and trustees is that their interests are not especially in education, that the trustees are mainly businessmen concerned with profit and loss and political expedience, caring more about property rights than human rights. I also believed that the proper role for the administration was secondary to roles of both the faculty and students. Proper administrative functions are those of organization, of coordinating the various faculties of the university, and in this sense they are not much above the services of grounds-keepers and secretaries. That administrators had all power with no restrictions was flagrantly unjust. There was never a demand that students take over the university. The most radical statement called for a committee composed

229

of equal numbers of faculty and students empowered to make policy decisions. A more moderate and fairly acceptable demand among students included representatives from the administration.

The demand for amnesty was based on the need for establishing this committee. If the protest at Columbia was more than a disruptive tactic and had anything of revolution in its conception, then any agreement by students to accept judgment and consequent punishment from the administration, regardless of how token its effect, was to recognize an illegitimate and irresponsible authority.

Life in Avery during the first few days of the strike was sometimes warmly communal, sometimes extremely boring. Sleep was difficult because of the stone floors and constant conversation. The first night I slept on the grass outside the front door. Meetings were frequent and interminable but necessary. To think that the students who liberated the buildings were merely frenzied radicals bent only on anarchy is simplistic. Our discussions were long and responsible. Many points of view were represented, and decisions came only after a majority vote.

Initially, the threat from the police did not seem real to me. I had never had any contact with the police before and thought of them (it now seems unbelievable) as a friendly source of information. As the days went by, however, many of our discussions concerned what to do about tear gas and Mace. My confidence began to waver. On each windowsill in Avery was a jar of Vaseline for protection against Mace. On the ground floor was a large vat of water surrounded by rags for use against tear gas. These precautions seemed to me to be overly dramatic, and I did not take them seriously. The atmosphere in Avery was not especially grim. We were well supplied with food. During the day we sat on a balcony on the third floor, from which we could see a good part of the campus. We listened to WKCR, the Columbia student radio station, faithfully. Ultimately, it was the only reliable source of information concerning the strike. Occasionally, I would leave the building to walk around the campus to talk to other students and to look with amazement at the lines of police that surrounded the campus. Their practice of checking the identification card of anyone trying to enter the campus not only was annoying, but also increased the existing tension, especially on the issue of Columbia-community relations. Legally, 116th Street is a public thoroughfare, although it runs directly through Columbia. It has little automobile traffic, but is used a great deal by pedestrians. Earlier in the year Columbia had built so-called "ornamental" gates at both 116th Street entrances. I was impressed by their exclusionary nature. They look most shuttable, and indeed were shut and reinforced by police barricades during the strike. The community was thus deprived of its use of the campus and 116th Street. During the strike there were several joint demonstrations by members of the community, one led by 37X Kenyata on one side of the gates and students on the other. Especially then the gates seemed to symbolize the separation that Columbia imposed between itself and the surrounding community.

When Stokely Carmichael and H. Rap Brown came to the campus, several hundred people ran toward Hamilton. WKCR announced that Carmichael and Brown had managed to force their way through the gates and were headed toward Hamilton to support their brothers. I believe that the administration's greatest fear during the occupation was that there would be some provocation at Hamilton. The black students there were silent and unmoving and therefore much more threatening than their white counterparts. Carmichael and Brown entered Hamilton, remained inside for about ten minutes, and emerged to read a statement of demands written by the students inside. Then they left with the promise that they were going to Harlem to organize their brothers. They never came back. Every day we heard rumors that the people of Harlem were coming to support the protest. This possibility must have seemed ominous to the administration. Of course, the Harlem residents never came, and, having worked in Harlem for the summer after the strike, I now see why. It will be quite a while before anyone will be able to organize the despair of Harlem.

During the last days in Avery I began to feel uneasy about why I was there. My reasons for entering the building were perfectly clear, but the reasons for remaining there became ambiguous. My biggest apprehension was that we at Avery were being misrepresented. Avery's position was not fanatically radical; we had no hardcore SDS members in our midst. It seemed to me, however, that everyone we elected to the strike steering committee returned to us radicalized. Maybe this was a good thing, a tribute to the strike committee that they were so persuasive or perhaps so right. Had I been a representative, I may also have become radicalized by SDS. But to me the rhetoric used by SDS was occasionally irresponsible and tended to create distrust and antagonism. I strongly believe that how you say something determines to a large extent what you are saying. My disagreement with SDS was not with their objectives but rather with their perspective. I have always supported, and still do support without reservation, the six demands. However, it seemed to me that in our particular position of power we might have been able to make some immediate and even radical changes in the university power structure. I also felt that we could make a meaningful gesture to protest the power structure in the society of which the university was a model. What SDS seemed to be saying was that it was impossible to change the university until society had been changed. I entirely agree with their criticism of the society. However, at that particular moment, when the source of our bargaining power lay in five buildings at Columbia, this seemed naive. I realized at that point that if our objective (without compromise) had been to change society, there could never be a dialog with anyone in power to grant our demands and we would undoubtedly remain in the building forever or get our heads beaten in by the police. On the night that the police finally came, the students at Avery staged a scenario which was intended to dramatize how the strike committee had envisioned the outcome of the strike. It was fanciful and, to me, horrifying. They did not believe that the police would come. Rather the university would be cordoned off. We, however, would be prepared, having stocked up on water, food, and candles. Replacements and provisions would be dropped to us by helicopters, and we could stay where we were forever and there have a free society. This I was not prepared to do. I did not think that the scenario was the least bit funny, and, frighteningly, neither did the strike committee.

After the scenario there was a discussion of the Fayerweather proposal, which was an attempt to establish a dialog with the administration by presenting the same six demands in other language. The word "amnesty" had become a stumbling block and a deadend. This proposal was voted down in Avery 31 to 34. I was a little dubious about the count and asked for a recount. This was denied because, I was told, it was extremely important to stock water at that moment. There was discontent and many of the more moderate members left. After the water was secure, the meeting resumed. I made a dramatic and angry speech accusing our chairman of misrepresenting us. I said that I thought that the scenario was a mockery and that I was not prepared to stay in Avery Hall until society changed. People applauded, but immediately someone from the strike committee began a long, dreary speech about the free university and allocation of funds. There was never a recount. I left.

As I reached the edge of the campus, I saw the battalions of police. Some emotional gut reaction turned me around. To this point I had made a strong commitment not only to the strike but to the people of Avery, and this did not seem like the time to leave them for whatever intellectually sound reason. It was too late to get back in the building, so I joined those sitting down in front of it. I think that I actually imagined that by sitting there I could somehow keep the police out. Standing in front of us, arms linked, was a line of faculty members. The professor in front later had his ribs broken and suffered a concussion. From my vantage point I could see the boots of the tactical police force. One policeman was holding some sort of monstrous looking tool used to cut through chains. We sang "We Shall Overcome."

I cannot be objective about the police and will not try to be. They behaved abominably. At Avery there was absolutely no resistance to them. I saw my friends dragged feet first down a spiral marble staircase and hit on the head with handcuffs and blackjacks. I was kicked and thrown onto the pavement by one delirious plainclothesman. But the police were not the issue. It is the nature of police, I now believe, to act in this manner. Much of the anger that was immediately directed against the police should have been brought to bear on the man who called them there and the power that gave him that authority.

After the first arrests I was not involved in any direct confrontation with the police. I am sure that this was caused by my fear. Every time, even now, that I hear a siren, I feel nauseous. I helped maintain the strike by attending only liberated classes until the end of the year; I did not get my degree in June. There were unending and innumerable meetings which sought to utilize what had happened to change and improve specific curriculums. The whole atmosphere of Columbia was enervated. Student support, with the exception of the rather pathetic jocks who liked things "the way they were before," was overwhelming.

The strike, if it accomplished nothing else, woke up Columbia and a lot of people with it. The university will never be the same and it will probably be better. I gained a whole new awareness of myself and the world around me. As a direct result of what I learned during the strike, I worked all summer in a tutoring program in Harlem. I believe that I have been radicalized by the revolution at Columbia. I no longer have any faith in the present political system nor the power system that underlies it. I abhor violence, but in secret moments I think that a revolution may be the only hope for this country.

The Economic Context
of the Student Role

Edgar Z. Friedenberg

Education in our society is usually assumed to be a form of investment in one's own future. Data are cited abundantly to show that high school graduates earn tens, and college graduates hundreds, of thousands of dollars more in a lifetime than the hapless dropout. Joseph Kahl's early study concluded that in his small but revealing sample of working-class New England high school seniors, "school and the possibility of college were viewed by all the boys as steps to jobs. None was interested in learning for the subtle pleasure it can offer; none craved intellectual understanding for its own sake."[1] Education in America is valued primarily as the gateway to opportunity (as the bitterness of the conflict over recruitment on campus for employment in war-related industry, hardly in itself an educational activity, attests).

If education were not viewed as a form of investment in one's future, it would have to be viewed as a form of involuntary servitude. Not merely the rationale but the very constitutionality of the education code depends on the assumption that schooling is a service to students as well as a social demand upon them. Coercion to attend college is less direct, operating chiefly through the student deferment of the Selective Service Act and the high unemployment rate for younger workers. But together these two factors eliminate the more highly remunerated alternatives to college attendance, while the expectation that leaving college before graduation to take a job will lead to a dead end and a considerable net financial loss reduces the attractiveness of job opportunities that do exist.

Life in school and college is parsimonious; the standard of living of middle class people is lower while in college than at any other time in their lives, as the Cox Commission noted with naive astonishment in its recent report.[2] Students accept a marked decline in their standard of living and expect to receive either no remuneration or a pittance scholarship because they assume that the gateway to opportunity is a tollgate. The toll must be paid both in kind, through their academic work, and in a high rate of tuition. Yet education is also regarded as in the interests of society—students are taught the skills, habits, and attitudes required to keep its systems going; punished for failure, or resistance, or ineptitude in attaining them; and identified by a credential that tells society what to hope or fear from them. Their education, then, may also be looked upon as a subsidy to their employers, public or private, to which both tax revenue and their unpaid or underpaid labor contributes. Since both private corporations and the military now routinely provide massive programs of inservice training for which participants are paid their normal salary and maintained in the field at their usual standard of living, it is clear that students, who receive no comparable consideration, are treated as a special, pejoratively defined economic category.

The idea of paying students for cultivating the skills on which society depends for its continuation strikes most adults as absurd, extravagant, and quite literally subversive, because the immediate effect would be to undermine the set of economic sanctions that plays a major part in youth control in school and in the family. Besides, we could not afford it. Total expenditures for public, exclusive of higher, education in the United States now run about 30 billion dollars per year.* To pay each of some 14 million high school

* The U.S. Book of Facts, Statistics, and Information (Statistical Abstract of the United States) for 1968 gives the figure $27,946,000,000 for the fiscal year ending June 30, 1967. Costs have been mounting at the rate of about $1.5 billion per year since 1956. (Tables 176 and 178, pp. 126-27)

students in the country $2,000 a year, far less than the federal minimum wage for the number of hours in the school week, would double this cost. Yet to say that the society cannot afford to pay students to attend school is, after all, a political rather than an economic statement. The gross national product, which itself expands to meet added economic demand, though not infinitely, is now at about a trillion dollars a year; how it is to be divided reflects the combined effects of political power, institutional inertia, and the value assigned to each constituent group in the population by our ideology. All these factors operate to the disadvantage of youth.

On the other hand, there can be no doubt that youth, in the role of student, legitimates an enormous economic enterprise that is very profitable to others. That $30 billion goes a long way, particularly when you add to it the $10 to $12 billion spent for higher education. It is harder to be precise about the figures for higher education, because it is harder to say just what a college is and which of its costs are related to education. We are accustomed to considerable self-deception with regard to the costs of higher education. Colleges and universities habitually claim in their fund drives that tuition covers so small a fraction of the costs that every student is, in effect, on scholarship. This is true if you arrive at per pupil costs by dividing total annual budget by enrollment. But most of what takes place on campus has very little direct relation to instruction, while the fact that instruction of a kind does go on makes nearly everything else that takes place both academically respectable and tax-exempt. It is hard to conceive, for example, that the kind of war and counter-insurgency research that has led, I think justifiably, to massive student protest could have been conducted in the United States anywhere but on a university campus. Until the very recent development, largely in the wake of the student protest, of the quasi-independent research institute, there was no institutional instrument that could offer technically competent research scientists the salaries and job security sufficient to attract them away from academic posts; and the institutes still have not acquired comparable prestige. A distinguished scholar or scientist who has agreed to devote his talents to the suppression or extermination of the insurgent poor colored people who live nearly everywhere else but here clearly needs all the security and prestige he can get to be happy in his work. And so far only the university can provide it, although the new giant diversified industrial combines like Litton Industries or General Dynamics may develop laboratory complexes able to take over this function, leaving the university much poorer and slightly more honest. The university will not, I expect, find itself happy ever after in the marketplace; but meanwhile life goes on, with undergraduate instruction kept cheap on the sweated labor of graduate students at $3,000 a year.

It is fortunate that our school and college years coincide with our greatest muscular strength and agility, for the student who enters the enormous American educational enterprise intent on climbing soon finds that much of it rests on his back. A satisfactory credential attests primarily to his agility through the years in managing the climb without shaking the structure. A lot of people are counting on it for shelter. There are more than a million elementary school teachers and about 800,000 high school teachers,* backed by myriad bureaucracies and service staffs. There are well over half a million on college and university faculties. And all these depend for their livelihood and social identity on the acceptance by students of up to two decades of unpaid or underpaid labor predicated on the assumption that he will more than regain through the rest of his life what he has foregone during his school years. To send a young college graduate reluctantly to his death in Vietnam is worse than murder—it is confiscation.

But the peculiarities of our economic system, which concentrates unemployment heavily among the younger members of the labor force, makes it doubtful that many students could get jobs if they were not obliged to remain in school. Table 1 illustrates this relationship between age and employment. The unemployment rate for the youngest members of the labor force, many of them high school

* *Statistical Abstract of the United States, 1968,* Table 181, pp. 129, 133.

dropouts and most of them poorly skilled, is four or five times as great as for middle aged persons.

Table 1
Relationship Between Age and Employment

	AGE				
	14-19	*20-24*	*25-44*	*45-64*	*65 or more*
Labor force (in thousands) (including armed forces)	4,913	6,139	22,156	17,054	2,131
Unemployed (in thousands)	938	445	865	636	92
Percentage of labor force unemployed	19	7.3	3.9	3.7	4.3

Based on figures for 1966. Extracted from *Statistical Abstracts of the United States, 1968,* Tables 315 and 317, pp. 222-23.

Economist John Rowntree and political scientist Margaret Rowntree, in their recent article on "The Political Economy of American Youth," note:

> Students are not paid for their labor. The U.S. Council of Economic Advisers estimates that earnings foregone by students would be between $20 and $30 billion a year. This is a minimum, since it assumes '75 to 85 per cent of students 16 years and over could find employment at from $1000 to $4500 per annum' [Council of Economic Advisers, 1967 Annual Report, p. 144] . . . . However . . . between 1950 and 1965, the percentage of the adult population (14 years old and over) in the military or in schools increased by 6.4%. To return to the 1950 enrollment-enlistment *proportions* of 15.1% of the adult population—to let the additional youths out of school and out of the armed forces—would put 8.7 million *young* people into the ranks of the unemployed, increasing the 1965 unemployment figures by 3.5 *times,* even if the teachers and officers were kept at their posts.[3]

There are about 32,000,000 Americans between the ages of fifteen and twenty-five; and it seems clear from the foregoing that our economy has no use and cannot provide very generously for those who are not in school or the armed forces. Indeed, the important function of the neatly dovetailed demands of the education codes and the Selective Service Act seems to be to keep youth out of the economy and in an unproductive and underpaid sector of the population. From this point of view the student deferment, otherwise so awkward in an ideologically egalitarian society, makes perfect sense, for economically the schools and the armed services are functionally equivalent, and both are effective in preventing young workers from becoming a dangerous drug on the market. The schools, however, have the more convincing rationale in maintaining that their students are really investing in their future, although the technical training programs of the armed services may in fact contribute more, at least for working class youth.

What does seem unarguable is that the legitimacy of the educational enterprise depends entirely on the validity of the claim that students are investing in their future. If that claim is not valid, then the whole coercive structure is a forty billion dollar a year boondoggle to which youth is subjected to keep it out of competition with its elders and under their direct day-to-day control; and to afford them employment as its wardens. Yet, the truth of the claim cannot be tested because youth is so completely captive within the military and education industries, as the Rowntrees call them, that there is no way of judging what it might be able to do with less formal instruction and more freedom if it had the chance. The very concept of "youth" in our culture is a consequence and an expression of its captivity. We have so conditioned ourselves to respond to the warning that half the population will soon be under twenty-five years old as presaging a takeover by youth, wild in the streets, that we hardly notice that age twenty-five is only young because we define it as young by the social sanctions with which we restrict youth. It is old enough, after all, to have raised a ten-year-old son or daughter in a society that supports the teenager's claim to adult status instead of defining him, as ours does, as childish.

The fact that people who stay in school longer earn more money than those who drop out sooner is not of itself sound evidence that schooling improves productivity. It is more likely to indicate what

240

is obviously true: that the schools and colleges, by issuing the credentials the society demands, control the access to economic opportunity. Moreover, the education code and Selective Service Act together make alternative ways of growing up and learning to live in society unlawful, so that alternative ways never have a chance to become institutionalized. Might it not be possible to devise them? As Paul Goodman has often stated, the idea that everyone ought to remain in school as long as he possibly can, and that a rise in the age at which one may lawfully set about one's business is an index of the level of civilization a society has reached, is a rather curious one to find in an America which is markedly anti-intellectual and has long prided itself on the contributions that relatively untutored men have made to its culture and its technology.

Suppose, heuristically, that the New York City Board of Education had unequivocally supported the plans of the Ocean Hill-Brownsville District for autonomy; had precipitated a citywide strike of teachers; had invoked the Taylor Act swiftly and ruthlessly and discharged the teachers; and had closed some schools, while keeping others open for parents, children, and teachers unsympathetic to the professional aspirations of their peers in the union to use as bases for exploring new ways of learning together. Suppose the Educational Testing Service, which gives the college entrance examination, or some other independent testing agency with a considerable library of established norms of achievement to draw on had agreed to let these young people take tests and transmit the resulting scores, interpreted on the basis of these norms, to the colleges to which they wished to apply for entrance? Would the young people have been worse off or better off than they are as a result of the services of New York City's dedicated cadre of teachers? We know that such a solution would have been politically impossible in a good union town like New York, that many of the teachers would have gone mad with rage and brought the city to its knees by fire and litigation. But would it have been educationally impossible? We do not know, though the most important contribution made by the people of Ocean Hill-Brownsville may be to have raised the

241

question in a society which regards schooling as sacred as long as only its youngest and least powerful members are subjected to it.

We know only that in our society students and their schools are locked by law and custom into a relationship that we hope is symbiotic and mutually sustaining, by which each defines the role and status of the other. The status assigned youth in this unequal partnership appears to be that of the exploited. The benefits adult members of society, and especially those in the education profession, derive from the way young people are defined with respect to them as students are obvious, large in magnitude, and clearly comprehensible in crude and immediate economic terms. The benefits students derive are deferred, hypothetical, and can only be enjoyed if the society continues through the decade with its basic socioeconomic processes and its values unchanged, and if those who are now young and promising accept those values and choose to perpetuate those processes. Is that what's happening? You bet your life!

Notes

1. Joseph Kahl, "Educational and Occupational Aspirations of 'Common-man' Boys," *Harvard Educational Review, 57:* 186-203 (1953).

2. *Crisis at Columbia: Report of Fact-Finding Commission on Columbia Disturbances* (New York: Vintage, 1968).

3. J. Rowntree and M. Rowntree, "The Political Economy of American Youth," *Our Generation* (Montreal, 1968).

"Bleep Kingman Brewer": A View From Calhoun College, Yale University, of the New Haven Black Panther Rally, May 1-3, 1970

Herbert Sacks

April 18, 1970

Today I completed a series of psychiatric interviews with eight Yale sophomores and juniors. They had been engaged in cross-cultural preparation for spending a year in a developing country under the aegis of the Yale College Experimental Five Year Program. The students' attention was riveted on the injustices which emerged during the pretrial proceedings of the Black Panthers accused of the slaying of Alex Rackley. The proximity of the state court house to the Yale campus made each of the students I saw a participant-observer in reality as well as in fantasy.

In their deeply felt moral outrage the students spoke with great expectation and some fear of the expected Black Panther rally on May 1 through May 3 on the Green, which faces the courthouse. Figures of 25,000 to 35,000 visitors were projected, including 300 from the Weathermen faction of SDS. A concert was planned at Ingall's Rink to attract students from other universities and colleges in the New England area into New Haven.

April 19

With some concern that I was overreacting, I called Master Richard C. B. Lewis of Calhoun College and discussed what I had learned from the previous day. I have often been impressed with his

243

patience when confronted by dogmatic positions which he helps students to elaborate, even though he may not share them himself. Calhoun College stands on the corner of Elm and College streets. It is a four and five story stone rectangle done in the best imitation of the residential college style of Oxford. In the structure of the Yale administration the masters are distinguished men in their own fields who have a special interest in the lives and development of the students.

Seven years ago I became one of the fifty fellows at the college. In practice, a fellow is supposed to institute contact with the students and share in the interdisciplinary brandy, cigars, and dining with men and women from the different faculties in the university. It was as a concerned fellow of Calhoun college that I called Dick Lewis on that Sunday morning. The university had not yet made known a public policy concerning the Black Panther rally. The master and I concluded that our choice was either to turn Calhoun into a bastion, shutting out visitors and closing the gates in a provocative, self-protective posture, or in a wiser gesture of friendship and peace, to open the college, providing food, lodging, and a health station to serve the visitors' needs. Lewis's judgment was to open the college, but to invite as well for May 1 to 3 only a few of his closest friends from the extramural world and a small group of faculty fellows who had a special interest in the quality of life in the college. The master also asked me to establish a first aid station and to move into the college during the rally days.

April 25

Events had moved swiftly within the university and a Yale College plan was adopted which incorporated the welcoming features of free food, housing and first aid facilities. Within the past two days Yale's president, Kingman Brewster, Jr., released a statement to the press that he was "skeptical of the ability of Black revolutionaries to get a fair trial in the United States" considering the political and social climate. Vice President Spiro Agnew, in an angry diatribe, urged Yale alumni to replace Brewster. Although many Yale faculty and students entertained reservations about Brewster's re-

244

marks, the Vice President's intemperate intrusion coalesced the Yale community behind Brewster.

I developed a plan for a first aid station with minimal capability. My assumption was that we would have to prepare for tear gassing, possible head injuries, adverse reactions from the use of hallucinogenic drugs, and the effects of fatigue and anxiety. An eager young junior, Bill Waterman, organized a health committee which prepared a first aid station in a series of rooms near the girls' entryway. The windows in these rooms were fitted with plastic sheeting and taped to seal them against the possibility of gas. Showers were available in these rooms in the event people were so thoroughly gassed that they would have to be washed off.

I attempted to recruit other physicians who were social acquaintances, colleagues, and old friends. The full-time medical academicians begged off because they had heard that a disaster contingency plan was underway at the medical center. I was unsuccessful with most of the others, who offered a variety of excuses. One distinguished surgeon told me:

> If Kingman could say that about the judicial system, he could say that about medicine, too. How would you like it if he made a statement saying if a patient required surgery, he doubted that there was any place in the country where it could be satisfactorily accomplished?

Two men, disillusioned in their past relationships with the university hospital, turned me down, remarking acidly that the only time the university called upon them was when it was in trouble. Others made similar excuses. I rationalized the rejections of help by my fellow doctors, believing that an extra doctor would not be much help if there were serious trouble.

Nonetheless, because I am a psychiatrist, I could not help wondering if my understanding of first aid management would provide enough expertise if disorders broke out.

April 28

I visited Courtney Bishop in the morning. He is an emeritus clinical professor of surgery, possessed of great equanimity and a

245

shrewd political understanding of doctors' function in society. Through the impetus of the medical mobilization he was able to deploy, within the hospital, physicians who had political reservations. Because of the critical proximity of the Calhoun gateway on Elm Street to the Green, he considered it appropriate if I moved forward with the plans I had drawn up.

Grave fears were expressed in the community and on campus about the reported thefts of 450 rifles and shotguns in three separate burglaries in the area. A cache of gasoline, supposedly for Molotov cocktails, was found in an Elm Street apartment, and two white men were arrested. Rumors that Weathermen and Hell's Angels would appear circulated in town.

April 29

I telephoned the local supply house for $75 worth of medical supplies. At noon the supply house cut off credit to the many callers who had no previously established charge accounts. Thousands of dollars worth of medical supplies had been ordered by neighborhood organizations and groups in the city, most of whom had never done business with this firm before. The news of the amount of medical supplies being purchased was disconcerting. I feared that the intensity of preparation might lead to a self-fulfilling prophecy by the participants in this unfolding drama. John Dempsey, a lame duck governor of Connecticut, had called up 8,000 National Guardsmen to support the forty Yale campus police and the 400 New Haven police. When Dempsey panicked and requested federal troops, the attorney general, with corroborative FBI information, was soberly pleased to supply 4,000 Marines and paratroopers at bases within hours of the city. Dempsey and State Senator Edward Marcus, majority leader in the state senate and aspirant for the Democratic U.S. senatorial nomination, earlier had denounced Brewster's "skeptical" statement.

April 30

Tonight I confirmed the medical arrangements and discussed the evolving political and security situation with Lewis and other fellows of the college. As we sat around the enormous living room at the master's house, Bill Kessen, professor of psychology and a significant policy-making figure in the life of the college, arrived. Pete Millard from the school of architecture and Bill Curran, executive fellow and associate treasurer of the university, responsible for many of the investment practices, were present. Also there was Dick Mooney, assistant foreign affairs editor for *The New York Times,* a Yale alumnus, who had been invited to come down for the three days by Lewis. Malcolm Boyd, Episcopal worker-priest, was also there. Contingency plans dealing with continued high volume, high density gassing requiring evacuation, and the possibility of Molotov cocktails being thrown into the rooms of the first and second floors on the College Street side of Calhoun were discussed. Meanwhile, the master gently arranged for the removal of a bedsheet painted with the words "DO IT" (the title of Jerry Rubin's book), which was hanging from a second floor window on College Street.

The chief marshal at Calhoun, a young, muscular junior, carefully presented the work of the student committees. Their plans had been coordinated on a university-wide level and they seemed thorough. During the fellows' meeting with the chief marshal, we agreed to ask visitors to leave helmets and gas masks in the guards' office as a token of their peaceful intentions, much like Western saloon keepers collecting the handguns of visiting cowboys. However, after the first few attempts by student marshals elicited overly suspicious responses, this tactic was abandoned.

May 1

I drove back to the college at 8:30 a.m. It was bright Spring. The streets were empty of children, parked cars, and traffic. Two miles away from the center of town, shops were closed, with explanatory signs in their windows. Closer in, storefronts were covered with plywood sheeting.

I learned that I missed the late arrival of Jerry Rubin and his wife, who asked to sleep in the master's house. The two departed early in the morning after having made their beds. At 9:30 a.m. I was notified that my telephone answering service was looking for

247

me with a "dire emergency." I phoned and learned that Dr. Ellis Perlswig, a child psychiatrist and an old friend and colleague, was looking for me. When I spoke to him, Ellis rapidly explained that the emergency concerned my neighbor, a significant figure in law and politics in the city of New Haven. On Monday, April 27, a group from the local Medical Committee of Human Rights (MCHR), an organization of physicians, nurses, social workers and other paramedical people who had come together as a consequence of the early civil rights marches, met with Police Commissioner James Ahern. A variety of suggestions involving disaster medical care were made to the mayor, but most important from the MCHR's viewpoint was their recommendation that a physician work in the lockups where demonstrators would be taken after arrest. The MCHR believed that this would provide the police protection against unfair charges of brutality and at the same time offer protection to those under arrest against the possibility of police excesses. Commissioner Ahern asked for a memorandum on these proposals to be presented to him on Tuesday, April 28. This was delivered to Ahern's secretary by Dave Duncombe, chaplain of the Yale University School of Medicine. When no response was forthcoming by Thursday, the MCHR checked with the police commissioner's office. Commissioner Ahern indicated that he had not received such a memorandum, and the secretary denied that she had even seen Duncombe. Ellis wished me to make use of my relationship with my neighbor to reach Mayor Bartholomew Guida, so that he could bring his influence to bear on the police commissioner. I called my neighbor but could not reach him.

By 1:00 p.m. many young people were streaming into the courtyard. Through the middle of the rectangle of the courtyard stood a long table serving green salad, bread, and familia, a mixture derived from the recipe of the Hog Farm Commune, composed of matzo, oats, raisins, and cereals. The small courtyard rapidly filled with buckskins and beards, brightly colored dresses, and olive drab knapsacks. Rock music blared from the windows of the students' rooms, and a balmy May Day atmosphere prevailed. I was wearing the physician's white coat at the master's urging; he felt my presence in and around the courtyard would signal our concern for the health and welfare of our visitors.

At 3:00 p.m. Phil Weyl, a second year medical student, sent an aide for me because we had our first real patient. A young man had collapsed outside our gateway on College Street, and the two marshals on duty had carried him into the courtyard. The patient was a red-headed, red-bearded nineteen-year-old in buckskins and blue denim shirt, perspiring profusely, looking very pale, and blowing off acetone into my face. A brief examination disclosed that he had a fast, thready pulse and was confused, disoriented, and hallucinating. He shouted that he did not want to be turned over to the pigs and knew that we would have him arrested. He would not give his name and refused to say what drugs he had taken. A member of our health team, a junior who had heavy experience with drugs in his earlier Yale years, threw himself down onto the patient's bed and embraced him, covering the patient's body with his own. He whispered intently into his ear that we would not turn him over to the pigs and that we had to know what drugs he had been taking. I quickly learned that our patient had been "shooting up" intravenous morphine and methedrine since noon and had not eaten in twenty-four hours. When the Yale student withdrew from the patient, I discovered that he had lived in Boston during the past two years panhandling and working at odd jobs to support his drug habit. I convinced him of the need to go to the hospital, called Ellis for a MCHR ambulance to take him to the medical center emergency room, and asked that he be entered in the records as John Doe.

Meanwhile, Jerry Rubin had been holding forth at Woolsey Hall for an audience of 900 people and had generated much laughter with his one liners. The one which was repeated most often to me by our students was: "You would no more take marijuana away from young people than you would take matzo away from Jews on Passover."

A period of anxious boredom began. Nothing was happening, and it did not appear that anything significant was going to happen.

249

From noon to 4 p.m. on the Green there was music with the speeches commencing immediately thereafter. In our shared concern Yale students and fellows assumed that the time for potential trouble was going to be between the termination of the speeches and 10 p.m.

At 5 p.m. a new flood of students from Cornell arrived, tired and hungry and carrying sleeping bags. They explained that they would not have come had it not been for the announcement of Nixon's Cambodian expansion of the war, which was tightly linked to the question of the national government's priorities and whether or not the Panthers could receive justice in New Haven. Many wore "Free Bobby Seale" buttons.

A monitoring committee had been established by the university to provide surveillance of the police and National Guard, demonstrators, and Yale students and to make clearly thought out and largely unwanted suggestions to the authorities as to how they could reduce the tension in the community. Bill Kessen reported to the committee his concern that National Guard troops had taken positions on York Street, which was two streets below us, and that these positions would have to be penetrated by the Yale students and the visitors on their return from the Green to Davenport, Stiles, and Morse colleges. He believed the presence of the troops to be a serious potential provocation and urged the immediate withdrawal of the guard.

Phil sent for me again, and this time our marshals had found, semicomatose in the courtyard, a black adolescent. We quickly learned that he was a student at Cambridge Academy in Boston, was named Ben, and that he had been having a great time on marijuana and wine since 3 p.m. He was "zonked" out of his head, hallucinated, but largely wanted to sleep. Ben fell into a deep sleep with ten Tollhouse cookies lying under his chin.

I went back to the gate listening to the repetitive speeches echoing and reechoing through the courtyard. A tall fellow with a mustache and glasses carrying a knapsack bounded through the gate and introduced himself as Boris, a Harvard physician. He said he had slept only four hours during the past night because he was a resident in a Boston hospital. I took him inside the information center, and he mumbled under his breath that he needed a girl to sleep with that night. In a few minutes he was dining on chicken and drinking the good whiskey in the master's house and brashly insulting, without any social sensitivity, Sid Lamb, professor of linguistics, who had just wandered through the living room in hopes of being helpful. At 7 p.m. my neighbor finally called back and agreed to clear the way for the MCHR letter to be delivered to John Murphy, the mayor's secretary.

Outside in the courtyard the marijuana smoke was hanging heavy. The courtyard had not been cleared by the speech-making on the Green, and forty people were sitting around eating familia and drinking iced tea. Young "groupies," fifteen or sixteen years old, with dilated pupils, tripped around the courtyard in pairs in a bizarre ballet.

Workshops in each of the colleges were to begin at 8 p.m., many of them led by the Chicago Seven. Dwight Hall, a center of volunteer activity at Yale and located across Elm Street, asked the master if Calhoun could take Rennie Davis, but Dick Lewis, after careful reflection, turned him down because the fire marshals had warned that more than seventy-five people in our courtyard would be dangerous.

At 9:15 p.m. Malcolm Boyd alerted me to a rumpus in the street. I left the aid station and rushed out to the gateway. Heading for the Green on Elm Street were 500 young people carrying revolutionary flags and shouting "liberate the Green." The crowds swelled swiftly as the colleges opening on Elm Street emptied. A passer-by explained that the trouble started at Branford College, where Jerry Rubin had been speaking. Working his audience up in his usual flamboyant style, Rubin had exclaimed that the time for political action was over and that problems would have to be solved in the streets. A young black participant in the meeting, identifying himself as a Panther, took Rubin's microphone and announced that two people had been busted and now was the time to liberate the Green. The audience flooded into the streets, overwhelming the marshals.

The traffic was still coming down Elm Street toward the Green, but between the four lanes of cars were tens of students. Above the sidewalk at Battell Chapel a young man wearing the yellow headband of the marshal was shouting through a strike poster shaped into a megaphone: "The Panthers say go back to your colleges, keep it cool, turn around!" I began to shout the same litany at the pushing mob on our own sidewalk and was joined by Lewis and Malcolm Boyd.

The most resistant in the crowd were the newspapermen and photographers from the television stations and study groups, such as the Institute of Documentary Anthropology at Brandeis. A press card, large camera mounted on one's shoulder, or a Uher tape recorder with a two-foot long styrofoam-covered microphone held by a sound man were sufficient authority to ignore admonitions for crowd control and safety. The marshals moved into the middle of Elm and College streets and were directing traffic down College Street away from the Green. A segment of 1,000 demonstrators had been turned around by nineteen-year-old Panther Doug Miranda on the Green and were heading away from the police toward the colleges again, and the flow toward the Green had been successfully stemmed.

Suddenly there was the call of "gas." Large balls of tear gas flew across the Green toward Calhoun and the gateway. The reports of the canisters being fired were repeatedly heard. Almost immediately the crowd dissolved, and I went back to the aid station to warn our team to seal the plastic to the window frames. Within minutes there was a flow of patients crying from gas. Several were coughing deeply, and a few were throwing up from the respiratory irritation. We set up a system which required our patients to doff their outer clothing, come through two doors, have their eyes washed out with normal saline solution, and then to depart for a rest area in the basement which had been properly sealed off. Within two hours we had treated almost 150 patients. As we worked with them, they had a great desire to talk about what happened, and I had an equally keen desire to understand something of their motivation in coming to the rally. My interest was largely focused on those who came in carrying helmets and gas masks.

A twenty-year-old Northeastern University, Irish Catholic sophomore from Boston, wearing a leather jacket and carrying his helmet, angrily told me that he came to New Haven because he wanted to fight with the pigs, who were at the forefront of the Establishment. I asked him what he had against the Establishment and he explained that it was because of "Venezuela." He indicated that 52 per cent of the gross national product of Venezuela is returned to the United States, and that the Establishment exploited Venezuela. I had visited Venezuela in February and related to him some of my observations about the country. He became enraged and jumped up and down calling me a "fucking bleeding heart liberal only interested in facts, facts, facts."

A seventeen-year-old high school dropout from Lowell, Massachusetts, who had not been home for a year and a half was busily sucking on a broncho inhalator because he experienced a moderate asthmatic episode precipitated by CS gas inhalation. He carried his helmet in one hand and his ski goggles in the other, and his gas mask hung from his belt. He answered my questions carefully and indicated that he was very suspicious of anybody who was a doctor because doctors and pigs too often worked together. His friend, about two years his senior, assumed a very protective role toward this boy and cautioned me not to ask the youngster questions because it made him "uptight."

When the gas cleared, I went out to the gate once more and began to reflect about the fragmentation of my own professional identity during the day's occurrences. I had been propelled into a partisan position by the events of the past few days. As an advocate, I behaved judgmentally and critically in defense of my position. This departure from my classical psychiatric role made me uncomfortable. In the psychiatric situation the doctor contracts with the patient to work together. He must deal with transferences and counter-

253

transferences, explore resistances, interpret defenses, and analyze dreams, even while he is reserving judgment and criticism. A physician who is a social activist and political reformer must defend what he believes, without recourse to the contract inherent in the psychiatric situation or the model of the doctor-patient relationship. At Calhoun I was white-coated, wearing white shirt and tie, carrying stethoscope in pocket, serving patients no matter what ideology they espoused. I thought of many of the doctors I knew who were deeply committed to social medicine and the silent criticism I made of them, believing that they were confusing the medical model with social ideology. I recognized that my previous position was wrong and prejudicial and that H. Jack Geiger and men like him were correct about being unable to separate the social role of the physician from purely medical functions.

More than this I was assaulted personally by the accusation that I was a "bleeding heart" liberal. The young people I spoke with tonight saw me as a copout, someone who was trying to steal their fire so that they could not achieve radical changes to remedy the exploitation and racism they saw in our society. Before the events of the past week I was disappointed that the university as an institution had not taken strong positions on behalf of legal and social justice. There were good reasons to spare the university from the winds of change, but now the interdependency of the community and the college and the anti-intellectual attacks from without have made isolationism reprehensible and suicidal.

What deeply concerned me was the relative passivity of what I have come to think about as the middle-of-the-road radical. Leaning against the Calhoun gateway, I thought that the middle-of-the-road radical is in the same position as the liberal he is contemptuous of, that his philosophic position is going to be coopted and distorted by the behavior of the militant radical. His message will be lost in the chaos which follows, and repression from the right will be inevitable.

Just before midnight I came back into the master's living room, where everybody was exhausted but happy that no heads had been

"BLEEP KINGMAN BREWER"

broken. While I was drinking beer in the kitchen, Abbie Hoffman and his wife returned looking for food and rest. Hoffman, a short, unshaven, tired radical, smelled as if he had been locked up in a cow barn for three months. He was a poignant fellow with superior intelligence, capable of great humor, and able to reflect carefully. He has been deeply involved in clowning on television, presenting himself as the fool, destroying the opposition by blatant attacks and unsubstantiated, illogical positions. In the kitchen he was a tired man eager to eat, and he was tenderly looked after by his attractive wife. When she disappeared into the corner of the kitchen, he would stop talking and furtively look for her, unrelieved until she reappeared. Bill Kessen asked him how old he was, and he quickly responded "thirty-nine." He was gently kidded a little about what kind of job he had, and what kind of work was that for a nice Jewish boy to be involved in at his age. He laughed and said that his present work was with the courts because he has three trials upon appeal.

Hoffman looked genuinely vexed as he explained that people blamed him for everything that happens in the streets. Because of the hassle in New Haven tonight, there was the likelihood that his Chicago trial bail would be revoked. He pointed out that his lawyer, William Kunstler, spoke at Columbia and directly cautioned against window breaking, but the students went out and broke windows anyway.

After the Hoffmans went to bed, Jerry Rubin and his wife appeared. Jerry wore velvet dungarees of many colors and a *T*-shirt. Like a little boy, he was very impressed and awed with the paneled living room in the master's house. He seemed proud of what had happened in the streets tonight, saying "it was heavy out there." He apparently saw no contradiction between his provocative behavior on the Green and his accepting the hospitality of the kitchen and the bed of the lavish house. I found it difficult to believe that he was a powerful sirocco of political and social change. I tried to generate some conversation which was not emotionally charged or political, but he seemed terribly tired and turned off.

255

May 2—1:30 a.m.

Phil Weyl called me and said that I had to look at a nineteen-year-old who was found wandering around the courtyard. Phil thought he was heavily into drugs, as he was leaning to the left and was dysarthric. When I arrived, I saw a poorly dressed boy wearing a St. John's University jacket. I realized that he had suffered from cerebral palsy in childhood. He had come to New Haven with an anti-Vietnam war group from New York City. During the day he had not eaten because he did not have much stomach for the familia.

When the gas was used tonight, he was separated from the group he had traveled with; their bus had departed and he was now unable to return to New York. He needed a bed to sleep in so he could return on Sunday. After spending time with him, I knew that he was distressed, anxious, unstable, in an alien setting where no one would understand him or feed him, and was undertaking more than his ego could handle. I went to the information center to find a bed for him. There were a dozen lumpy forms in sleeping bags across the courtyard. When I walked into the commons room to the left of the gateway, I counted nearly a hundred bodies huddled together, asleep without blankets, without sleeping bags, and in the clothes which they wore to the rally today. The information center, located in the fellows' room, was crowded with people trying to sleep or begging for housing.

As I stood awaiting a response to my whispered request that we give the last emergency bed to our friend from St. John's, a twenty-year-old black man leaned across the table. The white Yale student running the information center opened a tin of iced chocolate cake and offered the visitor a piece of cake. The black man turned it down saying that the piece was not big enough so the information center man guiltily offered him two pieces of cake. The black said indignantly that he would take it and then fished angrily into his pocket for coins which would make up 25 cents. The white Yale student did not wish to take the money and made the painful statement "we are all in this together, we are all brothers" (i.e., why should a visitor try to embarrass him by giving him money?). Nevertheless, the money was pressed upon him by the young black, which apparently was meant to demonstrate symbolically the cheapness of Yale men, of white men generally, and all of mankind's inhospitable failure to provide him a place to sleep.

I returned to the master's house ready to go to sleep and found Boris, the Harvard physician, drinking the master's liquor and eating some more chicken while he berated Leslie Fiedler, who had arrived at 3:30 p.m. from Buffalo. Fiedler is an old friend of Dick Lewis and a noted literary critic and professor at the State University of New York at Buffalo. The police arranged for a sixteen-year-old friend of his daughter to conceal a microphone on her person and then record incriminating statements alleging the possession of marijuana in his home. He is now out on bail.

Ollie, a friend of Peter Millard, arrived. He reported in vivid detail the scene in front of Phelps Gate, fifty yards up College Street from Battell Chapel, when the "crazies" moved through the crowd of unhelmeted radicals and observers, threw bottles and rocks at the police, who then fired tear gas back at them. The marshals tried to move the crowd back through Phelps Gate, which was then closed by the campus police. Bill Coffin emerged from Battell Chapel and urged the police to open the gates to let the fleeing people enter, but when the chaplain left, the campus police closed the gates again.

At 7:30 a.m. Ellis awakened me and had the MCHR letter in hand, explaining that he could not reach Murphy at home by telephone and asking me to deliver it by hand to him at City Hall. At 10:00 a.m. I dressed and walked to City Hall. There were three policemen on the corner of Temple and the Green, and I stopped to talk with them. The Irish sergeant was talkative and described how last night the police had been outnumbered six to one by the demonstrators. Furious with the out-of-towners who had come in to make trouble, the sergeant protested that New Haven police always got on well with Yale students. They were impressed that there were very few blacks in the crowd and that the Panthers had tried

257

very hard to keep the peace, using bullhorns and loudspeakers mounted on vehicles. It was increasingly apparent that the one black cop was uncomfortable and backed off from any approach I made which would require an exchange of words. As I walked on past the National Guard trucks, I felt viscerally repelled. I understood the hostility created in the young by the very presence of these trucks and soldiers.

In the Hall of Records a police officer phoned Murphy, who was "too busy to see anyone." I called Ellis, who advised me to see Lou Black, the press secretary to the mayor. I quickly explained my mission to Black and told him that I would like ten seconds with Murphy, who knew the contents of the letter I carried. He was agreeable, called Murphy, and discussed my seeing him. After several minutes there was a twenty second interruption, and Black changed his voice and said, "Oh, you say Murphy is not there, and you don't know where he is." He then hung up. I told Black indignantly that I have lived too long and that I had worked too long as a psychiatrist not to have to feel sorry for him because he had been compelled to lie to me. He smiled apologetically and threw his hands up, asking "What can I do?"

I returned to Calhoun and observed that I could possibly tolerate consumer fraud by corporations, presidential dishonesty, but not lying by cheap municipal politicians in a face-to-face situation. Pete Millard suggested that the city administration was so intimidated that it feared that any reasonable, flexible move would bring down the jerrybuilt structure it had contrived to deal with this crisis. I called Kenneth Keniston at the monitoring committee to relate the story and he behaved strangely on the phone. Ken and I had worked together for a number of years on the five-year bachelor of science program, and we knew each other well. This morning he related to me awkwardly, with many questions and interruptions that did not seem appropriate. After I had told the story, he mentioned that I had been tape-recorded. I felt offended by an old friend.

At noon Jerry Rubin glided into the living room, lurching into the piano and almost falling on his face in front of the coffee table. He then disappeared into the dining room enroute to the kitchen. I put down my newspaper, walked into the dining room, and quietly said that I thought he was dangerously high. If he wished, I could get something to bring him down. He responded bitterly that he did not like doctors, and he did not trust them. I went back to the living room, and Rubin then came out of the dining room shouting: "Why don't you get high with me?" I told him that I was high on life, and he suggested then that I had never used anything, to which I retorted, "How do you know?" He shot back that I had "nun's eyes" and I responded that nuns seemed to be leaving the church in large numbers. Abbie Hoffman came in and told me that Rubin was speaking this afternoon because Hoffman had lost the toss of the coin. Dick Mooney laconically observed that when Hoffman and Rubin awakened this morning, they searched through *The New York Times* for their names.

By midafternoon all the fellows were weary, and I was concerned about Lewis, who looked worn out from his repeated rounds. I walked over to the Green with Dick Mooney, who had heard a report from the master that a campus policeman had been picked up the previous night for carrying a dangerous weapon while driving a car. His name was Elbert Huckaby. Lewis saw this as an opportunity to start the "Free Elbert Huckaby" movement, a source of humorous relief in an atmosphere of uncertainty.

The crowds on the Green seemed larger by several thousand than the count on the preceding day. There were groups of students in buckskins and hats sleeping on the Green, and other groups of young men, who had doffed their shirts because of the warmth of the sun, were dancing in circles to the simple melody line "Fuck War."

The speeches started, and I found myself again turned off by them and not even able to follow the speakers. I was concerned about this development in myself because of my conscious sympathies for a fair trial for the Panthers, my outrage at the events in Vietnam and the move into Cambodia, and my deep concern about inequitable relationships between Yale and the community. I began to move back toward Calhoun across the Green when Jerry Rubin came on exhorting the crowd and warming them up. He delivered some of the same one liners that he had offered on the preceding day at Woolsey Hall and got the crowd to chant, with uplifted clenched fists, "Fuck Richard Nixon!" He then launched an attack upon the university, telling the students that student life and activities were like toilet training. He assailed Yale and said that the only reason that people experienced hospitality here was because Yale was scared of destruction, which I guessed was true enough.

He then tried to get the crowd to attack President Brewster, urging "All together, Fuck Kingman Brewer!" The crowd was cautiously responsive. I thought that was very funny and considered how hard it was going to be for the student broadcaster at WYBC-FM, the Yale station, to effectively use his "bleeper" button. For the last two days this poor broadcaster had suffered terrible incoordination in failing to punch the button at the right moment so that frequently he would censor inoffensive rhetoric and permit scatology to flow through the ionosphere. Later in the day a wag suggested selling a sweatshirt with the imprint: "Bleep Kingman Brewer!" And a politically conservative marshal was heard to say, "That guy Ruby never gets Brewer's name straight."

By late afternoon I was back in the courtyard and checking the aid station. Dick Mooney ventured that young people who get hung up in the rhetoric require it in the same way addicts have a need for hard drugs. Lewis was looking downcast, having received a phone call which raised the possibility of roving bands of marauders late at night who would "trash" the colleges. The master told me that some marshals were up on the roof with phones to identify early crowd movement so that marshals down below could be directed to points of confrontation and conflict. He recalled during the previous week a rumor had swept through the college that he had made a deal with the New Haven police department to put a machine gun nest on the roof in return for immunity for Calhoun College. As I drifted back toward the aid station, a young groupie came up to me holding her head and said, "Doc, do you have acid, (pause) oh, I mean aspirin?" I laughed for the first time all afternoon. The spirit of the people in the courtyard was downright sullen and hostile in contrast to the same time on the previous day. No Yale students were in sight. Fifty or sixty visiting students were lying around in bodily positions which did not suggest relaxation.

My answering service called with a patient referral from a psychiatrist friend in Cambridge. My friend was a graduate of Harvard Medical School, and I asked him to see if Boris was listed as a Harvard Medical School alumnus. He reported that Boris attended the Medical School from 1960 to 1963 but did not receive a degree. This sad news of our disturbed imposter friend confirmed a speculation Bill Kessen and I had shared last night, and Lewis soon asked Boris to leave.

That evening I went to a dinner party. At 9:30 p.m., not having heard anything from Calhoun, I decided to check in at the master's house and reached Malcolm Boyd, who lost his usual calm and shouted, "Come quickly, it's coming in heavily in the courtyard, they have started using gas again!" I left for a speedy trip back to the college. At Elm and York streets a detective stopped all traffic. I hopped out of the car and ran toward Calhoun. Halfway there I was crying profusely and breathing stertorously. I ran into some medical students who gave me several gauze bandages soaked in water to hold over my mouth.

In the aid station we were flooded by tens of young people, coughing and crying and vomiting in the courtyard. We must have provided good service, because we had several people whom we had treated on the previous night return, including one girl who had come down with fifty-five others from a commune outside of Boston. She was a pretty girl who did not really know what she was doing there except that she had been asked to come down, and it was kind of fun moving from town to town. Two weeks ago her group had trashed Harvard Square.

The mechanics of treating people who came in were well established, and I dashed over to the information center through the courtyard to discover about thirty people crying and coughing from

261

the effects of the thick gas. We escorted them down through the passageways in the basement and up to our treatment center.

It was hard to reconstruct the events triggering the police response. The "new politics corner" down on Elm and Church streets, three blocks away, was set ablaze at 8:30 p.m., either accidentally or by an arsonist. The fire started in the basement, spread, and then attracted a group of young people, who were led away by a Panther. There was the usual rock and bottle throwing and a response of tear gas from the police. Large amounts of tear gas were used, and at the time that I was running down Elm Street and turning into Calhoun at about 9:40 p.m., I could see the flashes of the tear gas launchers over on the Green and could hear the characteristic "crump, crump" sound of canisters being fired thirty or forty times more. The gas was sucked through the gateway and up through the courtyard like convection currents flowing across the hearth in a fireplace.

Once the gas cleared and our treatment unit had stopped providing service I went out to the gateway and viewed an alarming scene. On Elm Street in front of the Methodist Church, no more than thirty yards from the entrance to Calhoun, was an assemblage of twenty policemen wearing gas masks and helmets and carrying tear gas guns and canisters. Behind them were a loose formation of National Guardsmen with vehicles parked obliquely at the curb, ready to take off. The police were still firing occasionally on the Green, but the gas was not rolling toward us as it had earlier. The distance from the corner down to the gateway by the college was forty feet. In that space were packed about forty people muzzled in gas masks and helmets and armed with bottles and rocks. There was a great restlessness in the crowd on the sidewalk, and the marshals by this time were exhausted and somewhat ineffective.

I decided to talk to the police, to get them to withdraw. I walked out into Elm Street and spoke to the lieutenant, who indicated that his men were tense and jumpy. He did not want any more trouble but did not like the looks of the crowd on the sidewalk, and his men were now prepared to charge. I tried to encourage him to withdraw by citing the 150 students with conjuctivitis and other gas effects we had treated and was making headway when I looked up and found Bill Coffin standing next to me. He supported my withdrawal recommendation, adding that the students also would withdraw thirty yards. He started the police retreat and I went back to the sidewalk and instructed the marshals to get the young people moving back.

There was much resentment and many accusations of my having made a deal with the pigs. I asked some of the "crazies" if they wanted to have their heads busted or get gassed again. Speaking angrily and authoritatively, I said they seemed to be very much in love with humanity, but they did not give a damn about the people who were without masks and without protection for their heads. The largest number retreated into the college courtyard, having been assured that this was an area of dispersion where they would not be pursued by the police. Several clusters of helmeted and gas-masked militants remained. I asked one young man why he did not want to move, and he responded "I have had my head busted in Berkeley, Washington, and Chicago, why shouldn't I have it busted in New Haven?" Across his helmet was printed "Fuck you, pigs!"

Within ten minutes we had the sidewalk cleared, until a trio of young men, each more than six feet tall and weighing more than 200 pounds, insisted on passing through our marshals' ranks and walking up to the corner. They identified themselves as coming from Fair Haven, a conservative Italian-American community. I cautioned them against going to the corner, because it would provoke the police. They walked deliberately up to the corner, not once but three times. On the fourth walk I interrupted them and said loudly that there was a chance they could provoke a riot, but there was also the possibility that nothing would happen. But no matter what happened, I wanted them to remember that when they next went to confession and saw their priest, they would have this to report to him. They left sulkily, going through the courtyard of Calhoun and out through the gateway to College Street.

We began to have trouble with groups moving up Elm Street to the level of the gateway and wanting to come through to the corner.

The worst encounters were with blacks who wanted to see what was going on and would not take instructions from white marshals. We found a cooperative black youth who had introduced himself to me by saying, "Christ, these white radical bastards make me so nervous I can't sleep at night. When are they going home?" I felt now we had a new recruit, a yellow headbanded marshal who could deal with the blacks, and indeed he was effective. After the use of tear gas there was poorly contained rage toward the police and the National Guard on the part of the moderate radicals, i.e., those without helmets and gas masks. They required several explanations each time they attempted to push through the marshals' line.

I went back to the aid station, impressed with the relative ease with which one could turn back a milling crowd. Their readiness to be led by an authoritative figure was worrisome, whether it was I in a white coat or Jerry Rubin in velvet pants. A marshal called me fifteen minutes later to report a new threat. Coming down through the ranks of the police who were still standing at the level of the Methodist Church were five National Guard officers in full battle dress. Rock and bottle throwers were still present, and I saw the presence of the National Guard as an incitement to a real riot.

I walked into the middle of the street and confronted this group of five, identifying the leader through his nameplate as Colonel Pedersen. I suggested that their actions were a clear provocation, and if a riot developed, I would be careful to report this to the mayor's office, the news media, radio, and television. Pedersen seemed offended and asked me if I was coercing him. I told him that I was not coercing him, but that I was a doctor who was struggling to work with these young people, and I begged him to withdraw to positions behind the police. Much like their adversaries, the colonel and his men turned around and walked in the opposite direction.

Vastly relieved and a little bewildered at my success, I called Keniston again to report that we needed more marshals on the corner. He summarized my phone conversation to a recording secretary, and now I was annoyed that he did not want every detail.

When I returned to the gateway, the troops and police had departed and traffic flooded the four lanes of Elm Street. There were no crazies and no gas, but only the emptiness of the Green hinted that something had been awry.

The master's living room was quiet. The people sitting around looked half-dazed. Several of the fellows had mentioned that they wished that Rubin would come back so that they could have a quiet talk with him and tell him what they really felt about his demagoguery. There was strong feeling against him, despite the fact that Rubin did not cause the riot tonight. All were offended that Rubin had mounted the speaker's platform to condemn the university by accusing it of offering its hospitality out of fear. Lewis commented that Rubin never said thank you for kindnesses offered him.

With increasing fatigue, we sat talking. Were the rock and bottle throwers less threatening to our democratic society than the violence we created in Southeast Asia? How about the appeals to violence in the incendiary and divisive speech-making of Spiro Agnew?

I felt that the normative inner growth and development of the moderate radicals would provide for hopeful changes in their perception of themselves in the context of a continuingly inequitable world. This group has already inspired a moral resurgence in our hesitant clergy, compelled parlor politicians to give up obfuscating language and to declare themselves through action, and forced educator-administrators to abandon a policy of isolation from their faculties, students, and the communities in which their institutions reside. From the moderate radicals will emerge our leaders of the next twenty years. Unhappily, the positions of the center and the right are so fixed as a consequence of age and economic and political power that no amount of tactical yielding to the demands of youth can alter the basic intransigeance of the Establishment. I thought to myself that Rubin was right, that the university was frightened and through its fear was saved. However, it was rescued from chaos not just by opening up its doors and exposing itself to damaging elements, but rather by the active peace-making efforts of the marshals, Panthers, and the police.

It was hard to say goodbye to everyone, and the severe exhaustion took its toll. The basic issues still remained unsettled, despite the fact that in many ways the university was saved from itself and from the outside. In our collective embarrassment, we left the house individually, people like Malcolm Boyd and Leslie Fiedler leaving notes on the downstairs hall mirror.

We had spoken about a backlash which might result from the students' feelings of rage at those who had threatened them, and several of us felt that not a few may have been "conservatized" by the experiences of the past two days. Students and fellows together wondered about the possibility of a new divisiveness among the Yale students between those who left town versus those who remained to fight for preservation. There was now a new atmosphere of openness and communion between the students, faculty, and administration; each group had worked together to save something all believed essential to life and liberty in this great, troubled country. However, the inequities remain and the violence which begets violence continues from the government and from the militant left, and each accuses the other of having started it, utilizing a prior event to justify its continuance.

"Student Power" in Berkeley

Nathan Glazer

Whatever students may be doing to change the world, and they are clearly doing a good deal, it could turn out that in the end it will be easier to change the world than the university. This, it seems, is the inference to be drawn from four years of student rebellion at the University of California at Berkeley, where the present wave of student disorders, which has had such phenomenal impact in Italy, West Germany, and France, began.

Four years after the Free Speech Movement exploded in Fall 1964 the world looks very different, and the FSM looks like a prophetic turning point; but the University of California looks very much the same, and this paradox concerns me in this essay.

It may appear a case of distorted institutional loyalty to give Berkeley the primacy as the point of origin of the present wave of student civil disorder, and yet I think that what started at Berkeley in 1964 was different from the student violence of the years before —whether the student demonstrations of Japan in 1960, the endemic student violence of India, or the student rebellions of South Korea and Turkey that helped overthrow governments. There were five key differences:

1. The Berkeley student uprising occurred in an affluent country that, whatever the case with uneducated blacks, treated the educated well. There was no problem of unemployment for the educated (as there was in India, South Korea, and other developing

nations). Thus, the student uprisings could not be related to such issues as livelihood and status for the educated. It was new in that it could find issues that were crucial to students, despite their assurance of affluence.

2. It was new in that it was not directed against an oppressive national, local, or university regime, as "oppression" had been generally understood until that moment. In time the student movement was so successful that the civil government of local communities (such as Oakland and Berkeley), of the nation, and of the universities could be cast in an oppressive role, although they had generally not been seen in that light before. In contrast, much of the student disorder in developing countries was directed against military or dictatorial regimes; in Japan the regime was democratic, but was not considered so by many students and intellectuals. The new student movement that began in Berkeley was able to discover or create new issues pertaining to the basic constitution of a democratic government and the institutions within a democratic society.

3. It was new, too, in that it exploded at a time when there were relatively few great burning issues in the nation. One could still hope in the Fall of 1964 that civil rights legislation and social legislation would rapidly enough satisfy the demands of American Negroes (white backlash seemed a more urgent problem than black militancy), and Vietnam was not yet the overwhelming issue it was to become. But just as in Germany and France in 1968, student activists in Berkeley were able to create big issues on what most people felt was a relatively placid political scene.

4. It was new in its tactics. It found means of dramatizing its rebellion against an affluent and democratic society by forcing it to respond in ways that could be cast as repressive and authoritarian. The politics of confrontation was not original with the Berkeley students, but they nevertheless elaborated it in new and startling ways.

5. Perhaps the most striking novelty in the Berkeley student revolt was that the two ideologies which had played the largest role

in sparking student uprisings around the world, Marxism (in democratic countries) and liberalism (in dictatorial and Marxist countries), played only a minor role in Berkeley. Marxists of various
persuasions and liberals were of course involved, but neither the
classic demand for socialist revolution by the first, nor for civil
liberties and democratic reform by the second, could fully en-
compass the main thrust of the Berkeley student revolt. Marxism
and liberalism were rather two wings of a movement for which the
center was poorly defined. Participatory democracy, thoroughly
carried out in every institution and social process, was perhaps its
clearest feature. It is revealing that, when the Berkeley student rebels paused after their victory over the administration and cast about
for representative figures who might express their philosophy and
define their aims, they chose Paul Goodman, who is not a Marxist,
and invited him to the campus. Goodman considers himself an anarchist, and the dominant theme in his voluminous writings is specific
and his detailed attention is to small social structures and institutions that immediately affect people and their lives—predominantly
the school, but also housing, the neighborhood, local government,
the work setting. In radical contrast to the Marxists, who had
banned as utopianism all consideration of the details of how to reconstruct society, Goodman's main achievement is to analyze and
propose means of refashioning those details. If Marxists traditionally wait for the revolution, and in the meantime radicalize people
by demonstrating that no change but the largest can help them,
Goodman does quite the opposite. He hopes to show them that many
small changes can help them.

In summary, Berkeley to my mind is the first example of a student
rebellion that occurs in conditions where students are privileged,
their future is assured, where liberal, parliamentary democracy
prevails, and where the principal ideology of the student rebels is
neither Marxism nor liberalism but rather the effort to create a participatory and somewhat communal democracy. It is the first student
rebellion to have considered what is still wrong in a liberal, demo-

269

cratic, and permissive society, and by what tactics and strategy revolutionaries can bring larger numbers to agree with them that a great deal is wrong.

It is not easy to escape from the past, particularly when so many problems of the present resemble those of the past. Thus, Vietnam permitted and enabled Marxism again to become more prominent in the radical student movement. But the Berkeley revolt preceded any large concern with the issue of Vietnam and with the associated pressure of the draft, although these soon became the dominant issues of the movement. Moreover, the means of revolutionizing the masses inevitably are never entirely new. Thus it is known that when the police attack, one gains recruits and strength, and a good deal of attention must be devoted to the tactics that get the police to attack.

But what is new are the means of casting a liberal polity in the role of an oppressive one. Thus, the student activists stress the constraints of organization and government (any organization and government) and as a corollary emphasize the importance of participatory democracy, which concretely tends to mean that any mob is right as against any administrator, legislator, or policeman. (Fortunately, until now we have had left-wing rather than right-wing mobs, and they are milder.) In the thinking of the radical students the IBM card that facilitates student registration can be cast in the same role as the police control cards of the czarist state or the Soviet Union.

So the line that leads from Berkeley to Columbia, through the universities of Italy, West Germany, France, and England, marks something new. What is happening in Eastern Europe and Spain, in Brazil and Argentina, is easier to understand—it is the fight for freedom. But what then do the student uprisings of the affluent world represent? The answer is not easy. From the beginning there was a central ambiguity in the student disorders here (as there are in those of other affluent countries). Were students protesting primarily against their universities, the institutions of higher education, with their special constitutions, rules, requirements, culture?

270

Or were they protesting against their societies, with their unre-solved problems and their hypocrisies?

It is not easy to disentangle the two sorts of issues in practice, but they are clear in theory. On the one hand, we have issues that stem directly from the concrete institutional setting of higher education —relations among administrators, students, and teachers; roles in setting rules for the three groups; power to exercise discipline and to define the provocation; power to determine curriculum, criteria for admission and graduation, faculty appointments, and the like. On the other hand, we have the two great issues of American life in the late 1960s—the race issue and the Vietnam issue and what they reflect in society: racism, the dominance of the military, middle class fears of Communism encouraged by the mass media, the power of corporations, etc.

From the beginning in 1964 the university issues have played sec-ond fiddle to the political issues, even though this was often hard to see, for the actual battleground was generally the university and the representatives of the Establishment under siege were the univer-sity officials. But the university, in effect, was standing in for the world and its problems, which made for dilemmas in knowing how to handle student rebellion, but which also meant that the central structures and institutions of the university were really not the chief target. According to the radical students, the university had to be reformed, but mainly to permit the political resistance or inter-vention of students in a corrupt society to become more effective. One reason why the impact of the student revolt on the colleges and universities has been moderate up to now is that issues of educa-tional reform came up later and were secondary to the political issues.

In the thinking of the student radicals and their leaders, the pri-mary problem was the society, not the university. How then does the university get involved so prominently? The university gets in-volved because 1) the radical students demand that it offer a refuge and base for political action in the community; 2) they treat it as a surrogate for society in general, whether out of frustration, or because it was a nearer target, or to practice tactics and strategy for the larger offensive against the stronger institutions; and 3) they eventually hope to enlist it in their efforts at political education and mobilization.

In the first case the university simply, to use the language of the student radicals, "gets in their way." This was the origin of the Free Speech Movement: the students wanted the right to meet freely on campus, to raise funds, to recruit supporters, and to discuss the whole range of issues that concerned them, including the use of unlawful tactics in their political activities. This last was the sticking point in the first major Berkeley climax in December 1964, and it was left unresolved, with the faculty voting that only considerations of "time, place, and manner" should limit student political activity on campus, and the regents of the university insisting that considerations of legality should still limit the right to political activity on the campus. In the end a kind of compromise has emerged in which the radical students feel relatively unhampered in discussing the full range of present-day political issues and tactics, including of course a good deal that is unlawful, but in which the administration does not limit them unless major publicity is given to their actions. (Even then it simply works out a compromise to demonstrate to the regents and to the governor that it can exercise some power over political activity on campus.) As a result, when a "Vietnam Commencement" was proposed to honor those who refused to be drafted, there was a good deal of negotiation between the organizers of the commencement and the university administration as to where and when it should be held and just what its content would be. But it was held.

More significant has been the university's role as a surrogate or representative of society. Here some of the chief issues have been whether the university should give special placement examinations or report grades to draft officials (when standing in class was a factor in drafting students), whether the university should permit representatives from such government agencies as the armed forces and the CIA and from Dow Chemical Company to recruit em-

272

ployees on campus, and the role of the university in classified and weapons research. Here the university is acting as part of or as agent for society, and the radical students have had the convenience of an agent of society being near and also being more vulnerable to attack than some of the institutions it may be taken to represent. While in the first case, where the university serves as base and refuge, the radical students have insisted that the university make no judgment as to the legality or illegality of their actions and that it leave it to the civil arm alone to determine whether they have broken the law and should be limited in their political activity; in this second case the radical students insist that the university must make a judgment as to the morality of the activities it permits on the campus, and among those it must ban are any that serve the interests of the armed forces or the foreign policy of the government.

At Berkeley the role of the university as a surrogate and representative of those forces in society that radical students oppose recently has been in eclipse. The radical student movement has moved on from an attack on university practices in connection with Selective Service and military and government recruiting to a direct attack on Selective Service offices. The university has been superseded, first by the Selective Service headquarters in Oakland, and then by the police, with whom the radical students have clashed in Oakland in their efforts to close the Selective Service office. Radical student antagonism to the Oakland police is now allied with the militant and armed members of the Black Panther party, who have been harassed by the police. The city government of Berkeley and its police have been added to the list, because the police have opposed, with tear gas, the efforts of radical students to close a major street, ostensibly to hold a rally supporting the French students and workers. In addition, the radical students were active in organizing the Peace and Freedom party, which ran the writer Paul Jacobs for U.S. Senator, the former student leader Mario Savio for state legislator, and a variety of leaders of the Black Panther party for Congress and other posts.

But after one gets the university to move out of the way, and after one prevents, through the manufacture of disorder, the representatives of government agencies from recruiting on campus and cuts the universities' ties with defense research (not that this has been fully accomplished, but the mechanisms for doing so have (been well developed)—then what? The rules as to political behavior in a university are, after all, incidental to its chief functions, unless matters come to the point where unpopular (that is, nonradical) opinion is intimidated. This has happened at Berkeley and elsewhere, but it is owing less to the new rules, which are on the whole good, than to the attitude of the New Left to the expression of dissident opinion, which is bad. It also owes something to the ease with which people allow themselves to be intimidated. Similarly, just who recruits on campus and how much classified research is permitted is to my mind incidental to the central functions of the university. Classified research has never loomed large. The huge laboratories that various universities direct for the Atomic Energy Commission have been cut off from the university, administratively and sometimes physically. It is hard to see that they have had a major impact on the university, which is perhaps one reason why it has been hard for the radical students at Berkeley to launch an attack on the university's relationship with research facilities at Livermore and Los Angeles. These relationships could be cut without any significant effect on either the university or the laboratories, just as relationships with the Institute for Defense Analysis are now being cut by a number of universities.

The question remains: What about the heart of the university, the teaching of graduates and undergraduates, the day-to-day research of faculty and graduate students? How are they affected by the student rebellion? The structure of the university and its normal activities go on, suffering only minor impact from the events that have made student activism a major political issue in the state, the nation, and now in the world.

We have suggested one reason for this, that the radical students have really not been primarily interested in educational reform.

274

STUDENT POWER IN BERKELEY

During Paul Goodman's visit, for example, the radical students were more interested in him as a radical social prophet than as a radical educational reformer. Yet there has been all along an element of the radical student movement that, together with some nonradical students and a few members of the faculty, has been interested in educational reform since even before FSM, and FSM gave the reformers potentially much greater influence and a much larger audience. In the past this group's meetings attracted little interest. Meetings on educational reform after FSM attracted more student interest, although nowhere near the number that became involved in protest on the great political issues and in the confrontations with the university administration that the tactics chosen always seemed to lead to. And, revealingly enough, not one of these major confrontations with the administration since FSM has ever dealt with an educational issue. But if radical student interest in educational reform was not great, administration interest was. It is natural for educational administrators to assume or hope that student unrest and disorder must reflect and must be curable by institutional reform. Berkeley's Acting Chancellor Martin Meyerson in 1965 and Chancellor Roger Heyns, who succeeded him, were eager to sponsor changes in the university. The question was what changes?

The first expression about education of the student rebellion was the student-run free university. One was organized at Berkeley (it bears the unfortunate initials FUB), another at Stanford. At San Francisco State College, because of the greater strengh of student radicals, or the greater acquiescence of administration and faculty, the free university seems to have been in effect organized within the college, under the control of students, but giving credit for work. There are two points to be made about the free university as a means of revolutionizing the university. First, it is new. Radical and other ideological groups have always organized courses outside the university to push some specific outlook or to present material that they felt the university was slighting. Long before the free university one could take courses off campus on "Revolutions of Our Time

275

and Why They Failed," "Basic Principles of Marxism-Leninism," or the like. (Today's free university will generally have a course in guerilla warfare, picking up from Mao and Ché, and on the ideologists of black power.) There were other free, off-campus, noncredit courses that were and still are generally available around a university, often in the religious centers catering to students. Naturally, these courses would try to pitch themselves to student interests and would show a rapid flexibility in responding to current issues that the regular university departments would not. I imagine Kierkegaard was being taught in off-campus religious student centers before he got into the curriculum of many university philosophy departments; the off-campus pastors had a greater incentive to find something that might reach and excite students.

I review this background only because I believe that the free universities are not so different from these previous efforts to supplement university education, although they are on a larger scale. But of course the ambition of the free universities is greater than this, as their name implies; it is to teach new areas of learning and experience, by new means, all of which would not be allowed in an Establishment university. The problem is that almost anything that the law allows, and a bit more, is to be found in an Establishment-run university, and students get credit for it besides. I would guess that the summer universities now being launched in the wake of student unrest in France will have a greater impact, simply because their universities have been more conservative.

A second factor limits the effectiveness of the free universities for revolutionary purposes. Just as the off-campus religious centers have to offer courses that are responsive to student interest and fashions, so too must the free university. Perhaps the organizers would like to give courses in urban guerilla warfare, and they do, but there is nothing they can do to make them more popular than courses in drug experience meditation, sensitivity training, new forms of sexual and interpersonal relations, film-making, and a variety of other present-day youth interests. The free university is thus limited in its effect.

276

Another reason that its effect is limited is that the faculty, many of them young and only recently (or still) student radicals themselves, are by no means backward in adding to the curriculum new ideas which the radical students feel the university is suppressing. Frantz Fanon, Paul Goodman, Herbert Marcuse, and Ché Guevara get into regular courses of the university as fast as they get into the free university. This is perhaps one reason that drugs, meditation, and sex, which admittedly are handled in a more academic way, if at all, in the Establishment university, become a major stock-in-trade of the free university. And this, in turn, helps to explain why the phrase "repressive tolerance" is now so popular at Berkeley scene; it is Marcuse's explanation of how the Establishment draws the teeth of revolutionary ideas by spreading them through university courses and the mass media.

When the free university, the student-run university, gets within the fold of the university, its effects are greater but still not revolutionary. I have spoken of the student-run courses at San Francisco State College, given for credit. The same development has occurred at Berkeley as part of a number of experiments in education that flowed from the FSM. One of the results of the movement was the establishment of a faculty Select Committee on Education at Berkeley (the Muscatine Committee, as it became called after its chairman, Professor of English Charles Muscatine), which issued a large and substantial report.[1]

The committee reviewed the student rebellion at Berkeley, recognized it had many causes of which many were beyond the reach of the university, and then went on to urge reforms in education at Berkeley. It proposed no new or sweeping transformation of the university, although some of the faculty reacted as if it had. What it did propose were many small changes, and one major institutional change, all designed to support experiments and innovations in education. In effect, it proposed escape hatches for specific student and faculty interests, while the rest of the university was to go on its accustomed ways. Not clear as to how the curriculum of a huge university could be reorganized, the committee proposed a new in-

277

THE UNIVERSITY AS A MEDIUM

stitution, the Board of Educational Development, which would have the power to approve courses and studies outside the regular departments and would not require approval by the Select Committee or any other faculty committee.

These courses could be initiated by students or by faculty. If initiated by students, they required a faculty sponsor, although his role could be minimal. The board has been established, has been in operation now for two years, and has sponsored quite a number of interdisciplinary courses (twenty in the Spring 1968 quarter). There is as yet no new curriculum that has been proposed to the Select Committee. If one were, it could be approved. One of the most imaginative and unconventional courses it sponsored was one which sent forty students to Washington in 1968 to live with and observe the Poor People's Campaign. Students wrote papers, received credit, and were supervised by a faculty member. This course perhaps expresses best the kind of change the radical students would like to introduce, a course in which one becomes expert in political activism. However, even here the faculty sponsor imposed an academic discipline that some of the activists enrolled very likely felt to be external and irrelevant.

There is also now a student-run Committee on Participant Education to develop courses that students show interest in. (These do not give university credit unless the student makes a special arrangement with a faculty member, but in view of the number of acquiescent faculty members, this is not difficult to do.) These courses involve a few thousand students a year. The most popular was a course on (or in) meditation. They can be best considered something of a cross between extracurricular activities and course work. Once again, despite the popularity of Board of Education's and Committee on Participant Education's courses, the university—the departments and the research institutes, the faculty, the course work, the students—continued on its regular way, generally unaffected.

There have been other changes. Even before FSM, Joseph Tussman professor of philosophy, and some faculty colleagues of vari-

278

ous departments had been urging an experimental college to conduct the first two years of college education for some students. This would have replaced the normally disparate collection of courses students take by a single unified curriculum, based on the treatment of four major periods of civilization. This program was approved experimentally, and about 120 students and five faculty members plus graduate assistants were provided with a former fraternity house and full freedom. The program has graduated one class, and has completed the first year of work with another. It is not easy to come up with an unambiguous verdict of its results. One thing is clear, however. The experiment began with five regular faculty members, who were deeply committed, but it is now down to one, plus others brought specifically to teach in the experimental college. Rather than serving as a model for other experimental colleges, it seems questionable whether it can continue. The program merely confirms what everyone who has had some experience with experiments in higher education knows, that the departments and the disciplines define the greater part of college education, and it is very difficult to establish anything outside the regular departmental lines.

One must add that it is not clear that whatever could be established outside the regular departmental and disciplinary lines would be better than what exists within them. We should also add that the Tussman experiment, aside from the fact that its establishment was facilitated by the desire of the administration to encourage experiment as a result of FSM, has only loose connections with the student rebellion at Berkeley. It is neither student initiated nor student run, nor does the curriculum particularly reflect the new student interests. Although there is a great deal of faculty and student freedom about curriculum, it still consists of fixed readings in fixed periods of civilization.

The main thrust of student activism, in contrast, has been to further diminish the appeal of the notion of any fixed or required liberal arts curriculum. Here a good part of the faculty, with its specialist interests, agrees with the student radicals. The educational ideal of both, at this point, if they have any, is better expressed by the pure elective system than any available alternative.

While the Muscatine Committee Report, which moved somewhat in this direction, was approved by the faculty with the unenthusiastic support of student radicals, another educational report, which tried to move in the direction of a more coherent curriculum that would reflect the idea of a broadly accepted liberal arts education, was defeated by the faculty. At the time the Muscatine Committee was appointed, a second special committee (called the Herr Committee, after Richard Herr, the historian who chaired it) was formed to review the undergraduate program in the College of Letters and Science, the largest unit on the Berkeley campus. The committee proposed that the undergraduate program be made more coherent. Instead of the common arrangement whereby each undergraduate was required to take some work in a number of fields which supposedly defined the well educated man (science, social science, humanities, mathematics, languages, etc.) and was free to select what he would out of the wide range of courses offered in each field, the committee hoped that a more relevant undergraduate education could be structured, in part by developing special undergraduate courses attuned to the interests of students in other fields (science for literature students, and vice versa). This would mean either getting the faculty to develop such courses and programs or recruiting new faculty. In effect, it meant breaking the pattern of organization that is so well suited to a faculty committed to disciplines and research and is organized in powerful departments. In such a situation, which characterizes Berkeley and most universities, the undergraduate curriculum is arranged by treaties between groups of departments in the various major areas rather than by any agency reviewing undergraduate education from a nondepartmental perspective. The introductory courses and the courses designed for those from other fields, the so-called service courses, generally get little attention. The Herr Committee proposals meant that a faculty gathered on the basis of research interests and capacities and disciplinary orientations would now have to devote more

280

attention to undergraduate teaching and nondisciplinary concerns. In this case the interests of the faculty coincided with the interests of politically activist and other reform-minded students, who wanted as little restriction as possible in getting through their four years in college. The Herr Committee Report, as a result, did poorly, and its major proposals were voted down by the college faculty (only a small minority of whom in any case were interested enough to attend the meetings at which the report was discussed), in favor of a simpler student-formulated proposal.

The movement of the university toward greater fragmentation, greater specialization, strong independent departments, and a weakening concern with general education was either endorsed or at least not blocked by these changes.

Another major report, *The Culture of the University: Governance and Education,* is now under consideration by the faculty. This is the report of a faculty-student commission set up in January 1967 after another major blow-up at Berkeley. This one was occasioned by radical students who blocked military recruiters. When the administration called in the police, the predictable results occurred. The radical students gained a great deal of support, including that of liberal students and faculty, there was a student strike, and a faculty-student commission on governance was set up. The majority report of this commission is the first of three reports that expresses in some central way the ideas of the radical students.

The majority report, like the two reports before it, eschews any detailed discussion of the content of a desired education. (Who knows what that should be?) But it does know what is wrong with the present education. It argues:

> Some of the most thoughtful and serious students have come to repudiate many of the social goals and values they are asked to serve in the university and upon graduation. That repudiation is directed in part at the conditions of technological society which seem to threaten human dignity. The new world emerging seems to exact greater conformity, more routinized lives, more formalized relationships among individuals.

281

Faced with the crises of race, urban violence and decay, environmental degradation, and war,

> many students express intense dissatisfaction with the university, since it provides much of the knowledge and most of the trained personnel required by the technological and scientific society. . . . It is little wonder, then, that many students are no longer content to spend their college years preparing to "take their place" in such a society. Nor is it surprising that many students regard as irrelevant the miscellany of superficial, uncertain choices and professional training which often passes as the curriculum.
>
> Such discontent is deepened by the degree to which the university's atmosphere reproduces the characteristics of the society. The university is large, impersonal, and bureaucratic. The acquisition of specialized skills has often been substituted for education of persons, instead of supplementing it. . . .

The two crucial failures of the university, the majority report argues, are first "its failure to develop a student body which respects the value of the intellect itself," and students therefore suffer from "passionless mind and mindless passion" (as well as mindlessness and passionlessness, on the part of the majority of the students, who are characterized by apathy and careerism), and second, its domination by "service." The "function of providing useful knowledge and expert consultants to assist society in its efforts to satisfy human needs, has somehow gotten out of hand."

And the university is not well organized to deal with these problems: "Inertia and discouragement have combined to produce a situation in which fundamental educational problems are discussed only sporadically and then in so prosaic a fashion as to make education seem a dreary affair when compared with the drama of campus politics." The university should be an educational community, but it sees itself as if it were "any other pluralistic society populated by diverse interest groups and lacking a common commitment to anything more than the bargaining process itself."

It is somewhat disappointing to discover that the major recommendations of the report, spelled out at elaborate length, are first an extensive decentralization of all the functions of the university to the departmental level, together with a great increase in the role of students in educational policy-making at every level, from the departmental up and down; and second an elaborate system for exercising student discipline through various courts and panels and appellate bodies, whose aims is to ensure the fullest due process, but which strikes me as something only a lawyer could have written, and one suspects only lawyers could read or understand.

The majority report, despite the varied character of its writers and its strong commitment to a traditional view of higher education, has gained the support of the student radicals because it does offer them a greater field of action. But this report has been sharply criticized by a minority of two faculty members.

The majority report reflects to my mind many illusions: that the university can and should remain separate from society, criticizing it and failing to understand it but nevertheless gaining generous support from it; that service and practical knowledge are inferior to other kinds of education; that it is primarily administrative arrangements that prevent the kind of education that will involve radical students in their education rather than in transforming the world; that the modern university can or should be changed into a coherent educational community devoted to common ends (aside from those general ends of education, research, and service, which the majority finds inadequate); that the endless elaboration of due process and its required apparatus of courts, hearing officers, transcripts, and appeals bodies will solve some basic problem of the university; that extensive decentralization and student participation can be introduced without adding to the burden of a faculty that even now tries to escape duties of all kinds, aside from research and graduate teaching. One has the feeling that the university that would emerge from these proposals would be a delight to student politicians, but hardly to anyone else.

One outcome of the report will be more student participation in academic matters at Berkeley. But what is not clear is the extent to which this will, or can, affect the general structure of university

283

education. We have had much experience with student participation, at colleges such as Antioch and Bennington and in various graduate departments and professional schools on the Berkeley campus. I think it is a good thing, and student representation on committees may introduce valuable points of view. It does not transform education, however, and only demonstrates that the dilemmas of contemporary higher education are not simply of the making of conservative professors or administrators. And if students can be taught that by participation in faculty and administrative committees, well and good.

The radical student rebellion has not yet affected the central functions and character of the university. It is still dominated by departments and by a specialist-minded faculty. Research and publication are still the chief means by which faculty members gain status. Undergraduate teaching gets less attention than either graduate teaching or research and writing. Most college students are interested primarily in jobs, careers, and credentials, and no one has suggested how to change this, short of reversing the entire trend to mass higher education. The increasingly large support which universities need comes from states, the federal government, parents, corporations and alumni, on the assumption that universities are a good thing for society. From this massive support the functions of the university which traditionalists and radicals alike would like to see increased—social criticism and the liberal arts—are supported on a scale they have never known up to now. But I can see little prospect that the modern university can be transformed into the school of the revolution. In fact, I see a greater possibility that some universities will be destroyed in an effort to do so.

The new rebellion of black students has had much greater impact on the universities than the years of disorder by white student radicals. The explanation is simple. As I have suggested, the student radicals do not quite know what they want to do with the university, and many of their demands (for student participation, for example) can be accommodated without major upset. Radicals are to be found on many faculties, as they always have been, and Marx and his successors are in the curriculum. All this does not make radical students happy, because the academic tone changes all, but they have found no means to affect this, and their major thrust has been to such peripheral matters as to who recruits on campus and the university's formal relation with defense institutions.

In contrast, the demands of the black students have been concrete, directed at curriculum and university organization. Blacks want specific courses on American Negro and African history and culture. They want programs to recruit more black students, tutor them, and support them. They want more Negro faculty. Whereas the impact of the white student radicals has been met by administrators as that of an external invading army, which administrators have tried to appease with educational changes which scarcely interested them, the attack of black students has been directly on educational issues and can be met to some extent by changes in curriculum and student and faculty recruitment. There are nevertheless critical dangers to the university in the black demands. These concerns include the implicit demand for quotas of students and faculties and the sometimes-voiced demands for separate living quarters and exclusive courses for black students. Involved in both these demands is a potential attack on the ability of the university to maintain standards. But whereas the white radical students have fundamentally been interested in the university as a base for an attack on society, or as a surrogate for their attack on society, the black students are fundamentally interested in changing the university so that it can do a better job of getting them into society. The problem here is the illusions of many black students about just what is involved in getting into society. White radical students have convinced many blacks that getting into society is only a game unrelated to ability and effort.

A second reason that white radicals have not been able to change the university is that their faculty allies on political issues have been split and generally have been conservative on university issues. Even Herbert Marcuse has partially exempted the university, or at any rate the San Diego campus of the University of California where he teaches, from the devastating critique to which he subjects the rest of society. Many a faculty member who has said yes to getting out of Vietnam or getting military recruiters off campus has said no to greater student participation in the shaping of the curriculum or in the advancement and selection of faculty members.

A third reason that the radical students have not reshaped the university is that there is no outline or guide, no philosophy available, for reshaping the university. The traditional liberal arts curriculum is dead. It can excite little loyalty from anyone, excepting academic deans and the humanities faculty. The parts of the university which prepare people for the more concrete and obviously meaningful tasks in the world (engineering, the sciences, the law and medical schools) remain relatively unaffected by student disorder. Their students and faculty generally do not get involved. They do not see that the university needs reforming, or, if they do, they have positive and manageable proposals as to who will reform it and how it will be reformed. (David Riesman has reminded me that this is beginning to change and that law schools and, to a smaller extent, medical schools—though not yet engineering or the sciences—are now contributing a good share of student radicals, and in particular they are being deeply affected by the growing movement to involve more lawyers and doctors directly in service to the poor and to the ghetto dwellers. However, it is still my impression that the kind of nihilism that is so common among social science students when they consider the university and its functions is scarcely to be found among the law and medical students—they want to change their schools, hardly to destroy them, and I believe the discipline of professional education and the higher status their ordeal gives them within the university will prevent the radical alienation from their education that is now so common among social science graduate students.) It is the social sciences and the humanities that supply the rebels, student and faculty, and of these it is the softer rather than the harder fields, sociology rather than economics, English literature and history rather than foreign languages. The crisis of the university is a crisis of these areas. How should students in these fields be educated, for what functions, what resources should be devoted to education in these areas, to what ends? These radicals seek the overthrow or transformation of universities and wish society to be replaced by something as yet unclear.

Perhaps the most serious current radical effort to define a program for radicals in the universities is the Radical Education Project of Ann Arbor, which publishes the *Radicals in the Professions Newsletter*. All the dilemmas of student radicals in higher education are there exposed. The newsletter reports on the little triumphs of academic radicals, such as how, through "a little planning and initiative," the American Society for Aesthetics was persuaded to take a stand on Vietnam.

But when it comes to what radicals can do to transform the university into a truly radical institution, matters get more vague. One mathematics professor, writing on teaching mathematics radically, reports that he is still far from knowing how to do it. He has reached as far as emphasizing the concepts behind the formulas, which one imagines is the kind of thing conservative mathematics teachers might well agree with. One report advocates having students grade themselves. There are proposals for research projects and community projects that are not very different from others for which one gets credit or is paid. All good ideas, all good programs. But one asks whether they are truly capable of creating that totally different and transformed world that now excites the imagination of student radicals. And if they disappoint in achieving such an objective, as they must, will it not begin to appear more attractive to destroy the university rather than to reform it?

For one concerned for the universities a lengthy analysis in the newsletter of why universities and university faculties are really no places for radicals after all seems ominous. It is also ominous to me that a growing proportion of students feels a fundamental alienation from the university administration and the faculty. In 1964 Robert Somers, a Berkeley sociologist, conducted a poll on the campus during the excitement of FSM. Then 56 per cent of the students agreed that the campus administration could "usually be counted on to give sufficient consideration to the rights and needs of students in setting university policy." In 1968 after four years of moderate academic reform and with an administration far more responsive to student desires, the proportion agreeing with this formulation had dropped to 32 per cent. Only a slightly higher proportion in 1968 thought that faculty can "usually be counted on . . ." —48 per cent. There is no question about the increasing alienation of a very substantial part of the students. One finds the same phenomenon among Negro Americans, and in both cases I would argue strongly for greater participation, student and community. I do not think it will solve the basic problems particularly faster, but it may convince those who now think of themselves as oppressed classes that the problems are not easy to solve.

There have been bombings and fires and window smashing on the Berkeley campus, things which had not happened in the earlier years of intense student activism. Conceivably, the student radicals may decide on a scorched earth policy before they withdraw.

In the end one must judge whether the student radicals fundamentally represent a better world that can come into being, or whether they are committed to outdated, romantic visions which cannot be realized, visions which contradict other desires they possess and which contradict even more the desires of most other people. I am impressed by Zbgniew Brzezinski's analysis of the student revolution:

> Very frequently revolutions are the last spasms of the past, and thus are not really revolutions but counterrevolutions, operating in the name of revolutions. A revolution which really either is non-programmatic and has no content, or involves content which is based on the past but provides no guidance for the future, is essentially counterrevolutionary.[2]

The student radicals come from the fields which have a restricted and ambiguous place in a contemporary society. They remind me more of the Luddite machine smashers than the Socialist trade unionists who achieved citizenship and power for workers. This is why the universities stand relatively unchanged. Despite the universities' evident inadequacies, the student radicals have as yet suggested nothing better with which to replace them.

Notes

1. This report, *Education at Berkeley* (Berkeley: University of California Press, 1966), has been brilliantly analyzed in an article by Martin Trow, "Bell, Book, and Berkeley," *The American Behavioral Scientist, 11* (June 1968).

2. Zbigniew Brzezinski, "Revolution and Counterrevolution (But Not Necessarily about Columbia!)," elsewhere in this volume.

The Case for Student Power and Campus Democracy— a Contradiction

Boisfeuillet Jones

All persons except ideologs have difficulty in defining the proper nature of university government. Universities—so large, so complex, so contradictory in their socializing and criticizing roles—are interwoven into the American economy and society to such an extent that any hope for tangible, radical changes in their operation is pure fantasy. No doubt reform is needed at almost every level of university decision-making, but the positive benefits of reform must outweigh the dangers, and here lies a major dilemma.

In abstract terms the ideological style and rhetoric of student power and campus democracy are abundantly attractive. Their appeal, however, does not explain why student agitation against university governments has grown so rapidly in recent years. For decades critics cited the same faults in universities: the autocratic authority of officials; the apparent pervasiveness of big industry and government interests in supposedly neutral academic affairs; the advantages to the elite classes provided by universities; the impersonalization and regimentation characterized by large institutions and their highly specialized academic disciplines; the boredom of outmoded academic requirements; the incredible persistence in the lecture-exam rote system of instruction.

These inadequacies had not aroused widespread opposition, or even concern, among most undergraduates until the Vietnam war and the Selective Service System intruded onto the campus. Frustrated opposition to the all-too-clear war policy exacerbated campus protest and provided fresh examples to reinforce the traditional criticisms of universities.

The Vietnam war has intensified the ever increasing importance of colleges to middle class young men in a meritocratic society. College is no voluntary affair. To choose between going to college or going to the war is no choice. For all practical purposes the student cannot leave the college; so he strives for a say in the decisions which direct his life for four years and which set criteria on which his future opportunities could depend.

The ways in which colleges have dealt (or have not dealt) with the student and his role in an industrial society have promoted a single major idea of volatile potential, a political view of the nature of education. This concept holds that student participation in policy-making is not simply an immature quest for power; it is a way to make education become a process of self-determination. Or in other words, people learn by doing things and specifically by discovering the realities of collective decision-making.

This policy offers considerable educational advantages, as well as a few dangers. Loosening students from structures of authority implies that they will function more freely, learning from their own activities. They will have infinitely more flexibility than they now do at most colleges in selecting their academic courses and in devising fields of concentration. As alternatives to the lecture system, informal study methods, such as seminars, independent study and field projects can bring interest in scholarship to more students from nonconventional backgrounds. (Realistically, though, no revision in curriculum can hold the attention of the many young people who by family background or training are geared against intellectual pursuits.)

Political education includes self-determination of living arrangements. Colleges generally require on-campus residence, believing that the communal setup has significant educational values for undergraduates. And in metropolitan areas colleges assert that lower class town residents would suffer from inflated real estate prices if there were an influx of off-campus students. Within the compulsory residential environment, colleges have the additional responsibility of allowing students to run their own lives. It is one thing for colleges to exert authority when someone disrupts the actual academic process. It is quite another matter for the college to act as a substitute parent.

Most colleges, however, do act as parent and police for undergraduates. The school assumes the functions of a judge and enforces penalties. It is at best an ambivalent role for the college, which can result in double jeopardy when the administration invites police onto campus to handle a situation beyond its enforcement capability.

The present system of protection degrades students and in no way enhances their development to full maturity. Evidence supports the view that college protectiveness gives students a sense of special privilege. It therefore can be held partly responsible for the disrespect for civil law exhibited by some students. (The college, of course, should still offer help to a student in need of it and should maintain police for the entire school's protection.)

Equally detrimental are practices of some major colleges, such as the Ivy League schools, which avoid public fuss by maintaining a gentlemanly laxness in enforcement of rules, particularly of those relating to women and drugs. It would be better for colleges to abolish their archaic social rules altogether, permit each residential unit to enforce its own rules for maintaining peace and quiet, and allow police to handle matters of illegality.

This policy, which may be harsh on the previously sheltered freshman, will make the campus less of a sanctuary from police action in the short run; but it does not mean less independence for the individual student in the long run. The trend is already toward more local, state, and federal intervention on campuses, as amply demonstrated by the massive Stony Brook marijuana raid in January 1968 and by the congressional act to cut off federal loans to students who demonstrate illegally.

Campus activists have played into the hands of reactionary anti-intellectuals in some states. It would be best for colleges to give up

292

the task of keeping students in line with the laws and mores of society. Then a clear distinction can be made between laws and mere conventions so that outsiders will limit their campus enforcement practices to just the law and not make the colleges the target of political recrimination based on hostile political or social standards.

The major danger of a political definition of education is the great pressure to turn the university itself, not just its individual members, into a political body committed to certain aims. Some students want a political university that stands against the mainstream of American society or no university at all. This nihilistic view accepts one actuality, that the university cannot be totally pure and neutral because it serves the existing order. But it does not accept the second actuality, that the university goes far beyond any other institution in the United States as a center for questioning the status quo and criticizing official views.

The advocates of a political college neglect the obvious result: academic freedom, not the military-industrial complex, would be the victim. Transforming a university into a political action organization would first of all divert its members from the essential job of scholarship and criticism. Hence, the university's role would become shortsighted and opposed to new ideologies. The community of scholars would have to struggle continually for power on the basis of class and group interests.

Once a university became a partisan agency for action on behalf of a cause, it would totally lose the basis for its relative autonomy. The outside society and the government whose support and respect the university ultimately depends on for its income and independence, would place retaliatory curbs on it.

No wonder Richard Hofstadter spoke at the Columbia commencement of a "self-destructive strategy of social change." The possibility of changing a university in this way and to this extreme without changing society first simply does not exist. A political university would so antagonize the larger community that demands of wholesale repression from the right wing would appear.

293

Political purposes of a university require intolerance of certain ideological stands. A university's acceptance of such intolerance will only escalate the level of intolerance within the institution and provoke an opposite intolerance outside.

One reason for the disturbing avowal of a political university is that social protest for good causes in the last five years has taken the form of direct action—the civil rights movement, Vietnam war protests, draft resistance, teacher strikes for adequate salaries, ghetto capital, and educational projects. A second reason is the shoddy, two-faced behavior of many university officials in maintaining academic independence and objectivity. No university should permit classified research on official time, but many do. An individual faculty member should certainly have one day a week for any outside consulting he desires.

The position of a university official is different. Academic leaders, in contrast to faculty specialists and students, represent the university indirectly and commit it within a certain framework. It is something impossible to avoid. For that reason no university official should partake of any corporate membership which has political or ideological overtones. One university president, exhibiting incredible brass or myopia, declared that a university should be nonpolitical at a time when he himself was a trustee for the Institute for Defense Analysis.

The university officials, not the radicals are responsible for the subversion of the politically autonomous university. Take, for example, this statement from a leader of Students for a Democratic Society to a visiting committee of the Harvard Board of Trustees on January 23, 1967:

> From our view of the university as a center for free inquiry we believe that the university should be politically autonomous. It should preserve a forum for free political debate and the study of politically relevant problems, but it shall not either implicitly or explicitly become partisan in political affairs. This means that the university should preserve the right of its members to engage in responsible political actions, that it should insure an open platform for the ex-

pression of all political views, and also that it should carefully examine the political implications of any voluntary dealings with the government.

Nothing in the SDS statement suggests a radical departure from traditional notions of a liberal, nonpartisan university. Only on the question of "political implications of any voluntary dealings with the government" does the content vary from what former Harvard President Nathan Pusey, for example, might have said. Here SDS would cite as a violation of neutrality Harvard's practice of granting regular voting faculty positions to the military commanders of the ROTC units and academic credit for ROTC courses, which sometimes count a marching drill score more than the total written work of a term.

Providing class rankings for the Selective Service System's benefit was another questionable service which many colleges fulfilled unthinkingly. Most complaints of neutrality violation focus on apparent complicity with the Vietnam war. But there are other areas of politicial implication, too. The Columbia trustees' sponsorship of the Strickman cigarette filter and the Harvard Corporation's award of an honorary degree to the Shah of Iran were both disasters in this sense. Such actions undeniably throw the university's prestige behind the recipient. It would be better for universities to refrain from giving honorary degrees at all, except possibly to its loyal employes.

Freedom of political activity for individuals but not for institutions, student control of their own affairs, and freedom of curriculum choice can all be achieved practically in one way, the gradual decentralization of educational units into bodies of students small enough so that participatory democracy and free functioning do not degenerate into a manipulated relationship under the control of an elite steering committee.

There is nothing particularly ideological about the quest for decentralization. A few students feel that local, unconcentrated authority will check the centralized university machine which manipulates them for some national goal. But most students view

295

decentralization as a means to gain a dominant voice on decisions which affect their lives at college. People learn by doing things on their own power, not by having curriculums, schedules, and rules imposed from the top.

Power is not so much the issue as is the right to arrange one's own education and to know students and teachers as something besides numerical competitors and absentee overlords. A recent survey by the department of education at the University of Chicago found that less than 10 percent of Harvard's undergraduates were dissatisfied with the college, but that 20 percent considered the impersonality of student life and the lack of student voice in setting curricular policies as problems. These students wanted merely to reform a "good" college into a more meaningful and personal one.

Decentralization is nothing new. At institutions such as Columbia the president and trustees still wield authority on disciplinary and educational matters. But at Harvard actual educational power has long been delegated to the various faculties, departments, deans, and to some extent the residential houses. At Antioch and many West Coast institutions power has shifted further to student-faculty subunits.

The transferral of effective decision-making power from authoritarian presidents to senior faculty groups has actually been a reactionary step in some respects. Without administrative leadership, faculties rarely will permit curricular change. It is hard for professors to accept academic practices and ethics outside the framework of their own narrow, and sometimes narcissistic, professionalism.

At many colleges departmental semi-autonomy blocks changes in the educational system, often even if the faculty's dean personally favors such a move. Students can exert more pressure for constructive reform and decentralization upon faculty committees and departments, which tend to have acute fears of the interdisciplinary and nonconventional courses that will grow at the local level.

On matters of educational policy and appointments, the senior members of a department and the administration interchange in the role of proposer and approver. Rarely do questions reach the entire, bulky faculty. The departments and deans in turn tell students that faculty authority is legally delegated from the trustees and therefore not under the faculty's authority to delegate further, an old but still effective argument, which in itself provides a good reason for updating university constitutions to fit the current realities of faculty authority.

A result of the hazy decision-making process is that students who want to press for some reform often do not know exactly where to go for results. It is a frustrating business and has led to much rhetoric about "demystifying" the university. Part of the fault lies with undergraduate student governments and campus newspapers. These organizations more often than not devote their energies to eye-catching events and extravagant demands rather than focusing attention and pressure where substantive achievements are possible.

Although the educational and social unit within the college should be broken down to a level of humanized functioning, the need for a university superstructure remains. The United States is a highly technocratic and complex place, whether anyone likes it or not. It is foolish to suggest that students could—or should, or would —handle the financial or administrative operations of an educational community, however small.

Formal faculties are essential in 1) maintaining high standards of scholarship and teaching; 2) setting up the broad criteria under which students are free to operate; and 3) providing from its membership the administrators who have decision-making powers. A fourth faculty duty, which does not even exist at the more faculty-oriented universities like Harvard, should be the power of consent in selections of the president and deans.

Disciplinary matters dealing with obstruction of the educational process combines the first two categories of faculty duties. The third encompasses a number of administrative duties, such as admissions, school-wide extracurricular activities and sports, budgets and financial priorities. That leaves the president and trustees with authority to make some appointments, to approve faculty budgets on the basis of financial soundness, and to decide questions of investments and new additions to the university.

Few respectable scholars would tolerate student voice over academic appointments any more than they would accept similar control by trustees or politicians. The undergraduate, after all, is a transient and a layman like the politician. The whole question of permanent appointments would not arise if faculties were concerned with a candidate's published scholarship *and* teaching ability.

There is no reason that the university structure should necessarily operate on a plebiscite. Democracy could never really function in such a large and complex institution. The university as an entity is not geared to political dispute, but one-man, one-vote practices would lead to parliamentary bickering and away from freedom of inquiry and tolerance of opinions. And where does one draw a voter line in a democratic university? With faculty and students only? Or with administration, staff, and local residents who are also affected by major university policies?

Yet the superstructure should not follow the present practice at almost every major institution of making important decisions behind closed doors. Discretion is necessary in matters of faculty appointments, for it is a highly personal and sensitive matter. Otherwise, there is no reason that student opinion should not be heard at trustee meetings on financial and investment questions, or at faculty committee meetings on matters of general educational policy. Public discussion of major questions of political significance, such as whether to establish a multi-million dollar Kennedy Memorial Library in affiliation with Harvard, should occur before the trustees make a final decision.

At many universities the administration's dependence upon the goodwill of the faculty, and the faculty's only ultimate sanction through threat of resignation, necessitates an atmosphere of consensus without consistently divisive controversy. Such a balance is sensitive and vulnerable to pressure. As campus disruptions have illustrated, majorities do not matter so much when a minority is strongly aroused. Where delegation and checks exist, student and community opinion can have considerable influence on any given university issue.

The delegation system, however, foils student efforts to have any final decision-making power on a collegewide basis. A student subcommittee will never be independent of the full committee's judgment of the merits of a decision. And a full committee containing students will not be independent of the full faculty's vote, although at least the students gain initiative power this way.

Committee representation remains a far cry from student power rhetoric about developing a new and independent university force against the trends of today's society. Decentralization in itself assures that decisions on most matters are applicable only to the few people involved in a small community and not to all parts of the college or university. As one professor stated to a group of protestors, "the university is a hyperheaded thing if not a monster."

The fact that parliamentary procedures are generally useless in universities does not imply that students have no way to exert pressure. Nor does it mean that protest over substantive university policies is not a valid part of the decision-making process. It does mean, however, that a small professional administration and an informal dialog on university-wide problems constitute a major reason why some schools have held together in crises and have been run responsively at other times. Within a decentralized framework a large nonacademic administration is not necessary; students feel less isolated.

The Columbia upheaval made one point clear: students possess a great deal of power. If a small percentage of students decide to use this power, they can cripple any major academic institution. That there have not been more Columbia-type crises is remarkable. Students, even most radical ones, apparently would rather change their institution by working in it rather than committing it to a revolution. Students are no more monolithic than faculty or administration. Many are disenchanted with their educational experience; they plod uninspiringly through academic boredom, responding passive-aggressively if at all. But they are not alienated in any strict sense. The Vietnam war has served the one constructive job of catalyzing the normally quiet student into airing his grievances.

Deans of students often have the specific function of keeping in touch with the little guy, the regular student, who does not speak out on his needs in the fashion of the more shrill student leaders. In a sense the college administrator acts as a trustee for the inarticulate and apathetic. It is a difficult task in a fragmented student body.

For many students, formal teaching is preferable to self-concocted courses on contemporary social issues. There needs to be a blend of both. The establishment of bipartite legislative and judicial bodies of faculty and students will not solve major questions for the quiet student or for any student. But it will increase the lines of communication to university officers and faculty members. If the goal is to prevent massive disruption, decentralization and close educational ties with faculty are far superior to legislative channels.

Students, like all people, are most likely to feel strongly about symbolic issues. Because the university can deal only slowly (if at all) with the pressing questions of war, poverty, and racism, frustration and possibly physical confrontation on symbolic issues may occur. It is nonsense to claim that the lack of democratic voice leads to disruptive student tactics. Intense feelings cannot be channeled into institutions. The case for dealing with university reform is not to be made on grounds that it will stop further unrest. It should be made on grounds that a change in conditions would be reasonable and educationally beneficial.

There is nothing so sacred in any college's structure that it can remain unchanged with tradition alone as its justification. Universities in fact need to be shaken, but not broken. In some ways college students have never had it so good: breadth and freedom of curricular choice, relative independence on campus, and division of a centralized institution into smaller groups are all trends of the present and future. With several notable exceptions, administrative authoritarianism is dying out. The actual power of trustees and administrators over educational matters has dwindled, while the faculty's has increased. Ironically, student dissatisfaction with administrators grows at a time when the administrators do more of the time-consuming dirty work which students shun and faculty ignore. There remains the crucial question, how and to what degree can college education really be reformed? Certainly student pressure on faculty and administration key spots, as well as the evolution of the small educational unit, are steps in the right direction. But, as David Riesman and Christopher Jencks have reasoned the *The Academic Revolution,* the graduate school holds the central role in the university and dominates the college. It virtually controls university appointments, teaching, and even undergraduate studies in rigid professional classifications. Here reform is needed most.[1]

If the nation's most prestigious colleges would lead the way toward gradual educational reforms, then graduate schools would be under pressure to adapt approaches to fit a new type of clientele. At present, the prestigious colleges direct undergraduates to greater specialization early in their education. Despite the resulting warped and limited backgrounds, these students will fit easily into the professions of a technical society, leaving experimental institutions in an isolated and noneffective position in education.

The answer is not student democracy and activism at the colleges. That road leads to a dead end even if it had educational benefits; outer society and the federal government, the controllers of academic pocketbooks, would intervene against what they consider intolerable behavior. Society must change with the universities, if not before. And if reform at colleges is not piecemeal, it leads to impractical, indulgent, and unwise expression. The ensuing public attention can only bring disaster from a generally conservative government and people. The destruction of the university would mean less dissent rather than the breakdown of capitalist society that some radicals might want.

The obvious inequities of America's higher education system in a class-bound society cannot be eliminated by reforms in the college or university alone. As long as the distribution of power, wealth, and cultural privilege remains different in a family-oriented society, the children of the privileged will have the advantage in college admissions competition. As many educators have observed, motivation is the key to college admission and success. Elimination of meritocratic criteria and tuition costs would give the underprivileged and uninfluential even less chance of gaining access to college and increase the burden on the noncollege population even more, through higher taxes.

Advocates of platitudinous democratization of the university superstructure should perhaps ponder the hard realities of American society and politics before using society's one institution that is devoted to provoking social concern and thought to grind an ideological ax with a double cutting edge.

Note

1. Christopher Jenks and David Reisman, *The Academic Revolution* (New York: Doubleday, 1968).

Notes on Antioch Visit

Sue Keese

(These comments are drawn from a three-day diary Miss Keese kept while visiting the Antioch College campus as one of several student observers from Wittenberg College.)

We arrived at the Antioch Union early on a Thursday and I began almost at once to realize what would probably be my most consistent "discovery" about the campus: it could be a rather uncomfortable place for a visitor who fails to realize that people there are *not* watching him. A visitor searching for the proper thing to say or to do at Antioch will not be comfortable until he learns that the reason no one is showing him what to do is because very few of the students have bothered to give much thought to "how one behaves." There really are almost no norms. Once the visitor accepts this, he may learn that Antioch is an almost overwhelmingly comfortable place. The students seem to be confident of their right to be there and to pursue their interests in not the "correct" way, but the manner which seems most workable or desirable. They are frequently preoccupied and, besides, they assume that you also are capable of deciding what you want to do, and then doing it. They will not stand in your way and, to the visitor, it might often appear that this casual, almost indifferent attitude toward others is simply a lack of consideration.

Adrian's room was neat and sparsely furnished in an Oriental style. She had spent a year in Japan through AEA (Antioch Education Abroad). AEA was a wonderful program, she said. (Almost every one of the students I talked to said something of this sort. Most of them had either been abroad or were planning to go AEA, or otherwise, as Antiochians seem to be accustomed to arranging things for themselves.) Adrian had discovered Zen in Japan and she still practices it along with a small group of interested students who meet regularly to help one another. She had spent last quarter at Columbia in the Oriental studies department "with the best men in the field." That was one thing about Antioch: "The teachers just aren't that good. They're nice people, lots of them, but they're not brilliant." She was quick to assure me, however, that she was still glad to be at Antioch. Where else could she find so many opportunities for learning away from the campus? And she missed it when she was away. Antiochians, she told me, tend to congregate in cities all over the country, even abroad, partially because of the "strange chunks of time" during which they live off campus and perhaps also because there really was a sort of community among them. She laughed, "I can recognize Antiochians on the subway, even ones I've never met. You go up to them and say 'Don't you go to Antioch?' and they're going to the Museum of Modern Art, maybe, and say 'Why don't you come along?' And then there's the 'Moocher's Guide,' the co-op list. If you need a place to stay in any city, you go to the list to see who's in town. Then you call them up and say, 'How about lending me a piece of your floor tonight?' Of course, it works both ways; during div change especially you get more 'company' than you can handle!

"Actually, I think that we Antiochians are made to feel on many levels that we're quite different," Joan said. I asked her how. "Well, the work-study, the AEA, and just the nature of the students who come here. When I tell people where I go to school, there are three basic reactions: either they like you immediately, are impressed and all-for-it, you know; or they flare up and call you a Communist; or they've never heard of the place. If they've heard of it, their reaction is violent, one way or the other."

"Antiochians are a pretty egotistical group, really. You know, 'We're different, we're liberal, we're open-minded.' Now, whether this is only what people would like to believe . . . I don't know. I meet lots of people who feel as I do on many issues. . . . But it's true (although I don't have the statistics to back me up on this) that the reputation and structure attract certain types."

Later I went to Main Building, where the Educational Policy Committee meeting was being held. Teachers in casual clothes were stretched comfortably on chairs surrounding a long table. Present were three girl students, whom, in looking back, I imagine were rather "straight." Students and teachers were smoking, sipping soft drinks, and reading the syllabi, and when they referred to one another, they used first names. I asked if I might sit in and someone said yes. No one spoke to me or looked up at me until the meeting began. Then one of the professors asked, "Who are you?" and introduced me to the others.

The meeting was astonishingly well controlled, but without formality. Those present quickly reviewed what had been said last time, then discussed the topic for today. They were working on the grading system, trying to come up with a proposal to present to the community; the main suggestion this time, which came from one of the teachers, was that "the student has control over any information that the institution releases about him"; this, someone said, would imply that it was the faculty member's responsibility to keep a student informed about his impression of the student, but that it would be for the student to decide what goes into the record. Other more loosely structured grading systems had been proposed, and the group decided to present several alternatives to the community, perhaps by tape recording. They agreed to bring a tape next time to record discussions for and against the proposed systems. The meeting lasted exactly one hour, and by that time the talk had come full circle and was obviously complete.

"The main reason people get depressed here is because you're so much on your own," Sue said. "There's nothing like a dean's list for instance, so there's no competition for grades. Nobody knows who's 'good.' But it goes further than that. There's just no way of obtaining status, so you have to know yourself pretty well. You have to have something of your own to keep you going."

"Another thing, there's a lot of talk about community, but there's not too much community responsibility here. It's mostly all 'personal integrity.' Everybody gets involved in his own personal hangups—there's a sort of 'I don't give a shit' attitude towards others. The only way you can find out what's going on is from the bulletin boards."

Sue felt that she was "ruled out of a lot of things" at Antioch because she was straight, though she had never told anyone that she was, and she does not look that different from lots of people who are not straight. But she had never even had a chance, she told me, to refuse pot. Last year she had had a roommate who was a hippie. Sue had felt discriminated against; her roommate and her friends, all of the people, or most of them, who smoked a lot of pot, simply assumed that she would not understand. They were a bit defensive, she thought, and ruled her out of a lot of their activities. For all they knew, she said, she might be really anxious to try pot; she certainly had nothing against it. But she had not been given a chance.

"I've thought of transferring," she admitted. "But I don't know. If I weren't going AEA I'd probably consider leaving. But I don't think I could go anywhere else. If I left, I'd just go away for a while, and then come back."

In the Union one night a group of students carried lumber from a room upstairs to a car outside. I approached one of the boys, Lesley, an art major with long curly hair, who seemed to me rather effeminate, and asked what he was doing. They were taking down a display which some students had done as a special project. I followed him upstairs to where some of the others were working. No one looked at me, either to question my right to be there or to acknowledge my presence. Finally, I spoke to Vicky, a girl who seemed to be "around" a lot, to know a lot of people. She had curly hair, pulled back carelessly in a bun. She wore hoop earrings, jeans, a purple velour shirt, and lots of gold beads; her manner was confident and matter-of-fact, almost brusque. She made it clear that she was talking to me because she had to answer my questions, not because she wanted to. The display, she said, had been based on the Tibetan *Book of the Dead*. There had been rooms, walls levels, on beaverboard, with a flour-water-and-sawdust concoction "depicting the various levels of consciousness. How the states would appear if you could sustain them. I imagine it was analogous to what some people get on an acid trip." Then she excused herself abruptly and walked out. I introduced myself to another girl, who did not tell me her name, and told her what I was doing. Some of the others were listening by that time, and they were colossally uninterested; I imagine they were rather scornful about the "investigation," but that was my business. They were interested in their own.

I asked Claudia and Wendy about dating at Antioch. Wendy laughed sarcastically. "That's the big complaint around here. Girls gripe because they aren't called up till maybe half an hour before it's time to go out." Then immediately they began to defend that: "It's more natural. People don't date just to date."

"There's a very strong premium on honesty here," Claudia added. Wendy said, "Well, look at the dance. That's the only big social event of the quarter. [Laughter] You wear a dress. It's about the only tradition Antioch has." "And people don't like it, really," Claudia said. "They show up, but it's an artificial situation."

I asked what effect the three-month breaks had on dating patterns. Wendy said that everyone talked about it but that it had never bothered her. She had met Ronnie on a co-op job, and she and Claudia had first liked each other when they were in the same city during a work session. Steve and Claudia, on the other hand, had never been together on a co-op job, but "the reasons they liked each other were still there" when they both returned to campus. "If anything," Claudia said, "the work-study business tends to make personal relationships more intense."

I watched a group of people talking on the other side of the mailroom, a tall, long-haired foreign student with a British accent, two good-looking boys, one bearded, and two girls, one of whom (a

307

Puerto Rican student) stood out notably at Antioch for her exuberance. Unlike any of the other students I observed, she greeted most of the people who came into the mailroom. She semed to known everyone, and she laughed and smiled more than most students I saw.

A boy with long hair and a wild, bushy beard and wearing brown leather pants and jacket walked into the mailroom. Hannah (the Puerto Rican girl) called out to him, "What are you wearing?" He looked up from his mail. "A World War II flying suit." "Why?" "If you'd just come as far on a motorcycle as I have, in this weather, you'd want one, too."

After the others left Hannah told me that she had originally come to Antioch as an "exchange-type student," planning to stay for only one year. "But I couldn't go anywhere else after that. The students ARE something here." She decided to stay. She likes the responsibility she is given here. A very young-looking girl, with waist-length hair, walked in with a baby. While the girl was checking the mail box, Hannah played with the baby. (I had noticed, in the Union, quite a few students with babies. The babies seemed to be left to wander around freely. Their parents knew where they were, knew that they were more or less safe, and there was very little anxious nervousness about the children.)

I mentioned to Hannah that I had seen quite a few married students. Was it very common? She supposed so. But there was a high divorce rate, she thought. "Nobody I know who's married is married anymore. In fact, the only happily married couple I know isn't married; they have nothing to tie them down together except being in love."

Later that afternoon I went to the esthetics class which Joan and Adrian had recommended. The professor was rather unusual; a remarkably dense, unruly head of wavy gray hair was his most outstanding physical feature. He had been the moderator at the Marshall McLuhan discussion the night before.

But the class itself, though it was notorious (for mixed reasons) even at Antioch, and so not necessarily typical, was the ideal for my own purposes. Each student at each session was given three minutes to present a prepared "experience," something illustrating any esthetic point which seemed worthwhile to him. One presentation followed another without comment, unless there was time remaining at the end of the class. I will describe some of these presentations, because I think they provide excellent indication of the things Antiochians are thinking about—areas of interest, and various "notions" which I observed in less concrete manifestations throughout my stay.

Some students read selections from books which had impressed them. Only Sartre was chosen more than once, and no one read from anything like Hegel or Hume. As must be noticed from the attitudes I have already described, the existentialist temper, whether or not formally "adhered to" here, is almost a background for much student thought and action. Existential grasp, understanding of and action on the nature of each situation, seems more natural and obvious in the Antioch context than any sort of linear conceptualization of history, ethics, or assumptions. The sources which were used more than once were *The Tradition of the News* and *Art as Experience*.

One student had set up an experiment, and people in the class seemed satisfied and not at all surprised at its outcome. He had made a collage, with words like *Truth, Illusion, Reality, Falsehood, Man,* and *Art* and many bright colors. Then he asked the youngest member of the class to leave the room. "Is there anyone here over twenty-five?" he asked, and the professor raised his hand. He set the professor before his collage and gave him sixty seconds to describe what he saw. "Not much," the professor said. He thought for a while, and said very little until his time was up. Then the youngest student was brought in, and the experiment was repeated with him. Immediately he began pointing out the dichotomy between levels of reality, man's dilemma between life and death, and the relations of truth and illusion to society, until his time was up. Everyone, including the professor, grinned.

Another student placed two glass slides in a projector. With the lights turned off he began to play a tape which he had prepared of musical and sound effects, and he poured a cupful of beer between the slides. As the projected bubbles drifted down the side of the opposite wall, in time to the music, he poured in food coloring. As color struck the bubbles, a collision sound came from the tape.

One member of the class handed out slips of paper with instructions printed on them, and staged a happening. ("Happenings" are "happening" less often now at Antioch, I was told. For a while they were a popular classroom technique.) Another student illustrated beautifully, I thought, what seemed to me to be a prevalent hangup at Antioch, one which I would have trouble defining. She handed out numbered slips of paper with an expression on the back (mine was "Hello, it's so good to see you again"). Each number had a mate, and when the signal was given, students rose silently, holding out their numbers, found their mates, and for sixty seconds attempted, without speaking, to communicate the expression on the back to each other.

Another student used his time to state that he was not satisfied with the way the course had been going and wished to recommend an alternative plan. Later another student who had apparently prepared a presentation, "donated" his time to continuation of the discussion.

Adrian's friend Marshall was there, too (he had seen me, but not acknowledged me). For his presentation he turned off the lights, played an Olatungi African drum record and, after inviting the class to "get into it" in any way they chose, began to dance wildly to the drums.

A black student described an idea he wanted to try, a new experiment with musical notes, using arrows, squiggles, what-have-you, on a staff as a better means of expressing the jazz interpretations of such musicians as Coltrane and Mann. He called it "an experiment with order and my sensitivity to those musicians whom I'm using."

Still another student, a theater major, played a special tape which he was using to memorize lines for a play and demonstrated how much faster he learned the lines that way without thinking. Then he drew on the blackboard what he called "a theater major's concept of a dendritic pattern" and asked if, in the time remaining to him, anyone could please tell him what the hell was going on in his brain; he just wanted to know. The problem was discussed with interest for the remaining two minutes.

After the presentation the teacher asked if there was any discussion; after that, he could not get a word in edgewise. The students were comfortably dressed, and sat carelessly, some smoking, but always attentive. They continued the discussion of whether the course ought to be restructured. No conclusion was reached, but no one suggested that the matter be left to the teacher's discretion.

Adrian was curious to know what I had found out about drugs. She did not smoke pot often and had never tried LSD, but she, like everyone else I talked to, would not condemn them. "But it bothers me what they do to some people . . . who get preoccupied with them. There are a lot of kids around here who are pretty messed up," she said. She had a friend, she told me, who was a first year student. Before he came to Antioch he would come often to visit her. They talked of the school, and she encouraged him to apply, if this was what he wanted. "Now I see him on campus, walking around in a daze," she told me. "And I feel, somehow . . . responsible." She continued: "I hear the creative high on LSD is fantastic, but I'm sort of out of it. I just feel that I've got something much better with Zen. You know, I just don't need it."

Most of the boys' analyses of the LSD experience were rather pat, I had heard them all before. Chet, the biology major, did most of the talking. He considered himself a guide and had introduced several freshmen to LSD, including Michael. It was good to have a friend along, he said, someone you can groove with. And it is also an insurance against bad trips.

"If Michael here was high," Chet said, "and things started getting . . . well, getting bad, getting to him, he'd come to me. I'd see what was happening and just suggest to him, 'Don't you think you're being hypersensitive? Here, think about this,' and I'd sort of send him off in some other direction."

"It's a really special relationship . . . when you really get up there with someone, and you're really grooving together. It means more," Michael explained, "because you know that a guy's got all his inhibitions stripped away. He won't say anything he doesn't mean. I tripped out with my preceptoral fellow once, and he paid me a compliment, and it was the greatest thing that ever happened to me. I didn't look at him afterwards and wonder what his motives were, I just believed him."

Shortly after midnight I decided to leave and the boys said goodbye. The walk back from their dorm was dark but, once again, a typically Antiochian idea seemed to prevail in boy-girl relationships. It might be interpreted as a lack of consideration, but I feel that the reasoning behind it all is the assumption that "girls can take care of themselves." I saw many cases where girls were not escorted to and from dorms; doors were seldom held, and many dates are dutch. But, conversely, girls seemed to feel free to smoke on the street, to use their normal, free language around boys, etc. One of the male Wittenberg observers noted this and suggested that it was "hard to be a girl at Antioch." I asked some girls later whether they thought this was true, and the answer was always a flat no.

There is a slang term used quite frequently at Antioch: the verb *groove*. To groove with. You might picture it as a record groove: two people might be talking together and using the same words, but if they are not used to entertaining the same kinds of thoughts, if there are no common assumptions underlying what they say, then no matter how much the words seem to "agree," they are not talking about the same thing. They are not grooving together.

One way of telling who grooves, who is in it, a very superficial way but rather effective is to find out whether they understand—*get* is a better word—Bob Dylan. When I talked with Oren about "Mr. Jones" we both knew what we meant. It was a reference to a Dylan song where subject matter is more or less the whole hippie-straight dichotomy.

What Oren and I talked about that afternoon was what Antioch was about, what straight was about, and whatever else there is besides straight. You can read all the books, you can analyze it, and that is what Mr. Jones tries. But the emphasis on Antioch, and elsewhere, is on experiencing it. As Oren said, "You can understand it intellectually, but you can't know it until you feel it in your bones."

Oren called it "decadence," and, looking around the cafeteria I could see what he meant. You might call it "Nausea" (like Sartre's *Nausea*); it is what is happening to a lot of young people, and Antioch's peculiar structure—the co-op system, the availability of drugs—encourages or intensifies it. Students are peculiarly alone there, with no structure to orient themselves around. At Antioch it is very difficult to conceive of yourself in terms of what others think of you; you do not find out who you are in relation to others, but in relation to yourself.

Because others are not going to confirm your existence, then, you are left with yourself to confront. And it is depressing, because you do not know. So then you go out on your co-op job, and maybe you are impressed with yourself and with "The Great World." But you learn, then, that it is not the kind of world you want it to be. The values are rotten, you think, or the people are all measuring out their lives in coffee spoons. There are lots of overwhelming problems—racial discrimination, poverty, war—and these things seem absolutely natural to most of the people in the world, and you just cannot understand why, because they do not seem natural to you.

And to make it worse, most of the people "out there" think they know "The Truth." It is God, or reason, or money, or a philosophy. But you simply do not know *any* "Truth" at all—you even doubt, perhaps, that there is a single truth to be discovered.

So you come back to Antioch. And you look at whatever it is you have been living for, whatever your own values happen to be, and you look at the ideas you have been working with in school, and you realize that you have no place, either positive or negative, no relation whatever to the real world. And you realize that you are not afraid of failure; the problem, on the contrary, is that you feel that success within the existing society will have no meaning for you at all, that the best things which the system has to offer are quite unattractive to you.

That is where Oren's decadence comes in. You are not impressed with things anymore. You do not smile so much, because of the kind of thoughts you are thinking, but also because there is no longer a reason to smile if you do not feel like it: you are not trying to impress people, or to make large numbers of "friends" who do not mean anything.

Given these feelings (and, foolish as they might sound, and whether they ought to be true or not, they are what is happening to a lot of students), you might have become "political," say two or three years ago. Some Antiochians still do, but the school is astonishingly apolitical now. One of the reasons is the impotence which student demonstrators and civil rights workers have felt in the presence of problems which are overwhelmingly complex. ("We need another flood," one person told me.) Another reason is the disillusionment with the methods of the 1930s types and the FDR liberals, the discovery on the part of these totally alienated young people that the "liberals" like the "system," that they think that if it could only be perfected, or its deficiencies compensated for, then everything would be fine. But many of these young students do not want "more;" they want "different."

Given these things, Antiochians show a disillusionment with political philosophies in general; everything carried to its logical conclusion defeats itself. I talked to Carl Oglesby, the activist scholar in residence, about this. He found it, too, at Antioch. He told me that his political overtures met with a very poor response. It is significant, he thought, that when he decided instead to teach a course in "Absurdist Morality," he was amazingly well received. That was more like what Antiochians were ready for at this point.

At this point drugs come into the discussion and absurdism, and the vaguely non-Western, non-Aristotelian feeling you get at Antioch. I do not know where the word "straight" came from, but it is apt. Straight is staying on a line with the way society is going. Straight represents the kind of mindset, the frame of reference for which Aristotle is considered to be vaguely responsible. The opposite of straight (hippie is an unsatisfactory word, used only to separate from straight, and straight is used in much the same way as the Biblical Jews used the word "Gentile") attempts to see wholes, rather than linear concepts: it's getting less and less literate/verbal all the time (in a Marshall McLuhan sense, which is why he is so

314

important right now), more and more experiential, less and less intellectual in the old sense.

Marijuana and the mind-expanding drugs are inextricably tied up
in this particular scene. "What to do about it all," the phenomenon
which I just attempted to describe, becomes a matter of *The Yogi
and The Commissar,* except that in our society—and, whether they
like it or not, most Antiochians I talked to about this recognized that
they were caught up in whatever sickness it is that is infecting our
society—in this society and for these people neither the Yogi nor the
Commissar is satisfactory. Both ways are terribly right and terribly
wrong.

Turning on makes things a whole. It makes the old type words,
which in the past these students have become so hung up on, simply
decoration. Writing becomes the same thing as painting; reality (it
seems) becomes itself, instead of being clean, esthetically symbolized. You can experience things, instead of attempting to find their
significance. That is, from the hippie's point of view (or, say, from
Sartre's in *Nausea*), instead of softening reality with phrases and
meanings—taking a whole, breaking it up into separate words, and
projecting it in a linear sequence into time, which has not seemed
to work—the hippie can *have* a reality.

The arguments against this are good ones. The Antiochians I
talked to were tired of hearing them: "But isn't it giving up?" "Isn't
it losing your hold on reality?" "What will you ever accomplish?"
No one seems to have found a satisfactory answer to these questions, because (and this is where the hippie-straight dichotomy is
most acute) they are posed within an entirely different frame of
reference. "Giving up what?" "Whose reality?" "Accomplish?"

Many people are confused about where it is all leading. Susan, a
straight girl I talked to, didn't understand. It may have been unfair
that she was not given a chance to understand but the people who
do understand find a chance.

Walt was quite active in politics (SDS). He had just become involved with pot, and he quite frankly did not know "where he was
at." He saw before him an alternative: "There are an infinite num-

ber of same ways to go. I could go to a shrinker," he said, "and get adjusted. In a sense, you know, they're right. It's just an aberration. I just don't groove with the predominating scene. I could get it all fixed, because I really would like, you know, to get married and have kids and all that scene." He laughed and pointed to the tie which he was wearing. "I'm wavering, you see. I mean, because I know now that it's all rotten, and it's all phony, but, if I got adjusted, if I went to a shrinker and all, I would just know something else, the opposite of what I know now."

"So," he continued, "I could do that, and I have this feeling I might. Or I could get into this." He motioned to the room around him. "Where does that go? Nirvana, with everybody turned on and smiling in and fading out?" He simply did not know.

Lisa saw even more frightening implications. "We're here in school, right? Absorbing our own culture. So we go on absorbing, and absorbing, and then we learn about experience, right? Then it's all over. We've absorbed it all, and there's no more culture. No more history, just experience." She continued that this factor was what was hard for her to accept, that perhaps she was just too "literate." She needed something to tell her what was happening because the happening was not enough. "Maybe this is the best way," she said. "But unless I'm stoned, and not even really then, I can't get far enough out of my Western bag to want to want it."

Drugs are a personal thing at Antioch. The whole scene is quite different from the drug scene in New York, for instance. I could find no evidence of pot parties or anything like them. People turn on separately, or in twos or threes, and then go wherever they are going. But the most surprising thing about drugs at Antioch was the remarkable feeling of well-being with which students approached their use. To many students the matter of drugs was a tremendously important question (although certainly not in the *Life* magazine sense: "good vs. evil") but it was a personal question. The proverbial paranoia which dominates the use of drugs in a big city, where "everybody's" on to it and lots of people are trying to stop it, seemed to be missing entirely here. There was no fear of being seen "stoned on the streets," followed home, and raided. The college is apparently off-limits to the police; the students feel that they are protected. In New York there is a rather nihilistic approach to drugs, and getting busted is inevitable sometime or another. Groups like the Jade Companions have banded together, charging membership fees to create a pool to pay for their members' bail. At Antioch there is very little fear, and that seems to ward off to a certain extent the tendency toward clannishness, proselytizing, and other forms of "going off the deep end."

Oren and I talked for more than an hour, touching on many of these issues. We talked about books. It is significant, I think, that he was involved in the only thing approaching a book fad at Antioch: Herman Hesse. Perhaps *Magister Lude* and *Siddhartha*, and the students' interest in them, best characterize the apolitical, navel-inspection tendency at Antioch. Oren talked about the Glen, too, and how nice it was to be left alone and to go down there to figure things out.

It seemed to me that Jeff and his friends were more cheerful, lighter, and certainly more "groupy" than the "typical" apolitical Antiochian, although part of it may have been this particular occasion. They had gathered to visit with Johnny, a boy who had dropped out of school for a while and was working in Chicago, and as I understood it, he was a very special person, at least to these people. "One of the beautiful people," one of the girls told me later. I was quite taken with him myself; he said little and looked very gentle and unassuming. Later when some Wittenbergers joined the table and the hippie-straight problem became very strained, occasionally one visitor would ask a question ("What kind of fads do you have here?" or something like that) which would leave everyone at the table feeling awkward, almost speechless. Johnny would always be the one to break the ice; without being patronizing or ironic, he would attempt simply to answer the question, without exchanging "secret" glances with the others at the table.

There were several boys and three girls at the table. One of them,

Wissy, had bleached blonde hair (which is significant, because most girls at Antioch do not seem to want to be bothered with bleaching their hair; somehow it is tied up with the fact that Wissy is still "political"). When I arrived, they had been talking about Camus' *Resistance, Rebellion, and Death,* which Carl Oglesby had recommended to Jeff. Jeff introduced me to everyone. I smiled and asked if they were the political people. One boy protested "Not me! No!"

Jeff laughed. "Come on, Paul. You know you think exactly the same as I do, only you won't admit it." Everyone laughed at Jeff and winked at me.

"Come on, Jeff," I said. "I know you still think in a line." (I think it is significant that at this point everyone at the table knew what I meant.) Johnny nodded, and Jeff said, "Yeah, well maybe. Yeah, but . . ." Then he interrupted himself to point out someone to Paul—"Hey, see the guy over there with the Trotsky beard?"—and everyone laughed.

"It's a good thing you're not political, Jeff."

"But it's all changing, anyway. Like SDS," he said. I asked Jeff what SDS was doing now at Antioch.

"Nothing," someone said.

"Navel inspection," somebody added.

Jeff and the others explained that SDS was not really doing too much as SDS at that time. They are not recruiting new members right now. Their organization had grown up too fast. Now it did not matter too much whether they called themselves SDS or not; the most important thing was to figure things out, to examine their own values, to decide what they really meant by "freedom" and "power" and so forth. Most of their action, they said, was focused inward on the Antioch community.

As far as power camps were concerned, students were learning the real conflict of interest was not between students and administration, but between students, administration, and faculty. Students and administration, they felt, did not want to separate the community into camps, but the faculty was interested in preserving a separate identity and in protecting its own professional interests. All of this was coming out rapidly, now that the Troika was in office (one of the community managers was at the table) because they represented a desire for a more integrated community, and apparently they had been running into trouble with the faculty.

Someone bought an omelet, and we passed it around the table, everyone taking a bite when his turn came. I asked them what they thought of Carl Oglesby.

"He's a genius," Jeff said. Once again, the others thought that Jeff was a little extravagant (they loved him, but were obviously fond of teasing him about his sweeping statements), but everyone except for Paul, who simply shrugged, agreed that Oglesby was great.

I spent the best part of Saturday night with two other Wittenberg students at Carl Oglesby's home behind the Peace and Freedom Center in town. Most of what we talked about would be either repetitive or irrelevant to this "study," but I thought it interesting that Oglesby seems to have the Antiochians beat at their own game. When we entered his home, Dylan was playing on a record player and Carl's wife was sweeping the floor, which she continued to do, even when it meant pushing our feet aside with the broom. Then the Oglesbys talked for awhile and ate dinner, ignoring us completely. I felt almost that I was the object of tactics—would we "lose our cool'"? Later when an Antiochian came up from the Peace and Freedom Center, Oglesby continued to talk with us, without acknowledging the newcomer's presence; it was the first time I saw an Antiochian shift uncomfortably from foot to foot.

Later that evening we went to the midnight movie, as everyone had recommended, and sat in the balcony. The movie was "Davy Crockett," and there was a lot of heckling from all quarters. Everyone sang along with the theme song. The shouts certainly were different from those one might have heard at Wittenberg—"Smoke the Peace Pipe!" "Yeah!" seemed to go over well, especially with the white Antiochians (there were lots of townies), most of whom seemed to be with dates. But the balcony was dominated by a group of Rockefeller students, who were very drunk. (One of the students runs his own business, I understand, but liquor is out now for great numbers of students.) Their shouts consisted mostly of things like, "Red Power!" "White man take Indian lands." "White man lie." "Kill!" "Get Whitey!!"

Note on the Rockefeller students—Antiochians I talked to disagreed as to how successful the program was. Most of them seem to be confused, anyway, as to how to handle the black/white problem. "How can you define success in a program like this?" one boy said to me. "It depends on what you want to do, how you want to approach the thing, and what your goals are. Why should you get 'integrated'? What's so great about what we have?" Wissy put it a little bit differently: "Successful? Well, they're certainly separate and they stay separate. They're different and that's that. I guess it's had a considerable effect on the other Negroes at Antioch, though . . . but I don't know exactly what I mean by that. Antioch's sort of 'beyond liberal' if you know what I mean." A few other students said that they were glad to see the Rockefeller students starting a black power movement. They hoped that, out of respect (or something akin to that) the white kids would keep out of it.

The Adolescent Search

Character Formation Problems in Today's Adolescent

Manuel Brontman and Werner I. Halpern

Are we witnessing an alteration of middle class values? Is our ethic changing? What is acceptable behavior? Philip Rieff suggests that we are undergoing a cultural revolution whereby the old moralizing admonitions give way to therapeutic doctrines "amounting to permission for each man to live an experimental life."[1] This phenomenon is part of widespread ferment as people seek to exist in the modern world with its accelerating potential for comfort and for devastation. Within the framework of rapid cultural change, the family is called upon to promote a pleasing, yet individualizing, climate for its members. Parents are urged to be less arbitrary, while children are helped to acquire more self-confidence as both participate in the search for a new equilibrium in their relationship to each other. That there are significant problems associated with this process can be inferred from even a casual observation of the current scene. What seems to stand out is the need for changes in ways of conflict resolution. We believe that youth is most sensitive to the vagaries of this adaptive struggle. We will discuss some concepts which we consider crucial to understanding problems of young people growing up today.

Although clinical case studies may not be representative of behavior norms, they can nevertheless provide us with important understanding of prevailing interactional modes and coping styles. The following illustration is presented because it encompasses many of those issues which bear on the change and temper between the generations.

A nineteen-year-old college sophomore seeks help, ostensibly because he cannot decide whether or not to remain in school. He is long-haired with sideburns, flamboyantly clothed with knotted neck scarf and bell-bottomed pants, and a single earring in his left ear. He speaks in a calm, erudite fashion. He voices complaints about himself as if he were talking about a third party who must deal with his contemporaries in a hostile, argumentative fashion to be known as an irascible, corrosive person. He seems to delight in this description. Further discussion reveals distress over his indecisiveness and concern for his future. He has experimented with nonaddicting drugs. He describes himself as accepting—as his fancy pleases—a dual role of heterosexuality and homosexuality, with many experiences as an active or passive participant. In a well formulated and detailed way, he describes his aspiration to open a shop for master craftsmen where he will display and sell wood and leather craft, his own and others', in a rural setting. He and his associates would also raise their own food and subsist by the labor of their own hands. At the same time, while thinking out his plans, he lives quite well, on an unlimited checking account made available by his father. He describes his father as a self-made man who is a 'frustrated intellectual' in that he reads voluminously and makes a point of exhibiting his erudition. For the son he has been a cornucopia of material goods and cash, with only perfunctory interest in his academic work and only vague awareness of the intellectual and emotional struggles. When the son alluded broadly to homosexual involvements, the father acted as if he had not heard. Moreover, his chief concern was that the son's school standing be high enough to keep him out of the draft. The boy, in turn, showed sympathy for the father for being tied to a woman intellectually beneath him: "If I were my father, I wouldn't have married my mother." She was described by her son as mainly concerned with social facade, that is with keeping up a good appearance. A younger sister, whom he considers to be a "spoiled brat," is only peripherally involved with him. At the same time he maintains concern that his behavior shames his parents because they are unable to present him proudly to their social circle as their successful son.

The young man in the vignette makes every effort to achieve individuation and separateness in the face of his magnificent dependence on parents. Because of these irreconcilable interests he finds himself under increasing inner pressure to make a decision which will allow reconciliation of his various needs. Dropping out of school is viewed as a possible solution to his dilemma because he would then be able to dispense with support from home. When he reveals his idyllic fantasies of being in charge of a communal artist colony, we can detect a fusion of his striving for independence and his wish to return to a supporting and closed environment, but now on a level more acceptable to him. Although his fantasy only alludes to the necessity of providing for food and shelter, he apparently recognizes the need to struggle with the impersonal and the interpersonal environments. What is also evident is a desire to fulfill the hopes the father has for him without compromising his own integrity as a person who has aspirations in his own right. The plethora of resources available to him induces guilt when individuating feelings arise and evoke self-doubts when his efforts are scrutinized. Whereas the parents' expectation of their son is to make them proud in having succeeded with him where they had felt deficiencies in themselves, he tries to ward off such demands by alienating them or by making them feel ashamed of him. In their preference for non-engagement, the parents, and perhaps particularly the father, do not contribute the required opposition against which the young man can assert himself as is necessary for this important individuation phase.

This case illustration reflects several critical issues in character formation today. Some of the problems of the emancipatory strivings of adolescence have been amply discussed in terms of the loosening of infantile object ties,[2] of orienting the self toward one's future potential,[3] of undergoing an identity formation,[4] of internalizing standards of morality,[5] and of acquiring ultimately a capacity for social and sexual role assumption.[6] Our observations of the give-and-take process in family life suggest that the basic needs of the growing child are being responded to in ever-changing patterns. How the child eventually learns to deal with reasonable expectations, intrinsic human conflicts, self-definition, and a search for meaning is blunted in contemporary times by the ambiguities in the parenting processes in and out of the home. For example, the fluidity of limits, and the availability of multiple choices to the child, places the onus for decision-making prematurely on the shoulders of the child who does not yet feel potent. He is in effect deprived of the opportunity to consolidate his position as a young adult and to lay the groundwork for future participation in community life. There is no time or room for sufficient experience and practice during this period, designated by Erikson as a "psycho-social moratorium,"[7] to bring about the necessary incorporation of useful and goal-directed tools for effective problem-solving. Although we feel that ghetto youth have additional problems to contend with, the exigencies of their existence also demand that they assume responsibility for themselves at an early age, long before they are ready and without the strong but protective confrontation[8] with parental authority.

The traditional role of the family has been to provide generational continuity. On the individual level, parents expect the child to model himself after them as an extension of their existence into perpetuity. Through exhortations and admonitions, sanctions and strictures, parents convey the inherited values to children. In struggling with the imposition of values, children learn to assimilate the essentials of an ethical basis for human living. It follows that since the moral and judgmental bases of existence emanate from the established social order, the young must experience the presence of its authority if they are to fulfill their role as bridge builders to the future.

Is the family of today becoming an unstable consortium of parents and children with an uncertain leadership coming to rest in the hands of the young? Just what means of expression and operational modes are available to parents in dealing with a sense of frustration over mounting problems and over accumulating resources? We often hear a father say to a child "I want you to have what I did not have at your age," expressing the wish that the child should be a passive recipient of accomplished achievements. The father of a son involved in a protest activity on a college campus voiced this feeling as follows: "Why does he behave this way? I did all this for him when I was his age." As the parent becomes more aware of his limitations in an expansive world, he feels more compelled to blunt the possibility of failure in himself. The compensatory hope arises that the child has been invested with the power to overcome these limitations because he has been provided with so many more resources. The child, in turn, is deprived of his need to struggle for a sense of his own worth. He now has to struggle against these attempts at deprivation. He sets his own style in clothing and grooming. He chooses basic issues to polarize dissent. He differentiates himself from the usual behavioral expectations, although this process may operate essentially in the conventional moral framework.

In contemporary society the adolescent's struggle with authority can assume one of three basic forms: he can reject it; he can live with it; he can change it. It appears that the greatest number of adolescents are not inclined to be movers and shakers of the society in which they live, not even today.

A popular form of rejecting authority is to live outside the mainstream of society, a lifestyle exemplified by the hippies or voluntary poor. One wonders whether becoming a symbol of shame not only conveys rejection of parental values, but also assumes the proportion of a characterologic defense against despair over being deprived of experiential struggles. The child is made well aware of the family lore of the preceding generation, of the great feelings of gratification and satisfaction encountered in overcoming hardships. Our whole history, from pioneer days to the depression, suggests that considerable importance has been attached to the adaptive struggles of each generation.

The fifteen-year-old son of a physician who had struggled successfully from humble origins ran away from home repeatedly and spent varying periods of time in hippie communities on both coasts. He stated that education was overemphasized by his parents and that he "did not want to deliver." However, his efforts were bent on seeking out ever new adventures. At times, he was picked up by the police in an intoxicated state. His motto was "We are here to enjoy life." Yet, he also felt that everything expected of him was useless or meaningless for him. All he asked was to be left alone to manage his own life. What is of interest in this family was the mother's revelation that she had tried to protect the father from the boy and his attempts to struggle with the father, ostensibly because the latter's busy life would not tolerate such exchanges. Eventually, the boy left school and home for a marginal existence in the bohemian quarters of a large city.

For those who, in the main, choose to live with authority the pattern of accommodation may hide the struggles in irrelevant or transient episodes of assertive, antagonistic, or asocial behavior. Does this mirror the blunting of self-awareness in parents with respect to their own shortcomings? Although parents and children humiliate or shame each other, neither can face up to this process.

The father of a thirteen-year-old, who had come to clinical attention due to a single episode of stealing, felt that the boy's hair was growing too long. The boy did not comment on the father's criticism. When the father, a man whose achievements were gained with much effort and pride in his accomplishments, took him to the barber, the boy moved his head from side-to-side, blocking the barber's work. The father asked what the boy was doing. When the boy replied that he did not want his hair cut, the father observed: "Why didn't you say it right away?" and took the boy home. With this shaming maneuver the boy succeeded in getting his way. Further exploration of the family revealed a more widespread presence of mutual shaming. Thus, the parents were frequently heard to say, "Is this how a thirteen-year-old boy should behave?"

The existential encounter between parent and child is being side-stepped. In this vignette the father wishes to assume his authority role without recognizing his son's feelings and need for self-determination, that are a reality similar to his own. This sets up the opportunity for public humiliation of the boy, the father at the same time hoping to augment his own image. The boy, in turn, by refusing to submit threatens to shame the father publicly while simultaneously augmenting his own self-image. Underlying the boy's technique is a plea to the father to give him what he needs, namely, a perception of the son as a growing individual within the context of understanding, empathy, and structure. The father feels unable to respond to this plea because he needs the son to be a public reaffirmation of his tenuously felt achievements.

The young person who chooses to change authority can do so by an act of commitment to a struggle, by the example of participation in causes, by organizational means, by working toward social change, and by dialog through protest. These are often the young people who personify "the slowly awakening conscience of much of their country," sometimes without benefit of clear sanction, who have found respectable ways of becoming models for their elders.[9] The changes which came about through the civil rights struggle, VISTA, the Peace Corps, and campus rebellions were hardly thought possible a generation ago. Because these several youth movements are devoted to highly ethical ideals and moral principles, one suspects that this occurs in response to an unspoken wish for utopian resolutions of conflict and anxiety. The older generation, which exposes its shortcomings, invites this kind of shaming by youth who are overtly critical of their society in hopes of bringing about reform.

A seventeen-year-old high school student had become mildly depressed after he returned from a special summer program on a college campus some distance from home. He had enjoyed the relative freedom of the collegiate setting and being able to follow a curriculum of his choice. His parents now appeared to him conservative in outlook, overbearing in manner, orthodox in their beliefs. His school—he was now a senior in high school—was experienced with the same distaste for its compartmentalizing and conformist tendencies. He was in an academic track for bright students, a program which he considered to be irrelevant to his needs. When he struggled to be assigned to classes and teachers more in keeping with his professed desires, and still within the limits of established school criteria for graduation, he was strenuously opposed by his parents, teachers, and counselors, who wanted him to be blessed with scholastic honors. He endured in the struggle with the adults by repeatedly presenting his case logically and cogently. Although he expressed contempt privately toward those who were insensitively arbitrary, he frequently looked for such opponents to put them to shame by his "levelheaded thinking" in his search for wise competence.

It becomes obvious that the question of pathology among any of these coping styles depends not so much on the nature of the struggle with authority as it does on the varying perceptions of meaningfulness as defined by contemporaries. Is pathology the outcome of a failure in accommodation to well established precedent, or is it the inability to "do your own thing?" Observation would lead us to believe that youth who may turn away from or who may try to influence their community of origin are subject to the same definition of what pathology is as those who are troubled by their accommodation to it.

Much has been said about the primarily rebellious nature of the conflict which characterizes the breakaway adolescent.[10] Recent opportunities for experiential encounters in social, political, economic, and religious arenas by youth have reaffirmed something we had observed in clinical studies, the latent capacity of the struggling young to bring about modification of authority or its associated values.[11]

In connection with this shift in emphasis are changes in the expression of disordered behavior. Whereas the model of an earlier time was the youth who fought his parents' dearly held but ambivalently practiced ideology, the current prototype of rebellious offspring is the youth who by copping out, or by activist behavior, denounces his parents' lackluster ideology and pragmatic approach to living. His protestations are conveyed by public shaming of parents or other surrogates of authority in the hope of achieving reform, that is, to press them into resurrecting abandoned ego ideals.[12]

Is it possible that the extension of latency age patterns into and past adolescence has helped to bring about the kinds of deprivations which give rise to the current display of troubled behavior? For example, the expectation that the adolescent remain almost totally committed to being a student, a latency age, spongelike recipient of knowledge and a happily obedient pupil, runs counter to the developmental needs of child and parents at this critical juncture. The parents' uncertainties about their accomplishments may be an outgrowth of the unhappy prolongation of the parenting role from which they cannot extricate themselves. Within this process we see the communication of contrary messages to the adolescent, who is asked to remain the dependent student and, simultaneously, to show evidence of becoming an independent person.

There is also the hidden message of the older generation to youth that they must carry on the traditions and the struggle for resolution of unresolved problems. Parents hope to be relieved of these burdens, which they now must carry over much longer periods than was previously true. Youth is perceptive of these tensions as judged by the response to them. Youth can be observed to express, as well as act, for their elders' awareness of unachieved goals. However, the assumption of a protesting role also becomes incongruous in the face of the adolescent's fiscal fealty to parents. He has to find a way out of his dilemma and must learn to deal with diverse, often opposing forces. The energies for this are available to him because the whole maturational driving force is pointed in the direction of standing erect in both the physical and psychological sense.

Problems arise as the demands upon the self, which must match and compensate for real or implied deficits in parents, fall short again of being realized. Disillusionment over these efforts will lead some to escape the struggle and others to assume the burden of a self-disciplined idealism. These observations support the concept that among the forces that enter into character formation of young people, one must consider the effects of unresolved problems of the preceding generations and of the exigencies of the times.

Notes

1. Phillip Rieff, *The Triumph of the Therapeutic: Uses of Faith After Freud* (New York: Harper and Row, 1966).

2. Anna Freud, *Adolescence: The Psychoanalytic Study of the Child* (New York: International Universities Press, 1958); Leo A. Spiegel, "A Review of Contributions to a Psychoanalytic Theory of Adolescence" in *The Psychoanalytic Study of the Child, 6:*375-93 (1951).

3. Elizabeth Douvan and Joseph Adelson, *The Adolescent Experience* (New York: Wiley, 1966).

4. Erik Erikson, *Identity: Youth and Crisis* (New York: Norton, 1968).

5. Mary Giffin, Adelaide Johnson, and Edward Litin, "Specific Factors Determining Antisocial Acting Out," *American Journal of Orthopsychiatry, 24:*668-84(1954).

6. George E. Gardner, "Present-day Society and the Adolescent," *American Journal of Orthopsychiatry, 27:*508-17 (1957).

7. Erik Erikson, *Childhood and Society* (New York: Norton, 1950).

8. Wolfgang Lederer, "Dragons, Delinquents, and Destiny: An Essay on Positive Superego Functions," *Psychological Issues, 4,* monograph 14 (New York: International Universities Press, 1964).

9. Robert Coles and Joseph Brenner, "American Youth in a Social Struggle: The Mississippi Summer Project," *American Journal of Orthopsychiatry, 35:*909-26 (1968).

10. W. Schonfeld, "The Adolescent in Contemporary American Psychiatry," *International Journal of Psychiatry, 5:*470-78 (1960).

11. Robert Coles, "Psychiatric Observations on Students Demonstrating for Peace," *American Journal of Orthopsychiatry, 37:*107-11 (1967); Coles and Brenner, "The Mississippi Summer Project"; Coles and Brenner, "American Youth in a Social Struggle: II, The Appalachian Volunteers," *American Journal of Orthopsychiatry, 38:*31-46 (1968); Jerome D. Frank and Earl H. Nash, "Commitment to Peace Work: A Preliminary Study of Determinants and Sustainers of Behavior Change," *American Journal of Orthopsychiatry, 35:*106-19 (1965); Jerome D. Frank and Jacob Schonfield, "Commitment to Peace Work: II. A Closer Look at Determinants," *American Journal of Orthopsychiatry, 37:*112-189 (1967).

12. Gerhart Piers and Milton Singer, *Shame and Guilt: A Psychoanalytic and a Cultural Study* (Springfield, Ill.: Charles C. Thomas, 1953).

Sex and the Normal Adolescent

Daniel Offer

The aim of the Modal Adolescent Project was to examine the relative influences of internal psychological and external environmental factors on the functioning of adolescents. We were interested in studying the behavior of a specially selected group of middle class adolescents to assess their relative strengths and weaknesses and to learn what kind of psychological problems they have, how they cope with them, and, if they are not successful in handling problems, what the reasons behind their failures are.

In this study of the psychological world of normal teenagers[1] we have been interested in the nature of the adolescent's sexual experience, his attitude toward sex, and his sexual feelings and impulses. What kind of sexual problems does the adolescent have when he attempts to cope with sexuality, and how successful is he? If he fails to cope with his sexual feelings and impulses, why does he fail? We began working with our group of adolescents when they were entering high school. They are currently three years beyond high school. We examined the development of sexuality in a specially selected group of suburban adolescents from the age of fourteen to twenty-one.

We attempted to select a typical group of adolescents. We constructed a self-image questionnaire to tap significant areas in the psychological world of the adolescent. A typical student was defined as one whose answers fell within one standard deviation from

333

the mean in at least nine out of ten scales. Utilizing our question-naire as a screening device, we selected 103 typical boys from a total sample of 326 freshman boys in two local suburban high schools. In addition, we selected ten girls from thirty freshman girls in one of the schools. We have been able to retest seventy-three of the boys and all ten girls through the high school years.

All subjects were studied in the same way during the four years of high school:

Each subject was interviewed eight times during the high school years. All interviews were conducted in the school by a colleague and me. (Both of us are psychiatrists, and we each saw the same subjects throughout this study.)

Each subject was given a complete series of psychological tests (Rorschach, Thematic Apperception Test, and Wechsler Verbal IQ) administered by a clinical psychologist during the junior year.

All mothers and 70 percent of the fathers were interviewed once during their child's junior year to obtain additional information.

The subjects' school records were available to us. (These in-cluded the extensive behavior grading by teachers in the high schools.)

In the followup study after high school we were able to study 85 percent of the subjects. We interviewed them yearly and obtained followup information by mail.[2]

Obviously, our data concerning the boys is more complete and lends itself to statistical analysis. The data from the ten girls is lim-ited and will be utilized only for comparison. (It is discussed more fully in Offer and Offer.[3])

A significant number of our subjects (45 percent) had not begun dating by the end of the freshman year. The number of adolescents who dated increased slowly in the next two years so that by the end of the junior year 77 percent of our subjects were dating. However, most teenagers dated irregularly and did not seem either to relish the experience or think that it is important for teenagers to date. At the same time (junior year) those who did not care (23 percent) did not feel abnormal or self-conscious because they had not gone out with girls. According to our subjects, if anyone felt that teenagers should date, it was the parents, especially the mothers.

A typical example of a large number of our subjects' attitudes toward girls was the student on the football team who by the end of the sophomore year had never dated and felt he had not missed anything. As far as he was concerned, he would have plenty of time for "this sort of thing" in college. But even while he was expressing his indifference, his level of anxiety went up; when this was pointed out to him, he stated that he simply did not understand girls and wanted them to leave him alone.

We noticed a striking difference in our subjects when we interviewed them toward the end of their senior year. By now 95 percent were dating, and girls occupied a much more prominent place in the adolescent boy's life. The change was dramatic. It did not result solely from the fact that most teenagers were dating. More significantly, almost all of our subjects, including the football player, looked forward to their dates and enjoyed the relationship with girls. At this point the few teenagers who did not date stated openly that they would like to have dated, but they lacked the courage.

The dating experience is not a critical one for the adolescent in the first two years of high school. Although many teenagers do not "think much about girls" in the first two years of high school, they were very conscious of them. "I stay away from girls because I am too young, and we do not understand each other," they often told us. If the interviewer pressed the teenager and asked: "How do you know that you do not understand one another?" The reply will be quick and definite: "I know." Strikingly, after the boys talked with the interviewer about how they do not date and gave a rational explanation for refraining from it, they unconsciously brought their mothers into the picture. (The teenagers might tell us about their conflicts with their mothers or how much they like their mothers.)

Many of the teenagers complained that their mothers (and at

times also their fathers) teased them about their anxiety concerning girls. Seemingly, the more embarrassed the adolescent about girls, the more he was teased by his parents. For example, one subject told us that he liked his mother much more than his father. Next he said that he doubted that he would marry; he never thought about sex and never daydreamed about girls. He was the only subject to say that he probably would not marry. His other comments indicated that his negative responses were due to a fear of his inexperience. He feared growing older and the possibility of failures in new experiences. His mother, he reported, enjoyed joking about his lack of interest in girls. Her jokes made him uncomfortable. His parents may have turned a serious problem for the boy into something which could be handled by laughter.

As the teenager grew and matured, his interests in girls increased. Toward the latter half of the high school years the involvement became meaningful emotionally to the majority of our subjects. It seemed as if their curiosity about girls enabled them to overcome their fear of girls. Although the anxiety that they described while learning to ask a girl out was considerable, according to their own evaluation, the satisfaction that they received was worth it. In the beginning a major reason for dating was a social one. They shared their experiences with their peers almost immediately after they brought the girl home. The minute dissection that goes on among the boys telling each other what they did, right or wrong, is extremely helpful and suggestive. They try to do better next time, not so much because they enjoy kissing or petting, but so they can tell their friends. As their anxiety diminishes in their relation with girls, they begin to enjoy the dating encounter more, and eventually they can look forward to a date simply because they like the girl and want to share their experiences with her and her alone.

In comparison to the boys, the girls started to date much earlier. They were dating by the end of the freshman year, and all but one were actively dating by their junior year. They were more preoccupied with sexuality and often asked us what we thought of sex and "how far they should go."

Almost all our male subjects (more than 94 percent) had reached puberty by the end of the freshman year in high school as measured by the fact that their voices had already changed. The sexual behavior of our group of teenagers was, in general, limited.

During the freshman year among the small group that dated actively, kissing and necking were frequent ways of expressing affection. Our data agree with Reiss,[4] who reported that the majority of teenagers are conservative and restrained in their sexual behavior. During the junior year 30 percent of the subjects were active daters, defined here as those who were going steady or had gone on more than one date. Half of the active daters had experienced heavy petting. Ten percent of the total group had had sexual intercourse by the end of the junior year. No subject admitted participating in overt homosexual behavior. The subjects did state that they masturbated and denied having any problems associated with it. We did not collect any data concerning fantasies during masturbation.

Eighty percent of the subjects approved of premarital sexual intercourse but only at an age beyond high school. The main conscious reason that the teenagers gave for not engaging in sexual intercourse in high school was the fear that the girl would become pregnant. It seems that most of them think that anything goes, except intercourse, and that not because it was wrong, but because it was dangerous.

Talking about intercourse was like circling the mulberry bush. The students, if sufficiently at ease, were pressed by the interviewer for more exact responses. The student would retract the statement he had just made concerning, perhaps, the probability that intercourse would lead to pregnancy and then close the conversation with an irrational, "Well, I don't know why," "That is just the way it should be," or "Adults know what they are doing. Teenagers don't." Are you sure? "No." When told that pregnancy need not be the outcome of intercourse, the most frequent response was, "Well, in high school we're not mature enough to handle it." Too much sexual closeness was frightening. "We just are not ready for it," was repeated over and over. Statements claiming that a certain maturity level is necessary for intercourse are replacing fear of pregnancy response as the latter loses its realistic value.

Almost all the subjects (more than 90 percent) said that they daydreamed about girls, but only a small group (25 percent) stated that their daydreaming included girls they knew. In the latter case it was often an older woman. (Incidentally, almost all the subjects thought that their mothers were very attractive, impressions not always corroborated by our followup interviews with the parents.) The teenagers who did not date by the junior year daydreamed about girls in the abstract, movie stars, heroines from fiction, or even young and attractive teachers. The object of their fantasies was almost never a teenage girl they knew.

The frequency of dating increased significantly after high school. More than one-half (58 percent) of the subjects were dating once or twice a week. Many of the boys had steady girlfriends. Among this group of active daters were the boys (30 percent of the total group) who had had sexual intercourse at least once.

The other subjects (42 percent) who dated less often went out an average of once or twice a month. These boys could in turn be divided into two groups. There were the students who were lonely and regretted not having a girlfriend. There were also boys who claimed that dating once or twice a month was as often as they wished. They spoke of other interests, believing that in the future they could find a girlfriend.

Phil, who had told us that if he left home it would break his mother's heart, dated often and had a steady girlfriend. Nevertheless, he was roused to anger by the question: "Have you ever had intercourse?" Neither he nor his friends had ever had intercourse. "If you hear anything to the contrary about freshmen, the boys are bragging rather than being truthful."

An hour earlier Jerry had assured us that 90 percent of college students do have sex. Jerry, of course, had had intercourse many times. When the interview was finished, he remained to ask: "Do you think I'm oversexed?" As we saw earlier, Jerry had complained about the restraints his mother tried to place upon him. Now he was trying to break down the resistance of every girl he dated.

The development of intimacy with a girlfriend was beginning for a good number of the boys who dated at least once a week, yet in only one case was the interviewer told about the personality or the desirability of a particular girl.

How does today's teenager cope with sexuality? Obviously, the seventy-three boys and ten girls we have studied cannot be taken as representing the vast teenage population. However, our psychiatric data is consistent with our questionnaire results, which now have been given to 1,000 boys and 1,000 girls. Our results are also consistent with those of Reiss, Douvan and Adelson, and Simon, Cagnon, and Carms.[5] We can generalize our findings and say that our observations are representative of one segment of today's youth, a significant segment in number, though by no means representing the majority of adolescents. Our hunch is that it might describe accurately about one-third of the middle class population.

The most important finding is that the normal adolescent male does not experiment much with sexuality. He is slow in getting involved sexually with a girl, and fantasy plays as significant a role as the actual deed. Extrapolating from our total data we would say that about 10 percent of our study population have had sexual intercourse of the end of high school. The rate rises to 30 percent by the end of the freshman year in college. It goes up to 50 percent by the end of the junior year in college.

We believe that significant change has occurred in the teenager's attitude toward sex. Although the teenager (boy or girl) is very uncomfortable when he talks about his own sexual feelings and impulses, he likes to appear liberal when talking about such issues as premarital sex. This particular event is, after all, far in the future for the fourteen- or fifteen-year-old. Nonetheless, his moral stance is not as strict as it might have been thirty years ago. An interesting question might be raised, however, concerning the relationship between attitudes or values and behavior. It is possible that what we have described are the seeds, which in the next generation will lead to actual changes in sexual behavior in the kind of population we studied. First come the changes in attitudes, which eventually lead to changes in behavior. Assuming that the attitudes do not return to pre-World War II norms, the question of when we will see the change remains.

The lack of experience with sexuality does not mean that teenagers are not concerned with what to do with sexual feelings now. On the contrary, the area of sex was of prime importance in our subjects' lives throughout the high school years. They shared their intimate thoughts and feelings with their friends and kept their parents intensely curious as to their activities on a late date.

The kind of normal adolescent whom we studied is more concerned about the format and the code than about feelings. He wants to do the right thing. This concern with his place in the social field gives rise to questions like "Am I popular?" or "Am I attractive?" much more than, for example, "What kind of feelings do I have toward a specific girl or boy?" Although the feelings are scarce and the action often limited, whatever does occur attains a great significance for the adolescent. Their fantasy life is vivid, and kissing a boy for the first time may be equivalent unconsciously to becoming pregnant. Gratification from fantasy life may help the girl in avoiding her sexual impulses in early adolescence. She adjusts to them slowly and over a period of years. The adolescent girl, when she does act out, most frequently chooses the sexual route.

The adolescent boy has to learn to cope with aggression. He is not as concerned with sexuality in early and mid-adolescence as is the girl. For him learning to curb his aggressive impulses is more important than learning to handle his sexual impulses. When the adolescent boy acts out, it is most often aggressively, in delinquent or violent behavior.

Our subjects, as well as those studied by Simon and coworkers, have not started experimenting with sexuality early in life. We are reminded of the statement made by Freud that: "the postponement of gratification is an important element in the process of sublimation and therefore essential to development." In other words early sexual experiences might actually be harmful when the individual is not ready for them emotionally. This would be especially true for those students who shunned intimacy (Erikson) with a person from the opposite sex and utilized the sexual route to express unresolved conflicts, such as homosexuality, aggressive impulses, or strong oedipal attachments.[6]

Some of us might be surprised when we find that the sexual revolution is not yet with us. Another investigator, Karl Menninger, reported that the degree of sexual activity among our adolescent population as reported in the lay press is greatly exaggerated.[7] We agree with him, although it might be of interest to note that he made the remarks in 1926. Our findings stress that the majority of our normal adolescent subjects move slowly in the direction of heterosexuality.

Notes

1. Daniel Offer, *The Psychological World of the Teen-ager: A Study of Normal Adolescent Boys* (New York: Basic Books, 1969).

2. Daniel Offer and J. L. Offer, "Growing Up: A Follow Up Study of Normal Adolescents," *Seminars in Psychiatry,* *1*:46-56 (1969).

3. Daniel Offer and J. L. Offer, "Profiles of Normal Adolescent Girls," *Archives of General Psychiatry,* *19*:513-22 (1968).

4. I. L. Reiss, "Sexual Codes in Teen-Age Culture," *Annals of The American Academy of Political and Social Sciences,* *338*:53-62 (1961).

5. Elizabeth Douvan and Joseph Adelson, *The Adolescent Experience* (New York: Wiley, 1966); William Simon, John Gagnon and Donald Carns, "Sexual Behavior of the College Student," paper presented at the Academy of Psychoanalysis annual meeting, New Orleans, 1968.

6. Erik Erikson, *Identity: Youth and Crisis* (New York: Norton, 1968).

7. Karl Menninger, "Adaptation Difficulties in College Students," *Mental Hygiene 11*:519-35 (1927).

The Sounds of the
Tuned-in Generation

John F. Scott

The lyric themes of popular music appealing to adolescents in the late 1960s, in contrast to the idealized romantic themes of the 1940s, reflect a pronounced concern with personal and social values. "Who am I and where am I going?" and "What should I believe in?" are central questions for the tuned-in generation. Much of today's popular adolescent-oriented music reflects a sharp contrast to the Tin Pan Alley romantic notions of cokes, dates, and idealized romantic interludes characterizing the musical interests of previous adolescent generations. In part the rock music of the 1960s has served as an attempt of this youthful generation to communicate with their elders. Their music has become a meaningful form of personal expression.

The youth of the 1940s and the swing generation assumed a degree of comfortableness in their identity quest, but the tuned-in generation of the 1960s had made no such assumption. The latter's lack of a clearly defined sense of identity has only heightened their awareness of everyone else. Their beat, electrically amplified to deafening blasts of sound, repeatedly screams out their irritations with the discordant sights and sounds of their world.

The realistic and inevitable problem confronting all normal adolescent generations have been compounded for this adolescent generation by widespread anxiety and frustration associated with their thoughts about controlling their existence. They have become susceptible to uncertainties about their futures, with inevitable feelings of helplessness and insecurity. The problems that concern them, such as potential nuclear annihilation or the hypocrisies of adult values, are things about which they can do little, except to construct illusions. Under these circumstances the adolescent attempts through hostility and satire in music, expressed either directly (writing and playing rock music) or vicariously (listening or dancing to the music), to maintain an illusion of greater control over the threatening external forces. In one respect rock musical expressions become an adaptive defense against the pressing anxieties arising from uncertainty about role expectations in a society with conflicting and idiosyncratic values, demands, and expectations.

For this generation of older middle class adolescents, pot, protest, Playboyism, and people are important themes, whether in actual behavior or verbal preoccupation. They protest against the perceived ills of contemporary society with a sense of urgency about its future; they express anxiety (often in disguised forms) about interpersonal closeness; they react increasingly to the pressures of a Darwinian concept of the survival of the fittest within academic environments (particularly the high school neurosis about who goes to which college under what conditions); their sexual values have increasingly moved from a body-centered orientation to more of a person-centered orientation. (It's all right to "make out" on a casual basis, but you only sleep with someone you really care about.) They seek to experience creative success, so difficult to achieve individually in a technologically-oriented affluent society, by expanding their consciousness through the use of hallucinogenic drugs. In a society that they sense is turning them off, they turn on and speed along with stimulants to keep pace with the fast moving society, and with the help of the "ups" they can experience the feeling of keeping up. Perhaps as a result of the increased portrayal in the mass media, particularly television, the discrepancies between the haves and have nots are brought to their attention with an impact that no previous generation has experienced. Whether out of guilt about their own status in an affluent world, or out of a true concern

343

with human values about people and their needs, middle class youth, particularly, have shifted their attention to the discrepancies and the hypocrisies associated with the materialistic, depersonalizing hangup of their elders.

Functioning in a society that is increasingly youth-oriented (who but a youthful person is idealized on television commercials; gray hair is no longer acceptable even for men), youth is increasingly reminded of its power (it represents an enormous consumer market), and yet it knows that the power is still withheld by its elders. These same elders, in turn, in their roles as parents and socializers have become increasingly uncertain about what values to convey. Their inconsistent and hypocritical behavior has come under the scrutiny of an alert and sensitive youthful generation.

In response to these pressures, conflicts, and inconsistencies within a society that is in the midst of a value reorientation, the adolescent participant observer, through his music, has fostered a curious poetic sociological musical movement called rock. This musical expression, representing in part an abandonment of traditional commercial music, is not an isolated phenomenon. The rejection of old standards of values carries with it numerous manifestations in the life style of the young. Although every adolescent generation has manifested behavior reflecting a profound sense of loss, isolation, and a turning to the outside world for sensory stimulation, the tuned-in generation has become extremely sensitive to that outside world and has musically reported on its observations with startling and sometimes shocking lyrics.

For the first time in the history of commercial music, adolescents are writing, playing, and producing their own sounds. In the era of the big bands of the 1940s, writers wrote, singers sang, and musicians played music. Now with put-on names such as Ultimate Spinach; Blood, Sweat, and Tears; 1910 Fruitgum Company; and the Mothers of Invention; and gimmicks like style of dress and unique sounds, individual and group song writers and performers criticize the society and its values by direct musical assaults in lyrics often filled with double meanings. They express new attitudes toward

344

sex, drugs, relationships, and too often parents and the elder generation miss the point. (A "straight shooter" is no longer a Western hero and the Yellow Submarine trip is not a Boy Scout fun song.) Tragically, most parents of this tuned-in generation neither hear nor feel any desire to listen to what is being expressed, despite the larger and larger blasting electronic amplifiers the young musicans utilize to be heard.

Today's rock music has little similarity to the original rock and roll music of the 1950s, though there is a sequential relationship. Historically, music has always been one form of expression and outlet for discontented feelings. The trial and tribulation music of the blues and Negro spirituals in the United States extends back to the nineteenth century when it was spread by beggars, itinerant farm laborers, and traveling minstrel shows.

By the early 1900s, and the era of Bessie Smith, the blues began to have more elaborate accompaniment, including a jazz group. Black migration North brought it to the larger Northern cities where it was presented in theatres and dance halls. By the 1930s the sounds (called urban blues) that were to be the forerunners of rhythm and blues were expressing lust, pain, dirt, and fear and reflecting the pace and tension of urban living for the Negro.

By the time World War II had ended rhythm and blues had become firmly established among black listeners, although it was unheard of by the majority of whites in America. Rhythm and blues, with its amplified guitars and honking saxophones, reflected sounds that suggested primitive sexuality and raw emotions. Even if radio stations had wanted to play such sounds (which they did not), the suggestiveness of the lyrics would probably have prohibited their airing.

During the early 1950s whites in America became interested in a variation of the predominantly black-oriented rhythm and blues, and the period of rock and roll was born. Presented by performers such as Elvis Presley ("You Ain't Nothing but a Hound Dog") and Bill Haley ("Rock Around The Clock"), the music was loud and had a good beat, but the lyrics of rock and roll were yet to become

345

the message sounds of the 1960s. English groups such as the Beatles and the Animals were reflecting the rock and roll sound, but still representing an imitation of the Negro rhythm and blues.

By the 1960s true rock music had been established, branching out creatively to such sounds as acid rock and folk rock. English rock groups, particularly the Beatles and the Rolling Stones, were leaders in this direction. Concomitantly, the taboo against combining blues and gospel was violated by such performers as Ray Charles, and what emerged became identified as soul music, to be associated predominantly with blacks. Gospel music essentially described the wonderful life that awaited the true believers in the next world. It said, in essence, bear with the difficulties of devaluation and deprivation of this life in return for complete need fulfillment after death in the next life. Blues, in contrast, suggested that life, with all of its pain, be confronted and sorrowfully presented.

Rock music assimilated every sound within the spectrum of popular music: "urban and country, blues, gospel, hillbilly, Western, good-time (the ricky-tick of the 1920s) and Tin Pan Alley. It reached across the oceans for the sounds and rhythms of Africa, the Middle East, and India. It reached back to the Gregorian chant; and forward into the future for the electronic music and the noise collages of *musique concrete*."[1]

The lyrics of rock are often ambiguous, and many of the songs expound messages against the Establishment, against war, against hypocrisy. Based upon the rock sound, a rock culture has emerged. The culture reflects a shift in the attitudes of youth from control and inhibition to freedom and revolt. Whether expressed in the adolescent moralism of writer-singer Janice Ian, the bittersweet attacks on hypocrisy of Simon and Garfunkel, or the harshness and violence of The Doors, rock music has been rapidly assimilated into the world of today's youth. This integration has been aided by the mass media and by the affluent level of the society for many American youths, enabling them to purchase records and musical instruments with which they can imitate the sounds. Youth has found a means of expression for its concerns, anxieties, and commentaries about society. Thus its music represents one avenue to understanding its thoughts, feelings, and conflicts.

Between November 1967 and October 1968 we made an analysis of the weekly ratings of the top thirty popular records aired to the audience of a teen oriented radio station in a large, industrial New England city. (Appreciation is expressed to Radio Station WAAB, Worcester, Massachusetts, its staff and management for their cooperation.)

At any specific time period in the United States radio station programming policy, socioeconomic class, race, age of listener, and particular locale or regions will influence what songs will be most popular on a particular radio station. The radio audience of the station involved in this survey was predominantly white (the city's black population is approximately 1 per cent). The station viewed itself as being beamed to an older adolescent audience (high school and college age; there are ten colleges and junior colleges within the radio area). It is likely that the station's audience cut across all social class levels. This particular station's musical selections contrasted with those of other radio stations in the area playing mostly soul music; the Detroit sound (James Brown, Aretha Franklin); acid rock—the California sound (Big Brother and the Holding Company; Blood, Sweat, and Tears); or straight commercial popular music (Barbra Streisand, Jerry Vale).

This analysis was concerned primarily with lyrics of the music played, and we established categories for the songs, primarily in the top category songs that made a psychosocial commentary. No attempt was made to do a frequency count of songs classified into various categories. Our overall concern was with the themes expressed.

The music expresses the audible sounds of a tuned-in generation that has separated itself from the Establishment and conventional American life so as to create an identifiable gap. The music, in part, reflects the conflicts all adolescents experience between security and independence. A closer analysis, however, reveals an aggressive challenge to the Establishment's values and the protest voice of the young ridiculing adult standards. Beneath their put-on is a deep sense of anxiety and urgency about the world that in a short time they will be responsible for, and concern about the roles that they will perform in that society. Further, the lyrics express a concern about control of impulses in a society where great conflict and uncertainty about traditional controls exists.

We identified ten general themes with psychosocial implications and classified songs within each category. We presented them without intending to rank order, since we did not do a frequency count of the times a particular theme (via a particular record) was aired. Certain specific recordings aired during the survey will be identified for illustrative purposes for each category. The themes included:

1. *Sexual values.* This theme, as expressed in rock music, reflects a most pronounced shift from inhibitions to frank advocacy of the overthrow of old prohibitions. The Rolling Stones' recording of "Let's Spend the Night Together," leaves little doubt as to the intent of the invitation. Such open defiance of traditional sexual values is countered by songs dealing with the sexual response, urging restraint and warning of the heartaches of illegitimate pregnancy. The Supremes' record of "Love Child" sensitively depicts the hurt and pain associated with being illegitimate in a poverty environment and cautions about the dangers of premarital sex.

> . . . This love we're contemplating
> So worth the pain of waiting
> We'll only end up hating
> The child we may be creating
> Love child—never meant to be . . .
> Love child—always second best
> Love child—different from the rest
> Don't think that I don't want to please you
> But no child of mine will be bearing
> The name of shame that I'm wearing.[2]

O. C. Smith's recording of "Isn't It Lonely Together" compassionately tells of a forced marriage due to pregnancy:

> And we've got nothing in common
> But our name and our shame
> And the blame for letting passion's foolish
> Flame run wild
> And now we've got to cover up the fact
> With an act, to atone for our mistake
> And to protect the child.[3]

The latter two songs held top spots during the survey and obviously reflect the adolescent's conflicts about controlling impulses. Most impressive of all is the directness and honest portrayal of the range of issues associated with sexual expression in rock music, which contrast sharply with the "moon in June" themes of earlier popular music.

2. *Hypocrisy and anti-Establishment.* Perhaps no theme has been more fully expounded in rock music than that which attacks traditional American middle class values. Jeannie C. Riley's "Harper Valley PTA" attacks the hypocrisy of middle class suburbia, where PTA members are described as drunks, philanderers, and hysterics. Phil Och's recording of "Only A Small Circle of Friends" described people's lack of concern for their fellow man who is in distress, indifference to the plight of the poverty stricken, and inconsistencies in middle class values about pornography and drugs. "Skip A Rope" describes marital conflict and its effect on children, defrauding the government of taxes, and prejudice, all seen as the effects of parents and their values.

> Stab 'em in the back
> That's the name of the game
> And mommy and daddy are who's to blame . . .[4]

During the summer of 1968, singer-songwriter Ray Stevens' recording of "Mr. Businessman" held a top place on radio. This song attacks with biting, poetic lyrics the inconsistent, indifferent, hypocritical values of the American businessman, who spends Tuesday evenings with his harlot and Wednesday with "his charlatan analyst," who has air conditioned sinuses and doubts about his religious values; whose morals exempt him from "guilt and shame" about his involvement with his secretary; who seldom sees his children; who can wheel, deal, and steal with the best of his business competitors; and who needs to drink to keep going:

> Eighty-six proof anesthetic crutches
> Prop you to the top
> Where the smiles are all synthetic
> And the ulcers never stop.[5]

The song ends by questioning what it all means in the end.

Clearly these few illustrative songs point up the interest and observations of a generation asking itself if it wishes to mirror adult values in its own forthcoming adulthood. The rejection of values expressed in the lyrics emphasizes the difference between youth and its elders. Yet the youth of the 1960s seem to be in a dilemma about their own future role performance. What their music seems to say in part, often with sharp hostility, is that while they do not know what values they wish to pursue, they do not accept many of the existing Establishment standards that previous generations have accepted. Such rejection seems to find its ultimate expression in hippieism, the dangerous children's crusade of the 1960s, and acid rock sounds have been associated with the West Coast hippie movement.

3. *Drugs and their effects.* Groups like the Beatles, the Doors, and the Rolling Stones have devoted much lyrical content in their music to the effect of drugs, particularly of the hallucinogenic variety. At the same time, deliberate ambiguity imparts almost a put-on sophisticated quality to the songs. Relatively few adults associated the Beatles "Lucy in the Sky with Diamonds" with LSD or their comical drug song "Yellow Submarine" with tripping out. Their "Happiness Is a Warm Gun" describes shooting heroin:

> Happiness is a warm gun
> When I hold you in my arms
> And I feel my fingers on your trigger
> I know one can do me no harm.[6]

The theme associated with drug effects expresses, on the one hand, a state of confusion and, on the other, a hedonistic response to perceived reality pressures and sources of anxiety. Turning on or getting stoned for the tuned-in generation is probably the result of multiple motivational sources, but drug use, as described in songs, would seem also to emphasize the social-recreational aspect. Is it true that one is only truly able to relate, without the anxieties of possible social rejection, while under the influence of drugs? Psychedelic images (associated with the light show of the discotheques, so popular with the younger generation) represent a reaching out for the new, the different. In the midst of new structure and form that deny old inhibitions and prohibitons, new sensations are sought—the freedom to express long-denied emotions. Vicariously, drug songs hold out that kind of promised illusionary fulfillment.

4. *Cheating and deception.* The fourth theme identified in the survey described cheating and deception, usually involving extramarital affairs. The Union Gap's "Woman, Woman" asks the question "Woman, do you have cheating on your mind?" Clarence Carter's recording of "Slip Away" (a million seller) is clearly indicative of a man asking a woman to slip out of the house (presumably from her husband) to meet him, for he needs her. Perhaps the most popular of songs in this category was Simon and Garfunkel's recording of "Mrs. Robinson." (The success of the song was due in part to the success of the motion picture "The Graduate," which depicted Mrs. Robinson's trying to reassure herself about her ebbing youth via extramarital involvement with a college student.)

One cannot help wondering what life experiences the tuned-in generation's observations are based upon. One thing seems obvious —adultery and extramarital affairs as themes are part of the behavioral spectrum that this generation comments about.

5. *Society, its values, and its future.* Songs identified within this fifth category represented a variety of reactions to America of the 1960s. Some poke fun at middle class life style, as in Bobby Russell's recording of "1432 Franklin Park Circle Hero." Others lament the degree of violence in the United States and the world, as dramati-

cally presented by Simon and Garfunkel singing "Silent Night," in which a news commentator's voice in the background presents the evening news filled with descriptions of aggression, hate, and violence, which slowly drowns out the singing of the Christmas carol.

Perhaps the most impressive of all songs in this category was that of Spanky and Our Gang's recording of "To Give a Damn," a powerful poetic commentary of what it is like to live in a ghetto, that pricks the conscience of middle class America to give a damn about its fellow man:

> Put your girl to sleep some time
> With rats instead of nursery rhymes
> And wonder if you'll share your bed
> With something else that must be fed . . . .
> Suppose you lived there all your life
> Do you think that you would mind?[7]

A most provocative song that appeared in early 1968 (several months before it became popular with adults) was Ed Ames's recording of "Who Will Answer?" Using a combination of Gregorian chant, baroque instrumentation, and hard rock, the song questions where the answer can be found to the Vietnam war, man's indifference to suicide by his fellow man, finding fulfillment for "unmade dreams" through drugs, mistaken political strategy that could lead to nuclear annihilation, and the hippie movement.

With satire, hostility, and open frankness the lyrical content of this category of rock music dispels the myth of adolescent indifference and indicates that the younger generation is concerned about the values of present-day society with a degree of maturity that no previous youthful generation has expressed.

6. *Failure in Communication.* The communication gap is the much overworked concept of one generation's inability to talk to and be understood by an older generation. Although this has, to some degree, been characteristic of all adolescent-parent generations, it has assumed a sense of urgency now. Simon and Garfunkel's "Sound of Silence" ("People talking without speaking; people

hearing without listening") and their "Dangling Conversations" exemplify the concern with inability to communicate. The theme of such songs sees communication as being superficial and on a commercial level. There is no serious understanding because there is no serious communication.

Glen Campbell's recording of "Going to Phoenix" (one of the songs originally popular with the adolescents that became popular with adults) sums up the dilemma in the final lines:

> I tried to tell you so
> But you just didn't know
> That I would finally go.[8]

7. *Loneliness, sadness, and loss.* Loneliness and sadness have always been characteristics of adolescent feelings and have been expressed in their popular songs. Yet there is a quality of sadness in this seventh category of current sounds that seems more intense. Bobby Goldsboro's successful record of "Honey," describing the death of a man's wife after a successful marriage, is typical of the tuned-in generation's interest in death and loss. The Beatles' melodic recording of "Eleanor Rigby" expresses loneliness and sadness in one person that in turn is generalized to a whole group of people who live outside the modern world. ("All the lonely people. Where do they all come from? Where do they all belong?") Bob Dylan's music has also reflected a curious preoccupation with death. Perhaps the theme reflects the quest of the rock generation to confront life in the raw and, in turn, the kind of anguish most adolescents have experienced in the process of detaching themselves from their parents.

8. *Interracial romance.* In the midst of a nation embroiled in attempts to redefine relationships between the races it would be unlikely that the tuned-in generation would not, through its music, comment upon the relationships between blacks and whites. In the fall of 1967 the radio station surveyed was the only one, for a time, that would play teenage singer-writer Janice Ian's recording of "Society's Child": a white girl, bowing to parental pressure and

353

social ostracism by her peers and teachers, tells her black boyfriend she can no longer see him. But she holds hope for the future. A similar theme of rejection of a black boyfriend is expressed in the songs "Does Your Mother Know About Me?" in which the boyfriend expresses anxiety about possible rejection by his white girlfriend's mother. This theme is still a controversial one for radio stations, but three such songs gained popularity during the time of the survey, largely in response to adolescent demands for airing.

9. *Anti-war and anti-draft.* Most of the rock groups have expressed this ninth theme in their music, reflecting both an opposition to the government's Vietnam policy and a fear of nuclear annihilation. Barry McGuire's popular "Eve of Destruction" laments the latter theme, and Arlo Guthrie's satirical "Alice's Restaurant" ridicules draft induction physical procedures.

10. *Freedom.* This theme can be described in two ways: freedom for individual expression and freedom from oppression that minorities experience in this country. Several songs express youth's desire for freedom, with the underlying theme of adolescent struggle for independence. (This desire for freedom, however, is expressed equally for thought and behavior.)

Freedom from oppression is characterized by such a song as the Rascals' "People Got To Be Free," which represents a combination of gospel and rock sounds:

> Now that's the train of freedom
> It's about to arrive any minute now
> You know it's been long, long overdue
> Look out cause it's coming right on through.[9]

The freedom theme may very well mask adolescent anxieties about responsibility which await them in adulthood.

The lyrics of the music of today's youth, in contrast to that of previous youthful generations, is poetic and intellectual, often with ambiguity in each line. It has become the music of the college students as well as the high school dropouts attempting to break with tradition.

Rock music has become a platform for expressing a new morality. In contrast to the politeness and social restraints of their elders, the rock generation advocates a direct confrontation with life, whether it be birth or death, deprivation or leisure, survival or destruction. They have put down Organization Man and his materialistic quest and concerned themselves with the issues of life, poverty, sexuality, or any aspect of societal living.

Musically, they have faced the incongruities of the society of the 1960s. The tuned-in generation's parents, when they were young, handled their rebellion discreetly and in fear, if not of God then of their parents. This generation bluntly sounds its rebellion in song, and its music, so intertwined with the rapid value changes influencing it, becomes a badge of identity.

Perhaps youth's willingness to bear witness to the realities of living, instead of blocking them out as its parents did when they were young, is a reaction-formation to anxieties associated with survival in present-day society. Yet the issues youth raise are profound ones. Although limited in the practical solutions, it can offer at this time to those issues, the tuned-in generation's significant contribution may be, as the future adult generation, to go beyond identifying the issues, and to work to overcome the injustices and hypocrisies of current adult society.

Notes

1. Albert Goldman, "The Emergence of Rock," *New American Review* (New York, 1968), no. 3, pp. 118-39.

2. "Love Child." Copyright 1968. Jobete Music Company, Inc., Detroit, Michigan. Lyrics by R. Dean Taylor, Deke Richards, Frank Wilson. Used with permission of Jobete Music Company, Inc.

3. "Skip a Rope." Copyright 1964. Tree International, Nashville, Tenn. Used with permission. All rights reserved.

4. "Isn't it Lonely Together." Copyright 1968. Ahab Music Company. Used with permission. All rights reserved.

5. "Mr. Businessman." Copyright 1968. Ahab Music Company. Used with permission. All rights reserved.

6. "Happiness Is a Warm Gun." Copyright 1968. Northern Songs Limited. Used with permission. All rights reserved.

7. "Give a Damn." Copyright 1968. Takya Music Company. Used with permission. All rights reserved.

8. "By the Time I Get to Phoenix." Copyright 1967. Rivers Music Company. All rights reserved. Used with permission.

9. "People Got to Be Free." Copyright 1967. Slacsar Publishing Company Ltd.; c/o Steingarten, Wedeen & Weiss, 444 Madison Avenue, New York, New York 10022. Used with permission.

Being in the Combat Zone: a Study of Time and Behavior

Gary L. Tischler and John Perito

The current tour of duty in Vietnam is a time-limited one of twelve months duration. From the moment of arrival each soldier titrates his existence to the anticipated date of his departure. This leads to the construction of temporal barriers which wall off the present from both the past and the future. Being in the combat zone becomes an isolated and discontinuous experience, a rent in the fabric of existence; nevertheless, the inexorable reality of the experience intrudes with a forcefulness to which each man must respond. In the responses of individuals, time-related behavioral patterns can be delineated. We shall explore these behavioral patterns in detail to better illuminate the manner in which individuals come to terms with life in a combat zone.

The new arrival, trained in the "as if" soldiering of the garrison, comes to Vietnam with expectations colored by the fables of buddies, the family myths of wars gone by, the celluloid fantasies of Hollywood, and the cinematic purity of the ubiquitous television cameraman. These expectations quickly dissolve. At the point of debarkation a sea of new sights, smells, and sounds envelops each soldier. Because there are no front lines, the tide of war soon rolls up and touches him. Uncertain as to what stimuli represent cues of actual danger, he has difficulty in assessing the harm-producing potential of his current environment. The situation is very ambiguous. The ambiguity generates enormous anxiety, which the men

357

attempt to dilute through fusion with the group. Fusion is dramatically visible at points of debarkation, where the newly arrived stand and move only in groups. Their faces are dazed and frightened. Gradually, these faces fuse into a mask of a collective. The fusion has some benefit. It allows each soldier to say: "I am not alone. They are here as well. I am frightened, but they are frightened, too." Anxiety comes to be acknowledged by the group as a legitimate response in the face of a confrontation with an unknown replete with hazards and privations that are potentially finite.

The group, which has absorbed and diluted the anxiety of individuals, must now contend with its own collective state of anxiety. A quest for authoritativeness is initiated, its intent the finding of some person who possesses sufficient power and expertise to impose a degree of order on a frightening external reality. This person is endowed with omnipotence and omniscience. The group surrenders to his authoritativeness and derives reassurance from his presence. A sense of security suffuses the group, which helps attenuate collective anxiety.

Fusion with the group and the quest for authoritativeness help buffer the impact of the transition from one physical reality to another, but each man must still deal with the sense of isolation that results from being set apart from the dominant Vietnamese culture by race and religion and cut off from those significant objects which had previously acted as sources of support. To be isolated in an alien and hostile world is a threatening experience. When that isolation is compounded by the necessity of performing tasks which are both alien and potentially finite, then questions arise about the validity of many of the transcendent values and basic assumptions that had previously governed an individual's transactions in and with the world about him. He has not yet had sufficient time to learn or adequately test out measures for avoiding or minimizing harm within the context of a new reality when the measures utilized in the past are called into question.

The past, however, represents a known. Confronted by the unknown, each man escapes into the past to avoid the anomic anxiety that results from being suspended between two worlds. Similar reactions have been described in other transition states, particularly where men are propelled into extreme situations. These include descriptions of concentration camps,[1] communist prisons,[2] internment camps,[3] and disaster situations.[4] The escape is reflected in an "I was" rather than "I am" focus of conversations, an expectant wait for mail from home, painful but repetitive recapitulations of the last days before embarkation, and an idealization of all that has been left behind.

These behaviors are neither nostalgic exercises nor attempts to deny present realities. They represent modes of bringing into apposition the threads of past and present. Erikson[5] has demonstrated the potency of temporal discontinuity as a stress in combat situations. In the case of Sam, the Marine, he pointed out that a disruption in an individual's sense of continuity and sameness in time and space leads to a crisis of identity. It is as though one's life no longer hangs together. This is an experience with which each new arrival in Vietnam must contend. The escape into the past makes it possible to forge a symbolic bond linking the temporal dimension of the past to that of the present. This bond reestablishes a sense of continuity and sameness and materially reduces the anomic anxiety which the men are experiencing.

Thus, the basic experience of being in the combat zone during the first three months of the tour is one of dislocation. During the dislocative phase free-floating anxiety is attenuated through a fusion with the group and a surrender to authority. Anomic anxiety is dealt with by an escape into the past. The surrender to authority sufficiently reduces anxiety levels to a point where individuals can engage in the task at hand while learning new behaviors relevant to their current life situation. The escape into the past allows an individual to perform these tasks and master new behaviors without the threat of identity discontinuity. Where these mechanisms are successful, the adaptive capabilities of the men are materially enhanced.

By the fourth month the men have acquired a certain degree of mastery over their present environment. They have experimented with numerous behaviors and know the viability of each as a mode for dealing with particular situations. This, in turn, leads to greater proficiency both in judging what situations can or cannot be mastered and differentiating between actual and supposed hazards. The cost for leaving the combat zone prematurely is also known. It is calculated in terms of pain and bodily harm. For most this cost is unacceptable. While cost-knowledge plus an increased sense of mastery over an alien world make the present experience more tolerable, that which was left behind seems more distant and less palpable. The past can no longer adequately sustain the men who turn to the present for support and nurturance.

The acceptance of the present is heralded by a retreat from the past. Preoccupation with home and family lessen. Conversations begin to focus on day-to-day activities and the here-and-now. Such a retreat is not unique to combat situations. Bettleheim[6] described a similar response in inmates of concentration camps. After being in the camps for some time the inmates stopped speculating about their families and their past lives, and they became preoccupied with events inside the camp with many attempting to find a better place for themselves within the prison situation.

In Vietnam the retreat from the past is accompanied by a gradual emergence of an informal social structure founded upon a dominant materialism and given over to a quest for pleasure. This hedonistic renaissance parallels the realization that, while it may not be possible to avoid hazards inherent in the combat zone, it is quite possible to influence one's relative state of privation. The quest for pleasure appears first as soldiers begin to move out of their compounds into the restaurants, bars, and brothels in town. It reaches its zenith with rest and recreation leave (R and R), a programmed escape into the exotic. Materialism is in evidence everywhere. A tent in the support area will almost invariably contain a refrigerator well stocked with soda, beer, and even champagne. High fidelity and camera magazines abound, and the music coming from the stereo tape recorders competes with the vociferous arguments of the men over which camera, audio equipment, or luxury items to buy. The prime mover in the scene is the scrounger, a man with special talent in acquisition. Over the months he has built up an elaborate network of contacts. If you have hamburger, he can get you bread; if you have lues and do not want to go on report, he can see to it that you receive penicillin; if you want an item that is not presently in stock at the PX, he knows the wheres and hows of obtaining it. There is a price, which may be exacted in goods or services, as well as money.

But the informal social structure, this hedonistic pseudo-community, is not just an attempt to restructure reality and make it more palatable. The men have been in the combat zone for a considerable period and been forced to come to grips with the demands inherent in a highly ambiguous and anomalous situation. They have learned new behaviors and in the process, have surrendered a good deal of autonomous functioning in so doing. They have been exposed to death firsthand. All of this experience occurs in a setting that is essentially hostile, a setting in which they are cut off from the nurturing objects of the past. These men exist in a state of psychological bankruptcy. Their resources have been overdrawn. Their egos are depleted. The hedonistic pseudo-community with its intrinsic narcissism and acquisitiveness allows each man respite and an opportunity to replenish drained resources.

During the fourth through ninth months of the tour, depletion is the dominant experience. The hedonistic pseudo-community is the mechanism by which the men fortify themselves during the phase of depletion. Without this mechanism it would be extremely difficult to continue with the task at hand.

As the men enter the last three months of their tour, their attention shifts to the future. Previously, conversations about "the land of the great PX" had been subdued and tentative. Talk would last only for a few minutes and then give way to a consideration of the present. Now there is an aura of excitement and anticipation, as the men delve back to recollect the images of home, family, friends, and things forgotten. Elaborate plans are made about how the first few hours and days will be spent, and then the conversation drifts beyond the immediate future into the realm of hope and aspiration. They plan for college, jobs, and marriage. The future is ringed in ebullience and ideality.

Still, there is the present to contend with. In combat areas caution becomes the byword. A feeling of resentment that approaches loathing and hatred occurs when combat missions are ordered. Having survived at least nine months, no one wants to be "zapped" with the end of the tour so near. In support areas fewer people leave the compound. The number who leave decreases each week. The present lingers on, tempered with nostalgic reminiscences about the past months spent in Vietnam. Characteristically, however, these features are now talked about as though they had already been left. The magnetism of the future is so compelling that it blurs the realities of the present and inevitably causes each man to withdraw somewhat from both the environment and the group.

The experience in the combat zone during the last three months is one of disengagement. The men deal with disengagement by projecting themselves into an idealized future which exerts a magnetism that, in many ways, renders the present irrelevant. The idealized future acts as an internal support, strengthening the resources of the men and rendering them less vulnerable to the hazards, privations, and adaptive strains that abound in the combat zone.

Our exploration of the experience of being in the combat zone suggests that the time-limited tour unfolds in three distinct phases—dislocation, depletion, and disengagement. While there is some overlap and blurring of the phases, each phase is consistently present and occurs at a chronologically predictable time and is typified by a characteristic pattern of behaviors. Yet what of the vulnerability of the men to the experience? Does it exhibit a periodicity as well? To answer these questions we examined 200 referrals for evaluation and/or treatment by the psychiatric service of an evacuation hospital in Vietnam. We assumed that the men referred had encountered some difficulty in coming to terms with the experience of being in Vietnam. Referral is, of course, a gross index of vulnerability; nevertheless, it is measurable.

If one uses the number of referrals for psychiatric evaluation per unit of time spent in Vietnam as a measure of attrition, the first three months of the tour are the periods of greatest vulnerability.

Twenty-three percent of the men were referred during the first month of their tour, eleven percent during the second month, and thirteen percent during the third month. Thus, almost one-half of the men referred for psychiatric services had been in the combat zone for less than four months. Vulnerability decreases markedly after the third month. There is little variation in the number of referrals of men in the fourth through ninth months of their tour. After the ninth month, however, a gradual but progressive decrease again appears.

The data reveal a periodicity in vulnerability to the experience of being in the combat zone. The periods of vulnerability correspond in time with the phases of dislocation, depletion, and disengagement. Maximal vulnerability occurs during the phase of dislocation, decreased vulnerability during the phase of disengagement. The relationship between vulnerability and time spent in Vietnam is characteristic of all age groups, but the differential is most apparent in soldiers under age twenty-one. Sixty per cent of that group were referred during the dislocative phase. This contrasts with a figure of 40 per cent for men twenty-one and over. Perhaps the young are more vulnerable to the dislocative experience because youth is an interphase of life. It is a transitory period where an individual is involved in disengaging himself from parental bonds and forging an identity of his own. Psychological maturity is linked to the emulation of definite role models. A young man needs to absorb the major symbols and values of his culture. Youth's orientation is to the future. Psychological autonomy and self-regulation are very important during this life stage when a man moves toward something basically different from the past.

Many of the tasks of youth are dissonant with the initial experience of being in the combat zone. The impact of the confrontation with an unknown immediately raises the question of man's basic mortality. The threat of corporal dissolution is a very real part of being in a combat zone; hence, the world seems futureless. The mechanisms for dealing with the experience of dislocation raise psychosocial issues to which men under age twenty-one are particularly sensitive. Fusion with the group compromises self-regulation; the surrender to authoritativeness threatens autonomy; and the escape into the past activates feelings of dependence. Thus, the greater vulnerability of youth during the initial three months of the combat tour is the result of an inherent conflict between age-specific psychosocial tasks and adaptive demands imposed by the experience of dislocation.

We have examined the manner in which men come to terms with a limited and finite tour of duty in a combat zone. We have observed behaviors that unfold in time and others that are determined by time. For most individuals the concept of time as a determinant of behavior is alien. Rather they choose to view time as a dimension of man's physical universe and believe, like Moore, that:

> Time, like space, sets limits on human life and on the viability of social structures. Within those limits time and space are relevant but essentially passive or neutral conditions. They do not determine the course of life or the way patterns of social behavior will adapt to or use these 'natural' boundaries of social systems.[7]

This view depicts temporality as a flowing sequence of seconds, minutes, hours, days, months, and years. It is a structured unit within which behavior occurs.

Those of us who work with man as he strives to come to terms with the vicissitudes of the human condition, however, have come to appreciate the importance of the symbolic universe. From the moment that something is used to stand for or represent another thing, man interposes a symbolic system between receptors and effectors. He soon learns to utilize this system for modifying and manipulating physical reality and thus acquires a new method for coming to terms with the world around him. Symbolic processes inevitably play a role in human adaptation. This is true in extreme situations as well as in normal events.

In the symbolic universe, time exists as a complex distillate of internalized representations signifying that which leaves us, that which is now, and that toward which we are going. These representations serve as response initiators. During the dislocative phase a host of behaviors are generated as a result of a temporal orientation to the past. The same is true of the phase of disengagement, where the symbolized future molds behaviors. In both instances symbolic time acts as a determinant of behaviors which are fairly specific, behaviors which maintain a sense of intactness in the face of change, turmoil, and the threat of destruction.

Symbolic time is important not only as a determinant of behavior. It also allows an individual to compartmentalize life experiences. We described previously how a finite, limited tour of duty leads to the construction of temporal barriers which wall-off the experience of being in the combat zone from both the past and the future. The resultant encapsulation enables an individual to set the experience apart from the fabric of his existence. Thus set apart, the experience cannot interfere with an individual's self-actualization. We are not talking about repression, denial, or other defense mechanisms, but about a symbolic process, temporal encapsulation, which enables man to organize dissonant experiences so that they are less likely to intrude upon his trajectory into the future.

Notes

1. A. D. Biderman, "Life and Death in Extreme Captivity Situations," in *Psychological Stress*, ed. M. H. Appley and R. Trumbull (New York: Appleton-Century Crofts, 1967), pp. 242-264; V. E. Frankl, *From Death Camp to Existentialism* (Boston: Beacon Press, 1959).

2. R. J. Lifton, *Thought Reform and the Psychology of Totalism* (New York: Norton, 1963).

3. M. K. Oppler, "Cultural Induction of Stress," in *Psychological Stress*, ed. Appley and Trumbull, pp. 209-233.

4. I. L. Janis, "Psychological Effects of Warnings," in *Man and Society in Disaster*, ed. G. W. Baker and D. W. Chapman (New York: Basic Books, 1962), pp. 55-92.

5. Erik Erikson, *Childhood and Society* (New York: Norton, 1950).

6. Bruno Bettelheim, "Individual and Mass Behavior in Extreme Situations," *Journal of Abnormal and Social Psychology*, 38:417-452 (1943).

7. W. E. Moore, *Social Change* (Englewood Cliffs, N.J.: Prentice-Hall, 1963).

Epilog
Death in the Afternoon

Two hours before midnight on New Year's Eve, Lady Jane Seymour Brokaw Fonda Plemiannikov was not crying in her eggnog. She was coiled like Cleopatra's asp on the living room sofa of her father's lush townhouse on East 74th Street in a passion-purple sack sweater right out of "Margie," a medieval belt her brother wore in "Spirits of the Dead," a leather mini skirt, and "Barbarella" boots that soared almost as high as her Panavision thighs. "This is the end of a decade," she said confidently, "and I find it very reassuring that in my adult life I've experienced the end of a decade with a future that looks very positive. I'm very optimistic about the world tonight."

Obviously. That afternoon she stepped off a plane and learned she had just won the New York Film Critics Award for best actress of 1969 for her portrayal of a burned-out marathon dancer in "They Shoot Horses, Don't They?" Optimism was high. So was Jane. "You don't mind if I turn on, do you?" she asked impishly. Then her long fire-ice fingernails carefully rolled the tobacco out of a Winston, opened the cap on a dainty snuff box on her father's coffee table and replaced the ordinary old stuff that only causes cancer with fine gray pot she had just brought back from (where? India? Morocco? She couldn't remember; all she knew was it wasn't that tacky stuff they mix with hay in Tijuana, this was the real thing).[1]

Student energy has been building up throughout the spring of 1970. The issues have been familiar—ROTC, pollution, black power

367

—but the locus has shifted from the so-called better schools, few in number, to a strange covey of institutions. Berkeley, Harvard, and Wisconsin are still heard from, to be sure, but now there have been disasters at such disparate institutions as the University of Michigan, the University of South Carolina, MIT, and the University of Mexico. Even Johns Hopkins has encountered stormy weather which led its president, Lincoln Gordon, to say with some annoyance:

> It is a strange concept of the nature of a university community to suppose that any anonymous group has a proscriptive right to require my presence on short notice at a place and time of their choosing to reply to a series of demands based on premises that I believe contrary to fact and based on a rejection in the very wording of their letter with the whole notion of "negotiations, committees, and studies."[2]

From time to time one encounters some new names in the news. An example is Kent State University in Ohio, where there seems to be a persistent brush fire through much of the Spring, but Nixon's withdrawal policy from Vietnam, gradual as it is, seems to have defused some of the violence, and Agnew's voice and posture, as he inveighs against student radicals near and far, has come to take on the humorous dimensions of a nightly television show.

There are some new developments. The University of California at Santa Barbara seems to have replaced San Francisco State as the junior varsity for the Berkeley adventure, but its activities have shifted to an off-campus site. In a startling move students burn to the ground a branch of the country's largest bank. A temporary replacement is erected, but it, too, is destroyed. The students surge through the streets of this long-time conservative stronghold, breaking windows and setting fires, and angry confrontations ensue. One student is killed in the second assault on the bank, but the circumstances are confused; early reports from the police describe him as a rioter shot by an unknown sniper (presumably a student), while students contend that he was hit by police bullets as he was trying to put out the blaze.

Despite the fact that a young man has been killed, there is no public outcry. His name is not even mentioned on my morning newscast. I have been keeping an uneasy scorecard over the past few years. As best as I know, there were three students killed at Orangeburg, South Carolina several years ago in an incident related to an effort to desegregate a bowling alley. Two others died in Los Angeles in a campus struggle over control of the black student group. The People's Park quarrel in Berkeley in 1969 also resulted in one death.

This latest incident is reported by news media as if it is to be expected, almost like the sad toll of casualties from Vietnam. It is apparent that we can accommodate to anything. If we do not balk at 40,000 dead in Southeast Asia, it is possible to regard student deaths with the same weariness with which we accept Monday morning accident reports from the state police. A no-named boy has died in Santa Barbara; who can remember the names in Orangeburg or Los Angeles? Even Schwerner, Goodman, and Chaney have begun to fade. I cannot avoid feeling shock that it is possible to be shot dead at college, but the times are changing. The only apparent consequences of the Santa Barbara incident is a raft of bank bombings in towns surrounding colleges, and there are three or four in one night in East Lansing, Michigan, alone.

The year has been a strange one. Nixon is now in his third year of office, and he has scurried about being all things to all people. James Reston of *The New York Times* is not much taken with Nixon's style and has commented in cynical fashion about the President's Scylla-Charybdis stance:

> Mr. Nixon has reacted to all this recently like an actor on the world stage, each day playing a different role. One day there is Nixon the Unifier praising the Congress, and the next there is Nixon the Scrapper vilifying the Senate on Carswell and Haynsworth, or Nixon the Tough Guy dropping his "g's" at the Pentagon and characterizing the university militants as "bums."[3]

Reston's colleague, Tom Wicker, stated the matter even more trenchantly:

> Turning back the calendar by two or three years with the incomparable blandness that, in his Administration, invariably cloaks sophism,

the President decreed that "in devising local compliance plans, primary weight should be given to the considered judgment of local school boards—provided they act in good faith and within constitutional limits." A school board composed of P. T. Barnum, Harry Houdini, and Richard M. Nixon would not be able to devise more dazzling escapes from the clinking chains of desegregation than almost any old Southern school boards will be able to arrange through so generous a formula.[4]

On the other hand, those who make up what Nixon cleverly has chosen to call "the great silent majority" do like his performance, if public opinion polls are any measure, and although memoranda leaks (Moynihan and Hickel) have caused some cracks in the smooth façade, there is a growing feeling that middle America, if there is such a thing, feels that the country is moving in the right direction.

Occasionally, Nixon has lost his cool and made some wild gaffes. Late in 1968 there were his comments upon the Peace Moratorium in Washington. After a variety of efforts to discourage the event Nixon first indicated that he would be utterly unresponsive to whatever took place in front of his home. Later he let it be known that he had not even looked out the window, preferring to spend the Saturday afternoon, as did all good Americans, watching football on television. Despite Nixon's lack of interest, the march riveted the nation's attention on the opposition to war, and the evident discipline under trying cirumstances attracted congressional support for the first time. Several hundred thousand assembled in the Capitol and, Nixon notwithstanding, it was an impressive tribute to peace.

Our car had four people as we drove south toward Ohio. Washington seemed far off. After about two hours, however, we picked up momentum as the north-south tributaries joined the mainsteams, the Ohio and Pennsylvania turnpikes. Almost all of the cars were heading to the march. This was easy to tell as most of the passengers wore the uniforms of the peace movement: long hair, beards, mustaches, and old clothes. Washington seemed like a vortex. It was as if the whole country was falling toward this point.

370

Hitchhikers on the side of the road flashed peace signs instead of thumbs to stop cars. Once through the mountains of Pennsylvania, we were flying into the capital.

We reached Washington at about three o'clock Friday morning. It was more like a crash. We had no place to stay, and when the Moratorium Committee found us a room, we could not coordinate it with a place to park the car. Like waifs, we wandered around the city just fooling around. Then we walked into the March Against Death. Here were solemn people, carrying signs with victims' names. These were illuminated with flickering candles. The candlelight stretched for miles. We met a Mobe marshal who drove us to Arlington Cemetery to begin the march. They outfitted us with a candle, a victim's name, and a black armband. I marched for Albert Christey of Pennsylvania. For the first time the war became very personal rather than symbolic. I felt like I knew the soldier. For a moment I became the spirit of Albert Christey. When I came to the White House, a marshal signaled me to shout my victim's name. I shouted as loud as I could, hoping to knock Pat and the Dick out of bed.

We finallly found a motel at about seven o'clock in the morning. It was very cheap, and we sneaked four people into a single room. One person slept on the bed, while the other three camped on the floor; a weekend of asceticism seemed fitting. After getting four hours sleep we decided to look around Washington. The contrast is amazing; that so much shit can come out of such a beautiful city is poetic injustice. We walked from the Lincoln Memorial down to the Washington Monument (that phallus to the "Father of our Country") and then to the Smithsonian Institution. Most of the time we were just gadding about.

That night, across from Mobe headquarters, the Weathermen held a meeting and then marched to Dupont Circle dressed for battle with crash helmets, face masks, handkerchiefs for protection from tear gas, and stones and clubs. They began chanting the Weatherman war dance, "Ho! Ho! Ho Chi Minh; the N.L.F. is gonna win." They shouted over and over again until they were *worked up into a frenzy. I felt they were both very brave and very crazy as they readied themselves to get the shit kicked out of them. They have a hero mentality.*

    The theme reached a climax as they ran into the street to confront the waiting police. One girl ran up to a cop and shouted, "You fucking pig!" She hit him in the stomach with the thick staff of her Viet Cong flag. Like in a bad but familiar plot, the tear gas was fired. Then we split. I read in the paper the next morning that thirty were arrested. New Mobe denied any connection with the riot.

    We started moving early Saturday morning. Figuring parking would be at a premium, we left the car in Virginia and hitchhiked to the march. By 10:30 there were hundreds of thousands of people anxiously waiting for the march to begin. The starting gate was manned by Mobe marshals, who were being very sure that things did not begin before the permit said they should. The crowding was acute. I could not see, but I heard the neglectful father of New Mobe, Eugene McCarthy, give a short speech, and then we expected to move. But when 100,000 or 250,000 or 500,000 demonstrators (depending on the political persuasion of the newspapers you read, moving from right to left, respectively) try to take off at the same time, things happen very slowly. About an hour later we were finally in the street. As the March Against Death was solemn, the Saturday March on Washington was almost festive. Here was real solidarity. Everyone believed we would "overcome." It seemed impossible that "they" could ignore such a total (and, for the most part, lawful) demonstration. Marchers were happy. They wore buttons identifying themselves as "Effete Snobs"; describing Spider Agnew, the hated symbol of the reactionary right, as a "schmuck." Dick Gregory probably summed up our contempt best when he said, "Agnew is so dumb he can't chew gum and walk at the same time." The march moved for miles finally stacking up in the park under the Washington Monument. It was beautiful as these half million people became one.

    The demonstrators were entertained by Arlo Guthrie; Peter, Paul and Mary; and the anachronist, Pete Seeger. It was a tremendous

*performance by the unemployed "Communist" of the 1950s. The
world has finally caught up to Seeger.
The ride back home mirrored the ride to Washington. Our moods
moved from joy to bitterness as newcasters told us Nixon paid no
attention to the march. He spent the afternoon watching a football
game. Agnew wasn't even in the city.
Distance has proven that very little was won by this mobilization.
In a more realistic mood it was a long weekend for personal
catharsis.*

The march was to be succeeded by another equally dramatic but
longer performance each month. The national occurrence for November was scaled down to a series of local happenings for the pre-
Christmas trade, while December was an exceptionally cold month.
Somehow the winter wore down the initial enthusiasm and April
brought the sad news that the Vietnam Moratorium Committee was
disbanding.

Although its leader, Sam Brown, said "there was little prospect
of immediate change in the Administration's policy in Vietnam,"[5]
others attributed the Committee's demise to the results of Nixon's
November 3 "Vietnamization" speech. Even Brown acknowledged
in a midwinter speech that "Mr. Nixon had scored 'a tremendous
political coup by managing to identify himself with the cause of
peace.' "[6] Still the more recent polls this spring showed that only
48 percent of those interviewed approved of American policy in
Vietnam as opposed to 65 percent who supported Nixon in January.
Nonetheless, the marches seemingly were over, and one sponsor,
Marge Sklencar, commented disconsolately that "mass demonstrations were a political fad that has worn off." She compared the tactics of demonstrations with the civil rights sit-ins of the early 1960s.
"Sit-ins were popular and successful, but they ran their course," she
said. "But progress in civil rights didn't stop with the sit-ins, and
I don't think the antiwar movement is going to stop now."[7]

The fact that a woman was speaking for the Mobilization Movement should not be overlooked. One of the important corollaries of
the youthful demand for change was a sometimes shrill, more often

reasonable, demand by women for an equal voice in the country's destiny. At its worst it tended to regard brassieres as the symbol of male oppression and all of society's reactions to the feminine as a massive plot based upon old style Freudian polemics. At its best the movement sought to create understanding for the productive role of women in society and focused attention upon the feminine gender as a member of an underprivileged group. The latter faction generally could be found in politics, in the professions, or in the business world. Few could honestly question that there were now more women visible in those three arenas, and simple proof appeared in the society pages of the newspapers, which now featured numerous stories on "emancipated" women.

The other movers for women's rights were likely to be much younger, more radical, and at the same time more romantic in an anti-hero sense. Their struggle with men had a strangely personal quality, and while masculine society was its ultimate target, they chose to fight *mano a mano* with representatives of that hated society, often in communal relationships. The younger group likely has been scarred by their treatment in the peace movement where, for example, women were jeered at when they spoke at a rally in Washington in 1969. Further, girls in the civil rights movement commonly complained of their disdainful treatment by black male colleagues. This group flies its colors at Women's Liberation Front.

The tract of the older group is a well circulated pamphlet by Ann Koedt called "The Myth of the Vaginal Orgasm," which is based upon the fact that men deny that the female orgasm is clitoral in site. Not much is made of the fact that Mary McCarthy quietly (?) took on all of mankind on the entire orgasm issue as far back as 1947 in an article called "The Tyranny of the Orgasm," which appeared in the *New Leader* in April of that year. The professional complaints of these women make less controversial reading—the general societal malaise felt in midlife, the lack of vocational opportunities, the blocking of the creative impulses. They meet in seminars which often lead to action groups, and their center is the National Organization for Women. Both sectors have recently come

374

out in support of the American prostitute as the real heroine of the country—no sham, no fuss, doing an honest day's work for an honest dollar.

The history of this country has been based on violence. This society is at this point in time run by a few, and those few run it for profits. As an example, the health profession, rather than serving people and meeting their needs, is run on a profit basis. There are all sorts of inventions in terms of abortion, in terms of birth control, that aren't being introduced onto the market because money will be lost. Instead, thousands of women die every year from abortions, and others get pregnant because of the whole profit-making thing.

There are two roads to go in this country. One is people's struggling to survive because their needs are not met, because they have to work harder and harder for things that any humane government should provide for free; they either take it out on someone else; they become racists, they become chauvinists. The workers who cannot, who are struggling in shit jobs in a factory come home and take it out on their wives. They keep their wives down at home, and take it out on black people. That's one way of dealing with powerlessness. The other way is to begin to meet some of those needs that the government does not provide, because it is off slaughtering other people. This could be done by grouping together, beginning to analyze what is going on in this country, beginning to think of ways of solving it, beginning to get together to meet their own needs.

How do you get people together to understand from their own problems, their own lives? One theory that I hold to is that we can begin grouping collectively to try to understand the problems, to try and begin dealing with them. Nine months ago I left the city understanding all of these things, but did not see how I could be strong enough emotionally, together enough, to deal with all the problems that I understood. There was a lot in my own life that was really unsettled, and I came to New Hampshire four months ago quite by accident. I ended up at a household with people who were beginning to do sort of small-time political work, and we talked about the possibilities of redefining our lives in a place like New

Hampshire where there is still time, where there is still space and money, and of beginning to deal with the problems of the world; not just as they are reflected in the world but as they are reflected in our behavior. So we grouped together and began examining a lot of the fears and problems that we had in living with this society. We ran the gamut of our inability to deal realistically with money, our selfishness about possessions, of sharing things, of helping each other make decisions, of little petty things like housework, and how these issues reach the even bigger issues of male domination of women.

We were going to begin to try and do political work in New England. At the same time there developed a contradiction between what we wanted to see other people doing and the way we live our own lives. Our possessiveness about relationships, our competing with one another, our defining ourselves by the individual work that we did, rather than seeing it as work that we all did. My own concerns were about my possessiveness about a novel that I was working on. The way we began to break this down was to begin to open up these fears and peel off the layers that we all had built up around ourselves over the years to protect ourselves. For the past four months I've undergone an incredible experience that could be likened to a collective self-analysis or psychoanalysis that has been really helpful. I mean I really feel that it is possible to transform oneself in a way that is unheard of. I do not think there is a project like ours going on in the Western world.

I think that it is only through collective groupings that people will begin to realize that the problems that they face, although special in some cases, are pretty uniform, especially among women trying to have romantic relationships. In our collective and throughout the political movement, women are beginning to get together among themselves to talk about feeling like half-human beings. Most communes are very internalized but in terms of domestic things, we are challenging the roles that woman have always fit into.

All the domestic work is shared, as well as the heavy work. Women are beginning to learn about wiring, to learn about guns, to learn about cars. The idea is that we started out at the same level as the men did. Everybody does the housework and we have been incredibly efficient. It has to do with the consciousness that we have developed among ourselves from months of talking and of going through close criticism of each other.

I am very fortunate to have a boyfriend who is very conscious of the whole problem. It is not just a matter of petty things like housework; housework reflects another level of problems. Most of the women in the house are educated and are not used to, you know, have not been in the traditional domestic role, but at the same time it comes out in other forms. From the beginning we have shared housework, but that still does not explain a lot of women's insecurities about or dread of cars, of heavy work, of just feeling inadequate. The whole idea of women's liberation affects everyone's liberation. There are a whole lot of things that the whole women's liberation movement brings to all of society, to challenge its very bases. For example, the whole idea of competition, of authority, of elite, of skills. We all learn all kinds of things, and some are better at some things than others. The idea in this society is that the man goes out and the woman sits at home and slaves and there is no value attached to the work she does in raising the children. The men go out and are very detached from the basic kind of life. This must be changed. If it can be done, it can change marriage, it can change the way people relate to each other, it can break down the idea of someone's being dominant in a relationship. I think everything that is wrong in our society stems from men who have to do jobs that they do not like to make money. The money alienates them even from the meaning of their jobs so that they come home and take it out on their wives.

If you break down all the bad reasons for depending on someone, then maybe we will begin to learn those new reasons why two people should be together and really begin to understand the depth that two people can reach in their relationship. I am just beginning to open that up, all those things are broken down. I still want to go back and demand certain kinds of attention that I have demanded

377

from analysts, from my father, and from other boyfriends that always in the end ended in a disaster. It has only been through collective process, I mean, I have been fortunate enough to go through other sorts of processes, progressive schools, analysts, and at home, that it is only now through, you know, being able to really examine the motives in a group that I have been able to deal with some of this.

More than talk has been taking place, however. The SDS split into factions following its baptism of fire in Chicago in 1968, and its most action-oriented wing, the Weatherman, has undertaken a plan, reportedly developed in Flint, Michigan in the summer of 1969, to level society. Starting with a series of bomb scares last year, the group has moved onto the national scene with a panoply of dynamitings which make its first thrust, the Chicago window-breakings, seem like child's play. Their expertise with explosives stands at some distance from their dedication, and there have been several devastating accidents. There seems to be some kind of uneasy alliance between this group and the Black Panthers which is based upon practical rather than theoretical considerations. It is difficult to know whether Jerry Rubin is a Weatherman, or Eldridge Cleaver a Panther, but Cleaver's introduction to Rubin's book, entitled *Do It: Scenarios of the Revolution,* conveys the ambience:

> I can unite with Jerry Rubin around a marijuana cigarette . . . around being cool . . . I can unite with Jerry around hatred of pig judges, around hatred of capitalism, around the total desire to smash what is now the social order in the United States of America.[8]

The book itself closes with the happy prescription:

> Every high school and college in the country will close with riots and sabotage. Yippie helicopter pilots will bomb police positions with LSD gas. Revolutionaries will break into jails and free all political prisoners. Kids will lock their parents out of their suburban homes and turn them into guerilla bases, storing arms.[9]

It is this optimistic view of the future which occasioned Gail Sheehy's perceptive comment "the really new politics is a comic book."[10]

As the year goes on, there are at first scattered rumors, then more persistent ones, that some of our troops are in Cambodia. Senator William Fulbright is seen from time to time on the nation's screens, honest face seamed and lined, that curiously winning intonation of mixed Southern boy and Rhodes Scholar coming through, asking Nixon to confirm or deny. It is hard to hear the answer. Troops are in, but they are not in; or rather, in but not to fight; or were in but are no longer. These gleanings are from the voices of the President's associates, but Nixon himself puts his money where his mouth is on April 20 when he announces to nationwide television audiences that 150,000 more troops will come home from Vietnam this year, and this removal will leave less than half the number of Americans in Vietnam than were there when he took office in January 1969. Moreover, Nixon credits American patriotism for the withdrawal, suggesting that the enemy has failed to marshal opposition to the war in the U.S.: "Their [Hanoi's leaders] most fatal miscalculation is that they thought they could win politically in the United States."

The speech is greeted with editorial hurrahs, and the President's popularity is reported to be at a new high. Still, there are some doubters. If Vietnam is diminishing as a campus issue, there are others to take its place. The mood of the country is uncertain, and now in a peculiar way. The trial of the Chicago Seven has ended with unexpected consequences. Judge Julius Hoffman, whose legal deportment has caused many conservative lawyers to cringe, and the defendants, who have lost not a few friends by their assault upon the integrity of the entire judicial system and the Chicago system in particular, have come to the cross in the road. Judge Hoffman metes out heavy sentences with a curious punitiveness that convinces many that at issue is courtroom behavior rather than precourt crime and then flays the defense attorneys, sentencing all to lengthy jail terms for contempt of court.

While all are now out on bond, their presence as speakers on the campus has kept the pot boiling and a new kind of courtroom decorum is developing. In New York Judge John M. Murtagh delays a trial until some Black Panthers, held in jail and unable to meet bond, promise to behave when they are before his bench. The tinkerers are at work figuring how shields, soundproof cages, barred rooms equipped with television, or plastic bubbles may be used to keep courtrooms sleepy and drowsy as they used to be, while still protecting the right of the accused to be present at his trial. Along the way there is an unfortunate shoot-out at a Panther headquarters in Chicago, and the story that develops is frightening. Two blacks are dead and, as usual, confusion exists about who shot first. The police virtuously produce panels showing that the bullet holes mainly go from in to out, which suffices to satisfy the district attorney, who promptly arrests all found in the building and charges them with aggravated assault and attempt to commit murder.

The Panthers produce their wall panels showing bullets going from out to in and their supporters cry "police brutality." There are the usual solemn funerals, black leaders speak and threaten the end of the nonviolence movement, and liberal whites attempt to raise bail bonds for those imprisoned in Chicago and elsewhere. Evidence is rapidly produced to demonstrate that blacks charged with planning crimes are held on heavier bail than whites accused of committing crimes, and student radicals in the East begin a new round of demands upon university officials. They want the universities either to pay entirely for the bail of the jailed Panthers or at least to contribute sizably to the fund. The movement is fired by the fact that a Chicago Grand Jury throws out the indictment against the Chicago Panthers when a review of the evidence fails to support police allegations that the blacks were the aggressors in the incident.

The tone of this drive is sullen and dangerous, and not to be compared to the other social push of the Spring, the effort to get colleges to vote their General Motors stock for the pro-Nader forces. The latter thrust is a part of the growing interest in pollution, a matter widely hailed on all the nation's campuses as a "relevant" educational experience and one which draws upon the sympathies and support of all levels of academia. There are many pollution teach-ins, but few colleges respond to the opportunity to support Nader against pollution-responsible General Motors. Still, the feeling exists that this is not a central issue around which student dissenters can rally support. The Panther matter is more to the point. By curious coincidence, New Haven is the site of what rapidly has become known as "the Bobby Seale Trial." Seale is the member of the Chicago Seven who was bound, gagged, and chained in the courtroom for disruptive behavior and was finally separated from the trial by Judge Hoffman. His difficulties in New Haven are more quixotic. Along with others, he is accused of the torture-murder of a so-called black informer, a former Panther who was suspected of betraying the group. The hallowed Green, the portion of the campus where Yale athletic heroes have been pictured on the famous fence with the white "Y" on their blue varsity sweaters, now serves as command headquarters for students from all over the East who have come to protest the trial. As Yale begins to be shut down by student action, President Kingman Brewster soberly speaks out. He, too, feels that the Black Panthers cannot get a fair trial in New Haven or anywhere else in this country. He speaks of sending teams of Yale students to courtrooms in New Haven and elsewhere to observe the proceedings. The school is temporarily closed, but there is no violence. Both the Panthers and the students repeatedly express the determination to keep things cool, and the weekend crisis, at least, passes without unusual incident. No one knows what will happen later, but there is solid student support for Brewster's stand, although Agnew calls upon Yale's trustees to impeach their president for disparaging the judicial system. Other colleges are not so lucky. The National Center for Violence at Brandeis reports that almost 300 of the nation's colleges are currently in the throes of one kind of disorder or another, and one massive confrontation takes place at the University of Michigan, where black students demand an admission quota. A student strike ensues, violence occurs, gas cannisters fall freely, and the Board of Regents meets solidly for a seventy-two-hour period with Robben Fleming, the harassed president. When it is all over Fleming announces that the university will go to a 10 percent black quota, and that it will find funds for support of this increase "somewhere" in the existing budget by belt-tightening. The state legislature promptly announces that it will do some belt-tightening of its own in the next university budget, and there are also rumors that some members of the regents are angry at Fleming for his "capitulation" to radical demands.

Actions around the issue of minority admissions began one night, about three days before midterm examinations. I noticed a group of people gathered around the entrance to the Undergraduate Library when I went there to study. Instead of beginning a crowded, brightly lit study trip, the building was being darkened and people with bewildered, blank faces were filing out a door being held open by a university security man.

A friend who had been in the library explained this strange scene to me. About sixty black students, members of the Black Action Movement (BAM), had entered the library and begun removing armfuls of books from the shelves and piling them on the floor.

All this was done in silence, apparently without explanation to the library staff. The librarians had decided to close the library rather than risk further attack on their meticulously arranged shelves. The reason for the protest was that at that day's meeting of the university regents, they had appropriated some hundred thousand dollars to library maintenance, while cutting the budget for disadvantaged students.

White radicals were naturally excited that black students had begun political action, not only because it added to the quantity of dissent against university priorities and decision-making processes, but also because black protest is so legitimate, especially in the eyes of white moderates. Throughout the year white radicals, primarily SDS and Women's Liberation, had been demonstrating against industrial and military recruiting on campus. The radicals realized the potential of the BAM strike. The black demands were really quite conservative, yet we knew that the regents would turn down the proposals because they were student-initiated "demands." We knew the pattern; it had been used to secure a nonprofit student bookstore: students propose bookstores, regents reject proposal; 106 people arrested occupying administration building; university

382

*shut down by strike; regents approve bookstore. In the process po-
litical consciousness is increased as students observe how things
work.*

*For me this opportunity to increase awareness was the greatest
value of the strike. This was not only political awareness of the
power students do and should have and how this power can be developed, but more important to me was an increasing awareness of
how deeply ingrained we all are with what are essentially arbitrary
patterns of existence. The library action seems perfectly appropriate
to me. "What possible harm could there be in studying in a library?"
The strike forced everyone to ask similar questions about his own
activities. The answer is that the harm is not in doing things, but in
giving them closed-minded priority over the incredible mass of real-
life problems.*

*We did not hear from BAM again until two weeks later. On this
day BAM representatives were to present a list of eleven demands
to the regents for consideration. BAM called an afternoon rally
outside the Administration Building to await the regent's decision.
I attended the rally with an SDS "affinity group" of nine people.
We were divided into two lines, each with linked arms. This tactic
is part of SDS's general "decentralization," the reasons being that
the individual knows and can depend on the people near him in a
crowd, decisions can be made quickly, and protection is provided
if necessary. The regent's decision came down, accepting BAM's
figure of 10 percent black enrollment goal, but funding only 5-6 percent enrollment and ignoring most of the other demands.*

*Under BAM leadership and chanting slogans, the crowd marched
around outside and through some of the main university classroom
buildings. After about an hour the group of maybe 500 people returned to the Administration Building. Apparently not seeing us
coming President Fleming and two of the regents were walking
around outside of their fortress. When they were spotted, a part of
the crowd ran toward them, yipping in shrill voices. They got back
into the building, but one of the protestors grabbed a huge ring of
keys used to open the doors and held it up over the crowd in vic-*

tory. Maybe fifty people entered the building. My affinity group was wandering around on the outside of the crowd wondering what to do. Police in riot gear were arriving and slowly moving on the crowd. It was a very strange scene. People were everywhere, and the police just sort of formed lines. Our group kept backing away (to be away from police cars) and huddling. After a while the police started sweeping one way, then back the other, clubbing people in the crowd. We were very far away by then and could only see helmets, running people, and sort of a cloud of rocks in the air over the whole thing.

Our group started saying, "Don't run, walk, don't run, walk," which is what we did. It was sickening, everyone moving very slowly and helplessly. We couldn't see what was happening. We knew people were getting beaten but we didn't know who they were (I could see most of the SDS people I knew far out on the fringe, as we were) or what we could do. Several other affinity groups left, telling us that they were "going to do things" and would meet us later. Things mentioned were fire alarms, fires in wastebaskets, and turning on fire hoses in classroom buildings.

My group walked to a building. Two of us went through and located fire alarms, and we went back as a group and pulled a local alarm. We then ran to a nearby coffee shop and discussed methods of making torches, destroying university trucks, and decapitating parking meters. We were all nearly exhausted and also afraid. For all of us, pulling the fire alarm was our first illegal act, and we were pretty upset about it.

Strike leaders, purposely or otherwise, started the strike slowly, the result being that students had a chance to define their roles on a personal, fairly noncoercive basis. As the strike became more of a mass action, personal considerations were difficult to make, but at the beginning people had a good opportunity to evaluate their priorities. This was especially important for many of the women involved in the strike. For several weeks before, women had been trying to work out their role in the radical movement, including contemplation of splitting from the main organization of SDS. They used the opportunity of the strike to try all-women actions. The biggest of these was a march of about 300 women that wound its way around the city, blocking traffic and university parking structure entrances. They chanted encouragement to the men who were picketing classroom buildings. The women were very enthusiastic about this action and expressed feelings of great solidarity and satisfaction. They were able to find out many things about themselves both as individuals and as a group.

This became the most important aspect of the strike. The first day of picket lines found people horrified at the thought of missing a class. Symptoms of withdrawal appeared on their faces as they approached our lines. They could not cross, of course, because they would be branded as racist. However, as the strike progressed, students realized that classes were not an absolute, something that conformed to the natural order. As the strike progressed, especially during the last three days when BAM called off picketing, white radicals became more and more at odds with BAM leadership. There was no talk from BAM about significant reordering of university priorities or expanding the strike to deal with radical issues such as ROTC, recruiting, or university war research. Apparently the threats of Fleming and Michigan Governor William Milliken to call in the National Guard and state police, coupled with apprehension of being coopted, had frightened BAM into virtual capitulation.

The final settlement, which BAM accepted, was unacceptable to many white students on several counts. First was the issue of possible reprisals against student activists. BAM had stated that the strike would not be called off unless amnesty was granted for all participants. The settlement stated that charges stemming from the strike could be handled through normal university channels (faculty disciplinary boards) or brought directly to an "impartial judge" appointed by the university president. The second issue was where funding for the BAM proposals would come from. Students had asked for an appropriation directly from the regents. BAM accepted a plan that called for funding from departmental appropriation.

385

The money for department operations must come through the offices of two vice presidents, who are already at war with the deans of the various schools. The administration has already announced that no additional funding will be available for the departments, so the cost of the programs must be paid from faculty salaries. This threat that young, radical faculty, few of whom have tenure, might be let go was thinly veiled. In addition, several of BAM's original demands were not granted. This is strange, because BAM was negotiating from a position of absolute power, all university functions having been shut down. Many of us felt betrayed by the weak settlement. It was really sad to see all those people returning to their same dreary classes, claiming at the same time "victory" for the people.

As the warm weather comes on in late April, President Nixon finally confirms that U.S. troops are joining in ground operations in Cambodia to "clean out major enemy sanctuaries that were threatening to become a springboard for attacks on South Vietnam which would put American troops in an untenable military position." This simple admission of what is already a de facto situation begins what history may well record as the most fateful fifteen days of the year.

May 1 starts with the President's early morning visit to the Pentagon. The television shows him surrounded by cheering civilian employes who laughingly give the "V" sign, and perhaps buoyed by this enthusiasm for the shaky Cambodian adventure, Nixon makes an unnecessary mistake. After saying modestly that he has only done what he felt was right, he contrasts the behavior and courage of the military in the Cambodian struggle with the "bums who burn buildings and destroy books." And then follows the most "jingoist" statement of all. "We will not be a second rate power, we will not be defeated!"

Although the Pentagon seems overjoyed, late morning brings some sharp criticism. Nixon's man for all seasons, Senator Robert Griffin of Michigan, complains with considerable annoyance that "a minimum of communication" exists between the White House and Congress and reports that he "cannot altogether excuse the

President." As could be expected, the National Student Association calls for a nationwide strike on campuses and the old anti-war mobilizers once again pick up their previously discarded packs and begin to organize á massive demonstration in Washington for May 9.

Three uneasy days pass as congressional Democrats and not a few Republicans flail away at the President, and the nightly newscasts contain a strange mixture of characters. We see American soldiers enroute to Cambodia being asked whether they wanted to go there. A few say no, and a few even refuse to go, but the adventure begins to sound like a resounding public relations success. The enemy falls back with little fighting, and both the administration and the military relax as "large" stores of enemy ammunition and supplies are discovered. The mood at the colleges is undeniably bearish, and there are daily reports of increased opposition to the extension of the Vietnam war. At an embattled school in the rolling hills of Ohio, the National Guard is called in after an Army ROTC building is burned down. Students call the guardsmen names and throw rocks and sticks. There are a number of small skirmishes, tear gas is used to disperse the crowd, but something suddenly happens as the battle lines reform.

Following orders to clear the area, the guards begin to march down the hill once again. Suddenly they kneel and fire, and four students lie dead.

It was cold-blooded murder. We narrowly missed getting killed ourselves.

The students had been protesting President Nixon's escalation of the war into Cambodia and the bombing of North Vietnam.

The day of the massacre there had been an impromptu call for a student strike at Kent.

The statement from the National Guard that they started shooting in response to sniping is untrue. It was a one-sided shoot-out.

We were caught with hundreds of other students near a parking lot when suddenly a line of guardsmen turned toward us, knelt down, aimed—almost as if by an order.

Briefly, the events leading up to the bloodshed were this:

On Friday noon, May 1, there was a rally of about 2,000 to bury a copy of the U.S. Constitution. It was in response to Nixon's speech escalating the war. A serviceman with a silver star and a bronze star burned his discharge papers. Later the Black United Students held a rally.

That evening the guard was brought in.

Saturday night a crowd of several thousand burned down the ROTC building. When it burned, the guardsmen had orders to shoot anyone who cut firehoses.

On Monday, May 4, we both went down to the commons, an open field, at noon.

Someone climbed up on the base of a liberty bell and said, "It's time to strike. It's time to strike."

An Army jeep pulled up. There were four men, three guardsmen and one state trooper, in it. The trooper had a bullhorn. He said, "Please leave the area. Please leave the area. This is an illegal gathering. Leave before someone is hurt."

A few students—no more than a handful—were heaving rocks. Thousands of students were in the area.

A group of guardsmen approached. Before we knew it, we saw tear gas cannisters in the midst of us. People started running.

"Walk, walk" people shouted. The students walked. It was an orderly retreat.

Several truckloads of guardsmen pulled up, got out, formed a single line, fixed their bayonets, put on tear gas masks, and started coming up the hill. Gas cannisters were lobbed. Students threw them back.

We retreated again. The scary thing about it was that the guard was still coming, shooting tear gas.

The guard came down toward the hill. Maybe as many as a thousand students had regrouped on a hill near a parking lot. The guard came toward us. A few guys were throwing rocks—more like pebbles. They weren't big. One guardsmen brushed stones away with his hand.

Then the guardsmen got to their knees. They aimed. There was no sniper fire. If the commanding general claims there was sniper fire coming from a building, why didn't they shoot up at the building? Why did they shoot at the crowd?

At first no one was sure what was happening. There was a steady, loud rattle, like machine guns.

Someone yelled, "Those are only blanks."

Then we heard bullets whistling past our heads. Dirt flew up in our faces, where bullets were hitting the ground, landing only a few feet from us.

There was a tree about fifteen yards behind us. There were repeated sounds of thuds and splintering noises as bullets hit the tree. More bullets hit the cars in the lot, smashing the windshields, hitting the fenders and the sides of the cars.

One of us—Mike—dived behind a curb and lay flat. The other one—Fred—raced for a trash can and dived behind it. That's where we waited until the shooting stopped.

There was a steady rattling of bullets.

We saw one student run for the parked cars. He almost made it. Suddenly, he spun around, his legs crumpled underneath him, and fell, half behind the car. A student who had made it tried to drag the body behind the car but he wasn't able to.

A girl was screaming.

"They're not using blanks. They're not using blanks."

Another student fell over, dead.

A student collapsed to the ground, hit.

Suddenly after about thirty seconds the shooting stopped. We got up and looked around.

One girl was lying on the ground, holding her stomach. Her face was white.

There were others, lying on the ground. Some moved. Some didn't.

The prevailing mood in the whole area was one of panic. We heard a girl crying hysterically.

"Get an ambulance, get an ambulance," others were shouting.

A guy picked up one girl and held her in his arms. The front of her was covered with blood. "She's dead," he was shouting. "She's dead. I know she's dead."

Some guys were leaning over another girl and using jackets as makeshift compresses. Another was giving her mouth-to-mouth resuscitation.

Another guy was helped hobbling to a dorm. One leg had been shot.

One fellow lay in the parking lot. Just lay there.

There were sounds of ambulance sirens. The ambulances pulled up.

"Over here," some students were yelling. "Over here." Students were pointing down at the wounded, lying on the ground. "Please hurry, please hurry."

The attendant lifted one fellow onto a stretcher. One side of his head was puffed way out and his face was blue.

People were crying and screaming, saying this thing was uncalled for.

We blame Nixon for this. He's the man responsible for these murders. He sent the troops to Vietnam and sent more to Cambodia. The students are outraged.

What is there to do now? The answer is immediate, total withdrawal of troops.

Kent is closed now. The university's president sent all the students home.

But we want the killers brought to trial.

Right now, we're still in sort of a state of shock. We can still see the National Guardsmen firing.

Each of us tried to go to sleep last night. But you can't. You put down your head, and you keep hearing shots.[11]

Their names were Alison Krause, Jeffrey Glenn Miller, Sandra Lee Scheuer, and William K. Schroeder. Two were aged nineteen and two were twenty; two from Ohio, the others from the East. I heard the story first from Walter Cronkite early in the evening and was stunned. By the 11 p.m. news the father of one of the girls was shown piteously weeping and placing the blame on either Nixon or the war or both, I'm not sure. Then came the commander of the guard unit. He promised an investigation, a thorough one, and mentioned the single shot which came from the student side and which was to figure so crucially in the news over the next weeks.

Was an order given by an officer to shoot? The commander was evasive—perhaps yes, perhaps no. The investigation would clear this up. But he spoke earnestly of the immense provocation by the students. Finally, his name emerges. He is Brigadier General Robert Canterbury, and he is square-jawed and understandably defensive. Looking at his interrogators, the general tells it how it was: "Considering the size of the rocks being thrown and the nearness of the students, the guardsmen's lives were in danger and they could have been overrun."

An unidentified sergeant is interviewed. He comments laconically: "My friends and I don't think it was justified, but most of the fellows say if they are attacked like that, it's okay."

And then came two civilians:

"Anyone came in and tried to protect us, they [the students] called 'pigs,'" said a waitress at the Kent Motor Inn near the campus.

"I feel terrible about those children getting killed, but they must have provoked the Guard," said the elderly housemother of a Kent State fraternity.

All is peaches and cream on the "Today" show the next morning. Frank Blair quotes the President as saying flatly to the country that the needless deaths "should remind us all once again that when dissent turns to violence it invites tragedy." The fact that the statement misses the point by transferring the blame to the victims rather than those who shot impulsively is later noted by *The New York Times*. There are still more tales about a single shot fired, but the confusion grows, and a National Guard spokesman describes how nervous the troops were and how the shot sounded to some like a firecracker, and to others like a machine gun.

The scene switches to the weather, and then Hugh Downs and Barbara Walters are on. This happy morning, the topic is the crucial mini- or midi-skirt conflict, and Hugh develops an intellectual parallel between fashion and civilization, but perhaps the events of the previous night oppress him, for he hedges his thesis by a qualifier "civilization, or whatever there is of it." Barbara, ever ready to compromise, cautions Hugh about the danger of sounding "rash" and we are off as usual in the morning.

Barbara models the midi, but Hugh disapproves, explaining that he is not against midi per se, just that he is opposed to women throwing out a perfectly good wardrobe. The tempo of the argument mounts. Miss Walters, the Queen of Kitsch, puts the house skillfully in order: "All right, all right, are we going to wear midiskirts this year or are we going to stop shilly shallying . . . ?"

Mercifully, a commercial intervenes for "a product that's not lovable, but very likeable." It turns out to be Coronet Paper Towels and "other paper products," and the coyness of the introduction becomes clear. It is now a new hour and Frank Blair is back. Another Cambodian sweep is described, but this time there is heavy enemy fire, and then we are back to Kent State. The circumstances are described as a "three-second hail of fire," and Ohio's Governor James Rhodes asks for the FBI to investigate. Some thirty-seven college presidents call upon Nixon to pull out of Cambodia. They describe youth as now more alienated than ever before in our history. A London newspaper headlines the Kent story as "the death of a college," and Frank Blair concludes the news with the latest word from Agnew, who terms the shootings "predictable" and describes college war critics as "paranoids and tomentose exhibitionists who provoke more derision than fear."

During this sad day nothing very good takes place. By noon the Associated Press shows something between eighty to ninety colleges already shut down as a consequence of the Kent State disaster, but the President's press aide, Ronald Ziegler, says Nixon has no plan to see college presidents. The President does see 100 members of Congress, however, and promises to remove troops from Cambodia in six to eight weeks. He also indicates that no one will be sent deeper than twenty-one miles into Cambodia without congressional approval. When it comes to questions about dissent, Nixon is implacable. He is reported to pound the table, to reiterate that student militants are bums, and back once again to his last November mood, he argues that he will not be swayed by demonstrations.

By May 7, plans for a massive demonstration in Washington are solidified, and negotiations begin with District of Columbia authorities about the rules. Ziegler notwithstanding, Nixon meets with the heads of eight major universities, who later report he agreed to stop his own hostile comment about youth and to modify Agnew's words. The President denies the former, and the Vice President disclaims any knowledge of the latter.

The next day 250 colleges remain closed, and strikes all but officially close some 400 more. Nixon takes to the television to make his peace. The substance is the same as his assurances to Congress, but there is indeed something new; Nixon says he and the students want the same thing—an early end to the war. Agnew, at a speech at Boise, Idaho describes administration's critics as "a cadre of Jeremiahs . . . a gloomy coalition of choleric young intellectuals and tired, embattled elders." Just a little later, he, too, is to be found on both sides of the fence. When eleven professors from the University of Minnesota meet with Agnew and asked that he tone down his speeches, he concedes that his visitors have some valid arguments. At one point he is reported to have said that he had once taught night law school classes in Baltimore and "were I in your position, you know I might well be a member of your group."[12]

After his television appearance Nixon finds it hard to sleep. He calls aides during early morning hours to ask "How did I do?" He is understandably concerned over the impending demonstration just off his front lawn. In a surprising move he shaves and, accompanied by a few Secret Service men who later say they were "terrified," Nixon goes out to meet his critics.

I don't believe that I will ever go back to the capital for peace marches or moratoriums.

We arrived in Washington at 4 p.m. on "Spontaneous Moratorium Day." Our driver, Anne, decided to go sightseeing. Hungry after the all-night journey and frustrated because all one-way streets seem to

393

go the same way, annoyed that there are the Army vehicles buried in the central caverns of the federal building, we moved toward Arlington to find a cheap twenty-four hour beanery.

We hit Memorial Drive near the Potomac, as Anne drove to the Lincoln Memorial. We parked across from a black limousine and started up the stairs toward the stone emancipator. What I had at first thought was a D.C. policeman directed us up the right side.

As the three of us headed into the great memorial, Mary Beth saw a few of the "later to be" demonstrators flanked by five men in business suits. She gestured to me. After opening and then shutting my unverbalizing mouth, I moved to where the center of world controversy was addressing a handful of opponents.

President Richard M. Nixon, after a sleepless night, hoped to find solace under the eyes of Lincoln early that morning. Daily press across the nation reported what they termed the President's "monolog." I was accidentally there at least one hour before the first reporter and photographer had discovered where the man of "first and last" decisions was trying to bring himself together.

Thus, the sight of a sad-looking man on a sadder day. He looked as if physicians and Hollywood makeup artists had spent innumerable hours wiring and tacking this human sacred unknown into some presentable fashion. The blue suit and spit-polished shoes made a clown-like contrast to wrinkled face and graying hair: each wrinkle a question, each gray hair an answer.

Secret Servicemen and White House Guards eyed every gesture we made; a pocketed hand nervously going for a cigarette or arms moving in a sarcastic akimbo.

The banality of his speech was at first unbelievable. But realizing the barrage of questions he had answered the last few days, getting relevant thought across seemed at the moment a futile attempt.

His monolog was more travelog. He described visits to Communist countries, seeing the beautiful cities of Moscow and Budapest. If we could only see Southeast Asia, he said, and notice the lovely differences in these people. His visit to Prague and a Jewish ceme-

*tery led him to mention the horrors of killing and this area of
thought ended with a "terrible, terrible."*

*Someone mentioned that federal lands were given up and turned
over to the Indians. I thought of David Frye doing a Nixon imitation. The President, with folded arms, said, "Terribly proud people,
terribly proud."*

*Then he thought I said something about Alcatraz, which I didn't,
so he continued on with his days at college and on the West Coast
surfing. From two feet away his hearing seemed impaired. Most
likely his thoughts were.*

*I jumped in with "What about Cambodia, Mr. President?" He
lowered his head and simply stated "soon, soon." "Go to Europe,
Asia, see the world," he advised one very straight student, who retorted, "But where do I get the money?" Nixon answered, "Don't
worry, don't worry."*

*We had just driven through a city which still witnesses each day
the horrors of the 1967 riots: burned-out stores and homes lie waiting for money.*

*He spoke of cities; how we, the young, would take care of it all.
On pollution and specifically the oil slicks, he said, "Don't worry
about it. Our agencies are cleaning it up."*

*I don't know if it was fear or an ironic moment of respect for the
office, but all I had left in my head to ask was why the U.S. exhibit
at Expo '67 was turned into an aviary. In front of me was a lonely,
middle aged man who looked as if he had lost everything. His head
rarely rose as he rambled on and on. At one time his thoughts might
have seemed relevant, but on this warm May dawn it was sad, very
sad.*

*As I walked away a Secret Service man recorded my name and
address. When I asked why, he said, "The President might want to
send you a personal note." Most likely a security check. But it
doesn't really matter.*[13]

Washington was well prepared for the invasion. The White
House was surrounded by buses which were double-parked, and the

lights which usually bathe 1600 Pennsylvania Avenue in a white glow were turned out to the street so that it was impossible to see through the glare. There were 100,000 present. After Jane Fonda, now somewhat less optimistic than on New Year's Eve, opened the meeting with an affectionate greeting: "Hello, fellow bums," David Dellinger, an old hand at rallies, indicated the need for action, not words. He spoke out for solidarity with the Black Panthers, but the Panther speaker who followed was less sanguine, explaining he was tired of speaking at student rallies, after which everyone goes home with a satisfied feeling and does nothing. The weather was very hot, and the speeches tended to strike some previous participants as much like speeches they had heard before. There were few blacks, but there were a fair amount of nude swimmers in the capital's pools and fountains. There was also some disorder, most of it taking place after the rally ended and centering upon the Department of Justice, which was reported "trashed," the White House where an effort was made to tip over buses, and the Washington Monument, which bore the brunt of a late evening gas attack by D.C. police.

The radical newspaper, *Rolling Stone,* was not much impressed by the entire effort, saying:

> If the purpose of the rally was to 'petition' the government, and show the size of the anti-war movement, it was a failure. The events of the last week, and Nixon's own polls, already showed how great was the opposition to the Cambodian aggression. If the purpose was a symbolic attack on the White House, it was an equal failure. For though the rally was only yards from Nixon's back door, you couldn't even see the building unless you moved back about a block and looked over the buses that encircled it. The White House might as well have been 1,000 miles away.
>
> If the rally was meant to give people a chance to "dissent" from this newest atrocity, it's been tried before. Each dissent has been met with a new atrocity, and "responsible dissent," as they say, has been shown to be meaningless unless there's a "responsible response," which clearly is not forthcoming.[14]

On Sunday, May 10, the previous day's demonstration is officially pronounced "peaceful," and Nixon meets with his personal staff and cabinet officers, whom he had sent out in the streets to get their "gut" impression of the assembly.

The next morning sees a concerted student effort to try another approach to change. Armed with data and often accompanied by faculty, they speak with Congress and administration officials. There is much talk in the East of closing universities for a few weeks next Fall to allow students and faculty to work for and against political candidates. Although Princeton announced it will close, the Harvard faculty refuses, pointing out that politics are not central to the function of the university.

Some old Washington-watchers are unimpressed with both the prospects and the performance of the student lobby, complaining that the group had not done its homework. Consequently, they wasted their time talking to either those who were already committed to their position or to those who were irrevocably opposed to them. Once again, James Reston cut through to the heart of the matter:

> The student peace movement at this point is existing in the realm of ideas and ideals . . . It is concentrating on absolutes, general principles and national policies, but in a congressional election, the candidates have to deal with ambiguities, narrow prejudices and local interests. This is the gap the visiting students in Washington have not yet bridged.
>
> The problem now is a problem of practical politics and power. It is a very complicated problem, different in each constituency. Students have to deal with it in their own home districts in terms of local issues and with an understanding of the diverse and contradictory problems of local candidates. They cannot merely spout philosophy and send brilliant carpet-baggers into strange districts to tell the local yokels how to vote. . . .
>
> Accordingly, it will be interesting to see what the students do over the summer. They can separate and philosophize, or they can think

through their problem, and register, and organize congressional district by district, with local young men and women in charge. On that basis, with some general themes from the center and good leadership from the young lawyers at home, they can put force behind their idealism. But they cannot do it merely by visiting Washington and arguing general principles and noble ideals with distracted congressmen, who have to listen to all the voters and not just to the students home from college.[15]

There is little new on Cambodia on Tuesday, and the campus trashings and closing now are hardly newsworthy. There is a sad episode in Augusta, Georgia, where a sixteen-year-old is beaten to death in jail by two of his cellmates. According to the police, all are black. Reports spread in the community that the police did the killing themselves. There is widespread rioting and looting; at least fifty fires are started as 1000 National Guardsmen come in, and when the night is over, five blacks are dead. Governor Lester Maddox had warned beforehand that the troops were going in with live ammunition and further allowed as how "we're not going to tolerate anarchy in this state." His post-shooting statements were scarcely more conciliatory. He blamed the Black Panthers and the Communists; city officials, somewhat more guarded, assigned responsibility for the catastrophe to "militants and outside agitators."

By midweek Nixon is characterized by aides as "jaunty." They portray Nixon as "expecting the campuses to simmer down in a couple of months and predicting the Cambodian success will eventually permit Agnew to resume attacks on "anti-intellectuals"[16] within the university communities. Nixon and Agnew were reported to be turning down all invitations to address June commencement exercises, although cabinet officers will take on a few.

On May 14 there is some change in the administration stance. American diplomats have advised the President that Hanoi reads the public reaction to expanding the war as clearly indicating that Nixon does not have a broad base of support in the nation. Postmaster General Winton Blount, straightforward a few days back in Detroit, now takes a more conciliatory tack in Wilmington, Delaware. "The country must learn from our young people. I urge you to listen to them. Whatever the questions, whatever the answers, we have been on a collision course with reality. American cannot move to the third century of its freedom at war with its children."

Thursday was very warm in Jackson, Mississippi, the home of Jackson State College. On the evening before, a few hundred students, most of them black, were reported to have thrown stones at whites in passing cars in front of a girl's dormitory. In a move called precautionary by local authorities and provocative by students, the National Guard and local police began to patrol the campus. Some dormitory windows were broken and twelve people were arrested. The campus was restless all the next day, and most of the guardsmen were mobilized in front of the girl's dormitory that night when there was a report of a sniper shot from within the building. The response, a seven second barrage, yielded two more dead college students and eleven others wounded, three critically.

Before the week is out, Mississippi Governor John Bell Williams concludes his investigation clearing the police who acted in "self-defense."

> The police fired only after encountering physical assaults, gunfire and verbal abuse, Mr. Williams said. Any blame should fall "on the peace-breakers, not on the peace-keepers," he declared. . . . He said .32-caliber cartridges had been found at the scene, none of them from police weapons."[17]

On Friday, May 13, more colleges close, and many of those remaining open are on strike. In the White House Nixon presents the Congressional Medal of Honor to a dozen Vietnam heroes, saying sadly that some day the nation will appreciate their deeds. Later that afternoon he flies to his Florida home in Key Biscayne for a rest. He is greeted by a crowd of 1,000 Air Force families who hold signs saying "We support you. We trust what you are doing." Nixon is understandably pleased and he spends the next half-hour circulating about and shaking hands as the crowd sings "God Bless America" and "Let Me Call You Sweetheart."

There has been no official statement as yet on the Jackson State episode, but one is expected before the weekend is over.

On June 9 I am sitting quietly in the English Protestant Cemetery in Florence. I am the only person around, and a pleasant rain is falling. I have seen the grave of Elizabeth Barrett Browning. A previous caller has left a copy of the international edition of the *Herald Tribune* under the bench. Although it is slightly damp, I pick it up and glance idly at the headlines. They read: "Federal Investigators Find No Sniping at Kent or Jackson; Six at Augusta Shot In Back, Group Finds."

Notes

1. Rex Reed, "Jane: 'Everybody Expected Me to Fall on My Face,'" *The New York Times*, Jan. 25, 1970, p. 15D. Quoted with permission of *The New York Times*.

2. Lincoln Gordon, *Johns Hopkins Alumni Report*, July 1969, p. 3.

3. James Reston, "Washington: The President in Adversity," *The New York Times*, May 6, 1970, p. 42.

4. Tom Wicker, "Curbing the Man, Not the Office," *The New York Times*, March 20, 1970, p. 36.

5. Sam Brown, quoted in "Vietnam Moratorium Committee is Disbanding," *The New York Times*, April 19, 1970, p. 6C.

6. Ibid.

7. Ibid.

8. Eldridge Cleaver, "Forbidden Games," *New York*, April 6, 1970, p. 36.

9. Jerry Rubin, *Do It; Scenarios of the Revolution* (New York: Simon and Schuster, 1970).

10. Gail Sheehy, "Bombing on the Mind," *New York*, April 6, 1970, p. 35.

11. Mike York and Fred Kirsch, "Eyewitness Report of Kent Massacre," *The Militant, 34*, 18 (May 15, 1970), p. 1.

12. "11 Professors Ask Agnew To Cool Off His Rhetoric," *The Herald Tribune* (International Edition), June 5, 1970, p. 1.

13. Peter Sugarman, "Nixon at Dawn," *The South End*, Wayne State University student newspaper, May 11, 1970, p. 1.

14. John Morthland, "Nixon in Public: He Was Mumbling at his Feet," *Rolling Stone,* June 11, 1970, p. 12.

15. James Reston, "The Student Invasion," *The Herald Tribune* (International Edition), June 4, 1970, p. 8B.

16. J. F. Ter Horst, "15 Days in May—A Turning Point in U.S. History," *The Detroit News,* May 17, 1970, p. 15B.

17. "Mississippi Governor Justifies Slaying of Two Negroes," *The Herald Tribune* (International Edition), May 14, 1970, p. 7C.

Contributors

Manuel Brontman, M.D.
Staff Psychiatrist
Rochester New York Mental
   Health Center

Zbigniew Brzezinski, Ph.D
Professor of Government
Columbia University

John H. Bunzel, Ph.D.
President
San Jose State College

Eleanor C. Crocker
Graduate Student
Duke University

Arthur Feiner, Ph.D.
Supervisor of Psychotherapy
William Alanson White
   Institute
New York, N. Y.

Edgar Z. Friedenberg, Ph.D.
Professor, Department of
   Education
Dalhousie University
Halifax, Nova Scotia

Nathan Glazer, Ph.D.
Professor of Education and
   Social Structure
Harvard University

Werner I. Halpern, M.D.
Director, Children and Youth
   Division
Rochester New York
   Mental Health Center

Conrad Hilberry, Ph.D.
Professor, Department of English
Kalamazoo (Michigan) College

James Hitchcock, Ph.D.
Professor, Department of History
St. Louis University

Jane Johnson
Former Graduate Student
Columbia University

Boisfeuillet Jones
Former Student
Harvard University

Sue Keese
Former Student
Wittenberg (Ohio) University

403

Robert A. Klein, M.A.
Instructor in Pediatric
  Psychology
University of New Mexico
  School of Medicine

Maurine LaBarre, M.S.W.
Associate Professor of
  Psychiatric Social Work
Department of Psychiatry
Duke University Medical Center

Edgar A. Levenson, M.D.
Supervisory Psychoanalyst
  and Fellow
William Alanson White
  Institute

Morton Levitt, Ph.D.
Professor of Psychology and
  Associate Dean for Academic
  Affairs
School of Medicine
University of California at Davis

Mark Messer, Ph.D.
Assistant Professor, Department
  of Sociology
Adlai E. Stevenson College
University of California at
  Santa Cruz

Daniel Offer, M.D.
Associate Director
Institute for Psychosomatic

and Psychiatric Research and
Training
Michael Reese Hospital and
  Medical Center, Chicago

John Perito, M.D.
Practicing Psychiatrist
Washington, D.C.

Ben Rubenstein, Ph.D.
Lecturer
Marlboro (Vermont) College

Herbert Sacks ,M.D.
Associate Clinical Professor of
  Pediatrics and Psychiatry
Yale University School
  of Medicine

John F. Scott, Ph.D.
Director, Worcester
(Massachusetts) Youth Guidance
  Center

Nathan Stockhamer, Ph.D.
Director, The Young Adult
  Treatment Service
The William Alanson White
  Institute

Gary L. Tischler, M.D.
Associate Professor of Clinical
  Psychiatry
Yale University School
  of Medicine

Index

Morton Levitt is Associate Dean, School of Medicine, University of California at Davis.

Ben Rubenstein is a member of the faculty of Marlboro College, Vermont.

The book was designed by Mary Jowski. The typeface for the text is Linotype Baskerville originally cut by John Baskerville in the 18th Century; and the display face is Square Gothic designed by R. H. Middleton.

The text is printed on Marathon Offset paper and the book is bound in Holliston Mills' Roxite, vellum finished, over binders boards. Manufactured in the United States of America.